SACRED NARRATIVE

SACRED NARRATIVE

Readings in the Theory of Myth

EDITED BY *Alan Dundes*

University of California Press   *Berkeley · Los Angeles · London*

University of California Press
Berkeley and Los Angeles, California
University of California Press, Ltd.
London, England
© 1984 by
The Regents of the University of California

Library of Congress Cataloging in Publication Data
Main entry under title:
Sacred narrative, readings in the theory of myth.

Bibliography: p.
Includes index.
1. Myth—Addresses, essays, lectures. 2. Mythology—
Addresses, essays, lectures. I. Dundes, Alan.
BL304.S19 1984   291.1'3   83-17921
ISBN 0-520-05156-4
ISBN 0-520-05192-0 (pbk.)

Printed in the United States of America

1 2 3 4 5 6 7 8 9

A superstructure of theory is always transitory, being constantly superseded by fresh theories which make nearer and nearer approaches to the truth without ever reaching it. On the shore of the great ocean of reality men are perpetually building theoretical castles of sand, which are perpetually being washed away by the rising tide of knowledge. I cannot expect my own speculations to be more lasting than those of my predecessors. The most that a speculative thinker can hope for is to be remembered for a time as one of the long line of runners, growing dimmer and dimmer as they recede in the distance, who have striven to hand on the torch of knowledge with its little circle of light glimmering in the illimitable darkness of the unknown.

J. G. FRAZER, "Preface,"
Creation and Evolution in Primitive Cosmogonies (London, 1935), p. viii.

Contents

Acknowledgments

I wish to express my heartfelt appreciation to my dear wife Carolyn, not only for her many perspicacious comments on both the essays included and those not included, but also for her efforts to convince me not to entitle this volume "Mytheory." So much did she read on the subject that I feared at one point she might become a victim of myth taken identity. I thank all the authors and publishers of the essays selected for their kindness in allowing me to reprint copyrighted materials.

Introduction

A myth is a sacred narrative explaining how the world and man came to be in their present form. This definition has provided the guideline for the selection of essays included in this volume devoted to the serious study of myth. The critical adjective *sacred* distinguishes myth from other forms of narrative such as folktales, which are ordinarily secular and fictional. One can test the distinction between folktale and myth easily enough in Western cultures by placing one of the opening folktale formulas, for example, "Once upon a time," before one of the myths of the Old Testament, such as the creation of man, or the flood. Religious individuals would presumably be offended by the implication that such narratives were classified by the raconteur as folktales, that is, as secular, fictional narratives, rather than as sacred narratives. That myths are sacred means that all forms of religion incorporate myths of some kind. And there is nothing pejorative about the term *myth*. The term *mythos* means word or story. It is only the modern usage of the word *myth* as "error" that has led to the notion of myth as something negative (although it is true that Plato opposed myths because he felt they led men astray).

In common parlance the term *myth* is often used as a mere synonym for error or fallacy. "That's just a myth!" one may exclaim to label a statement or assertion as untrue. (The terms *folklore* and *superstition* may serve the same function.) But untrue statements are not myths in the formal sense found in this book—nor are myths necessarily untrue statements. For myth may constitute the highest form of truth, albeit in metaphorical guise. If one keeps in mind that a myth must refer minimally to a narrative, then one can easily eliminate most if not all of the books and articles employing *myth* in their titles. (One need only look under *myth* in the subject card index of the nearest large library to discover just how many book titles make use of the word *myth* and how few refer to myth in the sense of a sacred narrative.)

The study of myth is an international and an interdisciplinary venture. Scholars from around the world have contributed to the analysis of myth, and these scholars include students of anthropology, classics, comparative religion, folklore, psychology, and theology, to mention

1

several of the most prominent disciplines. This remarkable variety of approaches is represented by the essays in this volume. The initial essays, which are concerned with the definition of myth, include American anthropological folklorist William Bascom, Dutch folklorist Jan de Vries, Finnish folklorist Lauri Honko, British classicist G. S. Kirk, and theologian J. W. Rogerson. Another British classicist, James G. Frazer, applies the comparative method to a central myth in Genesis. Then follow theoretical considerations by an Italian scholar in the history of religion, Raffaele Pettazzoni; an American expert in the ancient Near East, Theodor H. Gaster; an American (but originally Romanian) scholar of comparative religion, Mircea Eliade; and a Swedish authority on American Indian religion, Åke Hultkrantz. These discussions take up the intriguing question of the relationship between myth and ritual. Swedish folklorist Anna Birgitta Rooth offers a typology of American Indian creation myths, and Japanese scholar K. Numazawa presents a unique interpretation of the world-parent myth (Sky-father and Earth-mother).

The functionalist approach is discussed by the champion of this method, social anthropologist Bronislaw Malinowski, who was born in Poland, as well as by anthropologist Raymond Firth (from New Zealand). A Dutch scholar in the history of religion, Th. P. van Baaren, extends Firth's notion of the adaptability of myth, while French scholar Eric Dardel gives a sensitive overview of missionary-ethnologist Maurice Leenhardt's extraordinary lifetime study of the meaning of myth.

Psychological considerations of myth are represented by Switzerland's C. G. Jung's delineation of the notions of collective unconscious and archetype in his essay on the child archetype; by an incisive critique of Joseph Campbell's approach to myth by Robert A. Segal, an American specialist in myth theory; and by my folkloristic application of Freudian theory to the widespread earth-diver creation myth. French anthropologist Claude Lévi-Strauss demonstrates the structuralist technique of analysis, and Hungarian folklorist Sándor Erdész, in a truly remarkable essay, shows how concepts of worldview are related to the content of traditional folk narratives. The final essay in the volume, by American classicist Dorothea Wender, reviews several of the principal theoretical approaches to myth by applying them in parody style to the legend of George Washington. A short bibliography of suggested further readings in myth theory brings the volume to a close.

From this sampling of theoretical writings on myth, the student will learn that there are disagreements about what myth is and how it should be analyzed. There has been a dramatic shift in theoretical orientation from the nineteenth century to the twentieth. In the nineteenth century, myth theorists were primarily interested in questions of origins. It was assumed by some authorities that myths prevailed in an early, usually the earliest, stage in an evolutionary scheme, or that myths were the result of primitive mythopoeic man's attempt to explain such natural phenomena as the rising and setting of the sun. Even the comparative method, which involved assembling different versions of the same myth, had as its goal the historical reconstruction of the original form of the myth.

After the diachronic theories of the nineteenth century came synchronic theories in the twentieth. Instead of speculating about possible origins, scholars turned to considerations of the structure and function of myth. Investigations of the formal attributes of myth and the purposes it served resulted from the empirical examination of myths in their actual cultural contexts. While nineteenth-century thinkers were content to muse about myths from the safety and comfort of their library armchairs, twentieth-century scholars often made a point of going into the field to experience firsthand the recitations of myth and their impact on living peoples. The substantial increase in the number of myths recorded from all over the world sparked new interest in studying the nature of myth.

Mythologists will surely continue to number specialists in their ranks. Scholars in classics are primarily interested in elucidating ancient Greek and Middle Eastern myths; Bible scholars are concerned with the presence of myth in the Old Testament; anthropologists study the ways myths encapsulate cultural patterns such as social organization; experts in the history of religion explore the role of myth in religious systems and rituals; folklorists are fascinated by the distribution of various myth types in different geographical and cultural areas; psychologists seek to understand myths as fantastic projections of basic human dilemmas or impulses. But no matter what the reason for studying myth, it is essential that one become familiar with the rich variety of theoretical approaches to the subject. "In the beginning" is how many myths start their story. We begin now our study of myth by turning to attempts to define the genre.

The Forms of Folklore:
Prose Narratives

WILLIAM BASCOM

The first task in the study of myth is to define what is meant by the term. What is myth and how does it differ from other forms of folk narrative such as folktale and legend? Nothing infuriates a folklorist more than to hear a colleague from an anthropology or literature department use the word myth *loosely to refer to anything from an obviously erroneous statement to an alleged "archetypal" theme underlying a modern novel or poem.*

Since the days of the Grimm brothers in the early nineteenth century, there has been general agreement among scholars as to generic distinctions between myth, folktale, and legend. William Bascom (1912–81), who was a professor of anthropology at the University of California, Berkeley, ably surveys these conventional folklore genres, drawing on the field reports of many distinguished anthropologists. By and large, Bascom's definitions of myth, folktale, and legend are shared by most folklorists.

In considering folk narrative genres it is important to distinguish between analytic and native categories. Analytic categories are those delineated or imposed by scholars; native or ethnic categories refer to distinctions made by the "native" members of a particular culture. Sometimes analytic and native categories are congruent; sometimes they differ. For instance, some native genre systems distinguish just two basic narrative categories: true narratives and fictional narratives. Myth and legend would thus be lumped together as "true" narratives in contrast to folktales, which would fall under the rubric of fiction. It is always of interest to note native narrative categories in the conduct of fieldwork, but analysts of folk narrative are not necessarily limited to native categories. They may prefer instead to employ what are purportedly cross-cultural categories, for example, myth, folktale, and legend.

In differentiating myth, legend, and folktale it may be useful to think in terms of a metaphor of an empty hourglass. The hourglass would represent true time. Folktale, which can occur at any time or outside normal time (cf. "Once upon a time"), would not be represented in the hourglass image. Let us consider the middle of the hourglass as the instant of creation, that is, the creation of the world and man. Myth would then occur before, up to, and at the moment of creation. The bottom of the hourglass is open-ended, signifying that there is no time before myth. It is extremely difficult to conceive of time and space before myth. There are relatively few examples of creation ex nihilo. *Typically, a creator takes some already existing matter and shapes it into man. Rarely is an explanation offered for the*

Reproduced by permission of the American Folklore Society and Mrs. William Bascom from the *Journal of American Folklore* 78 (1965), 3–20.

origin of the matter to be shaped. Even modern scientific theories, if their initial premises are questioned critically, cannot easily account for the ultimate origins of matter and the universe.

Legend, on the other hand, would fall in the upper portion of the hourglass, occurring after the moment of creation. Thus there could be legends of Adam and Eve that would take place after their creation (which would be a myth). The top of the hourglass, like the bottom, is open-ended, signifying there is no time after legend, just as there is no time before myth. There is no closure in some legends— the Wandering Jew still wanders; the Flying Dutchman still sails the seven seas; a haunted house is still haunted. The majority of legends tend to cluster around the top of the hourglass. While the hourglass metaphor is obviously based on a linear time model, it may prove to be heuristic in distinguishing myth from legend.

There is one additional point to keep in mind in reading Professor Bascom's valuable survey essay. This concerns the numerical or quantitative differences between the genres. Generally speaking, there are not so many myths in the world. True, there are various creations of the world, creations of man (and woman), accounts of the origin of death, etc., but in each culture there is a finite number of myths. In contrast, there are many, many more folktales. For every ten myths there are probably several hundred folktales. Yet however many folktales there may be, they do not compare in numbers with the abundance of legends. There are thousands upon thousands of legends. Every saint who has ever lived has inspired scores of legends. Political figures are frequently the subjects of legend. All the stories told as true about Jesus or about George Washington are technically legends. When one thinks of all the supernatural creatures reported—the fairies, ghosts, goblins, monsters, and revenants—one realizes just how many legends there are. And there are always new legends being created. The accounts of the Loch Ness monster and Bigfoot and UFOs are very much part of twentieth-century life. Myth, on the other hand, in the strict sense of the term, belongs to the past— even if it continues to have an important impact on the present.

For a useful entry into the elaborate set of narrative genres and subgenres employed by scholars, see Laurits Bødker, Folk Literature (Germanic) (Copenhagen, 1965). For a valuable discussion of the distinction between analytic and native narrative categories, see Dan Ben-Amos, "Analytical Categories and Ethnic Genres," Genre 2 (1969), 275–301 (reprinted in Dan Ben-Amos, ed., Folklore Genres (Austin, Tex., 1976), pp. 215–42). See also Lauri Honko, "Genre Analysis in Folkloristics and Comparative Religion," Temenos 3 (1968), 48–66.

This article is directed toward a definition of myth, legend, and folk-tale.[1] These three very basic terms in folklore are loosely used and have sometimes been as hotly disputed as the nature of folklore itself. Definitions and classifications are neither particularly interesting nor necessarily fruitful, but if any field of study needs clarification of its basic

1. Part of this article was presented at the meetings of the American Folklore Society in Detroit in December 1963; the balance was read at the International Congress of Americanists in Barcelona in August 1964. It has benefited from discussions at these meetings, as well as from comments by Archer Taylor, Alan Dundes, John Greenway, and others who read the original draft. I wish also to thank the Wenner-Gren Foundation for Anthropological Research for making it possible for me to attend the meetings in Spain.

terminology it is clearly folklore, which has so long been plagued by inconsistent and contradictory definitions. This article will contribute nothing, however, if it does not lead to some agreement among folklorists on these terms, whatever definitions may ultimately be accepted.

I make no claim to originality in the definitions proposed here. On the contrary, one of the main arguments in support of them is that they conform to what students of the folklore of both nonliterate and European societies have found, as will be shown. I have found them meaningful in some twenty years of teaching, and they seem so obvious and self-evident that I can only wonder at the disagreements which have arisen. Less conventional, but certainly not without precedent, is the proposal that these three important forms of folklore be considered as sub-types of a broader form class, the prose narrative. This provides a system of classification in which they constitute a single category, defined in terms of form alone, comparable to the form classes of proverbs, riddles, and other genres of verbal art.[2]

Prose narrative, I propose, is an appropriate term for the widespread and important category of verbal art which includes myths, legends, and folktales. These three forms are related to each other in that they are narratives in prose, and this fact distinguishes them from proverbs, riddles, ballads, poems, tongue-twisters, and other forms of verbal art on the basis of strictly formal characteristics. Prose narrative is clearly less equivocal for this broad category than "folktale" because the latter has so often been used by folklorists to mean *Märchen*. Its adoption permits us to equate the English term folktale with the German term *Märchen*, as I do here, and thus to dispense with the latter. Many American folklorists, to be sure, employ the term *Märchen* in English because they use "folktale" to include all of these three subtypes, but this is unnecessary, since prose narrative better serves this purpose. When the term prose narrative proves clumsy or inept, I suggest that *tale* be used as a synonym; this is admittedly more ambiguous, but one can appropriately speak of myths, legends, and folktales as "tales," and its counterpart in German, *Erzählung*, is similarly used.

I cannot recall how long I have been using the term prose narrative in my folklore course, but when or by whom it was introduced is of less significance than the recent trend toward its acceptance. Boggs used prose narrative to include myth, legend, and "tale" in his article on folklore classification (1949);[3] it has also been used in this sense by

---

2. For a similar attempt to define riddles, see Robert A. Georges and Alan Dundes, "Toward a Structural Definition of the Riddle," *Journal of American Folklore* 76 (1963), 111–18.

3. Ralph Steele Boggs, "Folklore Classification," *Southern Folklore Quarterly* 13 (1949), 166; reprinted in *Folklore Americas* 8 (1948), 6.

Davenport in discussing Marshallese folklore (1953), and by Berry in discussing West African "spoken art" (1961). "Folklore as Prose Narrative" is the title of the second chapter of the Clarkes' recent text book (1963).[4] One may also cite the Herskovitses' *Dahomean Narrative* (1958), and the founding of the "International Society for Folk Narrative Research," whose first meetings were held in 1962, although neither of these titles differentiate prose narrative from ballads. For a beginning of this trend perhaps one must go back to C. W. von Sydow's "Kategorien der Prosa-Volksdichtung" (1934),[5] or perhaps even to the statement in Frazer's *Apollodorus* (1921) which is quoted below. If we can adopt prose narrative as the comprehensive term for this major category of folklore, we may proceed to the definition of its main subdivisions.

Folktales are prose narratives which are regarded as fiction. They are not considered as dogma or history, they may or may not have happened, and they are not to be taken seriously. Nevertheless, although it is often said that they are told only for amusement, they have other important functions, as the class of moral folktales should have suggested. Folktales may be set in any time and any place, and in this sense they are almost timeless and placeless. They have been called "nursery tales," but in many societies they are not restricted to children. They have also been known as "fairy tales," but this is inappropriate both because narratives about fairies are usually regarded as true, and because fairies do not appear in most folktales. Fairies, ogres, and even deities may appear, but folktales usually recount the adventures of animal or human characters.

A variety of sub-types of folktales can be distinguished including human tales, animal tales, trickster tales, tall tales, dilemma tales, formulistic tales, and moral tales or fables. It is far more meaningful to group all these fictional narratives under a single heading, the folktale, than to list them side by side with myths and legends as has sometimes been done. Such a list can become almost endless if one adds all distinguishable sub-types, including those which are only of local significance. The definition of the sub-types of the folktale, such as proposed by von Sydow,[6] is an important second step, as is the definition of sub-types of the myth and the legend, but it may be premature be-

4. Kenneth and Mary Clarke, *Introducing Folklore* (New York, 1963).

5. Reprinted in C. W. v. Sydow, *Selected Papers on Folklore* (Copenhagen, 1948), pp. 60–68, with the title translated as "The Categories of Prose Tradition."

6. C. W. v. Sydow, *Selected Papers*, pp. 60–88. A consideration of various definitions of the subtypes of folktales, myths, and legends is beyond the scope of this paper, but I fail to see that von Sydow has demonstrated his claim that both steps must be made simultaneously, or his assertion that the distinction made between folktale and legends (*Märchen* and *Sage*) by the Grimm brothers is scientifically unsatisfactory.

Table 1
Three Forms of Prose Narratives

Form	Belief	Time	Place	Attitude	Principal Characters
Myth	Fact	Remote past	Different world: other or earlier	Sacred	Non-human
Legend	Fact	Recent past	World of today	Secular or sacred	Human
Folktale	Fiction	Any time	Any place	Secular	Human or non-human

fore agreement has been reached on the definitions of these three basic categories.

Myths are prose narratives which, in the society in which they are told, are considered to be truthful accounts of what happened in the remote past. They are accepted on faith, they are taught to be believed, and they can be cited as authority in answer to ignorance, doubt, or disbelief. Myths are the embodiment of dogma, they are usually sacred, and they are often associated with theology and ritual. Their main characters are not usually human beings, but they often have human attributes; they are animals, deities, or culture heroes, whose actions are set in an earlier world, when the earth was different from what it is today, or in another world such as the sky or underworld. Myths account for the origin of the world, of mankind, of death, or for characteristics of birds, animals, geographical features, and the phenomena of nature. They may recount the activities of the deities, their love affairs, their family relationships, their friendships and enmities, their victories and defeats. They may purport to "explain" details of ceremonial paraphernalia or ritual, or why tabus must be observed, but such etiological elements are not confined to myths.

Legends are prose narratives which, like myths, are regarded as true by the narrator and his audience, but they are set in a period considered less remote, when the world was much as it is today. Legends are more often secular than sacred,[7] and their principal characters are human. They tell of migrations, wars and victories, deeds of past heroes, chiefs, and kings, and succession in ruling dynasties. In this they are

---

7. African accounts of lineage origins, which are both highly esoteric and sacred, are in my opinion legends. Similarly, European saints' legends may also be sacred.

often the counterpart in verbal tradition of written history, but they also include local tales of buried treasure, ghosts, fairies, and saints.

These distinctions between myth, legend, and folktale may be summarized in Table 1. The headings Place, Attitude, and Principal Characters are added in an attempt to indicate subsidiary characteristics; arguments about them are welcome, but they are beside the point of this article. The definition of these three forms is based only on formal features (i.e., prose narratives) and the two headings of Belief and Time.

Myth, legend, and folktale are not proposed as universally recognized categories but as analytical concepts which can be meaningfully applied cross-culturally even when other systems of "native categories" are locally recognized. They derive from the tripartite classification employed by students of European folklore, and presumably reflect the "native categories" of the "folk" of Europe, but they are easily reducible to the dual classification recognized in those societies which, as we shall see, group myths and legends into a single category ("myth-legend"), distinct from folktales, which are fictional.

Myth, legend, and folktale are not necessarily the only major categories of prose narratives, under which all other kinds of prose narratives must be classified as sub-types. Reminiscences or anecdotes, humorous or otherwise, and jokes or jests may constitute the fourth and fifth such categories. Reminiscences or anecdotes concern human characters who are known to the narrator or his audience, but apparently they may be retold frequently enough to acquire the style of verbal art, and some may be retold after the characters are no longer known at first hand. They are accepted as truth, and can be considered as a sub-type of the legend, or a proto-legend. The Kimbundu and the Marshallese distinguish anecdotes from other legends, as we shall see, but the Hawaiians do not. Anecdotes are not well represented in any of the studies reviewed here. In contrast, jokes or jests do not call for belief on the part of the narrator or his audience, and in this resemble folktales. It may be possible to distinguish jokes from folktales and other prose narratives on formal grounds, but I am not aware that this has been done. In view of the importance of jokes in American folklore, they may seem to deserve a separate category along with myths, legends, and folktales, but this may be an ethnocentric view because little has been written about them outside of literate societies. Both jokes and anecdotes obviously require more attention by folklorists than they have received, but until more is known about them, particularly in nonliterate societies, I prefer to consider them tentatively as sub-types of the folktale and the legend.

In some societies the conventional opening formula which intro-

Table 2
Formal Features of Prose Narratives

1. Formal features (Form of prose narrative)	PROSE NARRATIVES		
	Myth	*Legend*	*Folktale*
2. Conventional opening	None	None	Usually
3. Told after dark	No restrictions	No restrictions	Usually
4. Belief	Fact	Fact	Fiction
5. Setting	Some time and some place	Some time and some place	Timeless, placeless
a. Time	Remote past	Recent past	Any time
b. Place	Earlier or other world	World as it is today	Any place
6. Attitude	Sacred	Sacred or secular	Secular
7. Principal character	Non-human	Human	Human or non-human

duces a folktale gives warning to the listener that the narrative which follows is fiction, and that it does not call for belief, and this notice may be repeated in the closing formula. These nominees serve as a frame to enclose folktales, and to set them apart from myths and legends, from normal conversation, and from other forms of serious discourse. This is true of the Ashanti, Yoruba, and Kimbundu of Africa and the Marshallese of the Pacific, among the societies cited here, and apparently of European folklore with its variants on "Once upon a time . . ." and ". . . they lived happily ever after." In addition, among the Marshall and Trobriand Islanders, and among the Fulani and the Yoruba, factual prose narratives are set aside from fictional ones by tabus against telling folktales in the daytime. As a hypothesis for further investigation one may postulate that if a prose narrative begins with a conventional opening formula (even if its meaning is unknown), and if it should be told only after dark, it is a folktale rather than a myth or a legend.

Provisionally, at least, one can establish a series of steps to be followed in differentiating myth, legend, and folktale, as outlined in Table 2.[8] These steps need not be followed in the sequence indicated, but

8. I am indebted to my colleague, Alan Dundes, for suggesting that the procedural steps be spelled out in this second table, and for other suggestions.

all of them should be investigated. Reliable conclusions cannot be reached on the basis of any single criterion, such as sacred vs. secular, nor from the contents of the texts alone. For the present, however, the definitions offered here are based only on steps 1, 4, and 5a, all others remaining tentative.

In these definitions the distinction between fact and fiction refers *only* to the beliefs of those who tell and hear these tales, and *not* to our beliefs, to historical or scientific fact, or to any ultimate judgment of truth or falsehood. It may be objected that this is a subjective judgment based on the opinions of informants rather than on objective fact, but it is no more subjective than the distinction between sacred and secular, and in practice it may be even easier to establish. Besides the nominees and tabus mentioned above, some languages have separate terms which distinguish fictional from factual prose narratives. Unfortunately these terms have not been reported as often as could be desired.

Folklorists who are exclusively interested in identifying tale types or in applying the historical-geographical method to the study of a particular tale type may find these distinctions irrelevant, because for distributional and historical studies prose narratives must be considered as a unit. However, for other purposes, including the understanding of the nature of prose narratives and their role in human life, these distinctions are important. As we have seen, myths, legends, and folktales differ in their settings in time and place, in their principal characters and, more importantly, in the beliefs and attitudes associated with them. In addition they often appear in different social settings, being told at different times of day or year, and under quite different circumstances. They may be told for different purposes or have distinctive functions. They may differ in the degree of creative freedom allowed the narrator, in their rates of change, and in the ease with which they spread by diffusion. They may also be distinguished by the presence or absence of conventional opening and closing formulas, stylistic differences, the manner of delivery, the identity of the narrator, and the composition of his audience, the degree and nature of audience participation, and the factor of private ownership. The fact that European folklorists from the Grimm brothers on have been concerned with the distinctions between these three categories is evidence enough that they are not important for the functional-anthropological approach alone.

Consistent with his view of magic, science, and religion, Frazer considered myths to be false science and legends to be false history. The attempt to distinguish beliefs which are scientifically true or false is of course valid and important for certain purposes, but when this distinction is made a criterion for the definition of myth or of legend, it only adds to the confusion. None of these three forms of prose narrative need be true, and least of all the folktale.

Moreover, it gives to myth a significance approaching the objectionable popular usage, as in "That's only a myth" or "That's just folklore," meaning simply something which is not true. An extreme expression of this view is to be seen in the proceedings of the Fourteenth Conference of the Rhodes-Livingstone Institute for Social Research, entitled *Myth in Modern Africa* (1960), where myth is equated with unverifiable belief. In the usage of folklorists for over a century, myths are not simply beliefs: they are prose narratives.

In passing from one society to another through diffusion, a myth or legend may be accepted without being believed, thus becoming a folktale in the borrowing society, and the reverse may also happen. It is entirely possible that the same tale type may be a folktale in one society, a legend ² . second society, and a myth in a third. Furthermore, in the course of time fewer and fewer members of a society may believe in a myth, and especially in a period of rapid cultural change an entire belief system and its mythology can be discredited. Even in cultural isolation, there may be some skeptics who do not accept the traditional system of belief.

Nevertheless is it important to know what the majority in a society believes to be true at a given point in time, for people act upon what they believe to be true. It is also worth knowing that certain narratives were formerly believed as myth or legend, and which tales are losing (or gaining) credence. Moreover, in many societies distinctions are made between prose narratives on the basis of whether they are considered fact or fiction.

Because a particular plot or tale type would be classed as a myth in one society and as a folktale in another, Boas said "it is impossible to draw a sharp line between myths and folk tales."⁹ This well-known but sometimes misunderstood statement, quoted out of context, may have deterred attempts to define these terms. Yet if one reads the relevant passages with care, it is apparent that Boas was not expressing the belief that distinctions between myths and folktales are impossible, but rather he was objecting to attempts to classify a particular tale type as myth or as folktale. He was also objecting to attempts to define myth in terms of explanatory elements, supernatural phenomena, or the personification of animals, plants, and natural phenomena, because these

9. Franz Boas, *General Anthropology* (Boston, 1938), p. 609.

may also occur in other kinds of prose narratives. I accept and endorse all of these objections.

Admittedly in an earlier statement Boas said that the strict adherence to one of these principles of classification would "result in the separation of tales that are genetically connected, one being classed as myths, the other with folk-tales. It goes without saying that in this way unnecessary difficulties are created."[10] These difficulties of course do not arise so long as one considers myths and folktales together under the rubric of prose narratives or "tales," as Boas presumably recognized subsequently, since this objection is omitted in his restatement in 1938. Moreover, in his earlier statement he proceeded immediately to suggest definitions which lead to the separation of genetically related tales. He proposed adherence to

> the definition of myth given by the Indian himself. In the mind of the American native there exists almost always a clear distinction between two classes of tales. One group relates incidents which happened at a time when the world had not yet assumed its present form, when mankind was not yet in possession of all the arts and customs that belong to our period. The other group contains tales of our modern period. In other words, tales of the first group are considered as myths; those of the other, as history.[11]

This distinction conforms closely to that made here between myth and legend. Boas refers to "folktales that are purely imaginative" and says that "folktales must be considered as analogous to modern novelistic literature." This suggests that the American Indians have fictional narratives, but from his discussion it is not clear whether they differentiate between true and fictional tales. However, this distinction can be justified on grounds similar to that offered by Boas for distinguishing myths from legends: that it is clearly recognized in the minds of many peoples in many parts of the world.

On the Trobriand Islands myths, legends, and folktales are clearly distinguished in terms comparable to the definitions proposed here; Malinowski's well-known statements may be summarized as follows:

> 1. *Kukwanebu* are "fairy tales" (i.e., folktales) which are fictional, privately owned, and dramatically told. They are told after dark in November, between the planting and fishing seasons. They end with a formalized reference to a very fertile wild plant and there is a vague belief,

10. Franz Boas, "Mythology and Folk-Tales of the North American Indians," *Journal of American Folklore* 27 (1914); reprinted in Boas, *Race, Language and Culture* (New York, 1948), p. 454.

11. Boas, *Race, Language and Culture*, pp. 454–55.

not very seriously held, that their recital has a beneficial influence on the new crops. Their main function is amusement.

2. *Libwogwo* are legends which are serious statements of knowledge. They are believed to be true and to contain important factual information. They are not privately owned, are not told in any stereotyped way, and are not magical in their effect. Their main function is to provide information, and they are told at any time of day and year whenever someone makes specific inquiries about facts, but they are often told during the season of trading voyages.

3. *Liliu* are myths which are regarded not merely as true, but as venerable and sacred. They are told during the preparation for rituals, which are performed at different times throughout the year. Their main function is to serve as a justification of the rituals with which they are associated.[12]

Similarly in North America, the Mandan, Hidatsa, and Arikara "recognize three classes of storytelling which approximate very nearly to the myth, legend, and tale [i.e., folktale] of Malinowski."[13] Despite the difficulty of classifying certain tales, these categories have also been successfully applied to Eskimo folklore. According to Essene:

Myths are often classified as those stories with a high emotional content, and particularly those having to do with religion. Myths often must be recited in a letter perfect fashion. In the previous selection, Lantis cites the essentially religious myths about Moon-Man and the Old Lady of the Sea. An Eskimo considers these stories to be the absolute truth. No explanation of Eskimo religion is complete without including such myths as these, which are accepted on faith.

Tales or folklore [i.e., folktales], while often containing elements of the supernatural, are generally recognized by the listeners as fiction. Normally, the story teller is allowed to vary a tale within certain limits. It is with tales that the narrator has the most opportunity to display his virtuosity as a story teller.

A third type of story, the *legend*, tells the purported history of a people. Though seldom even approximately accurate, it is usually believed to be completely true. Even skilled ethnographers are often fooled by the plausibility of legends, the more so if they hear the account from a skillful narrator. Careful analysis of a legend, however, usually shows a minute amount of truth mixed with many halftruths and many more pure inventions.

In most cultures of the world a fairly clear separation of myths, tales, and legends is possible. Difficulties arise when one story partakes of the

12. Bronislaw Malinowski, *Myth in Primitive Psychology* (New York, 1926); reprinted in Malinowski, *Magic, Science and Religion and Other Essays* (New York, 1954), pp. 101–7.

13. Martha W. Beckwith, *Folklore in America: Its Scope and Method*, Publications of the Folklore Foundation no. 11 (Poughkeepsie, N.Y., 1931), p. 30.

characteristics of two or even three of these types. Also the same story may be told in sacred as well as in profane settings. Eskimo stories are at times difficult to classify, but so far as possible the terms will be used here as defined above. . . .[14]

Citing Essene's statements, Lantis comments:

In Nunivak literature, the Raven and other animal anecdotes would be considered tales [i.e., folktales] by almost anyone. They may be improbable but are not mystical. To the listener, the characteristics and intentions of the animal characters are obvious, taken for granted, and he can have fun in identifying with them or in divorcing himself from them, laughing at the other fellow who is stupid. He has fun in the open disregard of mores and sanctions. There is pleasure in avowed exercise of imagination and ingenuity.

Nunivak war stories have no supernaturalism and are clearly legends. There is apparently no symbolism; traits of individuals and villages are portrayed directly. Again there is open identification with the war heroes and rejection of the enemy and the losers. There is, however, another element: horror instead of fun. The narrator says in effect, "We, Nunivakers, have suffered at the hands of these people." The emotional appeal is great, but again not mystical.

Most of the stories can be classified as myths. They deal with the supernatural, the mysterious. There seem to be two principal moods: yearning, wishing; and uneasiness, fear. Here is the best place to look for the subconscious. Myths utilize religious concepts and beliefs even when they are not "religious." Probably Essene's statement should be modified slightly: Myths may have no greater emotional appeal than war legends, but they tap different emotions and in a different way.[15]

These two statements have been quoted at length because they show how, even though some Eskimo stories are difficult to classify, these three categories can nevertheless be meaningfully applied. It is clear that the Eskimo have myths which are accepted on faith as the absolute truth, and legends which tell "purported history" which is "usually believed to be completely true." It is not clear whether the Eskimo themselves differentiate myths from legends, but they obviously distinguish both from folktales, which are recognized as fiction.

Similarly the Subiya and Lozi of Africa may, or may not, differentiate myths from legends, but they do distinguish both from fictional narra-

14. Frank J. Essene, "Eskimo Mythology," in *Societies Around the World*, ed. Irwin T. Sanders, vol. 1 (New York, 1953), p. 154.
15. Margaret Lantis, "Nunivak Eskimo Personality as Revealed in the Mythology," *Anthropological Papers of the University of Alaska* 2, no. 1 (1953), 158–59.

tives. Jacottet divides their tales into *contes* (folktales) and *légendes*, including *légendes religieuses* or myths about God and the origin of man. The myths and legends relate events in which the people believe, or at least recently believed; in the mind of the narrator they actually happened in the distant past. On the contrary, in the spirit in which it is told the *conte* or folktale is a purely imaginary tale.[16]

However, only two kinds of prose narratives, true and fictional, are distinguished in a number of other societies. Here again folktales are clearly recognized as fiction, but myth and legend apparently blend into a single category, "myth-legend." This is true for the Ponapeans and Hawaiians of the Pacific, the Dakota and Kiowa of North America, and the West African Fulani (Fulakunda), Efik, Yoruba, Ibo, and Fon (Dahomeans). It may also be true of the Eskimo, the Subiya, Lozi, Kimbundu, and Ashanti of Africa, and the Ifugao of the Philippines.

Thus Ponapeans distinguish their fictional narratives from myth-legends (*pathapath*) which deal with the creation of their island and its settlement, the totemic origins of their clans, the introduction of plant crops and useful arts, the magical erection of the impressive stone ruins at *Näniwëi*, and how a single king once ruled the entire island. The Ponapean myth-legend is secret and privately owned by specialists (*söupath*), and is taught to a son by his father in the privacy of the bedroom after the family was retired.

> Hawaiians use the term kaao for a fictional story or one in which fancy plays an important part, that of moolelo for a narrative about a historical figure, one which is supposed to follow historical events. Stories of the gods are moolelo. They are distinguished from secular narrative not by name, but by manner of telling. Sacred stories are told only by day and the listeners must not move in front of the speaker; to do so would be highly disrespectful to the gods. Folktale [i.e., legend] in the form of anecdote, local legend, or family story is also classed under moolelo.[17]

In North America the Dakota "distinguish two classes of tales—the 'true' and the 'lying'. . . . Other Indian tribes make somewhat similar distinctions."[18] Kiowa myth-legends or "true stories" include tales of the origin of the Pleiades, of Buffalo Old Woman, of Red Horse or Cyclone, and of rituals as well as "pseudo-historical stories" of hunting, raiding, fighting, and affiliations with other tribes. The Kiowa tale of

16. E. Jacottet, "Etudes sur les langues du Haut-Zambeze," *Bulletin de correspondance africaine, Publications de l'Ecole des Lettres d'Alger* 16, no. 2 (1899), ii–iii; 16, no. 3 (1901), iv.
17. Martha Beckwith, *Hawaiian Mythology* (New Haven, 1940), p. 1.
18. Beckwith, *Hawaiian Mythology*, p. 30.

Split Boys "is undoubtedly a myth or ritual tale, a 'true story' as the Kiowa put it, in distinction to the *pulhoeitekya*, lie or joke story." [19]

The Fulani also distinguish two categories of prose narratives, the myth-legend (*tindol*, pl. *tindi*) and the folktale (*tallol*, pl. *tali*).

> The *tindi*, which correspond a little to our legends, are considered by the Fulakunda as accounts of adventures having taken place in antiquity. They require a greater portion of truth than the *tali*, concerning which one never knows if they are not only fiction. *Tali* and *deddi* [riddles] are told at night. To do so in broad daylight is to risk the loss of a close relative: father, mother, brother or sister. The *tindi* can be told regardless of the hour. [20]

> The Efik possess a folklore classification of their own. Myths, legends and stories are classified as *mbuk*. . . . The term *ŋke* comprises the folktale, proverb, pun, tongue twister, riddle and tone riddle. The term *ata ŋke* "real *ŋke*" distinguishes the folktale from other forms of *ŋke*. . . . Myths, legends and stories are believed historically true, and deal with such incidents as the early history of the Efik, how Efik obtained the Leopard Society, revenge of supernatural powers on mortals, effects of magic medicine and witchcraft, and exploits of famous war chieftains. [21]

The Yoruba recognize two classes of tales: folktales (*alo*) and myth-legends (*itan*). Myth-legends are spoken of as "histories" and are regarded as historically true; they are quoted by the elders in serious discussions of ritual or political matters, whenever they can assist in settling a point of disagreement. Unlike myth-legends, folktales must not be told during the daytime, lest the narrator lose his way, and they have conventional opening and closing formulas. [22] According to an Ibo student in the United States, the Ibo similarly distinguish folktales (*iro*) from myth-legends (*ita*).

The Fon of Dahomey recognize the same two categories. The myth-legends (*hwenoho*), which include tales of the deities and the peopling of the earth, accounts of wars, and exploits of the ruling dynasty, are regarded as true. The folktales (*heho*) "tell of things which never existed and are inventions of people." "What is important is that the Dahomean names his abstractions, that he has words to define the categories he distinguishes. In his classification of narrative, he identi-

19. Elsie Clews Parsons, *Kiowa Tales*, Memoirs of the American Folklore Society no. 22 (1929), pp. xvii–xviii.
20. Monique de Lestrange, *Contes et légendes des Fulakunda du Badyar*, Études Guinéennes no. 7 (1951), pp. 6–7.
21. D. C. Simmons, "Specimens of Efik Folklore," *Folklore* 66 (1955), 417–18.
22. William Bascom, "The Relation of Yoruba Folklore to Divining," *Journal of American Folklore* 56 (1943), 129.

fies two broad categories, the *hwenoho*, literally 'time-old-story,' which he translates variously as history, as tradition, as traditional history, or as ancient lore; and the *heho*, the tale [i.e., folktale]. It is a distinction that the youngest story-teller recognizes."[23]

The Herskovitses, like Essene and others, have commented on the difficulty of applying these categories to specific tales: "Narratives overlap even in the two major divisions, and Dahomeans are hard put to it to give a categorical answer if asked to designate the type to which certain tales belong. This applies especially where the *heho* is of the type we would describe as a fable, or as a parable. Indeed a parable has been named by one informant as falling into the proverb group."[24] Nevertheless factual and fictional narratives are clearly recognized as separate categories in many societies, and, as they note, the distinction between them is recognized by even the youngest Dahomean story-teller.

Speaking more generally of West Africa, Berry says:

> Prose narratives are part of the cultural tradition of all West African peoples. A first and generally valid dichotomy would appear to be between fictional and non-fictional narrative. Under the latter heading I would subsume what have been variously considered as myths, legends, and chronicles. These are distinguished from tales proper, that is from fictional narrative, by the fact that they are regarded in context as true. Ethnographically at least, they are history. Myths, chiefly stories of the deities and origins of natural phenomena, are especially important throughout West Africa and a large body of mythology has been recorded. Legends which recount the origins of families or clans and explain the ritual and taboos of the ancestral code, are less well documented. Understandably so: They are told only for instruction within the group, and rarely to outsiders. . . . Fictional material includes in the main serious explanatory and moralizing tales, humorous trickster tales, and tales developed wholly or essentially in human society.[25]

A different picture is presented in the Marshall Islands of Micronesia, where Davenport reports that five kinds of "prose narratives" are recognized. Upon examination, three of these appear to be categories of the myth-legend, although Marshallese beliefs are in the process of change; none are introduced with the nominee which is used for fiction. Davenport's "myths" (*bwebwenato*) are clearly myth-legends. They "include such subjects as traditional history, genealogies, and explana-

23. Melville J. and Frances S. Herskovits, *Dahomean Narrative*, Northwestern University African Studies no. 1 (Evanston, Ill., 1958), pp. 14–16.

24. Herskovits and Herskovits, *Dahomean Narrative*, p. 16.

25. J. Berry, *Spoken Art in West Africa* (London, 1961), pp. 6–7.

tory tales of several kinds. . . . The myths are generally accepted as true, though today parts, particularly those which tell of the old gods and demigods, may not be so regarded." The "Edao stories" (*bwe-bwenato Edao*) are a cycle of humorous myth-legends about Edao, the local equivalent of Maui and other tricksters. "Even though they regard his doings as impossible, the people believe a man named Edao once lived in the islands. . . . This element of belief in the stories as well as in their content relates them to some of the modern myths." The "modern myths" (*bwebwenato i mol*) are humorous anecdotes about well-known persons. "These are the 'true' stories of today. Because their veracity is undisputed, they are very hard to get at, for the people do not class them with other forms of stories."

The "half fairy tale, half myth" (*inon-bwebwenato*) is a folktale (*inon*) which was formerly a myth-legend (*bwebwenato*). In the course of cultural change these narratives have become folktales; they are no longer generally believed, and they may be introduced by the nominee which indicates they are fiction. "This category, the least well defined of all, comprises the tales which are told as fairy tales, but which some people either still believe parts of or retain a reverence for, and so are unwilling to say that they are the same as other fairy tales [i.e., folktales]. Just which stories would be classified under this heading would vary considerably from village to village and island to island." The "fairy tale" (*inon*) is the folktale, and is clearly regarded as fiction. It "always begins with the word *kiniwatne*, which without specific meaning signifies 'this is a fairy tale; it may or may not have happened long ago; it is not to be taken seriously; it is not always supposed to be logical.' In ordinary discourse, a person exaggerating or telling an unbelievable story is accused of telling fairy tales." Folktales must not be told during the day lest the heads of the narrator and his listeners swell up as "big as a house."[26]

The distinction between true and fictional narratives is also made by the Ifugao of the Philippines and by the Kimbundu and Ashanti of Africa, but the data do not indicate whether or not myths and legends are distinguished. Thus it is not certain whether the Ifugao have legends or whether the Kimbundu have myths, or whether what Rattray calls "historical myths" are myths or legends. Here again all "true" tales may be myth-legends.

> This distinction between myth and folktale is always clear in the mind of the Ifugao. Myths—I think all of them—are used ritually; they enter into

26. William H. Davenport, "Marshallese Folklore Types," *Journal of American Folklore* 66 (1953), 221–30.

the framework and constitution of the culture and its world viewpoint; they are taken seriously, they are never, as myths, related for diversion. I have found only two myths that have folktale versions. In these instances the folktale versions are not taken seriously—the true version is believed to be the mythical one. . . . I hesitate to say that there exists in the mind of the Ifugao the distinction that Boas asserts always to exist in the mind of the American Indian, namely that the myth "relates incidents which happened at a time when the world had not yet assumed its present form and when mankind was not yet in possession of all the arts and customs that belong to our period. The other group (folktales) [i.e., legends] contains tales of our modern period." It will hereafter be seen that the Ifugao, on account of the manner in which he uses myths in ritual, is continually switching from present to past, and sometimes he muddles the two. . . . I define myths by the criteria of credence and function. A myth is a narrative that is believed, at least by the unsophisticated, and which enters into and bolsters the framework of the culture and its concept of the world. . . . Myths enter into nearly every Ifugao ritual, even into those of decidedly minor importance. The myth itself is called *uwa* or *abuwab* (in Kankanai *susuwa*); its recitation is called *bukad*.[27]

The Kimbundu of Angola also distinguish true and fictional tales, but Chatelain's evidence suggests that they have no myths. This would be a remarkable fact, if true, and it would make Kimbundu categories far less applicable to African folklore than he believed. According to Chatelain the Kimbundu distinguish three categories of prose narratives: folktales and two types of legends. One class of legends (*maka*) is that of "true stories, or rather stories reputed true; what we call anecdotes." They are entertaining, but they are intended to be instructive. "The didactic tendency of these stories is in no way technical, but essentially social. They do not teach how to make a thing, but how to act, how to live." The second class of legends (*ma-lunda* or *mi-sendu*) are historical narratives. "They are the chronicles of the tribe and nation, carefully preserved and transmitted by the head men or elders of each political unit, whose origin, constitution, and vicissitudes they relate. The *ma-lunda* are generally considered state secrets, and the plebeians get only a few scraps from the sacred treasure of the ruling class." In contrast, folktales (*mi-soso*) include "all traditional fictitious stories, or rather, those which strike the native mind as being fictitious. . . . Their object is less to instruct than to entertain. . . . They are always introduced and concluded with a special formula."[28]

27. Roy Franklin Barton, *The Mythology of the Ifugaos*, Memoirs of the American Folklore Society no. 46 (1955), pp. 3–4.
28. Heli Chatelain, *Folk-Tales of Angola*, Memoirs of the American Folklore Society no. 1 (1894), pp. 20–21.

Writing of the Ashanti of Ghana, Rattray says:

Each and all of the stories in this volume would, however, be classed by
the Akan-speaking African under the generic title of "*Anansesem*" (Spider stories), whether the spider appeared in the tale or not. There is a
clear distinction in the mind of the West African between all such tales,
ostensibly told in public for amusement, and those other records which
the European also classes as Folk-lore, but which are regarded by the
African as falling into a totally different category. I refer to the historical myths [i.e., myths, legends, or myth-legends], which—unlike these
Märchen—are the sacred and guarded possession of a few selected elders or a tribe. Such historical myths are, indeed, the "Old Testament" of
the African.

Before beginning a folktale the Ashanti raconteur stated "that what he
was about to say was just make-believe" through the opening formula
"We do not really mean, we do not really mean, (that what we are going
to say is true)," and he concluded, in one of their conventional closing
formulas, "This, my story, which I have related; if it be sweet, (or) if it
not be sweet; some you may take as true, and the rest you may praise
me (for the telling of it)." [29]
     Where these categories are most difficult to apply is in those cases
where the investigator has failed to consider, or at least to discuss, the
question of belief; yet the answer to this question is important, regardless of what definitions are accepted. Radin has pointed out that the
Winnebago have two stylistically distinct kinds of prose narratives. "In
the first, the *waika*, the actors are always of divine origin, the action
always takes place in a long past mystical era and the end is always
happy. In the other, the *worak*, the actors are human, the action takes
place within the memory of man and the end is uniformly tragic." [30]
One is tempted to consider the former as myths and the latter as legends, and to ask if the Winnebago lacked folktales. Yet earlier Radin
says that *waika* "includes all we would term myths and maerchen,"
while *worak* "includes some narratives that we would include among
the myths and maerchen. The majority, however, we would definitely
exclude from that category." Without knowing which, if any, tales are
regarded as fiction we are left in doubt as to what *waika* and *worak* are,

29. R. S. Rattray, *Akan-Ashanti Folk-Tales* (Oxford, 1930), pp. xi, xiii, 15, 49, passim.
     30. Paul Radin, *The Culture of the Winnebago: As Described by Themselves*, Indiana
University Publications in Anthropology and Linguistics, memoir 2 of the *International
Journal of American Linguistics*, supplement to vol. 15, no. 1 (1949), p. 76; *Winnebago
Hero Cycles: A Study in Aboriginal Literature*, Indiana University Publications in Anthropology and Linguistics, memoir 1 of the *International Journal of American Linguistics*, supplement to vol. 14, no. 3 (1948), pp. 11–12; "Literary Aspects of Winnebago Mythology," *Journal of American Folklore* 39 (1926), 18–52.

in what category the majority of *worak* do belong, and what Radin means by *Märchen*.

Lowie says:

> It is not at all easy to classify Crow tales. There are true myths like the stories about Old Man Coyote and Old Woman's Grandchild—stories that explicitly deal with a condition of life different from that of recent times and accounting for the origin of a natural phenomenon or of some established usage. But the line between these and more matter-of-fact tales cannot be sharply drawn, for marvelous happenings belonged to the routine of life until a few decades ago, as shown by reports of visions experienced by men I personally knew. Also the origin of certain institutions may crop up in relatively matter-of-fact settings. Nor do the Indians ascribe greater value either to the plainly mythical or the obviously non-mythical category.[31]

This last sentence refers to tale preferences, and not to sanctity or belief, and again Lowie leaves us in doubt as to the existence of fictional narratives; the balance of this statement is a reiteration of Boas's position. In a posthumous article Lowie says of Crow prose narratives, "Myths and folktales—not always distinguishable—are forms of fiction. One must also include tales of personal adventure, topical stories, and historical narratives, for all three admit of distinctly literary effects." Here he is obviously using fiction as an objective concept, leaving unanswered the question of whether myths and folktales were believed to be true. "Inevitably the several literary categories differ in their style, some conforming more closely than others to the colloquial forms. Even myths do not use identical formal patterns. Trickster stories generally begin with a set statement: 'It was Old Man Coyote. He was going around, he was hungry.' Nothing comparable occurs in hero tales."[32] Crow trickster tales, it would seem, are different from both myths and hero tales (legends); they are clearly not another type of legend, and they begin with somewhat conventionalized formula. But were they considered fictional or factual?

Such examples are too numerous to list, but Benedict's statement has been quoted so often that it calls for comment. "In Zuni, tales fall into no clearly distinguishable categories. The divisions I have used in this volume are for convenience of reference only, and have little to do with the literary problems of the narrator."[33] Considering her title, *Zuni*

31. Robert H. Lowie, *The Crow Indians* (New York, 1935), p. 111.

32. Robert H. Lowie, "The Oral Literature of the Crow Indians," *Journal of American Folklore* 72 (1959), 97–98.

33. Ruth Benedict, *Zuni Mythology*, Columbia University Contributions to Anthropology no. 21, vol. 1 (New York, 1935), p. xxx.

Mythology, one can only speculate whether she simply did not consider legends and folktales, or whether the Zuni have no "native categories" for their prose narratives. Even if the latter is correct, this is not to say that the three analytical concepts as defined here would not be useful if we had information on the question of belief, and on the other characteristics mentioned above. Perhaps their applicability would become apparent if Zuni tales were examined with the same care and detail as those of the Wind River Shoshoni.

The Wind River Shoshoni have a single term for all prose narratives (*nareguyap*) and do not distinguish between them linguistically, either on the basis of fact and fiction or of "the mythic primeval era and the historical present." Nevertheless they have myths, legends, and "fairy tales," and the latter are recognized as fiction, as Hultkrantz has recently shown in his penetrating analysis of their religious prose narratives.[34] Moreover, Hultkrantz's definitions of these forms parallel those offered here:

> The myth, as I understand it, is a narrative of gods and divine beings, whose actions take place in the period when the present world was formed (in principle, their actions are not bound by time). The myth is often sacred in itself, and it is always an object of belief. The legend deals with human beings, preferably heroes, and their supernatural experiences, and is regarded as a true description. The fairy tale (*Märchen*), again, makes use of the milieu and the personages of the myth and the legend, but without the dramatic action in which these are involved being considered true. There are, naturally, also profane *Märchen*, but these are without relevance in the present connection.

Despite the incompleteness of the evidence, and despite these variations in native categories, the definitions of myth, legend, and folktale offered here are analytically useful. They can be meaningfully applied even to societies in which somewhat different distinctions between prose narratives are recognized. They make it possible to say that the Trobriand Islanders and others distinguish myths, legends, and folktales as defined here, whereas the Wind River Shoshoni group theirs together in a single category; and the Yoruba and others class myths and legends in a single category which is distinguished from folktales. For certain analytic and comparative purposes, moreover, it is necessary to distinguish the different kinds of Shoshoni tales, and to distinguish Yoruba myths from their legends, even though the Shoshoni and the Yoruba do not do so themselves.

34. Åke Hultkrantz, "Religious Aspects of the Wind River Shoshoni Folk Literature," in *Culture in History: Essays in Honor of Paul Radin*, ed. Stanley Diamond (New York, 1960), pp. 552–69.

These categories also make it possible to say that although the Hawaiians have only two terms for prose narratives, one for folktales and one for myth-legends, their myths can be distinguished from their legends by the circumstances in which they are told. We can also say that in addition to the myth-legend and the folktale, the Marshall Islanders have separate categories for folktales which once were myth-legends, for a cycle of trickster myth-legends, and for humorous anecdotes; and that the Kimbundu similarly distinguish anecdotes from other legends. If true, it is also meaningful to say that the Kimbundu have no myths, and that the Ojibwa—to my knowledge the only society reported to lack fictional prose narratives—apparently have no folktales.[35]

If these definitions are analytically useful for the study of prose narratives in nonliterate societies, they can also be applied meaningfully to Euro-American folklore. In the United States, myths may be lacking, but folktales and legends are clearly distinguished. Halpert says, "I have known women story tellers who call tall stories 'damn lies' which they scorned to repeat; but they have no hesitation in telling me legends which they believed were 'true'."[36]

In fact, these categories of prose narratives are derived from the study of European folklore, and they have long been distinguished in similar terms by its students. Although both terminology and definitions have varied, the concepts of myths, legends, and folktales in English are comparable to *Mythen*, *Sagen*, and *Märchen* in German, and to *mythes*, *traditions populaires*, and *contes populaires* in French.

Janet Bacon in 1925 distinguished between myths, legends, and folktales, saying that "myth has an explanatory function. It explains some natural phenomenon whose causes are not obvious, or some ritual practise whose origin has been forgotten. . . . Legend, on the other hand, is true tradition founded on fortunes of real people or on adventures at real places. . . . Folktale, however, calls for no belief, being wholly the product of imagination."[37]

Her distinctions were adapted from the definitions proposed in 1921 by no less eminent a folklorist than Sir James Frazer, who wrote:

> As the distinction between myth, legend, and folk-tale is not always clearly apprehended or uniformly observed, it may be well to define the sense in which I employ these terms.

35. "The northern Ojibwa, for example, have no category of fiction at all; both their sacred stories and their tales are thought to be true. Consequently there is no art of imaginative fiction in this society, and no incentive to its creation." A. I. Hallowell, "Myth, Culture and Personality," *American Anthropologist* 49 (1947), 547.

36. Herbert Halpert, "The Folktale: A Symposium. 3. Problems and Projects in American-English Folktale," *Journal of American Folklore* 70 (1957), 61.

37. Janet Ruth Bacon, *The Voyage of the Argonauts* (London, 1925), pp. 3–5.

By myths I understand mistaken explanations of phenomena, whether of human life or of external nature. Such explanations originate in that instinctive curiosity concerning the causes of things which at a more advanced stage of knowledge seeks satisfaction in philosophy and science, but being founded on ignorance and misapprehension they are always false, for were they true they would cease to be myths. The subjects of myths are as numerous as the objects which present themselves to the mind of man; for everything excites his curiosity, and of everything he desires to learn the cause. Among the larger questions which many peoples have attempted to answer by myths are those which concern the origin of the world and of man, the apparent motions of the heavenly bodies, the regular recurrence of the seasons, the growth and decay of vegetation, the fall of rain, the phenomena of thunder and lightning, of eclipses and earthquakes, the discovery of fire, the invention of the useful arts, the beginnings of society, and the mystery of death. In short, the range of myths is as wide as the world, being coextensive with the curiosity and the ignorance of man.

By legends I understand traditions, whether oral or written, which relate the fortunes of real people in the past, or which describe events, not necessarily human, that are said to have occurred at real places. Such legends contain a mixture of truth and falsehood, for were they wholly true, they would not be legends but histories. The proportion of truth and falsehood naturally varies in different legends; generally, perhaps, falsehood predominates, at least in the details, and the element of the marvellous or the miraculous often, though not always, enters largely into them.

By folk-tales I understand narratives invented by persons unknown and handed down at first by word of mouth from generation to generation, narratives which, though they profess to describe actual occurrences, are in fact purely imaginary, having no other aim than the entertainment of the hearer and making no claim on his credulity. In short, they are fictions pure and simple, devised not to instruct or edify the listener, but only to amuse him; they belong to the region of pure romance. . . .

If these definitions be accepted, we may say that myth has its source in reason, legend in memory, and folk-tale in imagination; and that the three riper products of the human mind which correspond to these its crude creations are science, history, and romance.

But while educated and reflective men can clearly distinguish between myths, legends, and folk-tales, it would be a mistake to suppose that the people among whom these various narratives commonly circulate, and whose intellectual cravings they satisfy, can always or habitually discriminate between them. For the most part, perhaps, the three sorts of narrative are accepted by the folk as all equally true or at least equally probable.[38]

38. Sir James George Frazer, *Apollodorus* (London, 1921), pp. xxvii–xxxi.

Although Jane Harrison's definition of myth as the spoken correlative of ritual acts differs from that which is presented here, and indeed includes forms of verbal art which are not (or are not yet) narratives, she regarded myths as very different from legends and folktales. "It is this collective sanction and solemn purpose that differentiate the myth alike from the historical narrative [i.e., legend] and the mere *conte* or fairy-tale [i.e., folktale]."[39]

In 1908 Gomme had offered his definitions of these three terms:

> The first necessity is for definitions. Careful attention to what has already been said will reveal the fact that tradition contains three separate classes, and I would suggest definition of these classes by a precise application of terms already in use: The *myth* belongs to the most primitive stages of human thought, and is the recognisable explanation of some natural phenomenon, some forgotten or unknown object of human origin, or some event of lasting influence; the *folk-tale* is a survival preserved amidst culture-surroundings of a more advanced age, and deals with events and ideas of primitive times in terms of the experience or of episodes in the lives of unnamed human beings; the *legend* belongs to an historical personage, locality, or event. These are new definitions, and are suggested in order to give some sort of exactness to the terms in use. All these terms—myth, folk-tale, and legend—are now used indiscriminately with no particular definiteness. The possession of three such distinct terms forms an asset which should be put to its full use, and this cannot be done until we agree upon a definite meaning for each.[40]

As a cultural evolutionist Gomme viewed folktales as derived from myths, but he recognized that the folktale is neither sacred nor believed:

> It has become the fairy tale or the nursery tale. It is told to grown-up people, not as belief but as what was once believed; it is told to children, not to men; to lovers of romance, not to worshippers of the unknown; it is told by mothers and nurses, not by philosophers or priestesses; in the gathering ground of home life, or in the nursery, not in the hushed sanctity of a great wonder.[41]

Still earlier, in 1904, Bethe gave a series of lectures, later published as *Märchen*, *Sage*, *Mythus*, in which he argued that these three forms were sub-types of the "tale" (*Erzählung*):

39. Jane Ellen Harrison, *Themis* (Cambridge, 1912), p. 330.
40. George Laurence Gomme, *Folklore as an Historical Science* (London, 1908), p. 129.
41. Gomme, *Folklore*, p. 149.

Mythus, Sage, Märchen are academic concepts. Really all three mean the same, nothing more than *Erzählung*, the Greek word as well as the two German words. The word '*Märchen*' came to have its present current meaning at the end of the eighteenth century, as the Oriental *Märchen* became known. But it was only about a century ago that these three concepts were established and the words were forced into these meanings, with the result that '*Mythus*' means tales of the gods (*Göttersagen*), '*Sage*' narratives attached to particular persons, certain localities or customs, and '*Märchen*' the abundant unattached stories.[42]

Later in this work, Bethe offers his own distinctions between these three concepts.

Mythus, Sage, and *Märchen* differ from one another in origin and purpose. *Mythus* is primitive philosophy, the simplest intuitive form of thought, a series of attempts to understand the world, to explain life and death, fate and nature, gods and cults. *Sage* is primitive history, naively fashioned in hate and love, unconsciously transformed and simplified. But *Märchen* arose from the need for entertainment and serves only this purpose. Therefore it is free of time and place; therefore it takes what seems entertaining and omits what is boring, here in one way there in another, each time according to the narrator's taste. It is nothing but poetry, the quintessence of all works of fantasy of mankind.[43]

It is apparent that students of European folklore have long recognized both the significance of distinctions between myth, legend, and folktale and the fact that all three are different forms of "*Erzählung*" or "tradition" or "narrative." Usage has varied, but there is considerable agreement that myths include tales of deities and creation; legends deal with human characters who are considered historical persons; and while both myths and legends are believed, folktales are distinguished from them in that they are accepted as fiction.

Finally, if we go back to what are generally acknowledged as the very beginnings of the modern study of folklore, we find that the Grimm brothers made similar distinctions between *Märchen, Sagen,* and *Mythen,* devoting a separate major work to each. In *Deutsche Mythologie,* Jacob Grimm says:

The folktale (*märchen*) is with good reason distinguished from the legend, though by turns they play into one another. Looser, less fettered than legend, the folktale lacks that local habitation which hampers legend, but makes it more home-like. The folktale flies, the legend walks, knocks at your door; the one can draw freely out of the fulness of poetry,

42. Erich Bethe, *Märchen, Sage, Mythus* (Leipzig, n.d.), p. 6.
43. Bethe, *Märchen,* p. 117.

the other has almost the authority of history. As the folktale stands related to legend, so does legend to history, and (we may add) so does history to real life. In real existence all the outlines are sharp, clear and certain, which on history's canvas are gradually shaded off and toned down. The ancient myth, however, combines to some extent the qualities of folktale and legend; untrammelled in its flight, it can yet settle down in a local home. . . . In the folktale also, dwarfs and giants play their part. . . . Folktales, not legends, have in common with the god-myth (*göttermythen*) a multitude of metamorphoses; and they often let animals come upon the stage, and so they trespass on the old animal-epos. . . . Divinities form the core of all mythology.[44]

These are by no means precise definitions, but *Deutsche Mythologie* (1835) is clearly concerned with myths, *Deutsche Sagen* (1816–1818) is a collection of legends, and *Kinder- und Hausmärchen* (1812–1815) is a collection of folktales. One needs only to examine the contents of these three works to see how closely the three categories distinguished by the Grimm brothers correspond to the definitions offered here.

What is surprising, in view of this, is the seeming conspiracy of later folklorists to corrupt the meanings of folktale, legend, and myth—which the Grimms so clearly distinguished—with new definitions, new distinctions, and new usages. If it is now time to return to Thoms's original definition of folklore to reach some basis of agreement between humanists and social scientists, it is also time to return to the categories recognized by the Grimm brothers in order to reach some basis of understanding in folklore. It is time to agree upon English equivalents of *Mythen*, *Sagen*, and *Märchen*, and to agree upon their definitions.

As I stated at the outset, this article will contribute nothing if it does not lead to some agreement among folklorists on the usage of the terms myth, legend, and folktale. It is probably too much to hope that any system of classification or any set of definitions will be followed by the commercial entrepreneurs in folklore or by the many varieties of amateurs, but at least professional folklorists from both the humanities and the social sciences should be able to reach some agreement.

44. Except for substituting "folktale" for "fairy-tale" and "myth" for "mythus," the translation here follows Stallybrass. See Jacob Grimm, *Teutonic Mythology*, translated from the fourth edition with notes and appendix by James Steven Stallybrass, vol. 3 (London, 1882–83), pp. xvi–xvii. In the original *Mythen* and *Mythus* are less often employed than *Mythologie* because Grimm was attempting to reconstruct the mythology from fragmentary remains of myths.

Theories Concerning "Nature Myths"

JAN DE VRIES

The distinctions between myth, folktale, and legend go back at least to the Grimm brothers in the early nineteenth century, as Professor Bascom observed. It could also be plausibly argued that the serious, scientific study of myth began in the nineteenth century, although one can find precursors in previous centuries.

Myth, in the nineteenth century, was partly perceived as primitive man's functional equivalent of science. It was believed that early man, as he sought to explain or understand the forces of nature, articulated his speculations in mythical form. A host of competing theories were proposed, each advocating the preeminent importance of one natural phenomenon for mythopoesis, e.g., thunder, the sun, the moon, etc. Such theories were invariably universalistic and assumed that the particular natural origin of myth was common to all mankind.

Nineteenth-century theories of myth tended to be concerned primarily with origins, in contrast to twentieth-century theories, which emphasize the structure and function of myths. Sometimes the origins were presumed to be natural phenomena, as the rising and setting of the sun; sometimes they were merely geographical, as in the case of the Indianist school, which argued that European myths (and folktales) diffused from India.

In this brief survey by Dutch folklorist Jan de Vries (1890–1964), we get some sense of the intellectual ferment of nineteenth-century mythological schemata. Although few of these theories any longer enjoy any semblance of credence, they did stimulate the development of mythology as a legitimate area of academic inquiry. For more detail about the historical rise of mythological studies, see de Vries's longer work, Forschungsgeschichte der Mythologie *(Freiburg and Munich, 1961). For representative samples of earlier theoretical writings on myth, see Burton Feldman and Robert D. Richardson,* The Rise of Modern Mythology, 1680–1860 *(Bloomington, Ind., 1972). For a valuable historical account of the rise and fall of solar mythology, see Richard M. Dorson, "The Eclipse of Solar Mythology,"* Journal of American Folklore *68 (1955), 393–416 (reprinted in Thomas A. Sebeok,* Myth: A Symposium *[Bloomington, Ind., 1958], pp. 15–38, and in Alan Dundes, ed.,* The Study of Folklore *[Englewood Cliffs, N.J., 1965], pp. 57–83). For more on the study of myth in the nineteenth century, see Janet Burstein, "Victorian Mythography and the Progress of the Intellect,"* Victorian Studies *18 (1975), 309–24.*

From *The Study of Religion* by Jan de Vries, translated by Kees W. Bolle, © 1967 by Harcourt Brace Jovanovich, Inc. Reprinted by permission of the publisher.

At the start of the nineteenth century, religio-historical investigations were mainly confined to the Indo-European peoples. The study and growing knowledge of the ancient language of India and of the texts made a path far deeper into the past than the Greek or Germanic sources had allowed. And the overestimation of Sanskrit was not a disadvantage but a strong stimulus. Initially, it was felt that this sacred language of the Brahmans was virtually identical with the root tongue of all Indo-European languages. It took many years of painstaking comparative study to find that in many ways Sanskrit had deviated from that original language as much as had Greek and Latin. Sanskrit was merely among sister languages. At any rate, the result of the exaggerated attention paid to Sanskrit was that the ideas crystallized in the Vedas were treated as more ancient and original than those of classical antiquity.

The one-sided orientation toward the Vedas held a further pitfall. The Rigvedic hymns give mythical allusions and descriptions with an imagery inspired principally by nature. A figure like Ushas, the goddess of dawn—comparable to Eos in Greece—inspired the poet to sing of daybreak and the triumph of light. The great myth of Indra's struggle with Vritra, which the Veda says released the heavenly cows, seemed to be a story about thunder, which caused the long-awaited, long prayed-for rains to pour down. An idea developed that the Indian gods were powers of nature and that the myths were fanciful enactments of natural phenomena.

If one phenomenon seemed to be preferred, it was taken as the center of the mythological system. Thus, theories of thunder and storm were born and thus the theories about the sun and its manifestations.

The thunder mythology had its main proponents in Adalbert Kuhn and his brother-in-law Wilhelm Schwartz. Kuhn had begun his research into Indo-European culture on the basis of linguistics and became the founder of the Indo-European archaeology. Then, following the example of Jacob Grimm, he turned to the collection and study of popular traditions, and this brought him to mythology. His principal work, in 1859, *Die Herabkunft des Feuers und des Göttertranks* ("The Descent of Fire and of the Divine Drink"), is a book of high caliber, when seen in the light of his time, and still receives deserved attention. In his mythological expositions he begins with atmospheric phenomena, the passage of day and night, summer and winter, but especially with thunder and storm. By their nature the myths of Indra and the Maruts give an apt documentation. He also tries to support the coherence of the various Indo-European mythologies with linguistic data; this attempt was very important in a time when the coherence of the languages had just been discovered. It seemed obvious to compare Varuna with Uranos or Surya (Sanskrit: sun) and Helios (Greek: sun). Kuhn also saw a resemblance between the Indian Gandharvas and the Greek Centaurs. He related Saraṇyū, the mother of the Aśvins, to the Greek Erinys, which was more risky, as was his comparison of Hermeias with the Sanskrit Sarameya, the name of a dog. Kuhn's method did not bear up to criticism as the phonetic laws that determine the relation of languages gradually became better known and a scientific etymology became possible. The modern science of linguistics made quick work of the beautiful parallels he had established between Indian and Greek mythical figures. As a result, scholars hesitated for a long time to attempt the comparative study of Indian and other Indo-European names of gods. This was certainly at scholarship's expense, for in spite of everything, later research concluded that it is precisely in the area of religion that names and words can deviate from the "phonetic rule." Exceptional forms of this order could occur in the sacred sphere, where the usage of language was unlike profane speech. Taboo phenomena may have played a role in the peculiar conservation of religious words. Finally, a growing sophistication in the study of phonetics could make some comparisons of divine names acceptable, though the efforts looked unsure at first.

One cannot deny in the "nature mythologists" an intimate, romantic feel for the phenomena of nature. We read in Schwartz:

> The thunderbolt—the most universal and original magical fetish among almost all peoples—seemed to trace in the sky the source of rain, or, slightly differently, the thunder "opening up," or mythically expressed, "the unfolding flower of thunderclouds," brings on the stormy night with its shadows, or seems to disclose, as lightning tears the clouds, the mountains of the clouds with their radiant treasure.[1]

No nature mythologist lacked imagination, and this helped them in locating all sorts of physical phenomena in the ancient myths. Above all else, Schwartz expounds, Wodan (the chief Norse god) is the storm, and the comparison to the Indian Vayu immediately offers itself. The Indian deity, veiled in clouds, has his sphere of action in heaven. In the case of Wodan thunder and lightning are rather secondary accompaniments. They are central in the case of Donar or Zeus. Donar was believed to be a gigantic, demonic being, moving through the clouds, urging his thunderous steed around the sky in the wild commotion of the storm. The flash of lightning that shot underneath the clouds was believed to be the flash of his eye, which was shaded by the clouds as

---

1. Wilhelm Schwartz, *Indogermanischer Volksglaube* (Berlin, 1885), p. lx.

by a hat. But the flash of lightning could, at the same time, be a spear hurled from the heights, or a gleaming sword. These motifs could, in turn, be interpreted as the trappings of a hunting or a warrior god.[2]

In the same context Schwartz observes that in the "lower mythology" of the Germanic tribes, Wodan absorbed a great many elements that occur more faintly in Greek and Roman mythology and yet are analogous to the Indo-European popular beliefs. "Lower mythology" and "popular belief" were the new concepts coined by Schwartz. Since Jacob Grimm, popular traditions had been collected and examined with increasing intensity. Grimm saw them as precious survivals of a distant pagan past; the ancient myths, he thought, lived on in the fairy tales, and in the sagas he found the last traces of the pagan gods, who after Christianization had been brought to the state of trolls and giants.

Schwartz developed a different view. What is still alive among the folk, he thought, is not at all the echo of an ancient pantheon but the ground on which polytheism sprang up. Popular belief, or "the religion of the people," is precisely that belief in all those supernaturals, dwarves, giants, elves, and nixes that have had their home in the mind of the people since time immemorial. Moreover, this elvish populace is much more ancient and original than the great gods of the Greeks and Indians. Therefore Schwartz believed that the figures of the gods were born in the course of millennia by virtue of more highly refined ideas. To understand this higher religiosity we should find out what "the people" (*das Volk*) at one time believed and thought and what it still believes and thinks.

There is some sense in Schwartz's train of thought. Nineteenth-century research always began by assuming that all elements of civilization, and consequently also of religion, passed through an evolution; the schematic series of fetishism/polytheism/monotheism was familiar even to the eighteenth century. Its validity went unquestioned. And it is not impossible that in present popular religion much of the ancient lower mythology really does survive with the gods long since toppled by Christianity and transformed to demonic beings. It would be wrong to assume that the superstition leading a veiled existence among the people represents the primordial Indo-European beliefs, yet its testimony cannot be ignored. As long as one assumes—like Schwartz—a pantheon that was common to the Indo-European nations and must have preceded their division, the danger of overestimating the primitive beliefs in demons is not too great. It seems quite obvious that the anthropomorphic pantheon of an intelligentsia (as we know in the Vedic liturgies)—the work of sophisticated schools of

2. Ibid., p. 225.

priests—cannot have the same sway over the lower strata of the population. With the latter we certainly may assume there was a much sim-
pler and more naïve religiosity, in which spirits and demons figured
significantly, and where, from day to day, the great gods of the pantheon hardly played a part.

Nevertheless, Schwartz's conception of a lower mythology became
fatal for scholarly investigation. Before long, the collapse of the ideas
that Adalbert Kuhn had proclaimed—that Indo-European gods could
be inferred from similarities in names—also hurt the notion of a pan-
Indo-European pantheon. An incisive linguistic critique did not leave
intact much of the identifications that once were so striking. The one
god who was unaffected by this scholarly turmoil and who really
could have been worshiped by the Indo-Europeans was the ancient
skygod, for the identification of the names Dyaus pitar (Sanskrit), Zeus
pater (Greek), and Jupiter (Latin) could hardly be denied.

The net conclusion of the discussion was that, next to the worship
of the skygod, nothing must have existed but that popular religion or
so-called lower mythology. Gradually, in the course of centuries, the
variegated pantheon we know from the sources must have come into
being. Supposedly this happened after the Indo-Europeans had left
their "homeland." Each nation had its own names for the "secondary"
gods and thus proved to have discovered (or appropriated) them independently. This reasoning fitted miraculously well into the frame of
nineteenth-century historicism, which we shall discuss more elaborately later. It became a most appealing task to demonstrate how that
pagan pantheon had been slowly structured. This process was not so
much the result of a need for new gods because of growing cultural
complexity but rather of an interplay with alien civilizations, from
which whole sets of imageries and customs were borrowed. This hypothesis was already dogma in the study of Greek mythology: Zeus-
Ammon came from Egypt, Dionysus from Thrace, Apollo from Libia;
all those derivations that were held by the ancients themselves were
still immutable among scholars of the Greek pantheon. A foreign origin
seemed probable for other deities as well. The Romans were considered a nation that accepted almost completely a world of gods; did
they not appropriate the whole Greek pantheon? The Germanic people and their deities were treated similarly. Since the cultural superiority of the Celts was beyond dispute it was presumed that the
Germanic tribes who met Belgians and Gauls along the lower Rhine
received gods like Donar and Wodan from them. Even in the twentieth
century Gustav Neckel defended the thesis that the Germanic god Bal-
der had come to Scandinavia from the Near East through Thrace.

But let us return to the Nature Mythologists and the problems related to Schwartz's lower mythology. It was Wilhelm Mannhardt (1831–80) who became the nineteenth century's most successful student of this lower mythology. At the beginning of his work he was still an adherent of nature-mythological explanation after the manner of Adalbert Kuhn. But later the great significance of popular tradition for religio-historical study became clear to him. At the sacrifice of his own money and time he decided, independently, to collect accurate data by means of questionnaires, and his research went far beyond the borders of Germany. He concentrated on harvest customs. His results were published in 1865 in the book *Roggenwolf und Roggenhund*, followed by *Die Korndämonen* in 1868. In these works he explains that in popular religion certain beings—personal beings—were supposed to be present in the cornfield as "fertility spirits"; these spirits could be caught at the harvest time. Some curious customs involving the last sheaf of grain revealed this tradition to Mannhardt. In his main work, *Wald- und Feldkulte* (1875–77, "Cults of the Forests and the Fields"), Mannhardt assembled much material showing how closely the popular ideas of Greeks and Teutons corresponded and how the mysteries of Eleusis were rooted in similar ideas. "The same psychic process," he writes,

> which explains so many elements in tree worship, is also the germ of the Demeter myth. What I have in mind is the comparison of plant-life with human life. Not only that the growth, flourishing and withering of trees have been compared at an early date with the conditions and development of animals and man; but still more clearly perhaps in the language and customs of the peoples, a similar association of cereals and man comes to the fore.[3]

With Mannhardt the "folkloric" mythology begins its triumphal procession. It has had its day, and left a number of important insights. But like so many branches of study it became marred by onesidedness and exaggeration and provoked sharp criticism. The great importance of Mannhardt's ideas is shown most decisively by his influence on the English anthropologist Sir James Frazer (1854–1941). Frazer's books, *Spirits of the Corn and of the Wild* and *Adonis, Attis, Osiris*, give witness to this influence.

In a letter of May 7, 1876, to Karl Müllenhoff, Mannhardt writes:

> I am far from considering all myths psychic responses to natural phenomena—like Kuhn, Schwartz and M. Müller with their whole school—

3. Wilhelm Mannhardt, *Mythologische Forschungen* (Strassburg, 1884), p. 351.

and even farther from considering them exclusively sky phenomena (solar or meteoric); I have learned to value poetic and literary production
as essential factors in the formation of mythology and to draw the necessary conclusions. On the other hand, I am convinced that a part of the
earliest myths owed their origin to a poetry of nature which is not immediately comprehensible to us any more but needs to be explained by
analogies [to contemporary primitives]. That we can make these analogies does not imply a complete historical identity, but takes advantage of
a similar conceptualization and a similar predisposition on a similar de-
velopmental stage.[4]

This is an idea that in 1881, a year after Mannhardt's death, was to
be formulated by A. Bastian in his treatise *Der Völkergedanke im Auf-
bau einer Wissenschaft vom Menschen* ("The Function of 'Collective' or
'Ethnic' Ideas for the Science of Man"). Bastian discusses here the "*Elementargedanken*" ("elementary ideas"), which seem to be inherent in
the human psyche and for that reason can become manifest everywhere and in any age. It is a stimulating thought and has much weight
in some of its forms; it can restore the balance in the case when similar
beliefs in separate places are taken as emanating from a single place of
origin. Thus Mannhardt, who always evinced a touching modesty, is
one of the pioneers of modern scholarship in the areas both of folklore
and of the history of religions.

Later investigations showed, however, that the agrarian customs
and ideas existed far outside the Indo-European areas. We should not
attribute the popular beliefs as reconstructed by Mannhardt to an earlier stage of Indo-European culture but instead to much more ancient,
prehistoric substrata.

In his letter quoted above, Mannhardt mentions the name of Max
Müller (1823–1900), who was no doubt the most important nature
mythologist. He was not only a student of the history of religions but
also a great linguist. An eminent student of Sanskrit, he had immediate
access to the Indian sources—which was only partly true for Adalbert
Kuhn. Max Müller was also the first to edit Vedic texts and gained fame
by interpreting those archaic and often obscure hymns. Indeed, he
had everything needed for an intimate knowledge of Indian mythology.

But the spirit of one's time usually fixes one's interpretation. In Max
Müller's day the opinion was generally held that polytheistic religion
was a nature cult. This idea came from the Romantics, who were
strongly inclined toward nature-pantheism and panentheism. As we
have already noted, the Brahmanic metaphorical language readily allowed such views.

4. Ibid., p. xxv.

For Max Müller, the central point for the formation of the Aryan pantheon is not the terrifying thunder but the lovelier phenomenon of daybreak. He placed this phenomenon at the origin of the struggle of winter and summer and the return of spring. With a rather modern feeling for nature he delights in the dawn of day. "There is no sight in nature," he says,

> more elevating than the dawn even to us, whom philosophy would wish to teach that *nil admirari* is the highest wisdom. Yet in ancient times the power of admiring was the greatest blessing bestowed on mankind; and when could man have admired more intensely, when could his heart have been more gladdened and overpowered with joy, than at the approach of
>> 'the Lord of light,
>> Of life, of love, and gladness!'[5]

This must be regarded as merely the poetic rapture of a modern and very romantic person. Extravaganzas of this type were rebuked by Malinowski, who knew about primitive thoughts and feelings:

> From my own study of living myths among savages, I should say that primitive man has to a very limited extent the purely artistic or scientific interest in nature; there is but little room for symbolism in his ideas and tales; and myth, in fact, is not an idle rhapsody, not an aimless outpouring of vain imaginings, but a hard-working, extremely important cultural force.[6]

To illustrate the type of explanation presented by Max Müller, I want to mention the Indian goddess *Saraṇyū*. With Kuhn, he attaches importance to the similar sound of the Greek *Erinys*. Still he does not consider her the personification of the thundercloud but, again, the dawn of day. Therefore, he compares her to Ushas, and particularly so because both are the mothers of twins (Saraṇyū is especially known as mother of the Aśvins, celebrated twin deities in the Vedic pantheon). However, Athena is also a mother of twins. Hence Athena is another goddess of morning twilight; proof is the myth of her birth from Zeus's head, as the morning twilight is born from the eastern sky. (After all, the east in India is called "mūrdhā divaḥ" or forehead of heaven!) Now Athena's wisdom is explained, if only one thinks of the Sanskrit verb "*budh*," which means both "to awaken" and "to know," for the goddess who awakens men also leads them to knowledge.[7] It is not necessary any more now to waste words on such fanciful reasoning.

5. Max Müller, *Chips from a German Workshop*, vol. 2 (New York, 1869), p. 94.
6. Bronislaw Malinowski, *Myth in Primitive Psychology* (New York, 1926), reprinted in *Magic, Science and Religion* (New York, 1954), p. 97.
7. Max Müller, *Lectures on the Science of Language*, 2nd ser. (London, 1864), pp. 484 ff.

One point in the nature-mythological explanations needs to be clarified. How could the admiration for a phenomenon of nature ever give rise to a personal deity? How could the thrill—or with thunder, the fear or terror—develop into the mythology we know? This was the problem that haunted Max Müller. He did not rest until he found a solution—one that formed the keystone of his system. Being a linguist, he found his clue in the form in which primitive man expressed his feelings.

In the philologist Christian G. Heyne we met the idea that "primordial man," charged with emotion, recreated what he perceived in terms of imagination. This image occurs in a language of sense impressions because the primitive cannot form abstract thoughts. The abstract "causation," for instance, appears in the immediacy of "begetting." Max Müller developed a similar train of thought. He, too, believed that the primal language is not abstract but visual. Even in an expression such as "the day breaks," is there a pure concept of time or is there not rather an agent who can be expected to do something like "breaking"?

As long as the mind was sensual and filled with words, Max Müller argues, it was impossible to speak of evening and morning, of winter and spring without attributing to these something individual, active, sexually determined, and so, at last, a personal character. Either these phenomena were nothing—as in our own withered thought—or they were something, and in that case they could be conceived not merely as powers but as beings endowed with power.[8]

The sensual, visual nature of language appears also in the verbs. They have their full, primitive significance and have not yet faded into abstractions. The verb "to follow," for instance, presupposes someone going after someone else and must not be understood as "to appear later in time." Therefore, when it is said that the sun follows the dawn of day, we conceive a being loving another being and attempting to embrace it. For primitive man, sunrise was also that moment when the night gave life to a beautiful child.

If we assume such an imaginative language, we should expect shifts in meaning with the course of civilization and abstraction. However, Max Müller invokes another linguistic phenomenon: polyonymy and synonymy. Since most objects have more than one attribute, in the course of time each was given various names—polyonymy. Because one quality can be attributed to more than one object, it became possible to understand the word for this quality in different senses—that is, for one adjective to invoke various different objects—synonymy.

8. Müller, *Chips*, p. 56.

What this implies for the evolution of mythological ideas can be shown in the Indian tradition, according to Max Müller's reasoning. Śiva's or Mahadeva's myths, or Vishnu's and Krishna's myths, which were the starting-point of Creuzer's studies, are worthless; they originated late, as a wild and fantastic plant from the Indian soil. The Veda is the true theogony of the Aryan tribes; Hesiod gave no more than its caricature.[9] The human spirit, which always and by nature knows divinity, was compelled in a peculiar direction by the irresistible power of language, by the quirk in images of the supernatural. If we want to know this direction, we find it in the Veda. The gods in the text are masks without players, made by man and not his makers; they are *nomina* ("mere names"), not *numina* ("divine powers"): names *sans* reality, not ineffable real beings.

This development Max Müller called a "disease of language." The polyonymy and synonymy, which were once meaningful, confused imageries that were initially separate. A mythological phraseology appeared, because within a collection of predicates a single one was pushed to the fore and became the acknowledged proper name of a god.

The term "disease of language" is unfortunate and reveals the weakness of Max Müller's whole construction. After all, how could an unnatural linguistic process of confusion and mixture be responsible for a mythology that had been meaningful and trustworthy for generations? *Nomina*, not *numina*! How could one say such a thing about the gods of pagan polytheism, who move us time and again exactly because of their strong personal character? Indeed, were Zeus and Wodan, Indra and Donar no more than empty names? They were true gods—one could almost say of flesh and blood—so human were they in their imagery, so persuasive in their doings. They demanded veneration because of their powerful intervention in life; awe and confidence, fear and love were felt for them in accordance with their power and character. Mythology is not a disease of language; it is a reality immediately apparent to man; it has its being in all that is limitless and enigmatic in nature or in himself.

Max Müller's theory demonstrates once more the gap that lay between nineteenth-century man and the sundry faiths he knew existed. To the extent that modern man's soul detached itself from Christianity, to the extent that Christianity was allowed to deteriorate into a mere moral lore as the core was taken out of its dogma and the sense for its mystery got lost, to that extent also man's understanding for other religions disappeared. It seemed to him that these religions were so naïve

9. Ibid., p. 76.

that they could not have any connection with deep human experience. Max Müller's theory makes abundantly clear that he never fathomed belief.

He was a man of his time. For many years he had enthusiastic supporters. In England, G. W. Cox was his faithful disciple.[10] In France M. Bréal, who was at the same time a linguist and a historian of religion, as was Max Müller, propagated his theories.[11] A scholar of stature like A. Réville argued as late as 1881 that the mythical explanations of natural phenomena are poetic flights empty of every really religious element. Hence the cult is the imitation of a process of nature; Réville analyzes the elements he regards as separate symbols that nevertheless relate to a central idea and can unite in a complex cultic act.[12]

Analysis alone, no matter how subtle, is insufficient. So are constructions of thought, no matter how cleverly thought through. Only an accurate observation of primitive religious life will lead to worthwhile insights.

10. G. W. Cox, *The Mythology of Aryan Nations* (London, 1870); *An Introduction to the Science of Comparative Mythology and Folklore* (London, 1881).

11. M. Bréal, *Mélanges de mythologie et de linguistique* (Paris, 1877).

12. A. Réville, *Prolégomènes de l'histoire des religions*, 2nd ed. (Paris, 1881).

The Problem of Defining Myth

LAURI HONKO

The study of myth in the twentieth century differs dramatically from myth scholar-ship in the nineteenth century. The notion of myth as a pre-scientific "theory" of nature, supposedly peculiar to an early period or stage in human evolution, has given way to a vast array of new conceptions and approaches. In a remarkably succinct essay, Finnish folklorist Lauri Honko, professor of folklore and compara-tive religion at the University of Turku, provides a useful overview of twentieth-century definitions and theories of myth. Many of the theories mentioned by Honko will be discussed at greater length in later essays in this volume.

For other surveys of myth theory, see H. Baumann, "Mythos in ethnologischer Sicht," Studium Generale 12 (1959), 1–17, 583–97; J. L. Fischer, "The Sociopsycho-logical Analysis of Folktales," Current Anthropology 4 (1963), 235–95; Percy S. Co-hen, "Theories of Myth," Man n.s. 4 (1969), 337–53; and Robert A. Segal, "In Defense of Mythology: The History of Modern Theories of Myth," Annals of Scholarship 1 (1980), 3–49.

THE SEMANTIC SPAN OF THE CONCEPT OF MYTH

The first thing that one realises in trying to grasp the semantic im-plications of myth is that myth can cover an extremely wide field. Without resorting to an enumeration of the different ways in which the term is used nowadays, it is clear that myth can encompass every-thing from a simple-minded, fictitious, even mendacious impression to an absolutely true and sacred account, the very reality of which far outweighs anything that ordinary everyday life can offer. The way in which the term myth is commonly used reveals, too, that the word is loaded with emotional overtones. These overtones creep not only into common parlance but also, somewhat surprisingly, into scientific usage. That myth does, in fact, carry emotional overtones in this way is perhaps most easily seen if we think of terms such as prayer, liturgy, ritual drama, spell: they are all used for different religious genres but

Reprinted from Haralds Biezais, ed., *The Myth of the State*, Scripta Instituti Don-neriani Aboensis no. 6 (Stockholm, 1972), pp. 7–19, by permission of the author, the Donner-Institutet, and Almqvist & Wiksell Förlag.

would seem to be more neutral than myth. It appears to be difficult for many scholars to discuss myth simply as a form of religious communication, as one genre among other genres.[1]

All attempts to define myth should, of course, be based, on the one hand, on those traditions which are actually available and which are called myths and, on the other, on the kind of language which scholars have adopted when discussing myth. In both cases, that of the empirical material and that of the history of scholarship on myth, the picture that results is far from uniform. Among those factors which have influenced, and still do influence to some extent, the situation I should like to mention three. The first is: demythologisation; the second: the explanations provided by antiquity; and the third: modern theories concerning myth.

THE TYPOLOGY OF DEMYTHOLOGISATION

There are three main forms of demythologisation. It is possible to talk about a *terminological* demythologisation. This means that the actual word myth is avoided but the account, the story itself, is retained. To call the Resurrection a myth may be a dastardly insult to a Christian for whom the concept myth has a pejorative sense. He would probably prefer some such expression as holy story or sacred history: perhaps quite simply history, for in Christianity as in Judaism there is a marked tendency to transform religious traditions into history. Such a tendency is a culturally bound phenomenon: in some other cultures there may be noted a clear preference for the term story instead of history. Christian theologians are faced with certain difficulties when using the terms myth, history and sacred history. It is possible to imagine that someone might try to classify the Creation as myth, the Crucifixion as history and the Resurrection as sacred history.[2]

The second main type of demythologisation may be termed *total and compensatory*. Here the mythical tradition is rejected completely; such stories are unnecessary for the civilised mind, it is claimed. Then we are faced with two problems: how do we explain the continuing existence of myths and the influence they exert? How can we per-

1. The genre analytic aspect as well as some other aspects of myth research I have discussed in an article, "Der Mythos in der Religionswissenschaft," *Temenos* 6 (1970), 36 ff., and earlier in "Genre Analysis in Folkloristics and Comparative Religion," *Temenos* 3 (1968). Here I do not wish to repeat much of what I have already said, but I hope that the reader will consult those articles for further bibliographical references. In this paper the bibliographic apparatus will be reduced to a minimum.

2. Cf. Honko, "Der Mythos," p. 56.

suade others of the worthlessness of these stories? The first question has often been answered by means of evolutionary arguments. Comte, Dardel and many others have entertained ideas of a mythical period followed by non-mythical periods. However, historical developments have given the lie to such speculations. Philosophers who have been eager to abolish myth have realised that a vacuum is immediately created if the contribution made by myth to culture is explained away. They have therefore tried to provide constructive suggestions as to what might take the place of myth and its place in culture. David Bidney's answer runs as follows: "Myth must be taken seriously precisely in order that it may be gradually superseded in the interests of the advancement of truth and the growth of human intelligence. Normative, critical and scientific thought provides the only self-correcting means of combating the diffusion of myth, but it may do so only on condition that we retain a firm and uncompromising faith in the integrity of reason and in the trans-cultural validity of the scientific enterprise."[3] The renowned author of *Theoretical Anthropology* believes, then, in science, which will replace religion. He provides proof for the claim which is advanced from time to time that science is a religion for scientists. This somewhat trivial generalisation is of less interest to us here, however, than the fact that the advocates of demythologisation turn to compensation and substitution. A classic example of this is Plato's concept of an elite: he refused to admit Hesiod and Homer into his Ideal State. Another example is Auguste Comte, who tried to fill the gap left by demythologisation by founding the worship of "le Grand-Être."

The third type of demythologisation is of a *partial and interpretative* type. Advocates of this line of thinking explain that there is no justification for believing myths quite literally. Myths, they say, are symbols or representations: it is insight into what lies behind them that is important. In order to gain this insight we need the help of an interpreter who can explain what we shall believe. The origin of partial and interpretative demythologisation is often to be found in the fact that a philosopher notes that the religious tradition of myths is no longer enough: it no longer agrees with the other premises of the contemporary world scene. Instead of opting for the alternative of total demythologisation he tries to salvage something of the myths by interpreting them. This was what happened in Ancient Greece and, more recently, there has been Bultmann's campaign along the same lines, beginning in 1941. Without going through the whole of Bultmann's

3. D. Bidney, "Myth, Symbolism and Truth," *Myth: A Symposium*, ed. T. A. Sebeok (Bloomington, Ind., 1958), p. 14.

theology one gets the impression that he does not demand that the Creation, the healing miracles of the New Testament nor even the Resurrection be accepted as the complete truth. Instead he emphasises that the important thing is to gain insight into the essence of the Christian faith and find an existential solution to one's problems in the light of interpreted Christian traditions. Bultmann is not without his critics. In the debate between Bultmann and Jaspers, for example, the important difference between the two seems to be that Jaspers is able to accept that a myth may be capable of several interpretations while Bultmann tends to hold that a tradition can be reduced to a single meaning which has universal validity. Both regard the priest as playing a decisive role as interpreter, but Jaspers accepts interpretations adapted to certain situations. Bultmann, on the other hand, strives to discover the correct meaning of a tradition.[4]

THE INTERPRETATIONS OF ANTIQUITY

The part played by classical antiquity in mythological scholarship can hardly be overestimated. Ancient philosophers postulated some ten explanations for myths, which have been resurrected from time to time right up to the present. The significance of these theories did not begin to wane until the breakthrough of empirical research at the beginning of this century. To clarify what I mean by these theories concerning the explanation of myths here is a list:

1. *The mythographic interpretations* belong partly to religious practice and partly to literature. Hesiod in his Theogonia and Homer in his epics (or the compilers of these works) were believers in tradition and transmitters of it, but they probably allowed themselves some freedom of interpretation or poetic expression.

Criticism was levelled against the mythographers and "profanized" myths. There were demythologisers of the total and compensatory kind. So we have:

2. *Philosophical criticisms* of various kinds. The rejection of traditional myths is total, and compensations range from Xenophanes' monotheism and Heraclitus' somewhat pantheistic concept of λόγος to Plato's almost cynical view of religion as an instrument for dealing with uncivilised classes.

4. On the problem of demythologisation see, e.g., K. Goldammer, "Die Entmythologisierung des Mythus als Problemstellung der Mythologien," *Studium Generale* 8 (1955), 378 ff., and on the debate between Karl Jaspers and Rudolf Bultmann, *Myth and Christianity: An Inquiry into the Possibility of Religion Without Myth* (New York, 1958).

3. *The pre-scientific interpretation.* According to Thales water was the prime cause of all things, and Anaximander talked about ἄπειρον as a substance which was the material base of the universe. This natural science of physical origins did not severely contradict religion (Thales believed in a universe full of deities). The rejection as well as compensation remained implicit and latent.

There were those who wanted to rescue myths by means of partial and interpretive demythologisation. So we have, for example, the allegories of Theagenes such as:

4. *The allegorical explanation based on natural phenomena* according to which Apollo is fire, Poseidon water, Artemis the moon and Hera the atmosphere (cf. the "hymns" composed by Parmenides and Empedocles) and

5. *The allegorical explanation based on spiritual qualities* according to which Athena is wise judgement, Ares boundless unreason, Aphrodite desire and Hermes the discerning intellect (cf. Anaxagoras, who explained that Athena is art, Lethe forgetfulness and Zeus intellect).

6. *The etymological interpretations* were also aimed at creating the impression that myths "make sense." It was thought that the secret of the gods lay in their names and epithets. Plato derived, from the verb θεῖν, the theory that man created the idea of god by observing the regular movement of the stars. The Stoicist Kleanthes had two alternative etymologies for Apollo (verbs ἀπολλύναι "destroy" and ἀπολαύνειν "dispel").

7. *The historical (comparative and derivative) interpretation* was founded by Herodotus. The myths and gods were borrowed always *from* other cultures to the Greek. There were Libyan gods such as the one that later came to be called Poseidon or Egyptian gods like Zeus (derived from Ammon), Athena (from Neith), Apollo (from Horus). Interpretations of the names of gods and their attributes served as evidence. The "ethnological" view created an atmosphere of relativity and secularisation.

8. *The Euhemeristic interpretation* was also historical but in the sense that gods were explained to have developed from the biographies of human beings. Herodotus and Prodicus made suggestions of this kind. Later the worship of Heracles and Aesculapius and, above all, Alexander the Great served as contemporary examples. The idea of cult attributed to human beings, mainly kings and heroes, was systematically applied by the novelist Euhemeros in his writings (the tale of a visit to the island, Panchaia, where the genealogies of Greek gods, originally kings, etc., were found engraved on a golden pillar).

9. *The "sociological" interpretation or the deceit of priests, law-*

makers, rulers, etc., was introduced when the veneration of the wise leaders waned. The sophist Critias taught that the gods had been invented to maintain social order. Epicurus also referred to man's evil conscience as the prime source of myths and Polybius said that the ancestors had wisely introduced gods to restrain the ignorant masses by fear of the unknown. Socrates and Plato attributed much of the content of myths to the phantasy of poets.

10. *The psychological interpretations* are already discernible in the previous trend. Fear as a source of belief and worship was advocated by Epicurus, among others. It was Statius who coined the sentence: *primus in orbe deos fecit timor.* Prodicus taught that worship of the gods is based on gratitude, e.g., for a good crop, successful hunting; it is man's reaction to the favour and efficacy of cosmos and earth. The gods are benign powers: bread = Demeter (Mother Earth, protector of crops), wine = Dionysos, fire = Hephaistos.[5]

These explanations were designed to serve the elite: folk religion and official cults were not deeply affected by them. This has been the case ever since. You may follow the formation of various religions on the one hand, and the development of scholarly frames of reference on the other. They do not necessarily coincide or correlate.

MODERN THEORIES OF MYTH

Since the conception that we have of myth has continually to be revised in the light of modern scholarship a brief classification of present theories about myth, or of the angles from which myth is studied today, would not be out of place. I have compiled a list of twelve ways that scholars have used in their approach to the problem of myth: among these twelve approaches there may be distinguished four subgroups, namely, historical, psychological, sociological, and structural perspectives.[6] These approaches may sometimes be mutually opposed and in competition with each other but, nevertheless, I think that there are two facts which are today accepted by the majority of scholars. The first is that these theories in fact overlap and complement each other to some extent. The second is that myths are multidimensional: a myth can be approached from, shall we say, ten different angles, some of which may have greater relevance than others depending

5. For the theories of antiquity see, e.g., J. de Vries, *Forschungsgeschichte der Mythologie* (Freiburg, 1961), p. 43. Cf. J. de Vries, *The Study of Religion: A Historical Approach* (New York, 1967), pp. 3 ff.

6. Cf. P. S. Cohen, "Theories of Myth," *Man* 4 (1969), 337 ff., where the number of theories is more limited.

on the nature of the material being studied and the questions posed.

1. *Myth as source of cognitive categories*. Myth is seen as an explanation for enigmatic phenomena. The intellect needs to conceptualise certain aspects of the universe, to establish the relationship between different phenomena.

2. *Myth as form of symbolic expression*. Myth is placed on a par with other creative activities, such as poetry or music. Myth has its own laws, its own reality, its own forms of expression: it may be looked upon as a projection of the human mind, as a symbolic structuring of the world.

3. *Myth as projection of the subconscious*. Myth is seen in relation to a substratum shared partly by all humans, partly only by members of the same race, nation, culture (Neo-Jungian emphasis on socialization and cultural group instead of racial-genetic inheritance). Freud offered the concept of day-dreams as models for myth. The message is disguised and condensed; projection of the subconscious is controlled partly by tradition, partly by elementary facts of life.

4. *Myth as an integrating factor in man's adaptation to life*: *myth as world view*. In myths man is faced with fundamental problems of society, culture and nature. Myths offer opportunities of selecting different elements which satisfy both individual tendencies and social necessities. From these elements it is possible to create an individual, but at the same time traditional, way of viewing the world.

5. *Myth as charter of behaviour*. Myths give support to accepted patterns of behaviour by placing present-day situations in a meaningful perspective with regard to the precedents of the past. Myths provide a valid justification for obligations and privileges. Myths act as safety valves by making it possible for people to ventilate their emotions without socially disruptive effects.

6. *Myth as legitimation of social institutions*. Myths sustain institutions: together with ritual they give expression to common religious values and consolidate them.

7. *Myth as marker of social relevance*. Myths are not regarded as a random collection of stories: in a culture there is a clear correlation between the distribution of mythical themes and what is considered socially relevant in that culture.

8. *Myth as mirror of culture, social structure, etc*. Myths are considered to reflect certain facets of culture. This reflection is seldom direct or photographic but it may reveal values which would otherwise be difficult to detect.

9. *Myth as result of historical situation*. Stress is laid on the reconstruction of those events which were most decisive in the formation of the myths. Myths are appraised in the light of their historical back-

ground: their subsequent use and modification in view of new historical developments are placed in relation to their origin.

10. *Myth as religious communication*. Myths may be regarded as information which is transmitted from sender to receiver via different
media. Closer analysis of this communication process implies such
things as observing the redundancy in the language of religion and in
non-verbal forms of expression, the definition of the basic elements of
a message, etc.

11. *Myth as religious genre*. Myths are regarded principally as being
of a narrative nature: they are seen, however, in relation to other narrative genres and to non-epic genres of the kind which contribute to
spread the message of myth. This genre-analytical aspect of myth implies that traditional forms condition the nature of the communication process.

12. *Myth as medium for structure*. To this category belong those
methods of research which are often characterised as structural but
which deal in varying ways with the language, content and structure of
myths. The structure of myths may be analysed from a syntagmatic or
paradigmatic angle, for example. The concept of binary opposition is
one of the most popular watchwords in this respect.

A DESCRIPTIVE DEFINITION

What has been said above is intended to provide the background
against which the development and uses of the concept of myth may
be understood. Ideas as to what is comprised by the concept myth
vary considerably. Personally I favour a middle course between the ex-
tremes of too wide a definition and too narrowly drawn a definition.
As an example of far too wide a definition, so wide as to be almost
amorphous, there is the so-called mythopoetic conception which Cassirer represents, for instance.[7] I cannot believe that such an abstract
definition is either necessary or useful even for those who wish to
make use of the results achieved by Cassirer in his research on mythological symbols. On the other hand, Theodor Gaster's view may be
cited as an example of too narrow a conception of myth. According to
him direct proof is required that a story has been used in connection
with a rite before it can be accepted as a myth.[8]

As a descriptive and concise definition of myth I have in the past
used the following:

7. See Honko, "Der Mythos," pp. 38 ff.
8. Ibid., pp. 39 ff.

"Myth, a story of the gods, a religious account of the beginning of the world, the creation, fundamental events, the exemplary deeds of the gods as a result of which the world, nature and culture were created together with all the parts thereof and given their order, which still obtains. A myth expresses and confirms society's religious values and norms, it provides patterns of behaviour to be imitated, testifies to the efficacy of ritual with its practical ends and establishes the sanctity of cult. The true milieu of myth is to be found in religious rites and ceremonial. The ritual acting out of myth implies the defence of the world order; by imitating sacred exemplars the world is prevented from being brought to chaos. The reenactment of a creative event, for example, the healing wrought by a god in the beginning of time, is the common aim of myth and ritual. In this way the event is transferred to the present and its result, i.e. the healing of a sick person, can be achieved once more here and now. In this way, too, the world order, which was created in the primeval era and which is reflected in myths, preserves its value as an exemplar and model for the people of today. The events recounted in myths have true validity for a religious person. For this reason the use of the term myth in everyday language is from the scholarly point of view inexact (in ordinary language myth is often used expressly for something untrue, utopian, misguided, etc.). The *point de départ*, then, is criticism directed towards religious groups and traditions from outside and this criticism has always existed. Nowadays attempts have often been made to brand non-religious ideas, political ideas, economic teaching, etc., as myth."[9]

THE FOUR CRITERIA

In order to clarify more exactly what is meant by the definition given here it may be noted that it is built on four criteria: form, content, function and context.

In terms of its *form* a myth is a *narrative* which provides a verbal account of what is known of sacred origins. There are in addition, of course, brief intimations, allusions to myths and mythical symbols. These can be understood only if a certain narrative content can be considered a background for them. Mythical prototypes, exemplary figures and characters as well as repeated heroic deeds or creative acts can all be verbalised in the form of a narrative. The question is: can myths be expressed through the medium of other genres than narrative, for example, prayer or sacred pictures where there is no need to

9. L. Honko, *Uskontotieteen oppisanastoa* (Helsinki, 1971), s.v. "myytti."

recite the narrative content? When investigating a certain myth all the information that helps to perpetuate the myth must be included. There can be no limiting the material under investigation to the most traditional and fixed forms of the myth's manifestation: attention must also be paid to every individual, temporary, unique and non-fixed aspect of the use of the myth.

Myth can be brought to life in the form of a ritual drama (enacted myth), a liturgical recitation (narrated myth), in which case both verbal and non-verbal media (sermons, hymns, prayers, religious dances) can be utilised. Similarly myth can be manifested in religious art (ikons, symbolic signs). In addition to these codified forms we also have the way in which myth is transmitted in speech, thought, dreams and other modes of behaviour. A religious person may in the course of his experience identify himself with a mythical figure. Myth may totally dominate his behaviour, but it need not be verbalised. Since the material which empirical research into myth has to work with is so varied, it would perhaps be useful to have a term for the minimum amount of information that the human mind needs in order to create a recognisable version of a myth no matter what form or context the myth might adopt for its expression. Henry A. Murray's term "mythic imagent" might be used for this minimum.[10]

Myths vary greatly, of course, as to their *content*, but one link that ties them together is encountered in the fact that, in general, myths contain information about decisive, creative events in the beginning of time. It is no coincidence that *cosmogonic* descriptions occupy a central position in many mythological accounts. One has only to think of the part played by cosmogony in all three main types of ritual: calendar rites, rites of passage and rites of crisis. The importance of myths of creation as a kind of proto-myth becomes abundantly clear as soon as an attempt is made to list the countless examples which show how readily the origin of widely differing phenomena is linked with the creation of the world. Cosmogonic myths seem, in many religions, to provide a special authority for stories of how culture originated. But, of course, not all myths are cosmogonic in content if the word is used in its strictly literal sense. The most important thing perhaps, at least it would seem so to me, is the structural parallel between cosmogonic myths and certain other stories of the world's origin which the social group accepts as the ultimate source of its identity. In other words, the

10. He defines it as "an imagined (visualized) representation of a mythic event" and points out that a book of mythic stories on a shelf in the library is inoperative—a mere residue of past imagination—so long as it is never read, never generates influential imagents in other minds. See H. A. Murray, *Myth and Mythmaking* (Boston, 1960), pp. 320 ff.

term cosmogonic in this sense comprises all those stories that recount how the world began, how our era started, how the goals that we strive to attain are determined and our most sacred values codified. Seen from this point of view the 96th sura of the Koran, the birth of Christ, the life of Lenin, Che Guevara's death and Mao's speeches are all material which, under certain conditions, can be structured in a way which resembles ancient cosmogonic myths.

Myths *function* as examples, as models. From myths it is possible to obtain a more or less uniform explanation of the world at the basis of which lie the creative, the formative activities of the gods, culture heroes, etc. The mythical view of the world is experienced as something static: there are no changes, no developments. In principle it is possible to find exemplars and models for all human activity and all perceptible activity in the events of the great beginning. The religious person's share in this lies in the fact that he preserves these examples in his mind, he follows and copies them. Myths have, of course, numerous specific functions, but we may generalise and say that they offer both a cognitive basis for and practical models of behaviour. From this point of view myths can be characterised as *ontological*: they are incorporated and integrated into a coherent view of the world, and they describe very important aspects of life and the universe.

The *context* of myth is, in normal cases, *ritual*, a pattern of behaviour which has been sanctioned by usage. Myth provides the ideological content for a sacred form of behaviour. Ritual brings the creative events of the beginning of time to life and enables them to be repeated here and now, in the present. The ordinary reality of everyday life recedes and is superseded by the reality of ritual drama. What was once possible and operative in the beginning of time becomes possible once more and can exert its influence anew.

CONCLUDING REMARKS

The definition that I have tried to sketch here has been mainly intended to draw attention to the different levels which are relevant to the undoubtedly complex concept myth. If one differentiates between these four levels, namely, form, content, function and context, it is much easier to encounter the varied uses which the concept has acquired in scientific literature. By this I mean that it is possible to delimit and yet be flexible at the same time. There is no need to welcome with open arms just any traditions into the fold of myth research: but nor is it necessary to exclude, for example, studies of myth where the context criterion, i.e., a context of ritual, is not fulfilled. The degree of flexibility that can be achieved is dependent on the approach that the scholar has chosen. Should he wish to include both literary sources and oral material in different cultures and perhaps also in different genres, in order to cast light on all the manifestations of a myth motive, then it is pointless to demand that their function and context should correspond to those of the ideal type of myth. In such cases it has often been possible to circumnavigate the problem by speaking, for example, of a mythologeme instead of a myth. In this way one avoids deceiving the reader into believing that the subject under discussion is ritual text. For example, when, in a ballad recited by young girls in Ingermanland, a variant of a cosmogonic myth is included, it is better to refer to it as a mythologeme rather than as a myth to avoid giving the reader the impression that it is a ritual dance. It is thus a question of an expedient liberty at the level of context, which is justified as long as the scholar limits his claims strictly to the content. It would of course be desirable to say which of the criteria is or are the most decisive, but it would appear to be without justification to give a normative recommendation here. It is and will continue to be the task of every scholar to give the concept an operative definition, i.e., to give it a content which most effectively and consistently serves the ends which his own particular research situation demands. In the process, each of the criteria mentioned above should be carefully scrutinised in some way or other.

On Defining Myths

G. S. KIRK

Among scholars interested in myth, no group has written more on the subject than classicists. Although they are ordinarily primarily concerned with Greek or Roman myths and their ancient Near Eastern cognates, a few have ventured to consider myth in general. G. S. Kirk, professor of Greek at Cambridge University, is widely read in the theory of myth, and so his sophisticated discussion of the difficulties in defining myth provide a helpful perspective, supplementing the essays by Professors Bascom and Honko. For a more comprehensive treatment by Kirk, see his Myth: Its Meanings and Functions in Ancient & Other Cultures *(Berkeley and Los Angeles, 1970). For Professor Kirk's application of myth theory to Greek myths, see his* The Nature of Greek Myths *(Baltimore, 1974).*

There is no need to defend the relevance of Greek mythology to early philosophical thought. That thought emerged from a primarily mythological background, as Cornford showed, and it also developed, at least until Plato, in a cultural environment in which myths continued to be a dominant factor.

The remarks that follow are not concerned with myths in their literary variants, but rather with establishing some important methodological principles for the understanding of myths in their primary and perhaps pre-literary forms.

For there can be no doubt that the main Greek myths were formed before the spread of general literacy in the seventh century B.C. Homer, Hesiod, Stesichorus and others provided connexions and a kind of consistency, but the central themes of divine emergence as well as of heroic adventure seem to be Mycenaean at least, and probably much earlier still.

Our understanding of the constitution of these earlier myths must necessarily be defective, almost non-existent. Yet it has been unnecessarily handicapped, not only by reluctance to assess Asiatic and Egyptian parallels, but also by confusion about the range of myths in gen-

Reprinted from *Phronesis: A Journal for Ancient Philosophy*, suppl. vol. 1 (1973), 61–69, by permission of the author, Van Gorcum, and Humanities Press, Atlantic Highlands, N.J. 07716.

eral and their possible functions. The paucity of general treatments of myths, the evident satisfaction with descriptive surveys such as that by H. J. Rose, the tolerance of various absurd treatises that I refrain from naming, the indifference towards (and failure to review) substantial but difficult contributions like Fontenrose's *Python*—these things indicate that most Classicists are not really interested in the problems of myths, whether through ignorance that they still exist or as an after-effect of surfeit from the days of Jane Harrison, A. B. Cook and Gilbert Murray.

While Classical scholars have neglected the general implications of myths, these have been energetically explored by anthropologists, historians of religion, and psychologists. Unfortunately these other kinds of scholar have tended to be dogmatic and over-confident in their procedures, and to evade some of the important basic issues. Moreover their views are often affected by the false assumption that Greek mythology affords a pattern for all other myths. Classicists have been able to contribute little in the way of control or caution, and indeed have remained largely unaware of work on myths in other fields.

One of the chief impediments to progress has been the preconception—as strong today, in most quarters, as ever before—that all myths have the same kind of origin and function, and that what students of mythology should be pursuing is some all-embracing theory of myth. The results have been universalistic theories like those of the nineteenth-century nature-myth school (all myths are allegories of natural processes), or of Andrew Lang (they are primarily aetiological), or Malinowski (they are not aetiological, but are confirmations or "charters" of social facts and beliefs), or Jane Harrison developing Robertson Smith and J. G. Frazer (all myths arise out of the misunderstanding of rituals), or Freud (they are reflexions of unconscious fears and desires, as are dreams), or Kluckhohn developing Freud and Durkheim (they are parallel to rituals as "adjustive responses" to anxiety), or Jung (they are expressions of a collective unconscious and are determined by archetypal patterns of thought and symbol), or Ernst Cassirer (they are excited responses to special aspects of the world), or Radcliffe-Brown developing Malinowski (they are mechanisms of the social order), or Lévi-Strauss (all myths reproduce a common structure of mind and society), or Eliade developing Malinowski (their function is temporarily to reinstate the creative past), or V. W. Turner developing Durkheim and van Gennep (myths achieve a liberating restructuring of normal life).

Each of these universal theories (and none of them is presented as stipulative, or as valid for only one particular kind of myth) can be negated by citing many obvious instances of myth that do not accord with the assigned origin or function. Indeed the looseness of the term "myth" itself, and its wide range of applications in common usage (even apart from vulgar meanings such as "fabrication"), together with the failure of specialists to offer acceptable special definitions, suggest that it is a diverse phenomenon that is likely to have different motives and applications even within a single society—let alone in different cultures and at different periods. Any general theory that artificially restricts this probable multiformity by declaring that many apparent instances must be treated as something else, for example as "oral literature," or that denies it altogether, is likely to be incorrect. Formalistic definitions (e.g., "myths are tales that are believed to be true," or "myths are tales that are set outside historical time") are favoured by folklorists in particular and, once again, tend to exclude important blocs of *prima facie* mythological material for no particular reason. Moreover they tell us little about the nature of myths themselves; they simply isolate, not very accurately, one characteristic. There is, however, one useful distinction of this kind: the one outlined most prominently by Malinowski, between myths on the one hand and legends or sagas on the other—between essentially non-historical tales and those that include identifiable and conspicuous historical elements or are historicizing in intention. Naturally the distinction is not a hard-and-fast one. Much of the *Iliad* can be treated as legend (that is, the parts of it that describe the action before Troy in human and realistic terms); yet it overlaps myth in the intervention of the supernatural (the gods). The *Iliad* as a whole can be classified as "myth" in a very general sense, and finds its way into most surveys of Greek mythology; in any case there is much to be said for being too liberal rather than too exclusive in establishing a broad category, but the *Iliad* is also very different from non-historicizing traditional tales, whether about gods or about heroes, such as those about the succession of the earliest gods or about Heracles or Perseus.

Even theories of mythical expression (i.e., those that purport to define the kind of psychic process, usually unconscious, that gives rise to myths) are unlikely to be universal in application, and certainly all of them propounded so far are falsifiable by counter-instances. The wide range of morphological and functional variation—for example, even under the misleading heading of "aetiology," from practical charter-type uses to responses to abstract dilemmas of human existence; or in imaginative terms from simple wish-fulfillment to fantastic alterations of the pattern of life itself—suggests that the mental and psychic processes of myth-formation are themselves diverse.

At the same time there must be some general and universal quality of myths (to use rather Platonic language) by virtue of which we assign them this generic name. It will be agreed, at least, that myths are tales, stories. That is what the word comes to mean in Greek, and in this case usage and etymology are in accord. A mere description of a person or object, for example, whatever its other qualities, would not be accepted as a myth, nor would a prayer or a hymn (although a hymn, like many of the Homeric Hymns, may contain or refer to a myth). A more or less realistic account of a historical action is not a myth, although it may eventually take on mythical characteristics as did the tale of Croesus in antiquity, nor is a philosophical analysis of a social problem, or a legal charter. These are not myths, because they are not tales, even though they may serve similar purposes to those of some myths. A myth is a tale, and that is the basic element of any definition. Even the idea of a tale is, of course, somewhat imprecise: for example, is Hesiod's "myth" of the five races, in *Works and Days*, a tale or not? But generally speaking a tale is recognised as a dramatic construction with a dénouement, and most myths are of that kind.

If all myths are tales, not all tales are myths: a novel is not a myth, for instance, neither is a Christian cautionary tale (which is not to deny that they may contain elements of myth). By "myths" most people mean "primitive," unsophisticated and non-literary tales, tales that are told in non-literate cultures, that are repeated and developed by anonymous storytellers rather than being invented by an individual author with pen in hand.

It is a condition of our knowing any such tale from antiquity, at least, that it should have become traditional, should have passed down from generation to generation to be eventually recorded when literacy becomes established. That is what must have happened with many of the myths preserved by Hesiod and Homer. It is conceivable that literacy will happen to catch the odd tale that is pre-literate but not traditional, that is an invention of the time when writing becomes available; similarly in a partly-literate environment there may always be some passage from the non-literate to the literate side. So too an anthropologist observing a non-literate tribe may record the occasional tale that is not traditional, that is substantially the invention of a living storyteller who coincides with the anthropologist's visit. Nevertheless the vast majority of the tales that pass from a non-literate environment into literacy will obviously be traditional ones. Apart from anything else, in most non-literate societies, which are highly traditional, traditional tales will greatly outnumber new inventions at any one time, which is not to deny that they themselves may be under a constant process of elaboration and adaptation.

There is, however, a different and in some ways more specific basic definition that is much favoured by anthropologists at present: it is that "myths are sacred tales." That does not exclude the idea of their being traditional tales, but it goes much further in accepting only one kind of traditional tale. In my opinion this added exclusiveness has no advantages. It is true that many traditional tales are "sacred" in that they concern gods or spirits—for example most cosmogonical myths, a well-known class, are sacred in that sense. But other tales are not primarily about gods at all, and have no ancillary implications of sanctity or tabu. It is not helpful to regard many of the tales about Heracles as sacred, even if he is persecuted by Hera or helped by Athena; Deucalion's re-creation of men by throwing stones over his shoulder is not usefully specified as a sacred tale, even though the action is suggested by a god, is set in the early days of the world, and is the result of a divinely-caused flood. Most traditional tales in non-literate societies (which are usually highly religious) contain supernatural elements, and often "supernatural" will mean "divine" in these circumstances. But not everything that is supernatural is sacred. Nor should we be confused by specialized anthropological applications of the term "sacred," notably by the functionalist view that myths are expressions of the social structure and consequently of central importance in the life of the tribe and therefore "sacred." In short, although many myths in many different cultures concern gods and other sacred beings, or the period of creation, not all do so in any essential way, and therefore it can be misleading to focus on this quality as primary.

It seems that "traditional oral tale" is the only safe basis for a broad definition of myth. Even this will exclude whatever is meant by "a modern myth," as well as partly literary and historical developments like the Croesus tale already mentioned. But these and similar cases can reasonably be seen as secondary forms, and in trying to establish the essence of myths it makes sense to begin from the primary phenomena. Specific authorship and the use of writing affect not only the form but also the imaginative and emotional content of tales, and any kind of scholarly and self-conscious approach to myths (which can be traced in Greece to at least as early as the seventh century B.C.) tends to be destructive of some of their essential qualities.

The basic idea of the myth as traditional tale has its own important implication, which tends to be concealed if the definition is elaborated. Whatever the particular kinds and uses of such tales, their traditional quality and their narrative force cannot be infringed. In other words, in order to become traditional and remain so, a tale must have an appeal that continues from generation to generation (although perhaps with slight alteration of emphasis): either simply as a tale, because it is particularly neat and forceful (and so on), or as a tale with a special application or set of applications—as explanatory, problem-palliating, confirmatory, psychologically liberating and so on. If the applications are varied somewhat from generation to generation, or in the passage of a myth from one society into another, then its narrative core or plot must be such as to allow different emphases and interpretations according to different customs, needs and preoccupations. In one sense, a myth is always changing; in another, its narrative structure persists. Many traditional oral tales, often because of high factual and low fantastic content, tend not to assume practical or emotional and intellectual applications; they are what we term folktales or *Märchen*. It is sensible not to deny these the general title of "myths," since their themes interact with those of more imaginative and pregnant types.

Beyond their basic quality as traditional oral tales, therefore, myths may take on many different forms and functions—as associated with gods and rituals, as affirmations or charters of lands, titles, institutions and beliefs, as explanations at various levels and as problem-exploring and problem-palliating in various ways, and as providing different kinds of mental and emotional relief and support. No definition of myths can easily cover all these possible uses, which overlap each other but do not coincide. As already suggested, the different uses presuppose different interests, methods and kinds of imagination on the part of the tellers of tales, and different kinds of reaction on the part of their audience: a variation of interplay between individual and collective emotions, and between deliberate and spontaneous invention. The continuing factor, the $\dot{\upsilon}\pi o\chi\varepsilon\dot{\iota}\mu\varepsilon\nu o\nu$ that receives the different qualities, is the narrative structure itself: for example Prometheus has a subtly different role in Aeschylus from that suggested in Hesiod, and a different one again can be inferred for the pre-literate period in which the myth must have developed.

The rejection of universalistic theories of mythical expression, as a corollary of rejecting a universal mythical function, has some important implications for the concept of "mythopoeic thought." In fact it is one more nail in the coffin of a concept that has many weaknesses. Admittedly, if one takes human culture as a whole, whether synchronically or diachronically, one finds variations in degree as well as in kind of rationality. But not everything that is non-rational is necessarily mythical, and not everything is non-rational, or irrational, that is not consciously treated as rational. The polarisation between fully rational thought (which is usually held to begin, in the Western tradition, at some time after Thales) and non-rational or "mythopoeic" thought is logically indefensible and historically absurd. Greeks before Thales and indeed before Homer were quite capable of thinking rationally on a multitude of topics, not all of them concrete ones. They did not resemble the savages imagined by a Tylor, a Lévy-Bruhl or even a Durkheim, wandering around in a sort of imagistic haze, a prey to "collective representations," and connecting the objects of their experience solely by "mystic participation" and the like. Many of the thought-processes described in Homer would be perfectly acceptable to Aristotle—or Wittgenstein—given the range of problems to which they were applied. This is nothing like "mythopoeic thought," whatever that may mean, and even on many abstract topics early Greek modes of thought are not necessarily "mythical" in kind. There are different stages of abstraction and conceptualization. Some individuals think with concrete instances and visual images more than others, and the same is so with groups. Logical rules develop slowly, and even a "fully rational" society has its poets and musicians, who have their own rules, not to speak of its communal irrationalities. No society since the Palaeolithic era (at least) has operated without a good deal of practical reasoning, or depended on "mythical" or "mystical" procedures over all or most of the range of experience. The Greeks down to the time of Homer (or Thales, or the Sophists, or Aristotle, to name further stages of development) were strongly affected by their unusually rich mythology, and used it as a model for their view of certain aspects of experience. Even this is to be distinguished from "mythopoeic thought" in the sense of a kind of thought that expresses itself by making myths—which is, I think, a common implication. The use of specific exemplars, whether historical or fictitious, inhibits theoretical abstraction, but I am not sure that it differs in kind from many ways of thinking that are certainly not "mythopoeic." Indeed the special characteristic of much pre-Aristotelian Greek thought is not its mythical quality but rather its religious quality, which is different.

The approach to the problem of defining myths that has been recommended here is at least a flexible one; moreover it does not imply that other approaches (mainly exemplified in the different universalistic theories) are necessarily wrong in all respects. It is possible to accept that they may be substantially right for some classes of myths, while being misleading for others. Malinowski's idea of myths as charters is certainly correct for some myths, and Eliade's idea that myths reconstitute for a time a creative phase in the world's history is certainly applicable to some instances (including even some instances of charter myths). Other myths are undoubtedly concerned with restructuring experience, whether for psychological or for sociological reasons; it is only the theory that all myths have this function which is incorrect. Lévi-Strauss seems to me to be right in arguing that the significance of many Brazilian and neighbouring myths is to be found in their structural relation to the social forms of the Indians who have preserved and developed them; where he is not right is in arguing that all myths behave like this, and that the underlying structure is a universal one of the human mind.

Obviously this kind of flexible approach is liable to the charge of eclecticism, and I have already been accused (by E. R. Leach in *The New York Review of Books*, January 28, 1971, p. 45) of "giving almost everyone a run for their money," although the list of "runners" includes several—Müller, Kerényi, Dumézil, Stith Thompson—who have been given no sort of "run" at all, whom I have unduly neglected if anything. Yet the branding of any approach that allows the possibility of valid perceptions by previous scholars and thinkers as "eclectic" in the bad sense is obviously foolish. There is a profound difference between compounding the ideas of others into a mechanical mixture devoid of any special quality of its own, and the finding of some relevance and acuity in perceptions whose main fault, perhaps, lies in their claim to universality. It would be as strange if everything that has been said about myths is wholly wrong, as it would be if it had been wholly right. Progress in this field is to be made by recognizing myth as a broad category, within which special forms and functions will require different kinds of explanation. The analysis to be applied to a myth must be both flexible and multiform, and it must not reject earlier ideas because of their formal limitations or for fear of the bogey of "eclecticism."

On the other hand tolerance of different explanations of a myth can go too far, and I detect a danger of this in the use of the concept of "overdetermination." The idea is a useful one, borrowed from the psychologists in the first instance by E. R. Dodds, especially for problems like that of divine and human motivation in Homer. An act or decision like that of Helen sleeping with the cowardly Paris may be overdetermined, it may be the result both of "divine" pressures and of human or practical considerations. The two do not necessarily conflict, any more than they exactly coincide. A myth, too, can be used for different ends and have distinct if overlapping emphases. Yet "overdetermination" must not be used as a way of implying that it does not matter which application we identify, or that certain applications do not exclude others. Georges Devereux comes perilously close to this position in his contribution ("La Naissance d' Aphrodite") to *Mélanges offerts à Claude Lévi-Strauss*, ed. J. Pouillon and P. Maranda (Paris, 1970), p. 1230. There he argues that any myth, like any dream, is "surdéterminé," and therefore has more than a single explanation. Once again the universality is suspect: a folktale type of myth, for instance, may have narrative appeal and operate on no other level. Devereux goes on to argue that no particular kind of explanation can be rejected except by technical arguments on its own level—that a psychological explanation, for instance, cannot be refuted by the instancing of other kinds of plausible explanation. That, I believe, is correct, although it is interesting that in Devereux's chosen instance the psychological explanation offered is extremely improbable in relation to the form of the myth when accurately understood. The danger comes when "overdetermination" is loaded with further implications from psychology or sociology—in this case, when Devereux implies that an "external" social application of a myth will probably be balanced by an "internal" psychological application. Perhaps that is a concession to Lévi-Straussian structuralism at its most formalistic and least convincing, but in any case the different motives and functions of myths cannot be paired off against each other like that. Some myths are likely to have a psychological function and no social function—the tale of the escape from the labyrinth, perhaps—and many will have social implications without special psychological overtones.

At least Devereux sees the need for flexibility in the analysis of myths and in the listing of all their possible or probable functions and qualities. Many Classicists, on the other hand, seem to feel that the theoretical investigation of mythology is uninteresting or unimportant or both, and are content to accept any explanation provided that it is faintly exotic. Jungian archetypes and Harrisonian year-spirits are given a perpetually renewed lease of life for this reason.

In conclusion, I repeat that the remarks offered above are primarily methodological and have little to say about the poetry and the fantasy of myths; they belong rather to a necessary preliminary stage of discussion.

Slippery Words: Myth

J. W. ROGERSON

Another group of scholars vitally concerned with the nature of myth is theologians. Their approaches differ from those of students of comparative religion generally insofar as they tend to be especially concerned with the Bible. If one accepts that myths are contained in the Bible, particularly in the OT (Old Testament), then it is easy to see why theologians have been compelled to consider the nature of myth. To the extent that myth *was deemed pejorative, it was reasonable that there would be attempts to remove "myths" from the Bible either by editorial censorship or by explaining them away. The so-called "demythologizing" movement in twentieth-century Christian theology is a logical consequence of such a notion. On the other hand, to the degree to which* myth *was regarded as a positive form of human spirituality and creativity, its presence in the Bible was not considered a liability.*

In this brief essay by Professor J. W. Rogerson of the Department of Biblical Studies of the University of Sheffield, we find the concept of myth viewed from a theological outlook. For more on theological definitions of myth, see Christian Hartlich and Walter Sachs, Der Ursprung des Mythosbegriffes in der modernen Bibelwissenschaft *(Tübingen, 1952), and Robert H. Ayers, "'Myth' in Theological Discourse: A Profusion of Confusion,"* Anglican Theological Review 48 *(1966), 200–17.*

Those desiring to read further in the voluminous literature devoted to myth and the Bible should consult such works as James G. Frazer, Folklore in the Old Testament, *3 vols. (London, 1918), or the one-volume abridged edition (New York, 1923); Hermann Gunkel,* The Legends of Genesis: The Biblical Saga & History *(New York, 1964); Robert Graves and Raphael Patai,* Hebrew Myths: The Book of Genesis *(New York, 1966); and Brevard S. Childs,* Myth and Reality in the Old Testament *(London, 1960). Other representative studies include G. Henton Davies, "An Approach to the Problem of Old Testament Mythology,"* Palestine Exploration Quarterly 88 *(1956), 83–91; James Barr, "The Meaning of 'Mythology' in Relation to the Old Testament,"* Vetus Testamentum 9 *(1959), 1–10; John Carroll Futrell, "Myth and Message: A Study of the Biblical Theology of Rudolf Bultmann,"* Catholic Biblical Quarterly 21 *(1959), 283–315; W. H. Schmidt, "Mythos im Alten Testament,"* Evangelische Theologie 27 *(1967), 237–54; and Karin R. Andriolo, "Myth and History: A General Model and Its Application to the Bible,"* American Anthropologist 83 *(1981), 261–84. However, by far the most comprehensive treatment of the subject is J. W. Rogerson's excellent* Myth in Old Testament Interpretation, Beiheft zur Zeitschrift für die alttestamentliche Wissenschaft *no. 134 (Berlin, 1974), which places the theologi-*

Reprinted from the *Expository Times* 90 (1978–79), 10–14, by permission of the author and T. & T. Clark, Limited, Publishers.

cal scholarship in the context of general myth studies past and present. See also
Rogerson's Anthropology and the Old Testament *(Atlanta, 1978).*

How to define the word "myths" is a relatively easy matter. Most, if not all, biblical scholars would agree that myths are texts. In them, the gods or otherworldly agencies act freely in the affairs of man. How to define "myth" is another matter altogether. While most, if not all, biblical scholars would agree that the word myth may denote what produces myths, or may mean the understanding of the world which is contained in them, agreement would end as soon as these generalizations were made more specific. Some would argue that myths are produced by a naïve, pre-scientific outlook and that the world-view contained in myths must retreat as science advances. Others would regard myths as the product of a way of knowing different from science, expressing truths independently of the knowledge, or lack of it, of scientific causes. There are probably two main reasons for such differences of opinion, the one historical, the other theoretical.

For more than two thousand years, thinkers have paid close attention to myths. In an instructive article in the *Expository Times* twenty years ago, Professor C. K. Barrett sketched how myths were interpreted in Classical and later Greek, and pre-Christian Jewish writings.[1] To Professor Barrett's information we can add that a fourth-century-B.C. Sicilian, Euhemerus, put forward a theory of the origin of myths that has since come to be called Euhemerism. According to this theory, the gods of myths were actual historical persons who had been deified. In the early Christian centuries, myths and their content were attacked by Christian writers. Helped by the allegorizing of unseemly parts of the OT, Christian apologists were able to compare the debased morality and pagan religion of the myths unfavourably with the Christian religion, and, of course, in pagan circles, the myths themselves were interpreted allegorically. At the Renaissance and the Enlightenment, there was renewed interest in myths: a recently announced project to re-issue the major works of the Renaissance on myth will run to fifty-five volumes![2] The modern period of study of myth begins, however, with the Enlightenment.[3] What made this period different from the periods that preceded it was that new myths were discovered

1. C. K. Barrett, "Myth and the New Testament: The Greek Word μῦθο'," *Expository Times* 68 (1957), 345–48.

2. S. Orgel, ed., *The Renaissance and the Gods: A Comprehensive Collection of Renaissance Mythographies* . . . (New York, 1977–).

3. See B. Feldman and R. D. Richardson, *The Rise of Modern Mythology, 1680–1860* (Bloomington, Ind., 1972), pp. 3 ff.

from many parts of the world. These were not only the myths of the so-called primitive peoples, but, surprisingly, texts such as the Nordic mythology of the Eddas, first made widely known to European scholars as late as 1755.[4] Myths were clearly to be seen as a universal phenomenon among mankind, and further impetus was given to discovering what lay behind them.

This brings us to the second reason for the divergence of opinion about myth, the theoretical reason. The Enlightenment "discovered" in the primitives of countries such as North America the mentality of ancient man, and accordingly, began to interpret ancient myths in the light of what was thought to be known about contemporary "savages." But the simple equation "ancient man equals primitive man" concealed a whole mare's nest of questions, many of which are still live issues in social anthropology. How has culture developed? by all races evolving along identical lines of progress, some faster than others? or by diffusion, as a result of contact between peoples, such as borrowing and conquest? Is there such a thing as primitive mentality? What is the relation between being technologically undeveloped, and being artistically and philosophically undeveloped? According to what criteria can we make generalizations about human culture, or comparisons between peoples widely separated geographically and in time?

This article can be summarized so far by saying that the problem of myth, i.e., what produces myths and what they mean, is the outcome of the length of time that they have been studied and the complex questions about man and culture which are implied. To restrict the question of myth to its meaning in relation to the Bible is to court disaster. Time and again, myth (however understood) has been taken into biblical studies from other disciplines, and it is only by appreciating the wider study of myth that we shall avoid the "slipperiness" of the word, and the confusion that this inevitably brings. The article will first proceed to examine four main approaches to what myth has been thought to be, indicating something of its use in biblical studies. It will conclude with a brief consideration of Bultmann's understanding of myth in the famous demythologizing debate.

I

(a) Myth as Lack of Rationality

This can be described as the Enlightenment theory of myth. Myth is a defective understanding of scientific causes, but because man finds it

---

4. Ibid., p. 200.

necessary to explain phenomena, theories are put forward in the absence of scientific knowledge. One result is the personification of natural forces. The storm, the lightning, the thunder are understood as caused by persons, and as man in his savage state applies his own barbaric ways to these supernatural persons, so there arise myths about the brutal behaviour of the gods. The process of explanation can also go beyond natural forces. The absence of a body of scientific laws makes belief in what Enlightenment man would call miracle all too easy. This in turn assists belief in the constant intervention of gods or supernatural powers in the affairs of men, and we are brought close to myth as the opposite of history. Strange features of the landscape, or the presence of springs and wells, or of ruined mighty buildings are explained by stories of the acts of gods, stories which are unhistorical from the standpoint of modern knowledge. On this view, myth is a passing phase in the development of mankind, similar to the childhood of an adult. As a man leaves his childhood behind, so the human race has outgrown its mythical period, with the exception of modern-day primitive peoples.

When, at the end of the eighteenth century, some biblical scholars took the bold step of allowing that the Bible *contained* myths (earlier interpretation used the Bible to *criticize* myths) it was the Enlightenment view that was used.[5] It has been used in biblical studies ever since, and is certainly present in the opening statement of Bultmann's famous essay "New Testament and Mythology": "The cosmology of the New Testament is essentially mythical in character," i.e., it is the product of a pre-scientific outlook.[6] The Enlightenment view of myth contains a good deal of truth, and presents a challenge which no biblical interpreter can avoid. Whether it contains the whole truth is another question.

(b) Myth as an Aspect of Creative Imagination

In opposition to the Enlightenment view, the Romantic movement of the late eighteenth and early nineteenth centuries regarded myths as an expression of the deepest creative potentialities of man.[7] Myths were a constant source of inspiration to dramatists, poets and painters; they expressed profound truths about human existence, and therefore were not to be regarded merely as a relic of man's childhood. Indeed, the very simplicity of man in his earliest stages of development would

5. See my *Myth in Old Testament Interpretation* (Berlin, 1974), ch. 1.
6. R. Bultmann, "New Testament and Mythology," in H. W. Bartsch, ed., *Kerygma and Myth*, vol. 1 (London, 1953), p. 1.
7. See Feldman and Richardson, *Rise of Modern Mythology*, pp. 297 ff.

enable him to be open to intuitions of truth that would not be available to later, sophisticated ages. Myths were therefore not to be explained away as inadequate science, but to be interpreted symbolically.

This view of myth is what underlies the work of Jung on mythology, as well as modern symbolic interpretations such as that of Paul Ricoeur, which has yielded fascinating results when applied to the Bible.[8] It also figures in the arguments brought against Bultmann in the demythologizing debate. Thielicke, for example, maintained that mythology was an essential element in human thought, and he declared: "Both mythology and science are legitimate approaches to the truth. There is no question of the one becoming outmoded by the other in the process of historical development."[9] We shall see later that Bultmann also uses this sense of myth along with the Enlightenment view, but for the moment it is necessary to emphasize that the Romantic view cannot tell us whether there is a transcendent realm beyond the world of time and space. It is possible to account for myths in purely this-worldly, depth-psychological terms. If, with Thielicke, we wish to assert that "myth . . . employs subjective means derived from the human imagination to describe a reality which utterly transcends consciousness, and which possesses an objective validity in its own right. . . ,"[10] we need to be convinced on other grounds that there is a transcendent reality to which myths can give expression. In this connexion it is necessary to say something about the use of the word myth in religious education, where it has come to mean, more or less, parable. Thus, Gen. 1 is myth, i.e., it contains truths about God the creator, although the truths are expressed in terms of obsolete science. I would not regard this as a wrong use of myth—such is its range of meaning that the word can hardly be wrongly used. I would simply remark that to use myth in this way is to perform a double operation. First, it is decided on other grounds that Gen. 1 contains truths about God and the world; second, the word myth is used to allow us to accept these truths while rejecting the cosmology. There is nothing in the nature of myths as such to point us necessarily to this conclusion.

(c) The Social Role of Myth

In addition to being expressions of human creativity, myths have been seen as products of society, embodying common values and ideals,

8. On Ricoeur, see Rogerson, *Myth in Old Testament Interpretation*, chap. 9.
9. H. Thielicke, "The Restatement of New Testament Mythology," in *Kerygma and Myth*, vol. 1 (London, 1953), p. 158.
10. Thielicke, "Restatement," p. 160.

and expressing them in activities such as worship. In OT study, this view has been used positively as something present in the religion of the OT, and negatively as something found among ancient Israel's neighbours but rejected by the OT. The classical expression of its positive use was the myth and ritual theory of S. H. Hooke and his collaborators.[11] There was thought to have been a common pattern of culture in the ancient Near East in which annual rituals centring on the king and accompanied by the recitation of myths were performed so as to ensure the well-being and good order of the community in the following year. Although there was no explicit evidence for this in the OT, it was seen to underlie those psalms which speak of the kingship of God. It was suggested that the king was enthroned at a new year festival, possibly after he had undergone a ritual humiliation, and that he represented God in the ritual. Just as at the creation God had subdued the powers of chaos, especially those symbolized by the sea and by floods, so the rituals performed by the king would continue to guarantee the order established at creation. According to one view, Gen. 1:1−2:4 was read as an accompaniment to the new year ritual.

The negative use of this view of myth was as follows. It was part of the magical outlook of ancient Israel's neighbours that they saw the process of nature, especially of fertility, bound up with human activity. Man's life was dominated by the recurring phases of nature, but he could influence these phases, or at least ensure that they were beneficial, by corporate symbolic behaviour, accompanied by the reciting of myths. The religion of the OT broke with this pattern of religion. Its thought was dominated not by the cycles of the natural world, but by the promises of God being worked out and fulfilled in the historical process. Thus history was opposed to myth, not in the popular sense of true as against historically false, but in terms of conflicting views of reality. One view was a primitive and pre-scientific view, its attempt to direct natural forces being based upon ignorance of scientific laws. The other view, while no less pre-scientific, was enabled by God's redemptive action in history to be lifted above a crude relationship with the world of nature to a notion of transcendence in terms of a personal God.

There is perhaps no area of the employment of myth in biblical studies where so much has depended on what has been imported into the Bible from outside. There is a great deal of truth in the social view of myth as it is stated at the beginning of the section; as applied to the Bible it raises many questions. These include whether there was a pat-

11. For this section, see Rogerson, *Myth in Old Testament Interpretation*, chaps. 6–7.

tern of culture in the ancient Near East, and, if so, whether it has been correctly reconstructed in the light of the evidence available; whether, in contrasting the mythical, immanentist outlook of Israel's neighbours with the historical, transcendent view of the OT, full justice has been done to both sides. This is not to say that there is no place for the social view of myth in biblical studies; it is to say that it is an approach which needs to be applied with the utmost care, having regard to the many complex issues involved.

(d) Myth in Relation to History

The previous sections mentioned two ways in which myth can be opposed to history. In the debate with Bultmann about demythologizing it was suggested that myth can work in harmony with, and to the advantage of, history. According to Thielicke, "There are myths which are pictorial explanations of certain facts in history," and as an example, he cites the virgin birth, which is "the symbol of the historical fact that Jesus was the Son of God."[12] What is being said here, and also in OT studies,[13] is that if God is believed to be at work in the historical process, it will be necessary to present history in mythical ways. There will be a deliberate or unconscious use of images and symbols in order to bring out the divine purpose believed to be behind events. The Israelites will not simply move through the wilderness to the promised land; they will be accompanied by symbols of the presence of God: the pillar of cloud by day and of fire by night. To say this is not to have proved or disproved that the OT is correct in its presentation of the wilderness wanderings. Whether we accept that God guided Israel through the wilderness will depend, among other things, on whether we believe in God in the first place, and has nothing to do with the nature of myth. Granted belief in God, this view of myth, which stands close to the Romantic view, may assist us to interpret parts of the Bible.

The four approaches to myth outlined above show something of the complexity and range of meaning of the word, without by any means being exhaustive. The approaches have been deliberately separated out. That it is possible for the use of myth by one writer to be a complex blend of several different understandings of the word will now be illustrated from Bultmann's contributions to *Kerygma and Myth I*.

12. Thielicke, "Restatement," p. 162.
13. See Rogerson, *Myth in Old Testament Interpretation*, pp. 161–62, 171–72.

II

In an illuminating study of the presuppositions of Bultmann's thought, R. A. Johnson has argued that his view of myth is composed of the Enlightenment view, a view taken from the "History of Religions" movement, and an existentialist view in some way special to himself and influenced by Lutheran beliefs.[14] On the Enlightenment view, nothing need be said. The "History of Religions" definition is the sense of myth that Bultmann claimed he was using,[15] although Johnson shows that Bultmann's claim was an anachronism. From the "History of Religions" school, Bultmann took the theory that the Hellenistic culture in which Christianity emerged was dominated by the myth of the Primal Man or Heavenly Redeemer, which originated in Iran and was mediated by the Kyrios cult in the Hellenistic world. In writings of the period 1920–33, Bultmann meant by mythical in the NT anything derived from this saviour myth. He came via this view close to what is called above the Romantic view, in that he saw elements of the saviour myth being used in the NT in order to declare the identity of Jesus.[16] The existential view of myth was influenced by the work of Bultmann's pupil, H. Jonas, on Gnosticism.[17] Jonas regarded the Gnostic myths as an expression of the human spirit (cf. the Romantic view), but held that the way in which the myths expressed themselves, for example, in the claims that they made about the world, was a hindrance to the true understanding of the human spirit that they contained. Thus, myths carried within themselves the seeds of their destruction, a destruction that was necessary if their truth were to be grasped. Bultmann refined this understanding of myth by supposing that the objective claims about the world made by myths represented the desire for security also sought in Christianity in justification by works. Corresponding to the need to destroy the claims made by myths about the world was the doctrine of justification by faith, which destroys all human certainties in bringing man to rely upon God alone. Armed with these clues from Johnson, we can turn to Bultmann himself.

Not only does Bultmann set out from the Enlightenment view of myth, it is an undercurrent throughout his essays. The NT cosmology is pre-scientific; it comes from an age of mythical thought. Such thought regards divine activity in nature and history as an interference—as

14. R. A. Johnson, *The Origins of Demythologizing: Philosophy and Historiography in the Theology of Rudolf Bultmann*, suppl. *Numen* 28 (Leiden 1974).

15. Bultmann, "New Testament and Mythology," p. 10, n. 2.

16. Johnson, *Origins*, p. 99.

17. Ibid., pp. 119 ff., 216 ff.

what has been called miracle. So seriously does Bultmann take the modern world-view as he understands it that he cannot allow any room for the other-worldly at all. At the end of the day, the cross and resurrection are firmly confined to the world of time and space, being *traditions* about God's act in Christ intended to move us to faith, in which we realize our authentic existence.

Yet Bultmann is also critical of the Enlightenment view of myth. He speaks of a shallow Enlightenment failing to perceive truths in ancient myths, and rejects any idea that faith could be re-expressed in modern scientific terms. His attitude to the "History of Religions" approach is ambivalent also. Although he claims that his understanding of myth is the "History of Religions" understanding, he is critical of it. While admitting that the mythology of the NT is in essence that of the Jewish apocalyptic and Gnostic redemption myths, the NT is unique in combining such myths with an historic person, Jesus Christ. The NT witnesses a decisive event of redemption. At this point, however, the existential understanding of myth takes over, and, undergirded by the Enlightenment view, sweeps all before it. The "real purpose" of myth is to express man's understanding of himself in the world in which he lives. But this real purpose is hindered by the objective content of the myths themselves, and this content must be eliminated if faith is to grasp that myth's underlying understanding of human existence is true. This is why Bultmann cannot accept that myths may express other-worldly truths by means of traditional mythic symbols. To accept this, and to allow to myths some objective truth will be to make this truth the object of faith, but such faith will be a human construction not awakened by hearing the word of God.

To summarize, Bultmann deploys three views of myth in order to maintain his position. The "History of Religions" view is in fact a foil for the NT to allow for the uniqueness of the latter, because it brings the redeemer into the historical process. The Enlightenment view precludes any allowance for transcendence or truth about another world; these are part of the obsolete world view. In turn, this supports Bultmann's attempt, based on the existential view of myth, to do away entirely with the objective content of NT cosmology so that faith may be evoked by the hearing of the word alone. It will be obvious that Bultmann has no more derived all this from myths as such than have his opponents who believe myths to express other-worldly realities. Like them, he has accepted certain things on other grounds (e.g., the uniqueness of the NT, or the normative importance of a particular view of justification by faith), and has applied them to biblical interpretations with the aid of the concept of myth.

If we read a statement such as "the real meaning (or purpose) of myth is . . ." we should be on our guard. In the present state of our knowledge there is no such thing as the *real* meaning or purpose of myth. If we study the various attempts to account for myths and to say what they mean, our understanding of man and culture will be enlarged, and we may well discover insights that will assist biblical interpretation. The concept of myth itself, however, will not help us to decide whether there is a transcendent reality beyond this world, or how it might be possible to talk about it. Other factors will determine our attitude to these questions.

The Fall of Man

JAMES G. FRAZER

*As more and more myths were recorded by travelers, missionaries, colonial ad-
ministrators, and eventually ethnographers and folklorists, it soon became obvious
that few if any myths were totally unique. The comparative method, borrowed in
part from the comparative study of language, philology, could easily be applied to
myth. Through the comparison of similar myth plots in different cultures, scholars
attempted to reconstruct a hypothetical original form of a myth from which in
theory all later versions were assumed to derive.*

*According to unilinear evolutionary theory, which was inspired by the Darwinian
model, all peoples were believed to have passed through the identical successive
stages of savagery, barbarism, and civilization. Myths were assumed to belong to
the primitive period of savagery. As man evolved, so myth devolved. Progress for
mankind meant the opposite for myth. It was argued that sacred myth became
secular folktale in the barbarism period (barbarians were understood to be essentially "folk" or illiterate peasants), finally dying out completely among civilized societies. However, since it was postulated that evolution was truly unilineal, in other
words that the one line was entirely uniform, a curious form of the comparative
method was encouraged. Civilized investigators (at the end of the nineteenth century) who wished to know their own roots, their own ancestors, had only to look at
modern savage (primitive) peoples. These "savages," to continue to use the terrible
ethnocentric, racist label, were living in the present just as the ancient forebears of
the English, French, etc., must have lived in the past. By comparing the somewhat
fragmentary survivals still to be found among civilized peoples with the fuller and
"original" forms of the same item among contemporary primitive peoples, one
could elucidate many perplexing puzzles of modern civilization. (For an excellent
consideration of the intellectual milieu in which evolutionary theory flourished, see
J. W. Burrow,* Evolution and Society: A Study in Victorian Social Theory
[Cambridge, 1966].)

*In the light of this theoretical orientation, it is understandable why there was
so much interest in the reports made by missionaries and others from primitive
peoples. This data could be of great assistance in explaining confusing details of
present-day civilization. It was only a question of time before this version of the
comparative method was applied to the Bible. Among the unilinear evolutionary*

anthropologists, the name of James George Frazer (1854–1941) stands out. A classicist and library anthropologist, Frazer was one of the most widely read men of his age, especially in the areas of custom and myth. His thirteen-volume Golden Bough ranks as one of the most remarkable compilations of ethnographic data on magic ever assembled. Frazer's technique in nearly all his works was to gather together as many illustrations of a given magical practice or myth that he could. Anything in print was deemed a legitimate source. Through the assiduous citation of scores of examples, he hoped to discern patterns or at the very least provide the raw data for later theorists. Sometimes the sheer weight of the massive documentation so overwhelmed the reader that he tended to forget just what the materials were supposed to prove.

Modern-day anthropologists object to the fact that Frazer often wrenched ethnographic facts out of their cultural contexts to be fit into some Procrustean bed of his making. Still, reading Frazerian anthropology is a delightful experience, an esthetic experience, for he certainly wrote with uncommon grace and humor. By means of his works, he succeeded in bringing findings from obscure ethnographic reports and missionary memoirs to the rapt attention of a literate public.

One of the most dramatic examples of Frazer's method is to be found in his ingenious application of the comparative method to the fall of man in Genesis. By examining origin of death myths throughout the world (from "savage" societies) he felt he was able to explain features of the Genesis story hitherto not fully understood. The reader should keep in mind that, at the time that Frazer wrote, there was no easy means of locating large numbers of myth parallels. It was only by reading great masses of books and essays that one could compile sets of parallel texts.

Since Frazer's day, studies of various origin of death myths have been completed. It turns out that no one type is universal, but rather each cultural/geographical area has its own characteristic types. In Africa the most common myth revolves around a messenger's failure to deliver a message. Frazer had labeled this type the "Perverted Message." Typically, God sends the chameleon to mankind to announce that man will have eternal life, and the lizard with a different message to the effect that man will die. The chameleon dawdles on the way and the lizard arrives first, thereby ensuring that death enters the world. This is just one of more than a dozen types of African origin of death myths, according to the excellent comparative study by Hans Abrahamsson, The Origin of Death: Studies in African Mythology, Studia ethnographica Upsaliensia no. 3 (1951), 1–176. Other considerations of African materials include Bernhard Struck, "Das Chamäleon in der afrikanischen Mythologie," Globus 96 (1909), 175–77; Miklos Veto, "Le Rôle de l'homme dans les mythes de mort chez les Bantous de l'Afrique orientale et du Congo," Zaire: Revue Congolaise 15 (1961), 75–93; Denise Paulme, "Two Themes on the Origin of Death in West Africa," Man 2 (1967), 48–61; Dominique Zahan, "Essai sur les mythes Africains d'origine de la mort," L'Homme 9, no. 4 (1969), 41–50. Origin of death myths in American Indian tradition are different; see Franz Boas, "The Origin of Death," Journal of American Folklore 30 (1917), 486–91; R. Dangel, "Mythen vom Ursprung des Todes bei den Indianern Nordamerikas," Mitteilungen der Anthropologischen Gesellschaft in Wien 58 (1928), 341–74; and Åke Hultkrantz, "The Origin of Death Myth as Found Among the Wind River Shoshoni Indians," Ethnos 20 (1955), 127–36. A common type among the American Indians concerns a debate on the subject. The debate winner decides there shall be death in the world, whereupon his child is the first to die and he regrets his decision. In Oceania we find the most widespread origin of death myth to be yet another story. Supposedly man at one time

*possessed the power to rejuvenate himself by changing his skin like a snake. Frazer
refers to this type as "The Story of the Cast Skin." Usually an old woman who does
this frightens her grandchildren, who fail to recognize her as a young girl. They cry
for her until she resumes her old skin, and by this means death is mandated for
future generations. See Bengt Anell, "The Origin of Death According to the Traditions of Oceania,"* Studia ethnographica Upsaliensia 20 *(1964),* 1–32. *Other comparative studies of the origin of death include Goblet d'Alviella, "Coincidences
mythiques: L'Intervention des astres dans la destinée des morts,"* Bulletin de folklore *(Brussels)* 2 *(1892),* 183–92; *Obayashi Taryo, "Origins of Japanese Mythology,
Especially of the Myths of the Origin of Death,"* Folk Cultures of Japan and East
Asia, Monumenta Nipponica Monographs no. 25 *(Tokyo, 1966), pp.* 1–15; *Francisco
Demetrio, "Death: Its Origin and Related Beliefs Among the Early Filipinos,"* Philippine Studies 14 *(1966),* 355–95, *and Manabu Waida, "Central Asian Mythology of
the Origin of Death: A Comparative Analysis of Its Structure and History,"* Anthropos 77 *(1982),* 663–702; *"Myths of the Origin of Death: The Central Asian
Type?"* Temenos 18 *(1982),* 87–98.

*For samples of the reaction (not all of which was favorable) to Frazer's pro-
posed reconstruction of the fall of man in Genesis, see Samuel S. Cohon, "The Origin of Death,"* Journal of Jewish Lore and Philosophy 1 *(1919),* 371–96; *Alexander
Haggerty Krappe, "The Story of the Fall of Man,"* Nieuw theologisch Tijdschrift 17
(1928), 242–49; *and Paul Delarue, "Le Serpent qui vole à l'homme le secret de l'im-
mortalité,"* Nouvelle revue des traditions populaires 2 *(1950),* 262–75. *For other
examples of the application of the comparative method to biblical narratives, see
P. Saintyves,* Essais de folklore biblique: Magie, mythes et miracles dans l'Ancien
et le Nouveau Testament *(Paris, 1923); Alexander Heidel,* The Babylonian Genesis
(Chicago, 1963); A. Ohler, Mythologische Elemente im Alten Testament *(Düsseldorf,
1969); and Dorothy Irvin,* Mytharion: The Comparison of Tales from the Old Testament and the Ancient Near East *(Neukirchen-Vluyn, West Ger., 1978). For general
appreciations of Frazer, see R. Angus Downie,* Frazer and the Golden Bough *(London, 1970); Stanley Edgar Hyman,* The Tangled Bank *(New York, 1974), pp.* 187–291;
and Robert Ackerman, "Frazer on Myth and Ritual," Journal of the History of Ideas
36 *(1975),* 115–34.

---

1. THE NARRATIVE IN GENESIS

With a few light but masterly strokes the Jehovistic writer depicts for
us the blissful life of our first parents in the happy garden which God
had created for their abode. There every tree that was pleasant to the
sight and good for food grew abundantly; there the animals lived at
peace with man and with each other; there man and woman knew no
shame, because they knew no ill; it was the age of innocence.[1] But this
glad time was short, the sunshine was soon clouded. From his description of the creation of Eve and her introduction to Adam, the

1. Gen. 2:8–25.

writer passes at once to tell the sad story of their fall, their loss of innocence, their expulsion from Eden, and the doom of labour, of sorrow,
and of death pronounced on them and their posterity. In the midst of
the garden grew the tree of the knowledge of good and evil, and God
had forbidden man to eat of its fruit, saying, "In the day that thou eatest thereof thou shalt surely die." But the serpent was cunning, and the
woman weak and credulous: he persuaded her to eat of the fatal fruit,
and she gave of it to her husband, and he ate also. No sooner had they
tasted it than the eyes of both of them were opened, and they knew
that they were naked, and filled with shame and confusion they hid
their nakedness under aprons of fig-leaves: the age of innocence was
gone for ever. That woeful day, when the heat of noon was over and the
shadows were growing long in the garden, God walked there, as was
his wont, in the cool of the evening. The man and woman heard his
footsteps,[2] perhaps the rustling of the fallen leaves (if leaves could fall
in Eden) under his tread, and they hid behind the trees, ashamed to be
seen by him naked. But he called them forth from the thicket, and
learning from the abashed couple how they had disobeyed his command by eating of the fruit of the tree of knowledge, he flew into a tow-
ering passion. He cursed the serpent, condemning him to go on his
belly, to eat dust, and to be the enemy of mankind all the days of his
life: he cursed the ground, condemning it to bring forth thorns and
thistles: he cursed the woman, condemning her to bear children in
sorrow and to be in subjection to her husband: he cursed the man,
condemning him to wring his daily bread from the ground in the
sweat of his brow, and finally to return to the dust out of which he had
been taken. Having relieved his feelings by these copious maledictions,
the irascible but really kind-hearted deity relented so far as to make
coats of skins for the culprits to replace their scanty aprons of fig-
leaves; and clad in these new garments the shamefaced pair retreated
among the trees, while in the west the sunset died away and the shadows deepened on Paradise Lost.[3]

In this account everything hinges on the tree of the knowledge of
good and evil: it occupies, so to say, the centre of the stage in the great
tragedy, with the man and woman and the talking serpent grouped
round it. But when we look closer we perceive a second tree standing
side by side with the other in the midst of the garden. It is a very re-

2. Gen. 3:8, "They heard the sound of the Lord God walking in the garden." The
"sound" is clearly that of his footsteps, not of his voice, as the English version translates
it. The Hebrew word for sound (קוֹל) is ambiguous; it may signify either "sound" or
"voice."
3. Gen. 3.

markable tree, for it is no less than the tree of life, whose fruit confers immortality on all who eat of it. Yet in the actual story of the fall this wonderful tree plays no part. Its fruit hangs there on the boughs ready to be plucked; unlike the tree of knowledge, it is hedged about by no divine prohibition, yet no one thinks it worth while to taste of the luscious fruit and live for ever. The eyes of the actors are all turned on the tree of knowledge; they appear not to see the tree of life. Only, when all is over, does God bethink himself of the wondrous tree standing there neglected, with all its infinite possibilities, in the midst of the garden; and fearing lest man, who has become like him in knowledge by eating of the one tree, should become like him in immortality by eating of the other, he drives him from the garden and sets an angelic squadron, with flaming swords, to guard the approach to the tree of life, that none henceforth may eat of its magic fruit and live for ever. Thus, while throughout the moving tragedy in Eden our attention is fixed exclusively on the tree of knowledge, in the great transformation scene at the end, where the splendours of Eden fade for ever into the light of common day, the last glimpse we catch of the happy garden shows the tree of life alone lit up by the lurid gleam of brandished angelic falchions.[4]

It appears to be generally recognized that some confusion has crept into the account of the two trees, and that in the original story the tree of life did not play the purely passive and spectacular part assigned to it in the existing narrative. Accordingly, some have thought that there were originally two different stories of the fall, in one of which the tree of knowledge figured alone, and in the other the tree of life alone, and that the two stories have been unskilfully fused into a single narrative by an editor, who has preserved the one nearly intact, while he has clipped and pared the other almost past recognition.[5] It may be so, but perhaps the solution of the problem is to be sought in another direction. The gist of the whole story of the fall appears to be an attempt to explain man's mortality, to set forth how death came into the world. It is true that man is not said to have been created immortal and to have lost his immortality through disobedience; but neither is he said to have been created mortal. Rather we are given to understand that the possibility alike of immortality and of mortality was open to him, and that it rested with him which he would choose; for the tree of life stood within his reach, its fruit was not forbidden to him, he had only to

4. Gen. 3:22–24.
5. J. Skinner, *Critical and Exegetical Commentary on Genesis* (Edinburgh, 1910), pp. 52 ff., 94.

stretch out his hand, take of the fruit, and eating of it live for ever. Indeed, far from being prohibited to eat of the tree of life, man was implicitly permitted, if not encouraged, to partake of it by his Creator, who had told him expressly, that he might eat freely of every tree in the garden, with the single exception of the tree of the knowledge of good and evil.[6] Thus by planting the tree of life in the garden and not prohibiting its use, God apparently intended to give man the option, or at least the chance, of immortality, but man missed his chance by electing to eat of the other tree, which God had warned him not to touch under pain of immediate death. This suggests that the forbidden tree was really a tree of death, not of knowledge, and that the mere taste of its deadly fruit, quite apart from any question of obedience or disobedience to a divine command, sufficed to entail death on the eater. The inference is entirely in keeping with God's warning to man, "Thou shalt not eat of it; for in the day that thou eatest thereof thou shalt surely die."[7] Accordingly we may suppose that in the original story there were two trees, a tree of life and a tree of death; that it was open to man to eat of the one and live for ever, or to eat of the other and die; that God, out of good will to his creature, advised man to eat of the tree of life and warned him not to eat of the tree of death; and that man, misled by the serpent, ate of the wrong tree and so forfeited the immortality which his benevolent Creator had designed for him.

At least this hypothesis has the advantage of restoring the balance between the two trees and of rendering the whole narrative clear, simple, and consistent. It dispenses with the necessity of assuming two original and distinct stories which have been clumsily stitched together by a botching editor. But the hypothesis is further recommended by another and deeper consideration. It sets the character of the Creator in a far more amiable light; it clears him entirely of that suspicion of envy and jealousy, not to say malignanty and cowardice, which, on the strength of the narrative in Genesis, has so long rested like a dark blot on his reputation. For, according to that narrative, God grudged man the possession both of knowledge and of immortality; he desired to keep these good things to himself, and feared that if man got one or both of them, he would be the equal of his maker, a thing not to be suffered at any price. Accordingly he forbade man to eat of the tree of knowledge, and when man disregarded the command, the

6. Gen. 2:16 ff., "And the Lord God commanded the man, saying, Of every tree of the garden thou mayest freely eat: but of the tree of knowledge of good and evil, thou shalt not eat of it: for in the day that thou eatest thereof thou shalt surely die."

7. Gen. 2:17.

deity hustled him out of the garden and closed the premises, to prevent him from eating of the other tree and so becoming immortal. The motive was mean, and the conduct despicable. More than that, both the one and the other are utterly inconsistent with the previous behaviour of the deity, who, far from grudging man anything, had done all in his power to make him happy and comfortable, by creating a beautiful garden for his delectation, beasts and birds to play with, and a woman to be his wife. Surely it is far more in harmony both with the tenor of the narrative and with the goodness of the Creator to suppose, that he intended to crown his kindness to man by conferring on him the boon of immortality, and that his benevolent intention was only frustrated by the wiles of the serpent.

But we have still to ask, why should the serpent practice this deceit on man? what motive had he for depriving the human race of the great privilege which the Creator had planned for them? Was his interference purely officious? or had he some deep design behind it? To these questions the narrative in Genesis furnishes no answer. The serpent gains nothing by his fraud; on the contrary he loses, for he is cursed by God and condemned thenceforth to crawl on his belly and lick the dust. But perhaps his conduct was not so wholly malignant and purposeless as appears on the surface. We are told that he was more subtle than any beast of the field; did he really show his sagacity by blasting man's prospects without improving his own? We may suspect that in the original story he justified his reputation by appropriating to himself the blessing of which he deprived our species; in fact, that while he persuaded our first parents to eat of the tree of death, he himself ate of the tree of life and so lived for ever. The supposition is not so extravagant as it may seem. In not a few savage stories of the origin of death, which I will relate immediately, we read that serpents contrived to outwit or intimidate man and so to secure for themselves the immortality which was meant for him, for many savages believe that by annually casting their skins serpents and other animals renew their youth and live for ever. The belief appears to have been shared by the Semites; for, according to the ancient Phoenician writer Sanchuniathon, the serpent was the longest-lived of all animals, because it casts its skin and so renewed its youth. But if the Phoenicians held this view of the serpent's longevity and the cause of it, their neighbours and kinsfolk the Hebrews may well have done the same. Certainly the Hebrews seem to have thought that eagles renew their youth[8] by

8. Sanchuniathon, quoted by Eusebius, *Praeparatio evangelii* 1.10, καὶ πολυχρονι-
ώτατον δέ ἐστιν οὐ μόνον τῷ ἐκδυόμενον τὸ γῆρας νεάζειν. Here γῆρας is used in the
sense of "old or cast skin," as in Aristotle, *Histor. Animal.*, 7.18 (vol. 1, pp. 600a–601b, of

moulting their feathers,[9] and if so, why not serpents by casting their skins? Indeed, the notion that the serpent cheated man of immortality by getting possession of a life-giving plant which the higher powers had destined for our species, occurs in the famous Gilgamesh epic, one of the oldest literary monuments of the Semitic race and far more ancient than Genesis. In it we read how the deified Utnaphistim revealed to the hero Gilgamesh the existence of a plant which had the miraculous power of renewing youth and bore the name "the old man becomes young": how Gilgamesh procured the plant and boasted that he would eat of it and so renew his lost youth; how, before he could do so, a serpent stole the magic plant from him, while he was bathing in the cool water of a well or brook; and how, bereft of the hope of immortality, Gilgamesh sat down and wept.[10] It is true that nothing is here said about the serpent eating the plant and so obtaining immortality for himself; but the omission may be due merely to the state of the text, which is obscure and defective, and even if the poet were silent on this point, the parallel versions of the story, which I shall cite, enable us to supply the lacuna with a fair degree of probability. These parallels further suggest, though they cannot prove, that in the original of the story, which the Jehovistic writer has mangled and distorted, the serpent was the messenger sent by God to bear the glad tidings of immortality to man, but that the cunning creature perverted the message to the advantage of his species and to the ruin of ours. The gift of speech, which he used to such ill purpose, was lent him in his capacity of ambassador from God to man.

Im. Bekker's Berlin edition), who discusses the subject at length. The use of $\gamma\hat{\eta}\rho\alpha\varsigma$ ("old age") in the sense of "cast skin" is a clear indication that the Greeks shared the widespread belief in the renewal of an animal's youth by the casting of its skin.

9. Ps. 103:5, "Thy youth is renewed like the eagle." The commentators rightly explain the belief in the renewal of the eagle's youth by the moulting of its feathers. Compare J. Morgenstern, "On Gilgameš-Epic, xi. 274–320," *Zeitschrift für Assyriologie* 29 (1915), 294. "Baethgen quotes a tradition from Bar Hebraeus, that when the eagle grows old he casts off his feathers and clothes himself with new ones. Rashi, commenting on this same verse, is even more specific. He says that from year to year the eagle casts off his old wings and feathers and puts on new, and thereby renews his youth constantly." Strictly speaking, the bird referred to in this passage of the Psalms (נֶשֶׁר) is not the eagle but the great griffon-vulture, which abounds in Palestine. See H. B. Tristram, *The Natural History of the Bible*, 9th ed. (London, 1898), pp. 172 ff.

10. P. Jensen, *Assyrisch-Babylonische Mythen und Epen* (Berlin, 1900), pp. 251 ff.; R. F. Harper, *Assyrian and Babylonian Literature* (New York, 1901), pp. 361 ff.; P. Dhorme, *Choix de textes religieux assyro-babyloniens* (Paris, 1907), pp. 311 ff.; A. Ungnad and H. Gressmann, *Das Gilgamesch-Epos* (Göttingen, 1911), pp. 62 ff.; L. W. King, *Babylonian Religion and Magic* (London, 1899), pp. 173 ff. The first, so far as I know, to point out the parallelism between this passage and the narrative in Genesis was Rabbi Julian Morgenstern. See his instructive article, "On Gilgameš-Epic, xi. 274–320," *Zeitschrift für Assyriologie* 29 (1915), 284 ff.

To sum up, if we may judge from a comparison of the versions dispersed among many people, the true original story of the Fall of Man ran somewhat as follows. The benevolent Creator, after modelling the first man and woman out of mud and animating them by the simple process of blowing into their mouths and noses, placed the happy pair in an earthly paradise, where, free from care and toil, they could live on the sweet fruits of a delightful garden, and where birds and beasts frisked about them in fearless security. As a crowning mercy he planned for our first parents the great gift of immortality, but resolved to make them the arbiters of their own fate by leaving them free to accept or reject the proffered boon. For that purpose he planted in the midst of the garden two wondrous trees that bore fruits of very different sorts, the fruit of one being fraught with death to the eater, and the other with life eternal. Having done so, he sent the serpent to the man and woman and charged him to deliver this message: "Eat not of the Tree of Death, for in the day ye eat thereof ye shall surely die; but eat of the Tree of Life and live for ever." Now the serpent was more subtle than any beast of the field, and on his way he bethought him of changing the message; so when he came to the happy garden and found the woman alone in it, he said to her, "Thus saith God: Eat not of the Tree of Life, for in the day ye eat thereof ye shall surely die; but eat of the Tree of Death, and live for ever." The foolish woman believed him, and ate of the fatal fruit, and gave of it to her husband, and he ate also. But the sly serpent himself ate of the Tree of Life. That is why men have been mortal and serpents immortal ever since, for serpents cast their skins every year and so renew their youth. If only the serpent had not perverted God's good message and deceived our first mother, we should have been immortal instead of the serpents; for like the serpents we should have cast our skins every year and so renewed our youth perpetually.

That this, or something like this, was the original form of the story is made probable by a comparison of the following tales, which may conveniently be arranged under two heads, "The Story of the Perverted Message" and "The Story of the Cast Skin."

2. THE STORY OF THE PERVERTED MESSAGE

Like many other savages, the Namaquas or Hottentots associate the phases of the moon with the idea of immortality, the apparent waning and waxing of the luminary being understood by them as a real process of alternate disintegration and reintegration, of decay and growth repeated perpetually. Even the rising and setting of the moon is interpreted by them as its birth and death.[11] They say that once on a time the Moon wished to send to mankind a message of immortality and the hare undertook to act as messenger. So the Moon charged him to go to men and say, "As I die and rise to life again, so shall you die and rise to life again." Accordingly the hare went to men, but either out of forgetfulness or malice he reversed the message and said, "As I die and do not rise to life again, so you shall also die and not rise to life again." Then he went back to the Moon, and she asked him what he had said. He told her, and when she heard how he had given the wrong message, she was so angry that she threw a stick at him which split his lip. That is why the hare's lip is still cloven. So the hare ran away and is still running to this day. Some people, however, say that before he fled he clawed the Moon's face, which still bears the marks of the scratching, as anybody may see for himself on a clear moonlight night. But the Namaquas are still angry with the hare for robbing them of immortality. The old men of the tribe used to say, "We are still enraged with the hare, because he brought such a bad message, and we will not eat him." Hence from the day when a youth comes of age and takes his place among men, he is forbidden to eat hare's flesh, or even to come into contact with a fire on which a hare has been cooked. If a man breaks the rule, he is not infrequently banished from the village. However, on the payment of a fine he may be readmitted to the community.[12]

A similar tale, with some minor differences, is told by the Bushmen. According to them, the Moon formerly said to men, "As I die and come to life again, so shall ye do; when ye die, ye shall not die altogether but shall rise again." But one man would not believe the glad tidings of immortality, and he would not consent to hold his tongue. For his mother had died, he loudly lamented her, and nothing could persuade him that she would come to life again. A heated altercation ensued between him and the Moon on this painful subject. "Your mother's asleep," says the Moon. "She's dead," says the man, and at it they went again, hammer and tongs, till at last the Moon lost patience and struck the man on the face with her fist, cleaving his mouth with the blow.

11. C. J. Andersson, *Lake Ngami*, 2nd ed. (London, 1856), p. 328, n. 1, "When speaking of the moon, the Namaquas do not say, like ourselves, that it rises and sets, but that 'it dies and is born again.'"

12. Sir J. E. Alexander, *Expedition of Discovery into the Interior of Africa*, vol. 1 (London, 1838), p. 169; C. J. Andersson, *Lake Ngami*, 2nd ed. (London, 1856), pp. 328 ff.; W. H. I. Bleek, *Reynard the Fox in South Africa* (London, 1864), pp. 71–73; Th. Hahn, *Tsuni- ‖ Goam, The Supreme Being of the Khoi-Khoi* (London, 1881), p. 52.

And as she did so, she cursed him, saying, "His mouth shall be always like this, even when he is a hare. For a hare he shall be. He shall spring away, he shall come doubling back. The dogs shall chase him, and when they have caught him they shall tear him to pieces. He shall altogether die. And all men, when they die, shall die outright. For he would not agree with me, when I bid him not to weep for his mother, for she would live again. 'No,' says he to me, 'my mother will not live again.' Therefore he shall altogether become a hare. And the people, they shall altogether die, because he contradicted me flat when I told him that the people would do as I do, returning to life after they were dead." So a righteous retribution overtook the sceptic for his scepticism, for he was turned into a hare, and a hare he has been ever since. But still he has human flesh in his thigh, and that is why, when the Bushmen kill a hare, they will not eat that portion of the thigh, but cut it out, because it is human flesh. And still the Bushmen say, "It was on account of the hare that the Moon cursed us, so that we die altogether. If it had not been for him, we should have come to life again when we died. But he would not believe what the Moon told him, he contradicted her flat." [13] In this Bushmen version of the story the hare is not the animal messenger of God to men, but a human sceptic who, for doubting the gospel of eternal life, is turned into a hare and involves the whole human race in the doom of mortality. This may be an older form of the story than the Hottentot version, in which the hare is a hare and nothing more.

The Nandi of British East Africa tell a story in which the origin of death is referred to the ill-humour of a dog, who brought the tidings of immortality to men, but, not being received with the deference due to so august an embassy, he changed his tune in a huff and doomed mankind to the sad fate to which they have ever since been subject. The story runs thus. When the first men lived upon the earth, a dog came to them one day and said, "All people will die like the Moon, but unlike the Moon you will not return to life again unless you give me some milk to drink out of your gourd and beer to drink through your straw. If you do this, I will arrange for you to go to the river when you die and to come to life again on the third day." But the people laughed at the dog, and gave him some milk and beer to drink off a stool. The dog was angry at not being served in the same vessels as a human being, and though he put his pride in his pocket and drank the milk and beer

---

13. W. H. I. Bleek and L. C. Lloyd, *Specimens of Bushman Folklore* (London, 1911), pp. 57–65. The part of the hare's thigh which the Bushmen cut out is believed to be the *musculus biceps femoris*.

from the stool, he went away in high dudgeon, saying, "All the people will die, and the Moon alone will return to life." That is why, when people die, they stay away, whereas when the Moon goes away she comes back again after three days' absence. If only people had given that dog a gourd to drink milk out of, and a straw to suck beer through, we should all have risen from the dead, like the Moon, after three days.[14] In this story nothing is said as to the personage who sent the dog with the message of immortality to men; but from the messenger's reference to the Moon, and from a comparison with the parallel Hottentot story, we may reasonably infer that it was the Moon who employed the dog to run the errand, and that the unscrupulous animal misused his opportunity to extort privileges for himself to which he was not strictly entitled.

In these stories a single messenger is engaged to carry the momentous message, and the fatal issue of the mission is set down to the carelessness or malice of the missionary. However, in some narratives of the origin of death, two messengers are despatched, and the cause of death is said to have been the dilatoriness or misconduct of the messenger who bore the glad tidings of immortality. There is a Hottentot story of the origin of death which is cast in this form. They say that once the Moon sent an insect to men with this message, "Go thou to men and tell them, 'As I die, and dying live, so ye shall also die, and dying live.'" The insect set off with this message, but as he crawled along, the hare came leaping after him, and stopping beside him asked, "On what errand art thou bound?" The insect answered, "I am sent by the Moon to men, to tell them that as she dies, and dying lives, they also shall die, and dying live." The hare said, "As thou art an awkward runner, let me go." And away he tore with the message, while the insect came creeping slowly behind. When he came to men, the hare perverted the message which he had officiously taken upon himself to deliver, for he said, "I am sent by the Moon to tell you, 'As I die, and dying perish, in the same manner ye shall also die and come wholly to an end.'" Then the hare returned to the Moon, and told her what he had said to men. The Moon was very angry and reproached the hare, saying, "Darest thou tell the people a thing which I have not said?" With that she took a stick and hit him over the nose. That is why the hare's nose is slit down to this day.[15]

The same tale is told, with some slight variations, by the Tati Bushmen or Masarwas, who inhabit the Bechuanaland Protectorate, the

---

14. A. C. Hollis, *The Nandi* (Oxford, 1909), p. 98.
15. Bleek, *Reynard the Fox*, pp. 69 ff.

Kalahari desert, and portions of Southern Rhodesia. The men of old time, they say, told this story. The Moon wished to send a message to the men of the early race, to tell them that as she died and came to life again, so they would die, and dying come to life again. So the Moon called the tortoise and said to him, "Go over to those men there, and give them this message from me. Tell them that as I dying live, so they dying will live again." Now the tortoise was very slow, and he kept repeating the message to himself, so as not to forget it. The Moon was very vexed with his slowness and with his forgetfulness: so she called the hare and said to her, "You are a swift runner. Take this message to the men over yonder: 'As I dying live again, so you will dying live again.'" So off the hare started, but in her great haste she forgot the message, and as she did not wish to show the Moon that she had forgotten, she delivered the message to men in this way, "As I dying live again, so you dying will die for ever." Such was the message delivered by the hare. In the meantime the tortoise had remembered the message, and he started off a second time. "This time," said he to himself, "I won't forget." He came to the place where the men were, and he delivered his message. When the men heard it they were very angry with the hare, who was sitting at some distance. She was nibbling the grass after her race. One of the men ran and lifted a stone and threw it at the hare. It struck her right in the mouth and cleft her upper lip; hence the lip has been cleft ever since. That is why every hare has a cleft upper lip to this day, and that is the end of the story.[16]

The story of the two messengers is related also by the negroes of the Gold Coast, and in their version the two messengers are a sheep and a goat. The following is the form in which the tale was told by a native to a Swiss missionary at Akropong. In the beginning, when sky and earth existed, but there were as yet no men on earth, there fell a great rain, and soon after it had ceased a great chain was let down from heaven to earth with seven men hanging on it. These men had been created by God, and they reached the earth by means of the chain. They brought fire with them and cooked their food at it. Not long afterwards God sent a goat from heaven to deliver the following message to the seven men, "There is something that is called Death; it will one day kill some of you; but though you die, you will not perish utterly, but you will come to me here in heaven." The goat went his way, but when he came near the town he lit on a bush which seemed to him good to eat; so he lingered there and began to browse. When God saw that the goat lin-

16. Rev. S. S. Dornan, "The Tati Bushmen (Masarwas) and Their Language," *Journal of the Royal Anthropological Institute* 47 (1917), 80.

gered by the way, he sent a sheep to deliver the same message. The sheep went, but did not say what God had commanded her to say; for she perverted the message and said, "When you once die, you perish, and have no place to go to." Afterwards the goat came and said, "God says, you will die, it is true, but that will not be the end of you, for you will come to me." But the men answered, "No, goat, God did not say that to you. What the sheep first reported, by that we shall abide." [17]

In an Ashantee version of the story the two messengers are also a sheep and a goat, and the perversion of the message of immortality is ascribed sometimes to the one animal and sometimes to the other. The Ashantees say that long ago men were happy, for God dwelt among them and talked with them face to face. However, these blissful days did not last forever. One unlucky day it chanced that some women were pounding a mash with pestles in a mortar, while God stood by looking on. For some reason they were annoyed by the presence of the deity and told him to be off; and as he did not take himself off fast enough to please them, they beat him with their pestles. In a great huff God retired altogether from the world and left it to the direction of the fetishes; and still to this day people say, "Ah, if it had not been for that old woman, how happy we should be!" However, God was very good-natured, and even after he had gone up aloft, he sent a kind message by a goat to men on earth, saying, "There is something which they call Death. He will kill some of you. But even if you die, you will not perish completely. You will come to me in heaven." So off the goat set with this cheering intelligence. But before he came to the town he saw a tempting bush by the wayside, and stopped to browse on it. When God looked down from heaven and saw the goat loitering by the way, he sent off a sheep with the same message to carry the joyful news to men without delay. But the sheep did not give the message right. Far from it; she said, "God sends you word that you will die, and that will be an end of you." When the goat had finished his meal, he also trotted into the town and delivered his message, saying, "God sends you word that you will die, certainly, but that will not be the end of you, for you will go to him." But men said to the goat, "No, goat, that is not what God said. We believe that the message which the sheep brought us is the one which God sent to us." That unfortunate misunderstanding was the beginning of death among men.[18] However, in another Ashantee version of the tale the parts played by the sheep and goat are re-

17. J. G. Christaller, "Negersagen von der Goldküste," *Zeitschrift für Afrikanische Sprachen* 1 (Berlin, 1887–88), 55.
18. E. Perregaux, *Chez les Achanti* (Neuchâtel, 1906), pp. 198 ff.

versed. It is the sheep who brings the tidings of immortality from God to men, but the goat overruns him, and offers them death instead. In their innocence men accepted death with enthusiasm, not knowing what it was, and naturally they have died ever since.

In all these versions of the story the message is sent from God to men, but in another version, reported from Togoland in West Africa, the message is despatched from men to God. They say that once upon a time men sent a dog to God to say that when they died they would like to come to life again. So off the dog trotted to deliver the message. But on the way he felt hungry and turned into a house, where a man was boiling magic herbs. So the dog sat down and thought to himself, "He is cooking food." Meantime the frog had set off to tell God that when men died they would prefer not to come to life again. Nobody had asked him to give that message; it was a piece of pure officiousness and impertinence on his part. However, away he tore. The dog, who still sat hopefully watching the hell-broth brewing, saw him hurrying past the door, but he thought to himself, "When I have had something to eat, I will soon catch froggy up." However, froggy came in first, and said to the deity, "When men die, they would prefer not to come to life again." After that, up comes the dog, and says he, "When men die, they would like to come to life again." God was naturally puzzled, and said to the dog, "I really do not understand these two messages. As I heard the frog's request first, I will comply with it. I will not do what you said." That is the reason why men die and do not come to life again. If the frog had only minded his own business instead of meddling with other people's, the dead would all have come to life again to this day. But frogs come to life again when it thunders at the beginning of the rainy season, after they have been dead all the dry season while the Harmattan wind was blowing. Then, while the rain falls and the thunder peals, you may hear them quacking in the marshes.[19] Thus we see that the frog had his own private ends to serve in distorting the message. He gained for himself the immortality of which he robbed mankind.

In these stories the origin of death is ascribed to the blunder or wilful deceit of one of the two messengers. However, according to another version of the story, which is widely current among the Bantu tribes of Africa, death was caused, not by the fault of the messenger, but by the vacillation of God himself, who, after deciding to make men immortal, changed his mind and resolved to make or leave them mortal; and unluckily for mankind the second messenger, who bore the message of

19. Fr. Müller, "Die Religionen Togos in Einzeldarstellungen," *Anthropos* 2 (1907), 203.

death, overran the first messenger, who bore the message of immortality. In this form of the tale the chameleon figures as the messenger of life, and the lizard as the messenger of death. Thus the Zulus say that in the beginning Unkulunkulu, that is, the Old Old One, sent the chameleon to men with a message, saying "Go, chameleon, go and say, Let not men die." The chameleon set out, but it crawled very slowly and loitered by the way to eat the purple berries of the *ubukwebezane* shrub or of a mulberry tree; however, some people say that it climbed up a tree to bask in the sun, filled its belly with flies, and fell fast asleep. Meantime the Old Old One had thought better of it and sent a lizard post-haste after the chameleon with a very different message to men, for he said to the animal, "Lizard, when you have arrived, say, Let men die." So the lizard ran, passed the dawdling chameleon, and arriving first among men delivered his message of death, saying, "Let men die." Then he turned and went back to the Old Old One who had sent him. But after he was gone, the chameleon at last arrived among men with his joyful news of immortality, and he shouted, saying, "It is said, Let not men die!" But men answered, "Oh! we have heard the word of the lizard; it has told us the word. 'It is said, Let men die.' We cannot hear your word. Through the word of the lizard, men will die." And died they have ever since from that day to this. So the Zulus hate the lizard and kill it whenever they can, for they say, "This is the very piece of deformity which ran in the beginning to say that men should die." But others hate and hustle or kill the chameleon, saying, "That is the little thing which delayed to tell the people that they should not die. If he had only told us in time, we too should not have died; our ancestors also would have been still living; there would have been no disease here on earth. It all comes from the delay of the chameleon." [20]

The same story is told in nearly the same form by other Bantu tribes

---

20. H. Callaway, *The Religious System of the Amazulu*, part 1 (Springvale, Natal, etc., 1868), pp. 1, 3 ff.; part 2 (Springvale, Natal, etc., 1869), p. 138; Rev. L. Grout, *Zululand, Or Life among the Zulu-Kafirs* (Philadelphia, n.d.), pp. 148 ff.; Dudley Kidd, *The Essential Kafir* (London, 1904), pp. 76 ff. Compare A. F. Gardiner, *Narrative of a Journey to the Zoolu Country* (London, 1836), pp. 178 ff.; T. Arbousset and F. Daumas, *Relation d'un voyage d'exploration au nord-est de la Colonie du Cap de Bonne-Espérance* (Paris, 1842), p. 472; Rev. F. Shooter, *The Kafirs of Natal and the Zulu Country* (London, 1857), p. 159; W. H. I. Bleek, *Reynard the Fox in South Africa* (London, 1864), p. 74; D. Leslie, *Among the Zulus and Amatongas*, 2nd ed. (Edinburgh, 1875), p. 209; F. Merensky, *Beiträge zur Kenntniss Süd-Afrikas* (Berlin, 1875), p. 124; F. Speckmann, *Die Hermannsburger Mission in Afrika* (Hermannsburg, 1876), p. 164. According to Callaway, the lizard is hated much more than the chameleon and is invariably killed. On the other hand, according to Arbousset and Daumas, it was the grey lizard that brought the message of life, and the chameleon that brought the message of death; hence the chameleon is hated, but the harmless grey lizard beloved.

such as the Bechuanas,[21] the Basutos,[22] the Baronga,[23] the Ngoni,[24] and apparently by the Wa-Sania of British East Africa.[25] It is found, in a slightly altered form, even among the Hausas, who are not a Bantu people.[26] To this day the Baronga and the Ngoni owe the chameleon a grudge for having brought death into the world by its dilatoriness. Hence, when they find a chameleon slowly climbing on a tree, they tease it till it opens its mouth, whereupon they throw a pinch of tobacco on its tongue, and watch with delight the creature writhing and changing colour from orange to green, from green to black in the agony of death; for so they avenge the great wrong which the chameleon did to mankind.[27]

Thus the belief is widespread in Africa, that God at one time purposed to make mankind immortal, but that the benevolent scheme miscarried through the fault of the messenger to whom he had entrusted the gospel message.

3. THE STORY OF THE CAST SKIN

Many savages believe that, in virtue of the power of periodically casting their skins, certain animals and in particular serpents renew their youth and never die. Holding this belief, they tell stories to explain

21. J. Chapman, *Travels in the Interior of South Africa*, vol. 1 (London, 1868), p. 47.

22. E. Casalis, *The Basutos* (London, 1861), p. 242; E. Jacottet, *The Treasury of Basuto Lore*, vol. 1 (Morija, Basutoland, 1908), pp. 46 ff. According to the Basutos it was the grey lizard that was sent first with the message of immortality, and the chameleon that was sent after him with the message of mortality. Compare above, p. 87, n. 20.

23. Henri A. Junod, *Les Chants et les contes des Ba-ronga* (Lausanne, n.d.), p. 137; *Les Ba-Ronga* (Neuchâtel, 1898), pp. 401 ff.; *The Life of a South African Tribe*, vol. 2 (Neuchâtel, 1912–13), p. 328 ff.

24. W. A. Elmslie, *Among the Wild Ngoni* (Edinburgh and London, 1899), p. 70.

25. See Captain W. E. R. Barrett, "Notes on the Customs and Beliefs of the Wa-giriama, etc., of British East Africa," *Journal of the Royal Anthropological Institute* 41 (1911), 37. "The Wa-Sania believe that formerly human beings did not die until one day a lizard (Dibleh) appeared and said to them, 'All of you know that the moon dies and rises again, but human beings will die and rise no more.' They say that from that day human beings commenced to die." This is probably only an abridged form of the story of the two messages sent to man by the Moon through the lizard and the chameleon.

26. J. G. Christaller, "Negersagen von der Goldküste," *Zeitschrift für Afrikanische Sprachen* 1 (1887–88), 61. In this Hausa version the message sent by God to men through the chameleon is as follows: "When a man dies, you must touch him with bread, and he will rise again." This message the chameleon faithfully delivered, but men refused to accept it, because the lizard, outrunning the chameleon, had brought them this word, "When a man dies, you must bury him."

27. H. A. Junod and W. A. Elmslie; see above, nn. 23 and 24. The particular species of lizard which according to the Thonga (Baronga) outran the chameleon and brought the message of death is a large animal with a blue head.

how it came about that these creatures obtained, and men missed, the boon of immortality.

Thus, for example, the Wafipa and Wabende of East Africa say that one day God, whom they name Leza, came down to earth, and addressing all living creatures said, "Who wishes not to die?" Unfortunately man and the other animals were asleep; only the serpent was awake and he promptly answered, "I do." That is why men and all other animals die. The serpent alone does not die of himself. He only dies if he is killed. Every year he changes his skin, and so renews his youth and his strength.[28] In like manner the Dusuns of British North Borneo say that when the Creator had finished making all things, he asked, "Who is able to cast off his skin? If any one can do so, he shall not die." The snake alone heard and answered, "I can." For that reason down to the present day the snake does not die unless he is killed by man. The Dusuns did not hear the Creator's question, or they also would have thrown off their skins, and there would have been no death.[29] Similarly the Todjo-Toradjas of Central Celebes relate that once upon a time God summoned men and animals for the purpose of determining their lot. Among the various lots proposed by the deity was this, "We shall put off our old skin." Unfortunately mankind on this momentous occasion was represented by an old woman in her dotage, who did not hear the tempting proposal. But the animals which slough their skins, such as serpents and shrimps, heard it and closed with the offer.[30] Again, the natives of Vuatom, an island in the Bismarck Archipelago, say that a certain To Konokonomiange bade two lads fetch fire, promising that if they did so they should never die, but that, if they refused, their bodies would perish, though their shades or souls would survive. They would not hearken to him, so he cursed them, saying, "What! you would all have lived! Now you shall die, though your soul shall live. But the iguana (*Goniocephalus*) and the lizard (*Varanus indicus*) and the snake (*Enygrus*), they shall live, they shall cast their skin and they shall live for evermore." When the lads heard that, they wept, for bitterly they rued their folly in not going to fetch the fire for To Konokonomiange.[31]

The Arawaks of British Guiana relate that once upon a time the Creator came down to earth to see how his creature man was getting on.

28. Mgr. Lechaptois, *Aux Rives du Tanganika* (Algiers, 1913), p. 195.

29. Ivor H. N. Evans, "Folk Stories of the Tempassuk and Tuaran Districts, British North Borneo," *Journal of the Royal Anthropological Institute* 43 (1913), 478.

30. N. Adriani and Alb. C. Kruijt, *De Bare'e-sprekende Toradja's van Midden-Celebes*, vol. 2 (Batavia, 1912–14), p. 83.

31. Otto Meyer, "Mythen und Erzählungen von der Insel Vuatom (Bismarck-Archipel, Südsee)," *Anthropos* 5 (1910), 724.

But men were so wicked that they tried to kill him; so he deprived them of eternal life and bestowed it on the animals which renew their skin, such as serpents, lizards, and beetles.[32] A somewhat different version of the story is told by the Tamanachiers, an Indian tribe of the Orinoco. They say that after residing among them for some time the Creator took boat across to the other side of the great salt water from which he had come. Just as he was shoving off from the shore, he called out to them in a changed voice, "You will change your skins," by which he meant to say, "You will renew your youth like the serpents and the beetles." But unfortunately an old woman, hearing these words, cried out, "Oh!" in a tone of scepticism, if not of sarcasm, which so annoyed the Creator that he changed his tune at once and said testily, "Ye shall die." That is why we are all mortal.[33]

The people of Nias, an island to the west of Sumatra, say that, when the earth was created, a certain being was sent down from above to put the finishing touches to the work. He ought to have fasted, but, unable to withstand the pangs of hunger, he ate some bananas. The choice of food was very unfortunate, for had he only eaten river crabs, men would have cast their skins like crabs, and so, renewing their youth perpetually, would never have died. As it is, death has come upon us all through the eating of those bananas.[34] Another version of the Niasian story adds that "the serpents on the contrary ate the crabs, which in the opinion of the people of Nias cast their skins but do not die; therefore serpents also do not die but merely cast their skin."[35]

In this last version the immortality of serpents is ascribed to their having partaken of crabs, which by casting their skins renew their youth and live for ever. The same belief in the immortality of shellfish occurs in a Samoan story of the origin of death. They say that the gods met in council to determine what should be the end of man. One proposal was that men should cast their skins like shellfish, and so renew their youth. The god Palsy moved, on the contrary, that shellfish should cast their skins, but that men should die. While the motion was still before the meeting a shower of rain unfortunately interrupted the discussion, and as the gods ran to take shelter, the motion of Palsy was carried unanimously. That is why shellfish still cast their skins and men do not.[36]

32. R. Schomburgk, *Reisen in Britisch-Guiana*, vol. 2 (Leipzig, 1847–48), p. 319.
33. Ibid., vol. 2, p. 320.
34. H. Sundermann, *Die Insel Nias und die Mission daselbst* (Barmen, 1905), p. 68; E. Modigliani, *Un viaggio a Nías* (Milan, 1890), p. 295.
35. A. Fehr, *Der Niasser im Leben und Sterben* (Barmen, 1901), p. 8.
36. George Brown, D.D., *Melanesians and Polynesians* (London, 1910), p. 365; George Turner, *Samoa A Hundred Years Ago and Long Before* (London, 1884), pp. 8 ff.

Thus not a few peoples appear to believe that the happy privilege of immortality, obtainable by the simple process of periodically shedding the skin, was once within reach of our species, but that through an unhappy chance it was transferred to certain of the lower creatures, such as serpents, crabs, lizards, and beetles. According to others, however, men were at one time actually in possession of this priceless boon, but forfeited it through the foolishness of an old woman. Thus the Melanesians of the Banks Islands and the New Hebrides say that at first men never died, but that when they advanced in life they cast their skins like snakes and crabs, and came out with youth renewed. After a time a woman, growing old, went to a stream to change her skin; according to some, she was the mother of the mythical or legendary hero Qat, according to others, she was Ul-ta-marama, Change-skin of the world. She threw off her old skin in the water, and observed that as it floated down it caught against a stick. Then she went home, where she had left her child. But the child refused to recognize her, crying that its mother was an old woman, not like this young stranger. So to pacify the child she went after her cast integument and put it on. From that time mankind ceased to cast their skins and died.[37] A similar story of the origin of death is told in the Shortlands Islands[38] and by the Kai, a Papuan tribe of North-eastern New Guinea. The Kai say that at first men did not die but renewed their youth. When their old brown skin grew wrinkled and ugly, they stepped into water, and stripping it off got a new, youthful white skin instead. In those days there lived an old grandmother with her grandchild. One day the old woman, weary of her advanced years, bathed in the river, cast off her withered old hide, and returned to the village, spick and span, in a fine new skin. Thus transformed, she climbed up the ladder and entered her house. But when her grandchild saw her, he went and squalled, and refused to believe that she was his granny. All her efforts to reassure and pacify him proving vain, she at last went back in a rage to the river, fished her wizened old skin out of the water, put it on, and returned to the house a hideous old hag again. The child was glad to see his granny come back, but she said to him, "The locusts cast their skins, but ye men shall die from this day forward." And sure enough, they have done so ever since.[39] The same story, with some trivial variations, is told by natives of the Admiralty Islands. They say that once on a time there was

37. R. H. Codrington, *The Melanesians* (Oxford, 1891), p. 265; W. Gray, "Some Notes on the Tannese," *Internationales Archiv für Ethnographie* 7 (1894), 232.
38. C. Ribbe, *Zwei Jahre unter den Kannibalen der Salomo-Inseln* (Dresden-Blasowitz, 1903), p. 148.
39. Ch. Keysser, "Aus dem Leben der Kaileute," in R. Neuhauss, *Deutsch Neu-Guinea*, vol. 3 (Berlin, 1911), pp. 161 ff.

an old woman, and she was frail. She had two sons, and they went a-fishing, while she herself went to bathe. She stripped off her wrinkled old skin and came forth as young as she had been long ago. When her sons came from the fishing they were astonished to see her. The one said, "It is our mother"; but the other said, "She may be your mother, but she shall be my wife." Their mother overheard them and said, "What were you two saying?" The two said, "Nothing! We only said that you are our mother." "You are liars," she retorted, "I heard you both. If I had had my way, we should have grown to be old men and women, and then we should have cast our skin and been young men and young women. But you have had your way. We shall grow old men and old women, and then we shall die." With that she fetched her old skin, and put it on, and became an old woman again. As for us, her descendants, we grow up and we grow old. But if it had not been for those two young scapegraces, there would have been no end of our days, we should have lived for ever and ever.[40]

Still farther away from the Banks Islands the very same story is repeated by the To Koolawi, a mountain tribe of Central Celebes. As reported by the Dutch missionaries who discovered it, the Celebes version of this widely diffused tale runs thus. In the olden time men had, like serpents and shrimps, the power of casting their skin, whereby they became young again. Now there was an old woman who had a grandchild. Once upon a time she went to the water to bathe, and thereupon laid aside her old skin and hung it up on a tree. With her youth quite restored she returned to the house. But her grandchild did not know her again, and would have nothing to do with his grandmother; he kept on saying, "You are not my grandmother; my grandmother was old, and you are young." Then the woman went back to the water and drew on her old skin again. But ever since that day men have lost the power of renewing their youth and must die.[41]

While some peoples have supposed that in the early ages of the world men were immortal in virtue of periodically casting their skins, others have ascribed the same high privilege to a certain lunar sympathy, in consequence of which mankind passed through alternate states of growth and decay, of life and death, corresponding to the phases of the moon, without ever coming to an end. On this view, though death in a sense actually occurred, it was speedily repaired by resurrection, generally, it would seem, by resurrection after three days, since three

40. Josef Meier, "Mythen und Sagen der Admiralitätsinsulaner," *Anthropos* 3 (1908), 193.

41. N. Adriani and Alb. C. Kruijt, *De Bare'e-sprekende Toradja's van Midden-Celebes*, vol. 2 (Batavia, 1912–14), p. 83.

days is the period between the disappearance of the old moon and the reappearance of the new. Thus the Mentras or Mantras, a shy tribe of savages in the jungles of the Malay Peninsula, allege that in the early ages of the world men did not die, but only grew thin at the waning of the moon and then waxed fat again as she waxed to the full. Thus there was no check whatever on the population, which increased to an alarming extent. So a son of the first man brought this state of things to his father's notice, and asked him what was to be done. The first man, a good easy soul, "Leave things as they are"; but his younger brother, who took a more Malthusian view of the matter, said, "No, let men die like the banana, leaving their offspring behind." The question was submitted to the Lord of the Underworld, and he decided in favour of death. Ever since then men have ceased to renew their youth like the moon and have died like the banana.[42] In the Caroline Islands it is said that in the olden time death was unknown, or rather it was only a short sleep. Men died on the last day of the waning moon and came to life again on the appearance of the new moon, just as if they had wakened from a refreshing slumber. But an evil spirit somehow contrived that when men slept the sleep of death they should wake no more.[43] The Wotjobaluk, a tribe of South-eastern Australia, related that when all animals were men and women, some of them died and the moon used to say, "You up again," whereupon they came to life again. But once on a time an old man said, "Let them remain dead"; and since then nobody has ever come to life again, except the moon, which still continues to do so down to this very day.[44] The Unmatjera and Kaitish, two tribes of Central Australia, say that their dead used to be buried either in trees or underground, and that after three days they regularly rose from the dead. The Kaitish tell how this happy state of things came to an end. It was all the fault of a man of the Curlew totem, who found some men of the Little Wallaby totem in the act of burying a man of that ilk. For some reason the Curlew man flew into a passion and kicked the corpse into the sea. Of course after that the dead man could not come to life again, and that is why nowadays nobody rises from the dead after three days, as everybody used to do long ago.[45] Though nothing is said about the moon in this narrative of the origin of death, the analogy of the preceding stories makes it probable that the three

42. D. F. A. Hervey, "The Mentra Traditions," *Journal of the Straits Branch of the Royal Asiatic Society* no. 10 (December 1882), 190; W. W. Skeat and C. O. Blagden, *Pagan Races of the Malay Peninsula*, vol. 2 (London, 1906), pp. 337 ff.

43. *Lettres, Édifiantes et Curieuses*, new ed., vol. 15 (Paris, 1781), pp. 305 ff.

44. A. W. Howitt, *Native Tribes of South-East Australia* (London, 1904), pp. 428 ff.

45. (Sir) Baldwin Spencer and F. J. Gillen, *Northern Tribes of Central Australia* (London, 1904), pp. 513 ff.

days during which the dead used to lie in the grave, were the three days during which the moon lay "hid in her vacant interlunar cave." The Fijians also associated the possibility, though not the actual enjoyment, of human immortality with the phases of the moon. They say that of old two gods, the Moon and the Rat, discussed the proper end of man. The Moon said, "Let him be like me, who disappear awhile and then live again." But the Rat said, "Let man die as a rat dies." And he prevailed.[46]

The Upotos of the Congo tell how men missed and the Moon obtained the boon of immortality. One day God, whom they call Libanza, sent for the people of the moon and the people of the earth. The people of the moon hastened to the deity, and were rewarded by him for their alacrity. "Because," said he, addressing the moon, "thou camest to me at once when I called thee, thou shalt never die. Thou shalt be dead for but two days each month, and that only to rest thee; and thou shall return with greater splendour." But when the people of the earth at last appeared before Libanza, he was angry and said to them, "Because you came not at once to me when I called you, therefore you will die, one day and not revive, except to come to me."[47]

The Bahnars of Eastern Cochin China explain the immortality of primitive man neither by the phase of the moon nor by the custom of casting the skin, but apparently by the recuperative virtue of a certain tree. They say that in the beginning, when people died, they used to be buried at the foot of a tree called Long Blo, and that after a time they always rose from the dead, not as infants, but as full-grown men and women. So the earth was peopled very fast, and all the inhabitants formed but one great town under the presidency of our first parents. In time men multiplied to such an extent that a certain lizard could not take his walks abroad without somebody treading on his tail. This vexed him, and the wily creature gave an insidious hint to the gravediggers. "Why bury the dead at the foot of the Long Blo tree?" said he; "bury them at the foot of Long Khung, and they will not come to life again. Let them die outright and be done with it." The hint was taken, and from that day men have not come to life again.[48]

In this last story, as in many African tales, the instrument of bringing death among men is a lizard. We may conjecture that the reason for assigning the invidious office to a lizard was that this animal, like the

---

46. Thomas Williams, *Fiji and the Fijians*, 2nd ed., vol. 1 (London, 1860), p. 205.

47. M. Lindeman, *Les Upotos* (Brussels, 1906), pp. 23 ff.

48. Guerlach, "Moeurs et Superstitions des sauvages Ba-hnars," *Les Missions Catholiques* 19 (1887), 479.

serpent, casts its skin periodically, from which primitive man might infer, as he infers with regard to serpents, that the creature renews its youth and lives for ever. Thus all the myths which relate how a lizard or a serpent became the maleficent agent of human mortality may perhaps be referred to an old idea of a certain jealousy and rivalry between men and creatures which cast their skins, notably serpents and lizards; we may suppose that in all such cases a story was told of a contest between man and his animal rivals for the possession of immortality, a contest in which, whether by mistake or guile, the victory always remained with the animals, who thus became immortal, while mankind was doomed to mortality.

4. THE COMPOSITE STORY OF THE PERVERTED MESSAGE AND THE CAST SKIN

In some stories of the origin of death the incidents of the perverted message and the cast skin are combined. Thus the Gallas of East Africa attribute the mortality of man and the immortality of serpents to the mistake or malice of a certain bird which falsified the message of eternal life entrusted to him by God. The creature which did this great wrong to our species is a black or dark blue bird, with a white patch on each wing and a crest on its head. It perches on the tops of trees and utters a wailing note like the bleating of a sheep; hence the Gallas call it *halawaka* or "the sheep of God," and explain its apparent anguish by the following tale. Once upon a time God sent that bird to tell men that they should not die, but that when they grew old and weak they should slip off their skins and so renew their youth. In order to authenticate the message God gave the bird a crest to serve as the badge of his office. Well, off the bird set to deliver the glad tidings of immortality to man, but he had not gone far before he fell in with a snake devouring carrion in the path. The bird looked longingly at the carrion and said to the snake, "Give me some of the meat and blood, and I will tell you God's message." "I don't want to hear it," said the snake tartly, and continued his meal. But the bird pressed him so to hear the message that the snake rather reluctantly consented. "The message," then said the bird, "is this. When men grow old they will die, but when you grow old you will cast your skin and renew your youth." That is why people grow old and die, but snakes crawl out of their old skins and renew their youth. But for this gross perversion of the message God punished the heedless or wicked bird with a painful internal malady, from which he suffers to this day; that is why he sits wailing on the tops of trees.[49] Again, the Melanesians, who inhabit the coast of the Gazelle Peninsula in New Britain, say that To Kambinana, the Good Spirit, loved men and wished to make them immortal. So he called his brother To Korvuvu and said to him, "Go to men and take them the secret of immortality. Tell them to cast their skin every year. So will they be protected from death, for their life will be constantly renewed. But tell the serpents that they must thenceforth die!" However, To Korvuvu acquitted himself badly of this task; for he commanded men to die, and betrayed to the serpents the secret of immortality. Since then all men have been mortal, but the serpents cast their skins every year and never die.[50] A similar story of the origin of death is told in Annam. They say that Ngoc hoang sent a messenger from heaven to men to say that when they reached old age they should change their skins and live for ever, but that when serpents grew old they must die. The messenger came down to earth and said, rightly enough, "When man is old he shall cast his skin; but when serpents are old they shall die and be laid in coffins." So far so good. But unluckily there happened to be a brood of serpents within hearing, and when they learned the doom pronounced on their kind, they fell into a fury and said to the messenger, "You must say it over again and just the contrary, or we will bite you." That frightened the messenger, and he repeated his message, changing the words thus, "When the serpent is old he shall cast his skin; but when man is old he shall die and be laid in the coffin." That is why all creatures are now subject to death, except the serpent, who, when he is old, casts his skin and lives for ever.[51]

5. CONCLUSION

Thus, arguing from the analogy of the moon or of animals which cast their skins, the primitive philosopher has inferred that in the beginning a perpetual renewal of youth was either appointed by a benevolent being for the human species or was actually enjoyed by them, and that but for a crime, an accident, or a blunder it would have been enjoyed by them for ever. People who pin their faith in immortality to the cast skins of serpents, lizards, beetles, and the like, naturally look on

49. Miss A. Werner, "Two Galla Legends," *Man* 13 (1913), 90 ff.

50. P. A. Kleintitschen, *Die Küstenbewohner der Gazellehalbinsel* (Hiltrup bei Münster, n.d.), p. 334.

51. A. Landes, "Contes et Légendes Annamites," *Cochinchine française, Excursions et Reconnaissances*, no. 25 (Saigon, 1886), pp. 108 ff.

these animals as the hated rivals who have robbed us of the heritage which God or nature intended that we should possess; consequently they tell stories to explain how it came about that such low creatures contrived to oust us from the priceless possession. Tales of this sort are widely diffused throughout the world, and it would be no matter for surprise to find them among the Semites. The story of the Fall of Man in the third chapter of Genesis appears to be an abridged version of this savage myth. Little is wanted to complete its resemblance to the similar myths still told by savages in many parts of the world. The principal, almost the only, omission is the silence of the narrator as to the eating of the fruit of the tree of life by the serpent, and the consequent attainment of immortality by the reptile. Nor is it difficult to account for the lacuna. The vein of rationalism, which runs through the Hebrew account of creation and has stripped it of many grotesque features that adorn or disfigure the corresponding Babylonian tradition, could hardly fail to find a stumbling-block in the alleged immortality of serpents; and the redactor of the story in its final form has removed this stone of offence from the path of the faithful by the simple process of blotting out the incident entirely from the legend. Yet the yawning gap left by his sponge has not escaped the commentators, who look in vain for the part which should have been played in the narrative by the tree of life. If my interpretation of the story is right, it has been left for the comparative method, after thousands of years, to supply the blank in the ancient canvas, and to restore, in all their primitive crudity, the gay barbaric colours which the skilful hand of the Hebrew artist had softened or effaced.

The Truth of Myth

RAFFAELE PETTAZZONI

One's attitude towards myth depends in part on whether one regards it as contain-
ing truth—either literal/historical truth or metaphorical/symbolic truth. Most
human societies do distinguish at least two principal categories of traditional nar-
rative. One consists of true stories (myths, legends)—that is, stories that were or
are believed to recount actual events—the other of fictional stories (folktales), as
Professor Bascom observed in the initial essay in this volume. But this may be too
static a definition insofar as it is conceivable that myths may have been believed to
be true at one point in time but not at some later period. Does a myth cease to be
a myth if it is no longer believed to be true? Is belief a necessary criterion for the
strict definition of myth? To the extent that myths are part of organized religions,
aren't they usually believed to be true—even if only metaphorically or symbolically
so? Or is there a kind of double standard of truth? Typically, a myth is not believed
to be true by an analyst, who somehow assumes that it is or was believed to be true
by some native group. With such reasoning, "other" peoples have myths, while we
the analysts have religion and/or science. The fallacy here is that we analysts also
have myths—whether we believe them to be true or not.

The critical question of the truth-value of myths is addressed by Raffaele Pet-
tazzoni (1883–1959), who was a professor of the history of religions at the Univer-
sity of Rome. Scholars in comparative religion or the history of religion do not
limit themselves to the Judeo-Christian tradition or to such major world religions
as Islam and Buddhism. Rather they are interested in religious behavior and belief
worldwide. Professor Pettazzoni draws on data gathered from many peoples in
Africa, Asia, and especially native North America in his essay. For another fine essay
on myth by Pettazzoni, see his "Myths of Beginnings and Creation-Myths," in Essays
on the History of Religions *(Leiden, 1954), pp. 24–36. For other discussions of the*
*truth-value of myths, see Giuseppe Cocchiara, "Il mito come 'Storia Vera'," * Revista
d'etnografia *4 (1950), 76–86; Stephen J. Reno, "Myth in Profile,"* Temenos *9 (1973),*
38–54.

Myth, in the usual acceptation of the word, belongs to the realm of the
imagination, which as such is distinct from, even opposed to, the
world of reality. The gods, who are the characters in myth, are for us

---

Reprinted from Raffaele Pettazzoni, *Essays on the History of Religions* (Leiden, 1954),
pp. 11–23, by permission of E. J. Brill, Leiden. The essay was originally published in
Studi e materiali di storia delle religioni 21 (1947–48), 104–16, under the title "Verità del
mito."

fabulous beings in whom we do not believe. Criticism of myth goes back to pagan antiquity, to those first Greek thinkers, such as Theagenes and Xenophanes, who lived in the sixth century B.C. and already found the anthropomorphism of the Homeric gods incompatible with the ideal of deity. But myth is older than Homer and belongs to a world which did believe in the gods. This faith in myth, this religious reality of myths, which is already overshadowed in Homer, is on the contrary very much alive in primitive mythology, and the myths themselves are the proof of it, while explicit confirmation is provided by a number of testimonies furnished by the natives themselves.

The Pawnee, a North American tribe of Caddo speech, differentiate "true stories" from "false stories," and include among the "true" stories in the first place all those which deal with the beginnings of the world; in these the actors are divine beings, supernatural, heavenly or astral. Next come those tales which relate the marvellous adventures of the national hero, a youth of humble birth who became the saviour of his people, freeing them from monsters, delivering them from famine and other disasters, and performing other noble and beneficent deeds. Last come the stories which have to do with the world of the medicine-men and explain how such-and-such a sorcerer got his superhuman powers, how such-and-such an association of shamans originated, and so on. The "false" stories are those which tell of the far from edifying adventures and exploits of Coyote, the prairie-wolf.[1] Thus in the "true" stories we have to deal with the holy and the supernatural, while the "false" ones on the other hand are of profane content, for Coyote is extremely popular in this and other North American mythologies in the character of a trickster, deceiver, sleight-of-hand expert and accomplished rogue.[2]

In this connexion there is a story from the Wichita, who also speak Caddo and are akin to the Pawnee, which is full of significance. It tells of a contest between Coyote and an opponent as to which knew most, i.e., which knew more stories.[3] The contest takes place at night, and the two opponents, sitting beside the fire, tell each a story in turn. At a certain point, Coyote's opponent begins to show signs of fatigue, and is slower and slower at finding a new tale to match that told by Coyote, while the latter goes on without stopping or hesitating, as if his repertory were limitless. At last the opponent owns himself beaten, and is killed. Why does Coyote win? Because, says the tale, his stories are

1. G. A. Dorsey, *The Pawnee: Mythology*, part 1 (Washington, D.C., 1906), pp. 10, 13, 141, 428.
2. E.g., among the Crow, see Fr. B. Linderman, *Old Man Coyote* (New York, 1931).
3. G. A. Dorsey, *Mythology of the Wichita* (Washington, D.C., 1904), pp. 252 ff.

"false," i.e., invented and therefore indefinitely many, while those of his opponent, who, we should note, is a falling star, are "true," that is, they tell of things which have really happened, and consequently are as many as they are, no more. The tales of Coyote, who appears here, as usual, as a breaker of his word, a violator of women, and so forth, would seem probably to be accounts of his imaginary adventures, easily to be multiplied at will on the model of his real ones. Certainly the Wichita themselves differentiate "old" tales, which have to do with the beginnings and the first age of the history of the world, from "new" ones, which treat of the present age, and it is only the former which are "true stories" for them.[4]

Similarly, the Oglala Dakota, a tribe of the Western Sioux family in North America, distinguish "tales of the tribe," that is, of historical events which really took place, which are considered as "true tales," and "funny stories," mere inventions having no real substance, such as are above all the adventures of Iktomi, a figure corresponding to Coyote.[5] Analogously, the Cherokee, who are Iroquois, distinguish between sacred myths (of the beginnings of the world, the creation of the heavenly bodies, the origin of death) and profane tales whose object is, for instance, to give an explanation, often a humorous one, of the more outstanding anatomical and physiological peculiarities of certain animals.[6]

In Australia also, among the Karadjeri tribe of Lagrange Bay on the north-west coast, the sacred traditions dealing with the mythical age, and in particular those of cosmogonic contents, which are taught the novices during their initiation, are known as "true."[7]

In Africa, among the Herero, the tales which tell of the beginnings of the different groups into which the tribe is divided are supposed to be historically true, and consequently are distinguished from the many more or less comic tales which have no foundation in fact.[8] The Negroes of Togoland, again, think of their stories of beginnings as "absolutely real."[9] Similarly, the Haussa distinguish between sagas or histori-

4. Ibid., pp. 20–22.
5. Martha W. Beckwith, "Mythology of the Oglala Dakota," in *Journal of American Folklore* 43 (1930), 339. On the legendary cycle of Iktomi (*Inktomi* among the Assiniboin, *Isginki* among the Iowa, *Istinike* among the Ponca and Omaha) see also J. R. Walker, *The Sun Dance and Other Ceremonies of the Oglala Division of the Teton Dakota*, Anthropological Papers of the American Museum of Natural History vol. 16, no. 2 (New York, 1917), 164 ff.
6. J. Mooney, *Myths of the Cherokee*, Nineteenth Annual Report of the Bureau of American Ethnology, part 1 (Washington, D.C., 1900), pp. 229 ff.
7. R. Piddington, "Totemic System of the Karadjeri Tribe," *Oceania* 2 (1932), 374, 393; "Karadjeri Initiation," *Oceania* 3 (1932), 46 ff.
8. G. Viehe, in *Mitteilungen des Seminars für orientalische Sprachen zu Berlin* 5 (1902), part 3, p. 112.
9. A. W. Cardinall, *Tales from Togoland* (London, 1931), p. 9.

cal narratives and fanciful tales concerning human beings or the lower animals.[10]

Now it is precisely the tales of beginnings, the cosmogonies, theogonies and legends of superhuman beings who brought things into existence and founded institutions, which are myths. And yet we see that for those who have and tell these tales, they are "true," and as such quite clearly distinguished from "false" stories; and the difference is not merely in their content, but affects the very nature of myth, showing itself likewise in conspicuous external signs.

Indeed, among the Pawnee and the Wichita, the tales of beginnings, including those of the associations of shamans, are recited in the course of certain cult-ceremonials, during the intervals between one rite and the next, which is not done with the false tales.[11] Furthermore, the true tales, in contrast to the false, are not common property; among the Cherokee the stories of the creation, of the heavenly bodies, and the like were told (at night) in the presence of a small gathering.[12] Among the Pima, who live between California and New Mexico and speak a language of the Uto-Aztecan family, the myths were not told if women were present; only a few experts knew them thoroughly, and to them the boys were intrusted for four consecutive nights, to be taught how the world was made, whence the Pima had come, and of their conflicts with demons, monsters and fierce beasts.[13] Finally, while the false tales may be recited indifferently and with impunity at all times and in all places, it is not so with the "true" stories, which are told almost exclusively in winter or autumn, and only exceptionally in summer,[14] but in any case never in the day, but always at night or in the evening.[15]

10. C. K. Meek, *The Northern Tribes of Nigeria*, vol. 2 (Oxford, 1925), p. 147.

11. Dorsey, *The Pawnee*, pp. 13, 141, and Dorsey, *Mythology of the Wichita*, p. 16. Among the Tinguian of Luzon (see F. C. Cole, *Traditions of the Tinguian: A Study in Philippine Folk-Lore*, Field Museum Publication no. 180 [Chicago, 1915], p. 6), the medicine-men's tales are told only during the preparations for the sacrifice of a beast or other offering to the gods.

12. Mooney, *Myths of the Cherokee*, p. 229.

13. Fr. Russell, *The Pima Indians*, Twenty-sixth Annual Report of the Bureau of American Ethnology (Washington, D.C., 1908), p. 206. Among the Berbers on the other hand it is the (old) women who tell the tales, and men are never among the listeners; see H. Basset, *Essai sur la littérature des Berbères* (Algiers, 1920), p. 101.

14. Among the Berbers the tales are told in summer and in winter, but not by day (Basset, *Essai*, p. 103). Among the Yavapai of Arizona, the myths are told in summer, by night, and to tell them in winter is to run the risk of raising a great storm. This, however, is the custom only of the south-eastern Yavapai; see E. W. Gifford, *The South-Eastern Yavapai*, University of California Publications in American Archaeology and Ethnology, vol. 29, no. 3 (1932), 212. On the contrary, among the other Yavapai, those of the west and north-east, the myths are told (by old men, at night) in autumn or winter, by the fire (Gifford, "North-eastern and Western Yavapai Myths," *Journal of American Folklore* 46 [1933], 347). Among the Tinguian of Luzon tales of the mythical era are generally told during the dry season (Cole, *Traditions of the Tinguian*, p. 5).

15. Among the Bukaua (Papuans of New Guinea), the tales are told in the evening

It is thus evident that the myth is not pure fiction; it is not fable but history, a "true story" and not a "false" one. It is a true story because of its contents, which are an account of events that really took place, starting from those impressive happenings which belong to the beginnings of things, the origin of the world and of mankind, that of life and death, of the animal and vegetable species, of hunting and of tilling the soil, of worship, of initiation-rites, of the associations of medicine-men and of their powers of healing. All these events are far removed in time, and from them our present life had its beginning and its foundation, from them came the present structure of society, which still depends on them. The divine or other superhuman persons who play their parts in the myth, their remarkable exploits and surprising adventures, all this world of wonders is a transcendent reality which may not be doubted, because it is the antecedent, the *sine qua non* of present reality.

Myth is true history because it is sacred history, not only by reason of its contents but also because of the concrete sacral forces which it sets going. The recital of myths of beginnings is incorporated in cult because it is cult itself and contributes to the ends for which cult is celebrated, these being the preservation and increase of life. Among various peoples of Australia, during the initiation-ceremonies the stories of the mythical age are told, the endless journeyings of the totemic ancestors who were the progenitors of the individual clans, because these recitals, apart from keeping alive and reinforcing the tribal traditions, promote the increase of the various totemic species. To tell of

---

during the season in which tubers and grains ripen; see Neuhauss, *Deutsch Neu-Guinea*, vol. 3, pp. 479 ff., quoted in Lévy-Bruhl, *La Mythologie primitive* (Paris, 1935), p. 116. Among the coastal Yuki in California, myths are called "night stories," because told only during the nights (of winter), while to tell them or even to think of them during the day is to risk becoming humpbacked; see E. W. Gifford, "Coast Yuki Myths," *Journal of American Folklore* (1937), p. 116. Among the California Miwok, myths are told (by old men) in the season which follows the first winter rains, and always at night; see C. Merriam, *The Dawn of the World* (Cleveland, 1910), p. 15, cited by Van Deursen, *Der Heilbringer* (Groningen, 1931), pp. 28–30. Among the Thonga, who are southern Bantu, stories are not told by day, but only in the evening, and anyone who tells them in the daytime will go bald (see H. A. Junod, *The Life of a South African Tribe*, 2nd ed. vol. 2 [London, 1927], p. 211). Among the hunting peoples of Siberia and those of the Altai, the tales are told in the evening at that time of year when hunting parties go out; among the Ostiaks of Yenissei it is forbidden to tell tales in summer, until the streams begin to freeze; among the Abkhases and other peoples of the Caucasus, and also among some other nomadic Iranian peoples, the prohibition against telling them by day is in force; see Zelenin, "Die religiöse Funktion der Volksmärchen," *Internationales Achiv für Ethnographie* 31 (1910), 21 ff. The same customs and prohibitions are in force for the recital of legends both in the Mediterranean countries and elsewhere in Europe. Thus, an Irishwoman who was a storyteller would not hear of telling her tales in the daytime, because it brings ill luck; see Bolte-Polivka, *Anmerkungen zu den Kinder- und Hausmärchen der Brüder Grimm*, vol. 4, p. 5.

the creation of the world helps to preserve the world; to tell of the beginnings of the human race helps to keep mankind in being, that is to say the community or tribal group. The recital of the institution of the initiation-rites and shamanistic practices has power to ensure their efficacy and their duration in time. Thus in ancient Mesopotamia, to recite the "Creation-epic" at the *akītu* or New Year festival was as it were to repeat the creative act; it was as though the world began again, and thus the year was truly inaugurated in the best manner, as a new cycle of time initiated by a new act of creation.[16]

That is why myths are true stories and cannot be false stories. Their truth has no origin in logic, nor is it of a historical kind; it is above all of a religious and more especially a magical order. The efficacy of the myth for the ends of cult, the preservation of the world and of life, lies in the magic of the word, in its evocative power, the power of *mythos* in its oldest sense, of the *fa-bula* not as a "fabulous" narrative but as a secret and potent force, akin, as its very etymology shows, to the power of *fa-tum*.[17] "It is said that it is so and therefore it is so"; that was the sentence in which an Eskimo of the Netsilik tribe expressed forcefully the magical truth, that is, the power to make real which the spoken word possesses. He was referring especially to the Netsilik narratives, which "are both their real history and the source of all their religious ideas."[18]

This evocative power of myth is reflected likewise in certain practices which often accompany its telling. Among the south-eastern Yavapai of Arizona, anyone listening to the story of the dying god ran the risk of falling ill,[19] with the result that when the narrative was

16. Cf. the chapter "Babilonia" in my *Confessione dei peccati*, vol. 2 (Bologna, 1935), pp. 91 ff.; also my article "Der babylonische Ritus des Akitu und das Gedicht der Weltschöpfung," *Eranos-Jahrbuch* 19 (1951), 404–30.

17. A thought of the invariability prescribed for magical formulae arises when one reads that among the coastal Yuki of California the teller of a tale must recite every word of it without the smallest variation (Gifford in *Journal of American Folklore* [1937], p. 116). Among the Miwok of California, the myths which make up the religious history of the people are handed down from generation to generation by word of mouth with no omissions or additions (Merriam, *The Dawn of the World*, p. 15). Among the Haussa of the Sudan, if the teller of the tale introduces a variation into the text of it, even of an insignificant word, the listeners correct him (Meek, *The Northern Tribes of Nigeria*, vol. 2, p. 153).

18. Knut Rasmussen, *The Netsilik Eskimos* (Copenhagen, 1931), pp. 207, 363.

19. The myth of the god or hero who dies (and rises again) is common to sundry peoples of southern California, as the Luiseño, Diegueño, Mohave and others. See Constance Goddard Du Bois, *The Religion of the Luiseño Indians*, University of California Publications in American Archaeology and Ethnology vol. 8, no. 3 (Berkeley, 1908), 145; T. T. Waterman, *The Religious Practices of the Diegueño Indians*, University of California Publications in American Archaeology and Ethnology 8, no. 6 (Berkeley, 1910), 338 ff.; A. L. Kroeber, "Two Myths of the Mission Indians of California," *Journal of American Folklore* 19 (1906), 314; R. Pettazzoni, *Miti e leggende* vol. 3 (Turin, 1953), pp. 201 ff.

ended every listener would get up, stretch and shake himself, with the
intention of freeing himself in this way, as he believed he could, from
the besetting malady.[20] Among the western and north-western Yavapai,
when the elder has finished telling a story (at night), he says to the
young people, boys and girls, who have listened to him, "Now get up,
and before the dawn appears, run to the river to wash your faces, because this is a 'great story,' and if you do not, you will go lame." [21] Analogously, among the Cherokee, when anyone had been present at night at
the telling of the myth of Kanati and Selu, that is, of the origin of corn
and of game (therefore a sacred legend, a "true story"), with all the explanations and comments belonging to it, he must "go to water" at dawn,
before eating, in other words bathe in running water, while the medicine-man occupied himself with certain of his ritual performances on
the bank.[22] Or, according to a parallel testimony,[23] after spending the
night in hearing stories,

> At daybreak the whole party went down to the running stream, where
> the pupils or hearers of myths stripped themselves, and were scratched
> upon the naked skin with a bone-tooth comb in the hands of the priest,
> after which they waded out, facing the rising sun, and dipped seven
> times under the water, while the priest recited prayers upon the bank.

This shaking, washing and blood-letting were all processes of riddance, having in view the same end, namely to free the hearer from the
harmful influences which he had contracted while listening to, in
other words during the evocation of, those imposing or even sinister
events, such as the death of the god among the Yavapai, which, thus
evoked, might by sympathetic potency bring about the death of the
listener.

Riddance is also the aim of certain formulae often employed at the
end of the narration. Among the Thonga, a Bantu people, the narrator
is accustomed to end his story with these words, addressed to the
story itself, "Run away, go to Gwambe and Dzabana!" This is as much
as to say, "Depart to the spirit-world," for Gwambe and Dzabana are
the first man and the first woman, who as ancestors of the human race
are the rulers of the realm of the dead, the country of spirits.[24] Among
the Berbers also, narratives begin and end with formulae, which vary
from tribe to tribe, but generally speaking, the introductory ones have

20. Gifford, *The South-eastern Yavapai*, p. 242.
21. Gifford, "North-eastern and Western Yavapai Myths," p. 347.
22. J. Mooney, "Myths of the Cherokees," *Journal of American Folklore* 1 (1888), 98;
Pettazzoni, *Miti e leggende*, vol. 3, p. 490.
23. Mooney, *Myths of the Cherokee*, pp. 229 ff.
24. Junod, *Life of a South African Tribe*, vol. 2, pp. 211, 349.

a propitiatory force ("may God give us good and death to our enemies!"), the concluding formulae have an apotropaic meaning intended to transfer the evil influences to some animal, for instance the jackal, or to some character of the story itself.[25]

The same principle of an utterance intended to cause a riddance governs the confession of sin, which indeed is, in its elementary forms, also associated with acts of riddance, such as washing, stripping, burning, drawing blood, vomiting and spitting. With all these, the sinner means to put the sin away, or take it out of himself, or shake it off his back, and for this reason also he confesses it, because by doing so, that is by putting it into words, he evokes it, "expresses it" in the most literal sense, and so expels it from his own person.[26] The same principle holds good also for a dream, which often leaves the dreamer under the oppression of its phantasms and the influence of its boding apparitions. To drive these away, according to the ancients, it was useful to wash, especially in sea-water,[27] as the enchantress Kirke does in the *Argonautica* of Apollonios of Rhodes (iv, 663, 670).[28] But another beneficial process was to tell the dream in the open air and in the sunlight,[29] as we are informed in a scholion on the *Electra* of Sophokles *à propos* of Klytaimestra's dream related by Chrysothemis (*El.* 424, foll., cf. 644 foll.). The ancients, says the annotator, "were accustomed, as a rite of riddance, to tell their dreams to the sun." The intention is still the same, to rid the person in question of the residual influence of the ghosts and spectres seen in the dream, nightly phantoms which the sun scattered and drove back to their own realms of darkness.

It is not without cause that among peoples who live by hunting myths and tales of beasts are told on the occasion of hunting-parties. Thus among the Pawnee the tales already mentioned, the "true stories," of the mythical hero who saved his people from hunger by slaughtering buffaloes, used to be recited by hunters taking part in an expedition, because this remarkable "bag" in the myth, by the very fact of being told, that is spoken aloud, and therefore evoked, had the power to assure good success to the actual hunting.[30] Analogously, the Korwa,

25. Basset, *Essai*, p. 104.
26. See my *Confessione dei peccati*, vol. 1–3 (Bologna, 1929–36) and vol. 1–2 (Paris, 1931–32). See also "Confession of Sins: An Attempted General Interpretation," in Raffaele Pettazzoni, *Essays on the History of Religions* (Leiden, 1954), p. 49.
27. Aeschylus *Persae* 201 ff.; Aristophanes *Frogs* 1340, with the scholiast there.
28. The natives of Morocco spit when they awake from a bad dream (E. Doutté, *Magie et religion dans l'Afrique du Nord* [Paris, 1909], p. 408). Among the Akamba, who are Hamitised Bantu of East Africa, if anyone has had a bad dream, he takes a burning brand, puts it out and throws it away, saying, "May my ugly dream go away like this brand." See G. Lindblom, *The Akamba* (Uppsala, 1919–20), p. 212.
29. Euripides *Iphigeneia in Taurus* 43.
30. Dorsey, *The Pawnee*, p. 141.

who are Kolarians of Chota Nagpur in east-central India, before they go to hunt, are accustomed to tell each other stories of hunting, assured that this contributes to the better success of the enterprise.[31] Among sundry people of Siberia, as the Buriats and others, and of the Altai, hunters are wont to tell stories in the evening in the communal hut, because, as they say, the spirits of the wood, who are the natural protectors of the beasts, are so fond of hearing them that they immediately crowd in and stay there invisible until the end, forgetting their protégés, which being thus left to themselves fall a prey more easily to the hunters.[32] This however is a secondary rationalistic motivation, which misses the real meaning of the narratives. These must originally have been told to attract, not the spirits, but the beasts themselves, of which the guardian spirits who watch over single species are after a fashion a transfiguration, an animistic hypostasis.[33]

The fact is that the tales told by the hunters of Siberia and the Altai are nothing else than tales of animals, as indeed the myths of the Bushmen, who are still more primitive hunters, are mostly stories of beasts. The rock-paintings of these same Bushmen also represent for the most part figures of animals and hunting-scenes, for the same magical principle is at work in these representations as in the recital of the myths; the picture is credited with a sympathetic potency fitted to promote the reproduction of the thing portrayed, that is the multiplication of the animal in question or the repetition of an equally productive hunt, and the like. For in the sphere of magic the picture that is drawn or painted has the same power as the word that is spoken, and anyone who possesses the effigy of a person has that person himself at his mercy, like him who knows his name; and anyone acquainted with the myth of the origin of an animal or vegetable species has in his power all the individuals of that species,[34] as anyone who can draw the capture of a bison on a rock is master of all bisons.

And this is equally true of prehistoric epochs and for the oldest rock-paintings of palaeolithic, mesolithic and neolithic huntsmen, for these pictures are mostly figures of animals and hunting scenes. And

31. R. V. Russell, *The Tribes and Castes of the Central Provinces of India*, vol. 3 (London, 1916), p. 577.

32. D. Zelenin, "Die religiöse Funktion," pp. 21 ff.; cf. K. Menges, "Jägerglaube u. -gebräuche bei Altajischen Türken," *Muséon* (1932), p. 85.

33. Cf. Uno Harva, *Die religiösen Vorstellungen der Altaischen Völker* (Helsinki, 1938), pp. 391 ff.

34. Among the Cuna of the Isthmus of Panama, a formula alluding to the origin of a given species confers the power of attracting the creatures of that species; to know the origin of a plant is the necessary and sufficient condition for the success of its medicinal action (Erl Nordenskiöld, "La Conception de l'âme chez les Indiens Cuna de l'Isthme de Panama," *Journal de la Société des Américanistes* [1932], pp. 6, 15, 24).

as these are for us the oldest monuments of graphic art, it has been thought that correspondingly the beast-tale,[35] from the Bushman myths to Aesop's fables and beyond, represents the oldest form of human story-telling, since both the art of those distant days and this primitive "literature" go back to the rudimentary culture of hunting and food-gathering, and both come from the spirit of magic, which is the spirit properly belonging to that ancient humanity, as yet sunk in animalism, always uncertain of to-morrow, always at the mercy of the unknown, always awaiting lucky happenings, such as a fortunate capture of game or the discovery of fruit-bearing bushes.

But this primitive humanity was already, for all its magic, a religious humanity. There never was, as Frazer supposed, a magic epoch earlier than religion, as there never was a religious epoch earlier than magic. Assuredly, the myths of beginnings with their great figures of creative Beings, Creators of the world and of the human race, of life and of death, are nearer to what *we* mean by religion. But the idea of a Supreme Being who creates, as a purely logical concept of pre-mythical thought, such as W. Schmidt postulates, is a wholly arbitrary construction. A pre-mythical stage is no more and no less an abstraction than the pre-logical stage of L. Lévy-Bruhl; human thought is mythical and logical at the same time. Neither is religion pure rational thinking which knows nothing of myth, as Andrew Lang supposed. Like magic, so also myth is already religion. The idea of the creative Supreme Being among primitive peoples is nothing but a form of the myth of beginnings and as such shares in the character of myth, at once magical and religious.[36] This character is, as we have said, the very truth of myth, an absolute truth because a truth of faith, and truth of faith because a truth of life. The myth is true and cannot but be true, because it is the charter of the tribe's life, the foundation of a world which cannot continue without that myth. On the other hand, the myth cannot continue without this world, of which it forms an organic part as the "explanation" of its beginnings, as its original *raison d'être*, its "prologue in heaven."[37] The life of myth, which is at the same time its "truth," is the very life of its natal world of formation and incubation. Apart from this, the myth can indeed survive, but a surviving myth is no longer true, because no longer living; it has ceased to be a "true" story and become a "false" one.

As already stated, the tales of Coyote, the prairie wolf, among sun-

---

35. Cf. Zelenin, "Die religiöse Funktion," pp. 28 ff.

36. See "Myths of Beginning and Creation-Myths," in Pettazzoni, *Essays*, pp. 26–27.

37. [The reference is to the famous scene with which the action of Goethe's *Faust*, part 1, begins—trans.]

dry peoples of North America, are "false." They form an extensive cycle of narratives concerning his adventures, which are far from edifying, since they consist of frauds, practical jokes, intrigues, lies, traps, swindles, deceits, thefts, love-makings, fornications and vulgarities of every kind, in sharp contrast to the loftiness, seriousness, dignity and impressiveness of the myths of beginnings, which are "true stories." But the figure of Coyote has not only these despicable attributes; Coyote appears frequently as a sort of demiurge, the benefactor of humanity, the lawgiver, the founder of institutions, and sometimes even as Creator, subordinate and in opposition to the Supreme Being.[38]

The complex and contradictory nature of Coyote's aspects results from the composite process which gave rise to his figure. Originally, Coyote clearly goes back to that primitive world of hunters in which life depends above all on hunting, and the good result of a hunt depends on the beasts, and in the first place on the Lord of Beasts who has them in his power. That is what Coyote was to begin with. As such, he was a rudimentary Supreme Being, as is, in other North American mythologies, the Hare or the Crow, as in Africa the praying mantis among the Bushmen, the spider or the elephant elsewhere, and such he remained as long as that primitive world from which he sprang lasted and continued. But when that world passes, its Supreme Being passes with it, that is to say the Lord of beasts, or Lord of the bush and of the game in it.[39] Then Coyote yielded up his place to another Supreme Being, the Creator, and survived only as the Creator's opponent and implacable adversary, a figure without dignity, a "false" figure confronted with the "truth" of the new Supreme Being, as his legends henceforth are false in face of the truth of the creation-myth.

A day will come when the myths of beginnings too will lose their "truth" and become "false stories" in their turn, in other words fabulous. This will occur when their world, built up on the ruins of the first one, collapses in its turn to give place to a later and different structure. This indeed is how history proceeds, in a series of disintegrations and reintegrations, dissolutions and rebirths, in the everlasting alternation of life and death. And when, by reason of internal degeneration or overpowering external forces, a world breaks up and another rises on

38. So among the (north-eastern) Maidu of California, see R. B. Dixon, *Maidu Texts* (1912), pp. 4 ff.; cf. his "System and Sequence in Maidu Mythology," *Journal of American Folklore* 16 (1903), 32 ff.; R. Dangel, "Der Schöpferglaube der Nordcentralcalifornier," *Studi e materiali di storia della religioni* 3 (1937), 31 ff.

39. H. Baumann, "Afrikanische Wild- und Buschgeister," *Zeitschrift für Ethnologie* 70 (1938 [1939]), 208–39; cf. A. Dirr, "Der kaukasische Wild- und Jagdgott," *Anthropos* 20 (1925), 139. See further my forthcoming book, *The All-knowing God* (London, 1955), epilogue.

its ruins, when one form of culture fades, to be replaced by another, the organic relationship of its constituent parts comes to an end. Disintegrated, disjointed, sundered, they lose all cohesion and fall a prey to dispersing centrifugal forces. Then the myths too, fragments among the fragments, stripped now of their genuine religious character and constitutionally foreign to the new structure, which has an ideology of its own, are thrust to the margins of the new life, until, utterly severed from their matrix and with every bond that held them loosened, they go on the ways of the world, passing from mouth to mouth as mere sport and amusement.

This does not mean that all profane tales are ancient myths desacralised. Many, and perhaps from the literary point of view the most interesting, were profane from the beginning, pure inventions and fictions, "false stories" which never had been "true stories." But by the side of these are others, of more remote origin, which from having been myths, that is to say "true" stories, as they were to start with, have become fabulous, "false stories," tales to laugh at, "a theme of laughter and of sport." [40] By this same process Coyote, from being a rudimentary demiurge and afterwards the adversary of the Creator, a distant forerunner of Satan, of the Devil, the "Spirit that still denies," degenerated into a sacrilegious buffoon, a jesting cheater, a vulgar harlequin. It was the same procedure by which another literary *genre*, the drama, which was once a liturgical performance, changed into a secular entertainment, the same through which, in another department, pictorial art got free, as an end in itself, from the primordial magico-religious paintings of prehistoric caves, and in yet another, the mystic bull-roarer of primitive initiation-mysteries degenerated into the ludicrous function of a plaything for little children, [41] and an ancient holy rite founded upon the course of the sun ended by becoming a ball-game. [42]

40. ["Argomento di riso e di trastullo," a line from a well-known poem of Giacomo Leopardi—trans.]

41. Cf. chap. 1 of my book *I Misteri* (Bologna, 1924).

42. Cf. Alice C. Fletcher and Fr. La Flesche, *The Omaha Tribe*, Twenty-seventh Annual Report of the Bureau of American Ethnology (Washington, D.C., 1911), p. 197; Father P. H. Meyer, "Wunekau, oder Sonnenverehrung in Neuguinea," *Anthropos* (1932), p. 427; W. Krickeberg, "Das mittelamerikanische Ballspiel u. seine religiöse Symbolik," *Paideuma* 3, nos. 3–5 (1948), 118 ff.

Myth and Story

THEODOR H. GASTER

The idea that sacred myth can in the course of time become secularized is not new. The Grimms, for example, believed that secular folktales were the "detritus" of ancient myths. But one school of myth interpretation argued that myth itself derived from earlier ritual. This so-called myth-ritual approach enjoyed a great vogue around the turn of the twentieth century. It was especially popular among students of Near Eastern mythology. As myth texts were assumed to represent reflections from ritual, the nineteenth-century preoccupation with searching for origins centered on reconstructing the supposed rituals which had given rise to the myths. Most commonly the initiating ritual was said to be a calendrical or seasonal one. So as the death of winter yielded to the birth or rebirth of spring in predictable cyclic fashion, so there were myths of renewal like the cleansing effect of a primeval deluge in which an older world was destroyed and a new one created.

The myth-ritual approach was applied to cultural materials as diverse as dances, dramas, games, and nursery rhymes. (See, for example, Lewis Spence, Myth and Ritual in Dance, Game, and Rhyme [London, 1947].) Most of these myth-ritual reconstructions lacked credibility, and even if there were a ritual origin for a given myth, no explanation was ever offered as to the origin of the ritual. The question of the ultimate origin then of myth was left unanswered. If myth came from ritual, where did the ritual come from? Yet the interrelationship of myth and ritual is not a trivial issue, for there are certainly documented instances of myth and ritual co-occurring. Perhaps the sanest statement on the subject was made by anthropologist Clyde Kluckhohn when he observed, "In sum, the facts do not permit any universal generalizations as to ritual being the 'cause' of myth or vice versa. Their relationship is rather that of intricate mutual interdependence, differently structured in different cultures and probably at different times in the same culture."

Myth-ritual interpretations did have a salutary effect on the study of myth insofar as they encouraged literary scholars to look beyond the verbal texts of myths. Myths were not to be studied solely as ends in themselves but as reflections of other aspects of the cultures in which they were found. One of the most fascinating ideas was that just as myth and ritual could be construed as parallel phenomena, so earthly forms such as temples might be isomorphic with presumed other-worldly forms. Man's attempts to replicate in ritual what he held to be the reality depicted in myth meant that there could be a conscious attempt to have man-made microcosms modeled after what was perceived as a macrocosm.

Theodor H. Gaster, a modern myth-ritualist and specialist in comparative reli-

Reprinted from *Numen* 1 (1954), 184–212, by permission of the author and E. J. Brill, Leiden.

gion and folklore especially of the Near East, articulates his view of myth. Gaster tends to see myth and ritual as parallel expressions, but not as derivative one from the other. For more of Gaster's approach to myth, see his Thespis: Ritual, Myth and Drama in the Ancient Near East *(Garden City, N.Y., 1961). For a sample of the abundant myth-ritual scholarship, see S. H. Hooke, "The Myth and Ritual Pattern of the Ancient East," in S. H. Hooke, ed.,* Myth and Ritual *(London, 1933), pp. 1–14; E. O. James, "Myth and Ritual,"* Eranos Jahrbuch *17 (1949), 79–120; Stanley Edgar Hyman, "The Ritual View of Myth and the Mythic,"* Journal of American Folklore *68 (1955), 462–72; Claude Lévi-Strauss, "Sur les rapports entre la mythologie et le rituel,"* Bulletin de la Société Française de Philosophie *50 (1956), 99–125; William Bascom, "The Myth-Ritual Theory,"* Journal of American Folklore *70 (1957), 103–14; Phyllis M. Kaberry, "Myth and Ritual: Some Recent Theories,"* Bulletin of the Institute of Classical Studies *5 (1957), 42–54; S. G. F. Brandon, "The Myth and Ritual Position Critically Considered," in S. H. Hooke, ed.,* Myth, Ritual and Kingship *(Oxford, 1958), pp. 261–91; Francis Lee Utley, "Folklore, Myth and Ritual," in Dorothy Bethurum, ed.,* Critical Approaches to Medieval Literature *(New York, 1960), pp. 83–109; and Robert Ackerman, "Frazer on Myth and Ritual,"* Journal of the History of Ideas *36 (1975), 115–34. For Kluckhohn's important essay, see "Myths and Rituals: A General Theory,"* Harvard Theological Review *35 (1942), 45–79. For a critique of the approach by a classicist, see Joseph Fontenrose,* The Ritual Theory of Myth *(Berkeley and Los Angeles, 1966). See also Robert A. Segal, "The Myth-Ritualist Theory of Religion,"* Journal for the Scientific Study of Religion *19 (1980), 173–85.*

I. A NEW APPROACH TO MYTH

1. Sciences are like small children that constantly outgrow their clothes but are compelled, all too often, by the negligence or penury of their guardians, to "make do" with last year's outfit. Of no science, perhaps, is this more true than of Mythology.

During the past fifty years, the science of mythology has reached— if not maturity, at least adolescence. In the first place, thanks to archaeological excavations in the Near East, we now possess a richer body of ancient mythological literature and a wider acquaintance with ancient religious beliefs and practises than ever before.[1] Consequently we are now in a position to recognize a number of controlling processes and patterns hitherto unsuspected. In the second place, the intensive work of field anthropologists has now made it clear that Myth can no longer be studied merely as a branch of literature or art, but belongs also—and more fundamentally—within the realm of religion and cult, mythological stories being recited, in many societies, not for

1. Translations of most of this new material are now available in *Ancient Near Eastern Texts Relating to the Old Testament*, ed. James B. Pritchard (Princeton, 1950). This volume is here referred to as *ANET*.

entertainment or diversion, but as part and parcel of ritual procedures.[2]

Nevertheless, the full implications of these developments do not appear even now to have been adequately apprehended. For, although the field of inquiry has certainly been enlarged, the science of mythology continues to be dominated, by and large, by the perspectives of an age in which it was still primarily a *literary* study and in which a myth was regarded as an essentially *verbal* phenomenon—that is, as a type of *story*. The "truth" of Myth, for example, is still all too often identified with the veracity or historicity of particular *narratives*; the relation of Myth to Ritual is still conceived, in most cases, as one of a thing *told* to a thing *done*, while investigations into the nature of the basic myth-making process tend to concentrate on accounting for the element of fantasy *in tales*, and usually resolve themselves into what are really disquisitions on the psychology of poetry or poetic imagination.[3]

The Redefinition of Myth

2. The point that clamors for recognition is that Myth has now turned out to be a far more comprehensive thing than was previously supposed. It has acquired not only a new context but also a new dimension. Consequently it can no longer be contained within the old categories, but demands both redefinition and a fresh approach. We are, in fact, face to face with the birth of a new and wider science of which traditional "literary" mythology is but one aspect.

What name may best fit that new science, or rather its basic subject, is a question of terminology which may safely be left to the future; the important thing at present is to define and delineate it. In this discussion, therefore, we shall simply call it Myth (with capital M), and for its purely verbal expression—that is, for what is conventionally styled *a myth*—we shall, by way of distinction, employ the term "mythological story."

3. Taking our cue from its cultic function rather than from its mere literary or artistic content, Myth—in this larger sense—may be defined as *any presentation of the actual in terms of the ideal*. It is an ex-

2. See especially B. Malinowski, *Myth in Primitive Psychology* (London, 1926). Note also H. Leenhardt, *PCHR VII* (1951) (Proceedings of the VII Congress for the History of Religions [1950], Amsterdam, 1951), p. 89: "Le mythe n'est pas un récit, il est vécu. Il ne faut pas déduire de là qu'il ne s'agit point de mythe puisqu'il n'y a pas de récit, mais accepter que le mythe soit vécu avant d'être conté."

3. This applies, for instance, to Ernst Cassirer's *Sprache und Mythos* (1925) and to Susanne K. Langer's treatment of the subject in her suggestive volume, *Philosophy in a New Key* (New York, 1948), pp. 138–65. Langer says explicitly: "Myth begins in fantasy, which may remain tacit for a long time; for the primary form of fantasy is the entirely subjective and private phenomenon of *dream*."

pression of the concept that all things can be viewed at once under two aspects—on the one hand, temporal and immediate; on the other, eternal and transcendental. The present generation, for example, is but the immediate, punctual avatar of an ideal community which transcends the here and now and in which *all* generations are immersed, in the same way that a moment is immerged in time. All that it does and suffers is but a concentration in the actual and empirical of that which transpires simultaneously and automatically on an ideal, preterpunctual level.[4]

The Relation of Myth to Ritual

4. The purpose of *ritual* is to present a situation formally and dramatically in its immediate punctual aspect—as an *event* or *occurrence*, something in which present and actual individuals are involved. That of *myth*, on the other hand, is to present it in its ideal, transcendental aspect—as something transpiring (rather than occurring) concurrently in eternity and as involving preterpunctual, indesinent beings of whom living men and women are but the temporal incarnations.

5. A simple illustration will best clarify the point. It is commonly believed among primitive peoples that at the end of a year or cycle the life of a community stands in need of regeneration; the sun has to be relumed, the succession of the seasons re-established, and the fecundity of the human, animal and vegetable kingdoms to be re-assured. *Magnus ab integro saeclorum nascitur ordo.* To this end, certain functional procedures are adopted under communal auspices and sanctions. This is Ritual. At the same time, however, the revival adds a new lease to the ideal continuum; it is not only the immediate generation that is revitalized, but also *eo ipso* the transcendental entity of which it is merely the present phase. The presentation of the procedure in this aspect is Myth.

To speak in terms of practical expression: if a king or headman performs a certain act in order (say) to produce rain or avert pestilence, the corresponding myth will portray that act in terms of something done on a transcendental plane by immortal suprahuman beings. If, for instance, the king or headman ritually engages and discomfits the demon of overflowing or impounded waters in order practically to ensure the prosperity of the crops during the ensuing year, his action will be presented in the concomitant myth as the defeat of the Dragon by the tribal god (or the weather-god) or by, e.g., "Saint George."

4. On this concept, see the present writer's *Thespis* (New York, 1950), pp. 4–5.

6. *Au fond*, therefore, Myth is cosubstantial with Ritual. They are not—as is often supposed—*two* things artificially or schematically brought into relationship with each other, but *one* thing viewed from two different angles or through two different prisms. To be sure, in point of formal articulation, a particular mythological story may be later than a particular ritual procedure, or vice versa. This, however, is a sequence or precedence of *forms of expression*, not of abstract and ultimate essences. It by no means implies, as Robertson Smith maintained,[5] that Myth *per se* is but an offshoot or projection of Ritual; nor, as some more recent writers have contended,[6] that Ritual is but a subsequent enactment of Myth. Both of these theses are alike misleading because they dichotomize what is essentially a single phenomenon and because they represent as genealogically successive what are in fact but concomitant aspects of the same thing.

The Various Expressions of Myth

7. The basic mythic idea—that is, the concept of an intrinsic parallelism between the real and the ideal—is in itself implicit in the very process of apprehending phenomena or of attributing significance to them. A major function of religion, however, is to render it explicit, i.e., to articulate it through outward media. Of these, the *verbal* medium—that is, the mythological story—is but one. There are also several others, and all of them must be considered together if the true character of Myth itself is to be properly understood.

8. *God and King*. One of the most striking of these alternative media is the concept of Divine Kingship.[7]

5. W. Robertson Smith, *Religion of the Semites* (London, 1927), p. 18.

6. E.g., D. G. Brinton, *Religions of Primitive Peoples* (New York, 1899), p. 173. Among other pronouncements on the relation between Myth and Ritual, the following may be quoted:

Jane Harrison, *Themis* (Cambridge, 1912), p. 328: "The primary meaning of myth in religion is just the same as in early literature; it is the spoken correlative of the sacred rite, the thing done; it is *to legomenon* as contrasted with, or rather as related to, *to drōmenon*." This confuses Myth per se with its mere verbal articulation.

S. H. Hooke, *Myth and Ritual* (Oxford, 1933), p. 3: "The myth is the spoken part of the ritual: a description of what is being done. The original myth, inseparable in the first instance from its ritual, embodies in more or less symbolic form the original situation which is seasonably re-enacted in the ritual." The same confusion, *plus* a fallacious assumption that the original myth was archetypal; see below, §30.

Fr. Heiler, *PCHR VII* (1951), p. 160: "Der Kult erzeugt den Mythus." This requires a definition of "der Kult" and a little more precision about the process implied by "erzeugt." Van der Leeuw's classic dictum that myth is "word circumscribing event" is likewise too vague. It could apply equally well to narrative in general.

7. See A. M. Hocart, *Kingship* (Oxford, 1927); I. Engnell, *Studies in Divine Kingship in the Ancient Near East* (Uppsala, 1945); C. G. Seligman, *Egypt and Negro Africa: A Study in*

The true nature of the relationship between the king and the tribal god is that they are two aspects of the same phenomenon, viewed respectively from the standpoint of the real and of the ideal. The *king* personifies or epitomizes the "spirit" or character of a living community, as it exists in a particular moment of time. The *tribal god*, on the other hand, personifies or epitomizes the "essence" of that community conceived as an ideal, transcendental entity of which the living generation is but the present phase. To put the matter in contemporary terms: the king would be the reigning sovereign of Great Britain, while the tribal god would be "the Crown" (or, possibly, John Bull). *Mutatis mutandis*, the relationship is of the same order as that of God the Son to God the Father in normative Christian theology.

9. An illuminating illustration is afforded by the concept of the *devarāja*, or "god-king," in ancient Cambodia. "The *devarāja*," we are informed,[8] "is not the deified sovereign, but rather the permanent principle and essence of kingship (*rājyasāra*)." But—and this is the significant point—it is conceived to be concretized and punctualized in the "basic self" (*sūkṣmāntanātman*) of each successive ruler, and it may even be symbolized by an image or idol. Here, therefore, we have, in a more or less precise formulation, just that immergence of the punctual in the ideal of which we have been speaking.

10. A close parallel is the ancient Egyptian belief that every pharaoh was an embodiment of the god Horus, and the picture may be further clarified by reference to contemporary African usage. The king of the Loango, for instance, is styled *pango*, which means "god." He is thus, as a Christian might put it, "very God of very God," cosubstantial and of the same essence—θεός, not merely θεῖος. Similarly, the king of Ganda is called *Llare*, "Almighty God," and is believed to control the punctual and immediate manifestations of nature. Here again, he is not a deputy or vicar, but an incarnation. "*God*" is likewise the title of the king of Ruanda, while among the Kaffitshos, he bears the name of the chief deity, *Heql*. In the same way, too, the people of Landa hail their king with the cry, "Greetings to our *god*," and when the chief of the Biu dies, it is said that "*God* has fallen."[9]

11. Sometimes the mode of expression is less direct: it is said only that *upon his death* the king "becomes a god." This, for example, is a

Divine Kingship (London, 1934); G. Widengren, *The King and the Tree of Life in Ancient Near Eastern Religion* (Uppsala, 1951); P. Hadfield, *Traits of Divine Kingship in Africa* (London, 1949); H. Frankfort, *Kingship and the Gods* (Chicago, 1948); C. J. Gadd, *Ideas of Divine Rule in the Ancient East* (London, 1948); T. H. Gaster, "Divine Kingship in the Ancient Near East," *Review of Religion* 9 (1945), 267–81.

8. G. Coedès, *PCHR VII* (1951), pp. 141 ff.

9. These examples are taken from Hadfield, *Traits of Divine Kingship*, pp. 12–15.

common expression in ancient Hittite texts,[10] and Johannes Friedrich has pointed out a parallel in Mexican usage.[11] Even here, however, the basic concept is the same, and the same mythopoeic process is at work. For what is involved is not (as is all too commonly supposed) a process of *deification*—that is, of *con*version into a superior type of being—but rather a *re*version of the avatar to that more comprehensive essence which it temporally and temporarily embodied. In other words, the punctual and actual recedes at death, and being then continues only in the aspect of the eternal and ideal.

12. *God and Hero.* Another and allied expression of the basic Mythic Idea is the institution of Hero Worship.

Worship, it should be observed initially, is more than mere respect; it entails not only veneration but also awe; not only piety, but also subservience. Accordingly, when a national hero or a deceased ancestor receives *worship*, he receives something more than an expression of esteem or than mere funerary or posthumous honors. What we have to ask, therefore, is precisely *why* he is thus distinguished from all other mortals or from that vast majority of the dead who can inspire only feelings and rites born of numinous apprehension or, at best, of sentimental reverence. The answer is that he is recognized as possessing some special extra quality which sets him apart from them, and that quality consists precisely in the fact that he is, or was, but the punctual vessel and vehicle of an ideal and indesinent essence. It is this preterpunctual essence, and not his earthly personality, that is really being adored. As Lord Raglan has excellently expressed it: "The king is worshipped when alive; he continues to be worshipped when dead, not because he is dead, but because he is believed to be in some way alive."[12]

13. Thus, when we find Agamemnon recognized in Sparta as Zeus Agamemnon,[13] it is not Agamemnon, but Zeus—that is, the indesinent being which he embodied—that is the object of worship; Agamemnon is simply a particularizing symbol, an empirical point of focus. Similarly, when we find ancient Mesopotamian kings (e.g., Shulgi of Ur) receiving divine honors either in their lifetimes or after their deaths, and when we find the sign for "god" prefixed occasionally to the writ-

---

10. Fr. Hrozny, *Sprache der Hethiter* (1917), p. 171; A. Goetze, *Kleinasien* (Munich, 1933), p. 83.

11. Johannes Friedrich, *Zeitschrift für Deutschen Morgenländischen Gesellschaft* 89 (1930), 283; cf. W. Krickeberg, *Märchen der Asteken und Inkaperuaner* (Jena, 1928), pp. 90 ff.; E. Seler, *Sahagun* (Stuttgart, 1927), p. 437.

12. Lord Raglan, *The Origin of Religion* (London, 1949), p. 80.

13. See on this, A. B. Cook, *Zeus*, vol. 2 (Cambridge, 1925), pp. 1069 ff.

ing of their names,[14] we are not to infer that they were *promoted* to a higher than mortal status; all that is really implied is that the preterpunctual aspect of their office was duly and formally acknowledged. To put it concisely, such expressions as "Zeus Agamemnon" and "god Shulgi" do not mean "*deified* Agamemnon" and "*deified* Shulgi," but rather "*ideal* Agamemnon" and "*ideal* Shulgi," and connote an aspect of being which they always inherently possessed. The conventional use in this context of the term "deification" (or *Vergöttlichung*) is, indeed, utterly fallacious;[15] for the phenomenon with which we are confronted is rather that of "divinity" (or *Gottheit*) pure and simple. What we have, in fact, is simply another expression of the intrinsic parallelism between the real and the ideal—a foregleam, as it were, of the great affirmation that "In the beginning was the Word, and the Word was with God, and the Word was God. . . . And the Word became flesh and dwelt among us."

14. *Correspondence of the "Heavenly" and the Earthly.* A third expression of the basic Mythic Idea may be recognized in the common notion that earthly cities, temples or religious institutions have their duplicates in some other, transcendental sphere, often identified with the heavens.

The ancient Egyptians, for instance, believed that the nomes, or administrative divisions, of their country matched the several "fields (i.e., territories) of the gods" on high, and that many of their temples had been built on a pattern laid down by the gods.[16] The Mesopotamians held a similar belief. A text discovered at Ashur, the older capital of Assyria, states, for example, that Esagila, the famous temple of Marduk in Babylon, corresponds to an edifice erected by the gods in heaven,[17] while an inscription of Gudea, the governor of Lagash (c. 2250 B.C.), relates how he beheld in a dream the goddess Nisaba holding a tablet on which were depicted "the holy stars of the building of the temple," and how that goddess was accompanied by a god who proferred a "blue-

14. Cf. Ch. Jeremias, *Die Vergöttlichung der babylonisch-assyrischen Könige*, Der alte Orient, vol. 19, no. 3–4 (Leipzig, 1919); T. Fish, "The Cult of King Dungi [Shulgi] During the Third Dynasty of Ur," *Bulletin of John Rylands Library* 11, no. 2 (July 1927), 1–7.

15. E.g., in Ch. Jeremias' treatise mentioned in the preceding note, and in Goetze's brief treatment of the subject in *Kleinasien*, p. 83.

16. A. Moret, *Du caractère religieux de la royauté pharaonique* (Paris, 1903), p. 131. Note, however, the remark of H. H. Nelson in *Biblical Archaeologist* 7 (1944), 47: "I can find no indication that this interpretation of the temple was other than secondary. At any rate, the cosmological significance ascribed to the temple did not determine its form. The structure came first, and the interpretation dealt with what already existed." Even so, the secondary interpretation may have been a mere later articulation of a primitive concept.

17. *Keilschrifttexte aus Assur religiösen Inhalts*, no. 164, 38 ff.

print" of it.[18] Similarly, in the Biblical account of the building of the Tabernacle, it is said that God showed Moses a plan of it on Mount Sinai,[19] while the Islamic writer Ibn al-Ferkah declares that the building on al-Haram was planned by the angels and carried out by Adam.[20]

15. Sometimes it is a city, not a temple, that is credited with a transcendental counterpart. Jewish tradition asserts, for instance, that there is an "upper" as well as a "lower" Jerusalem[21]—an idea which is echoed in sundry passages of the New Testament (notably in the Book of Revelation)[22] and thence forms the theme of several mediaeval Christian hymns.[23] Similarly, in Psalm 87:3, Zion is apostrophized as "the city of the gods"[24]—that is, as the earthly duplicate of the heavenly abode—and with this may be compared the name Amarapura, "City of the Gods," borne by the ancient capital of the kings of Burma.

16. Analogous also in point of basic concept is the Jewish doctrine that the Law which was given to Moses on Mount Sinai was but a copy of the ideal, primordial Law (Torah) which abides eternally with God,[25] or the Mohammedan idea that the Koran is but the transcript of a celestial archetype—the so-called "Mother of the Book."[26]

All of these ideas go back ultimately to a recognition of the intrinsic parallelism between the real and the ideal.

17. *Name and Person.* The Mythic Idea likewise finds expression in the primitive belief—attested especially in magic—that the *name* of a person is an integral part of his being.[27] For this belief rests on the ul-

18. Thureau-Dangin, *Die sumerischen und akkadischen Königsinschriften* 140, 19, 20 ff. (The oft-quoted passage from the "Bellino Cylinder" of Sennacherib is to be otherwise interpreted; Gadd, *Ideas of Divine Rule*, p. 94.)

19. Exod. 25:9, 40.

20. Matthews, *Journal of the Palestine Oriental Society* 15 (1935), 531; cf. J. Pedersen, *Israel*, vol. 3–4 (1940), pp. 263, 693.

21. Taᶜanith 5a; Hagigah 12b; Pesiḵta 21.144b; L. Ginzberg, *Legends of the Jews*, vol. 5, p. 292. The idea is mentioned also in apocryphal and pseudepigraphical literature: Test. 12 Patr., Dan. 5; Syr. Apoc. Baruch 4:3, etc.; cf. G. H. Box, *Liber esdrae*, vol. 4 (London, 1912), pp. 198 ff.; A. Kahana, *Ha-sepharim ha-ḥiṣônîm*, vol. 1 (Tel Aviv, 1917), p. 369.

22. Gal. 4:26; Heb. 12:22; Rev. 3:12; 21:10.

23. E.g., in the anonymous seventh-century hymn, "Urbs beata Ierusalem / dictu pacis visio / quae construitur in caelis / vivis ex lapidibus / et angelis coornatur / ut sponsa comitibus" (J. S. Phillimore, ed., *The Hundred Best Latin Hymns* [Glasgow, 1926], no. 18). The words *dictu pacis visio* are based on a fanciful derivation of Jerusalem from Hebrew *r-ʾ-h*, "see," and *shalôm*, "peace"). Cf. also Abelard's famous "O quanta qualia sunt illa sabbata," stanza 2: "Vera Ierusalem / est illa civitas / cujus pax jugis est / summa jucunditas; / ubi non praevenit / rem desiderium / nec desiderio / minus est premium."

24. Heb. ᶜîr ha-elôhîm. The words are to be construed as epexegetical of the preceding, "Glorious things are spoken of thee," not as a vocative.

25. Cf. Ginzberg, *Legends of the Jews*, vol. 1, p. 3; vol. 2, p. 153; vol. 6, p. 307.

26. Sura 48:3; 55:77; 85:22.

27. Cf. the Indic doctrine of *namarūpa.*

terior assumption that personality consists not only in the visible, corporeal self but also in some wider, preterpunctual essence of which the *name* is a peculiarly appropriate symbol inasmuch as it indeed represents the individual even when his body is absent or defunct. The name stands, in this context, in exactly the same relationship to the body as the god stands to the king, or the "heavenly" to the earthly in the examples we have cited; it connotes the personality conceived on the ideal as well as the empirical plane.

18. *Myth and History.* Nor is it only persons and things that are conceived as possessing a transcendental counterpart. The same holds true also for historical events. The best example of this is, perhaps, the Jewish tradition that *all* the generations of Israel, not merely the actual fugitives from Egypt, were present *in spirit* at Mount Sinai when the Covenant was concluded.[28] Here a punctual situation is presented explicitly as something that also transpired *eo ipso* on a durative, preterpunctual plane. In the same way, when (say) the recent war between Great Britain and Germany is represented as a conflict between the British lion and the German eagle, something more is involved than mere pictorial metaphor; for the lion and the eagle stand respectively for each of the two countries *conceived in its ideal, continuous aspect*, so that a struggle which actually took place at a particular moment of time is thus portrayed in its concomitant ideal aspect.

Insofar as the mythopoeic process is concerned, it is, of course, completely unimportant whether or not an alleged historical event really took place; it is sufficient if it be imagined to have done so. For the basic Mythic Idea is part of the *conception*, not the *actuality*, of an event.

Limitations of Mythic Expression

19. As soon as the Mythic Idea is articulated in outward forms, its basic significance is inevitably compromised; for the very process of articulation involves a reduction of that which is essentially transcendental to the idiom of empirical concepts and categories.

This attenuation can be illustrated most conveniently from ancient Oriental cultures.

20. The intrinsic parallelism between king and god, for example, tends to be represented under the figure of *genealogical descent* or of an actual *conferment* of properties and status.

28. Cf. Ginzberg, *Legends of the Jews*, vol. 3, p. 97.

Thus, the Egyptian pharaoh is a son of the god Re ͨ;[29] the Babylonian king is suckled at the breasts of the goddess Ishtar;[30] and the Hebrew monarch is formally adopted by Yahweh at the moment of his installation: "I have installed My King on Zion, My holy hill. . . . Yahweh hath said unto me, 'Thou art My son, this day have I begotten thee'" (Psalm 2:6–7).[31]

Alternatively, the emblems of kingship are believed to be stored on high and to be bestowed, as an act of divine favor, upon each succeeding sovereign. In the Babylonian Story of Etana it is said expressly that, during a period of divine displeasure, when the city of Kish was left without a king, crown and sceptre remained in the treasuries of Anu, the supreme god,[32] while Hammurabi, king of Babylon, declares that the insignia of royalty were conferred on him by the god Sin.[33] Similarly, in Psalm 110 (which appears to have been composed for an enthronement ceremony), "Yahweh sends forth the sceptre of thy prowess, (saying), 'From Zion do thou rule in the midst of thy foes.'"[34]

Again, the "authority" of the king—that is, his power to govern the community in accordance with what is believed to be the natural norm (Egyptian mu'at; Hebrew ṣedeq; Sanskrit ṛta)—is referred not to any innate divinity but to specific endowment by a superior god. "God, give Thy judgments to the king, and Thy gift of right-doing (Hebrew, ṣidqatĕkā) to the king's heir," cries the Hebrew psalmist (Ps. 72:1); while in Hittite texts, the ruler is said to be favored with the divinely-bestowed quality of parā-handātar, a kind of "holy spirit" which enables him to direct affairs aright.[35]

29. Breasted, *Ancient Records*, vol. 1, §786 (Khenzer): Pharaoh is called "son of his (Re ͨ s') body." Similarly, Re ͨ says to Sesostris III: "Thou art the son of my body whom I have begotten"; cf. S. A. B. Mercer, *The Religion of Ancient Egypt* (London, 1949), chap. 14, pp. 248 ff.

30. Cf. *Thespis*, p. 179.

31. Compare Re ͨ s' declaration to Sesostris III, as quoted in n. 29. The preceding words, usually rendered "I will publish the decree" (Heb. asapperah el ḥôq), are probably to be emended, with Torczyner, to "I gather thee unto my bosom" (ôsîfĕkä el ḥêqî). This is a sign of adoption; cf. J. Grimm, *Deutsche Rechtsaltertümer*, 4th ed., vol. 1 (Leipzig, 1899), pp. 219, 638; F. Leibrecht, *Zur Volkskunde* (Heilbronn, 1879), p. 432. The Count of Edessa so adopted Baldwin.

32. Etana A.1.11 = *ANET*, p. 114b.

33. *Cuneiform Texts from Babylonian Tablets, Etc. in the British Museum*, part 21 (London, 1905), plate 40.

34. The traditional text mars the point by punctuating, "Y. sends the sceptre of thy prowess from Zion, (saying), Rule thou," etc. But the sceptre is sent *from heaven*; only the wielding of it proceeds from Zion.

35. Cf. A. Goetze, *Hattusilis, Mitteilungen der Vorderasiatisch-Aegyptischen Gesellschaft* 29, no. 3 (1925), 52–55. H. G. Güterbock, *Forgotten Religions*, ed. V. Ferm (New York, 1950), p. 99, defines it as a "special force governed by the gods." It is equated with the Accadian mišaru, which is, approximately, "equity"; cf. L. Oppenheim, *ANET*, p. 269b, n. 1.

So deeply, indeed, does this notion of *conferment* take root that it in turn gives rise to a set of secondary symbols: the "power and the glory" are *rubbed* into the king by unction or anointment, or *pressed* upon him by the laying-on of hands, or passed to him by a symbolic clasping of the divine hand.[36]

21. Similarly, in the field of hero-worship, the innate divinity of the hero is often portrayed under the image of positive deification; after his death he is *translated* to a higher realm or caught up into heaven, as witness the innumerable legends of "assumptions."

22. So, too, the intrinsic *identity* of real with transcendental cities (or temples) tends to be conveyed in terms of an artificial *identification* of an earthly with a heavenly structure. The transcendental "holy city," says the Book of Revelation (21:2), came down *out of heaven* from God, and elsewhere it is actually recognized in the stars. In Mesopotamian belief, for example, the terrestrial city of Sippar had its duplicate in the constellation of Cancer, and that of Babylon in a combination of Aries and Cetus ("the *Iku*-stars"), while the ideal Tigris was seen beside Pisces (*Anunîtu*), and the ideal Euphrates in the vicinity of Cygnus.[37] Similarly, under the Han dynasty of China (206 B.C.—221 A.D.), the capital was laid out to correspond to the configuration of the Great Bear and the Little Bear joined together, with the palace in the position of the Pole Star, and this pattern persisted, with but slight modifications, throughout later ages.[38]

Here, too, once the basic Mythic Idea has been thus reduced to empirical categories, a secondary symbolism is in turn created, the relationship between the real and the ideal being represented as one between the local and the universal. Temples and cultic sites are then believed to portray the world in miniature.[39] In Vedic ritual, for example, the sacred mound is taken to symbolize the universe, its base representing the earth, its top the sky, and the intervening portion, the atmosphere.[40] Similarly, in Iranian tradition, Zoroaster is said to have dedicated to Mithra a cave specially dug out in the hills and so con-

36. Cf. Isa. 45:1 (of Cyrus). There is an exact parallel in the "Clay Cylinder" inscription of Cyrus, line 12 (*ANET*, p. 315b): "(Marduk) sought out a righteous king as his favorite, whose hand he would grasp"; see S. Smith, *Isaiah XL–LV* (London, 1949), p. 73.

37. II R 51.2, 58 ab.f.; *Cuneiform Texts from Babylonian Texts, Etc. in the British Museum*, part 19 (London, 1904), plate 19, iv, 58 ff.; B. Meissner, *Babylonien und Assyrien*, vol. 2 (Heidelberg, 1925), p. 110.

38. J. J. L. Duyvendak, *PCHR VII* (1951), p. 137.

39. See on this: M. Eliade, *Traité d'histoire des religions* (Paris, 1949), p. 324. On the survival of this idea in the construction of Byzantine temples, cf. O. M. Dalton, *East Christian Art* (Oxford, 1923), pp. 243 ff. Cf. also H. P. L'Orange, *Studies in the Iconography of Cosmic Kingship in the Ancient World* (Oslo, 1953), pp. 9–17.

40. Śatapatha Brāhmaṇa 13.8.1, 17, etc.

structed as to symbolize the universe which that God had created.[41] The temple built by Solomon in Jerusalem seems likewise to have been reared upon a cosmic pattern, the twin columns (Jachin and Boaz) representing the pillars which supported the sky, and the "sea of brass" in the courtyard the cosmic ocean.[42] Whether or not Babylonian temples were built on this model is as yet undecided among specialists,[43] certain it is, however, that they too possessed their equivalent of the nether ocean (*apsu*), and that the canopy over the divine throne was sometimes called "heaven."[44]

Even altars lent themselves to this symbolism. Thus, as Albright has pointed out,[45] the plan of the altar sketched by the prophet Ezekiel (43:13–17) presumes that it was to consist of *three* stages, and it is significant that the lowest of these is called "the bosom of the earth" (Hebrew, *ḥêq ha-areṣ*) and the highest "the divine mountain" (Hebrew, *har'el*), terms which clearly indicate a cosmic pattern, and the former of which is likewise used by Nebuchadnezzar to denote the foundation platform of the temple tower (E-temen-an-ki, "House of the Foundation of Heaven and Earth") of Marduk in Babylon.[46]

23. It is most important that these limitations of expression be

---

41. Porphyry *De antro nympharum* 6.

42. See fully: I. Benzinger, *Hebräische Archäologie*, 3rd ed. (1927), p. 329; R. Patai, *Man and Temple* (London, 1947), chap. 4, pp. 105 ff.

43. It is often stated that the seven-staged *ziggurat* of Babylonia represented the seven heavens. A. Parrot declares, however (*Ziggurat et Tour de Babel* [Paris, 1949]), that this cosmological interpretation is secondary; and J. Nougayrol (*Symbolisme cosmique et monuments religieux*, Musée Guimet [July 1953], p. 13), likewise expresses skepticism. H. Frankfort asserts that the ziggurat represents the cosmic mountain, and this view is adopted also by H. G. Quaritch-Wales, "The Sacred Mountain in Old Asiatic Religion," *Journal of the Royal Asiatic Society of Great Britain and Ireland* (1953), p. 24.

44. On the *apsu*, see *Keilinschriftliche Bibliothek* 3.1.13. E. Forrer, *Glotta* (1938), p. 186, claims that artificial oceans also existed in Hittite temples. Lidzbarski, *Ephemeris* vol. 3, p. 9, would recognize a reference to the *apsu* in the seventh-century B.C. inscription of Zakir of Hamath, b. 9–11: "I built temples thr[oughout] my [land], and I built the . . . [and] the *ʾa-p-š*."

A "golden 'heaven'" (*šamê ša ḫuraṣi*) is mentioned in Behrens, *Assyrisch-Babylonische Briefe* (Leipzig, 1906), pp. 64 ff., and a wooden one, overlain with jewels, was placed by Nebuchadnezzar over the statue of the goddess Gula at Babylon (*Vorderasiatische Bibliothek* 4.164.12). The word "heaven" is also used in this sense by the woman Ishtar-bêl-dāini in her oracle to Esarhaddon in IV R 61 (cf. S. Langdon, *Tammus and Ishtar* [Oxford, 1914], p. 131). In the Syriac Peshitta, "heavens" is used as the rendering of "rafters" in 1 Kings 6:16. Pertinent also is the following lemma in Hesychius: OYPANOΣ·Πέρσαι δὲ τὰς βασιλείους σχηνὰς χαὶ αὐλάς, ὧν τὰ χαλύμματα χυχλοτερῇ, οὐρανοὺς [ἐχάλουν]; see L'Orange, *Studies*, pp. 22 ff. On the other hand, this linguistic evidence should not be pressed unduly, for the usage may be altogether figurative, like the Latin *coelum cameras* in Vitruvius 8.3, the modern French *ciel*, "vault," and the Greek οὐρανδς in the sense of "roof *of the mouth*."

45. *Archaeology and the Religion of Israel* (Baltimore, 1942), pp. 148–55.

46. Ibid., p. 152.

clearly apprehended, for otherwise we are in danger of letting them obscure the true nature of the basic Mythic Idea. This, indeed, is what has very largely happened in recent studies. In the case of divine kingship, for instance, the conventional idiom has been taken at face value, and on this basis elaborate theories have been constructed in which the king is represented to be the actual offspring of a "sacred marriage" or a human being specifically selected and delegated by a superior deity.[47] The truth is, however, that he is nothing other than the deity himself in his punctual aspect, the imagery of physical descent or special selection and designation being simply a concession to empirical forms of articulation.

II. THE MYTHOLOGICAL STORY

Myth and Tale

24. All of the foregoing paves the way for a fresh approach to the *mythological story*.

A mythological story (or myth) is not—as is commonly supposed—just any story of the supranatural that happens to be believed.[48] It is a story that gives verbal expression to the Mythic Idea; in practical terms, a story that is specifically associated with a cultic situation or that ultimately ascends thereto. It stands, in fact, in the same relationship to Ritual as the god stands to the king, the "heavenly" to the earthly city, and so forth.

25. By means of this more limited definition the obstinate problem of what basically distinguishes a myth from a tale is at once resolved. The difference lies not in their subject matter nor in the credence that is accorded them, but in their function and motivation. A myth is, or once was, *used*; a tale is, and always was, merely *told*. The former presupposes an actual or original counterpart in cultic performance; the latter does not.

Thus—to confine ourselves to examples drawn from the ancient

47. This is the basic error, for instance, of Engnell's *Studies in Divine Kingship in the Ancient Near East*; see the present writer's critique in *Review of Religion* 9 (1945), 267–81.
48. Cf., for example, Webster's definition: "Myth: a story, the origin of which is forgotten, that ostensibly relates historical events, which are usually of such character as to serve to explain some practise, belief, institution or cultural phenomenon. Myths are especially associated with religious rites and beliefs." Similarly, *The Standard Dictionary of Folklore, Mythology and Legend* (New York, 1950) defines myth as "a story, presented as having actually occurred in a previous age," explaining the cosmological and supernatural traditions of a people, their gods, heroes, cultural traits, religious beliefs, etc."

Near East—the Babylonian Epic of Gilgamesh is a *tale*, since there is no evidence that it was ever anything more than a collection of heroic legends told for entertainment or edification. The so-called Epic of Creation (*Enuma elish*), on the other hand, is a *myth*, because the sequence of its basic incidents—the defeat of a cosmic marplot, the recognition of the victor as king, the establishment of the world order, and the creation of man—corresponds to the typical pattern of New Year rituals and of religious ceremonies of seasonal "regeneration" in many parts of the world, and because it was actually recited as part of the service for the New Year (Akîtu) festival,[49] and sometimes also at the dedication of new temples.[50]

Similarly, the Ugaritic Poem of K-r-t, which deals solely with the adventures and misadventures of a legendary king of Hubur, is a *tale*, no matter how many deities figure in it; while the Poem of Baal is a *myth*, since its narrative of the rain-god's victory over the draconic lord of the waters (Yamm) and over the spirit of death and infertility (Môt), his enthronement in a newly-built palace, his regalement of the gods, the appointment of a temporary king ('Ashtar) during his forced absence, and the like, run parallel on a transcendental plane to the characteristic program of seasonal rituals.[51]

So, too, the Hittite story of Kessi the huntsman[52] or of Ullikummi, the monster made of stone,[53] is pure *tale*, whereas that of the Weather-god's battle against the dragon Illuyankas[54] is *myth*, since not only was it formally recited at the Puruli festival in summer, but it also corresponds to the general pattern of "dragon-slaying" mummeries which are so common a feature of European seasonal festivals and which ascend to pragmatic rituals designed originally to subdue the malevolent and threatening spirits of overflowing or impounded waters.[55] (Representative instances are the Saint George mummeries in England, the annual dragon-slayings at Fuerth and Ragusa, and the many French "dragon-parades" assembled by Sébillot and Dontenville.)[56]

49. See the program of the Akîtu ceremonies translated in *ANET*, p. 332b, lines 280–85.

50. Weissbach, *Miscell.* no. 12.23; Zimmern, *Zeitschrift für Assyriologie* 23.369; Langdon, *Scientia* 15.239.

51. See *Thespis*, pp. 115–222.

52. J. Friedrich, *Zeitschrift für Assyriologie*, n.f. 15 (1950), 235–42, 253–54; T. H. Gaster, *The Oldest Stories in the World* (New York, 1952), pp. 144–58.

53. H. G. Güterbock, *Journal of Cuneiform Studies* 5 (1951), 135–61; 6 (1952), 8–42; Gaster, *The Oldest Stories*, pp. 110–33.

54. Goetze, *ANET*, pp. 125–26; Gaster, *Thespis*, pp. 317–36; Gaster, *The Oldest Stories*, pp. 134–43; O. R. Gurney, *The Hittites* (London, 1951), pp. 181–83.

55. Cf. *Thespis*, pp. 321 ff.

56. P. Sébillot, *Le Folklore de France*, vol. 1 (Paris, 1904), pp. 468–70; H. Dontenville, *La Mythologie française* (Paris, 1948), chap. 5, pp. 132 ff.

26. Our more limited definition of the mythological story also enables us to disencumber the discussion of it of many extraneous topics which continue to invade it, and to concentrate such discussion where it properly belongs. Instead of indulging in fanciful speculations about the origin of the imaginative process in general, or spinning gossamer theories about the "pre-logical mind" or the connection of myths with dreams, we are able to focus our attention squarely upon a specific cultic phenomenon, without being diverted or seduced by the consequences of comprehending it within too wide a category. In other words, we can now eliminate from the study of *myth* such questions as how the wolf could have been imagined to have disgorged Red Riding Hood's grandmother whole, or why the prince's kiss should have been able to awaken the Sleeping Beauty. The process involved in the invention of such fantasies is now seen to have nothing whatsoever to do with *myth*, and the investigation of it belongs rather to an inquiry into the nature of *tale* or, indeed, of poetic imagination in general.

The Evolution of the Mythological Story

27. The mythological story passes through four main stages of development. These are determined by a progressive attenuation of its functional character. They may be termed for convenience: (a) the primitive; (b) the dramatic; (c) the liturgical; and (d) the literary.

(a) In the *primitive* stage, the story is the direct accompaniment of a ritual performed for purely pragmatic purposes, and it serves to present the several features of that ritual, *pari passu*, in their ideal aspect—that is, as incidents in a transcendental situation. This stage, however, is—like the original Aryan or Semitic language—more of a schematic postulate than a documented fact. It is what is presupposed by all the subsequent stages, but it would be difficult to find concrete examples of it; by and large, it can be reconstructed only by a process of "working backwards."

(b) In the *dramatic* stage, the ritual or cultic performance has already been toned down into an actual pantomimic representation of the story. The latter therefore serves as a mere libretto or "script."

The clearest example of this stage is afforded by the Saint George mummeries in England. The purely functional significance of slaying the dragon at crucial seasons of the year has long since receded. The performance has become a mere theatrical portrayal of the story of Saint George, and in each case the accompanying recitation is nothing but a "book of words" composed expressly to fit the action.

More ancient examples may also be cited. Perhaps the most striking of these is the Egyptian "Coronation Drama" composed during the First Dynasty (c. 3300 B.C.) and re-discovered, in 1898, in the precincts of the Ramesseum at Thebes.[57] Here, the leading features of an annual festival involving the re-confirmation of the king are presented not only in the story but also in the accompanying cultic performance as the installation of Horus as king of United Egypt after the discomfiture of Set. There is, however, no question of mere mythic transcendentalization; the participants in the performance play the parts of the protagonists in the story. Indeed, at the end of almost every scene there is, in the text, a rubric specifically identifying the personalities and places of the performance with the *dramatis personae* and localities of the story.

Another good example of this stage is the Ugaritic *Poem of the Gracious Gods*, discovered, in 1930, at Ras Shamra, on the north coast of Syria.[58] Our copy dates approximately from the latter half of the fourteenth century B.C., but the composition itself may well have been traditional and therefore even more ancient. This text (which is unfortunately incomplete) divides clearly into two parts; the first containing rubrics and snatches of songs for a ritual ceremony, and the second a more or less connected story leading up to the birth of certain "gracious gods" in whose cult, apparently, that ceremony took place. Here we have a curious mixture of the first and second stages of the Mythological Story. In Part I, for instance, the purely functional procedure of trimming vines is represented mythologically, in an accompanying chanty, as the emasculation of an indwelling spirit of fertility.[59] Similarly, so it would seem, the token ploughing of a special plot of sacred soil (a rite paralleled in many parts of the world) is represented, by a familiar and widespread metaphor, as the impregnation of two great goddesses.[60] Part II, on the other hand, is a libretto pure and simple. The primitive functional procedure of the "sacred marriage" has become an incident in a formal drama, portraying the supreme god's espousal to certain divine brides and the subsequent birth of the gods to

57. The standard edition is that of K. Sethe, *Dramatische Texte zu altägyptischen Mysterienspiele*, vol. 2 (Leipzig, 1928), pp. 83–264; cf. also, *Thespis*, pp. 383–403.

58. For the cuneiform text, see Ch. Virolleaud, *Syria* 14 (1933), 128–51. The text is transliterated in C. H. Gordon, *Ugaritic Handbook* (Rome, 1947), no. 52. For translation and commentary, see *Thespis*, pp. 239–56. (A revised treatment will appear in the forthcoming Italian edition of *Thespis*.)

59. Lines 8–11.

60. Lines 13, 28. The text reads *(w)šd šd ilm sd Aṯrt wRḥm*. This has been variously interpreted. We render: "And plough the field, the field divine, even that field which is (really) Asherat and the Virgin (i.e., ʿAnat)." The explanation will be that the act of ritually cultivating a patch of sacred soil is mythified, by a familiar figure, as the insemination of the goddesses of fertility. The idea links up with the "woman = field" image.

whom the ritual (or festival) was evidently dedicated. Moreover, it has already degenerated, like the Saint George mummeries and their analogues, into a piece of popular fun, for the theme is treated not in the manner of a solemn "mystery" but as rank burlesque.[61]

(c) In the *liturgical* stage, the story no longer marches *pari passu* with the ritual, but has sunk to the level of a mere general recitation designed to set forth the overall significance of a religious ceremony. Nevertheless, although the precise and systematic parallelism between the sequence of its incidents and the elements of the ritual has now disappeared, the story still retains its association with cult by being included in the formal "order of service." In this form, it is, of course, no longer necessarily the ancient "book of words" piously conserved, but, as often as not, the creation of contemporary writers or of a succession of writers, and it is usually tricked out with all sorts of secondary and subsidiary elaborations.

A good example of this stage is the Hittite Story of the Dragon Illuyankas, to which we have already referred. The text says clearly that this story was originally recited at the Puruli festival,[62] and the contents march, as we have observed, with those of the European dragon-slaying mummeries. But there is nothing to prove that the tale was *acted out*. It has become a mere recitation, though at the same time the very fact that it forms a part of the liturgy betrays its ultimate origin in a more functional prototype.

Of the same order is the Babylonian "Epic of Creation" (*Enuma elish*). Although, as we have seen, the plot of this poem comports with the program of the New Year (Akîtu) ceremonies, there is no evidence that it was recited *pari passu* with the performance of them. On the contrary, we know that it was intoned by a priest (*urigallu*) as a formal recitation before the statue of the god.[63] It therefore ranked solely as a liturgical chant.

To this stage, too, belong many of the mediaeval Christian hymns associated with the liturgy of saints' days. Not infrequently, these are simply poetic narratives presenting an abstract Christianized "sublimation" of ritual practises originally observed at the "heathen" prototypes of these festivals. Take, for example, Adam of St. Victor's famous *Laus erumpat*, composed for Michaelmas.[64] Based on the twelfth chapter of the Book of Revelation, this relates how the archangel vanquishes

---

61. Throughout the text actions are explained, by means of verbal *double entendre*, in a sexual sense bordering on the fescennine.
62. *Keilschrifttexte aus Boghazköi* 3.7.1.3–4.
63. See above, n. 49.
64. Cf. *Thespis*, pp. 104–6.

Satan and drives him from heaven. Anciently, as we can tell from parallels and survivals in popular usage, the defeat of the sinister marplot and of noxious demons in general was actually achieved in mimetic ritual at this crucial season of the year, but this particular poem was not accompanied by any such performance: it was, and has remained, a mere liturgical recitation.

(d) In the *literary* stage, the mythological story has become a mere *tale*, severed altogether from any ritual observance. The Homeric Hymns and several of the more narrative Hebrew psalms (e.g., Pss. 74:10–17, 89:2–19, 93) afford good illustrations of this final development.[65] In both, the ancient content is very largely preserved, but there is also a marked degree of purely artistic elaboration, and there is no clear evidence that they were designed for specifically liturgical use. Indeed, it is characteristic of this stage that the traditional material is often used only as the background for a poetic treatment of historical (or allegedly historical) events.

Sometimes, to be sure, it is difficult—even impossible—to decide whether a particular mythological story belongs to the liturgical or to the literary stage.

The Ugaritic Poem of Baal is a case in point. The sequence of incidents in this poem corresponds closely to the typical program of seasonal rituals. There is a combat between the god of fertility and his rivals, an enthronement of the victor, the construction of a new palace for him, the interim appointment and subsequent deposition of a deputy, a regalement of the gods, and so forth. Moreover, there is comparatively little extraneous matter or purely literary elaboration, i.e., very few subsidiary motifs are introduced. The probability is, therefore, that this poem was actually used as a liturgical recitation, even if it does not ascend to the yet earlier stage of dramatic representation. There is, however, no conclusive proof of this, and the possibility must therefore be allowed that we are dealing solely with a literary version.

This difficulty obtrudes itself especially in connection with the now familiar theory that some of the Biblical psalms, e.g., those which begin "The Lord is become king," were really cult-texts used in the New Year ceremony of enthroning the god. The objection to this theory is that the psalms in question may belong rather to the *literary* stage of mythic expression—that is, they may be purely literary survivals of the ritual pattern, just as are the many mediaeval Jewish hymns in which the enthronement of God or the holding of a heavenly assize are stressed as special features of the New Year liturgy.

65. Cf. *Thespis*, pp. 74–87.

Mythic Expression in Story

28. In the primitive stage of the mythological story, the intrinsic parallelism between the real and the ideal is brought home explicitly by the constant correspondence of word to act in the cultic performance. But even in the later stages, it is not left entirely to inference.

In the first place, the sacred scriptures which embody such stories are regarded in most religions as possessing not only a plain and historical, but also a symbolic and transcendental sense. Yaska points out, for instance, that in the religious tradition of India, the Vedic hymns are believed to carry a triple significance: one related to ritual practise (*adhiyajna*), one related to the sphere of the divine (*adhidaiva*), and one related to spiritual experience (*adhiyatna*); and this view is expressed also in the Upanishads.[66] Similarly, it has always been a firm principle of both Jewish and Christian hermeneutics that the historical narratives of the Bible are informed by a timeless as well as a punctual significance,[67] that, for example, *all* the generations of Israel, and not merely the fugitives from Egypt, were present in Spirit at Mount Sinai and concluded the covenant with God.

Secondly—and this is far more important—even in its more sophisticated stages, the mythological story presupposes activity on a level somewhat different from that of the actual and empirical. Its heroes and other leading characters can violate the normal laws of nature; they can change shape and sex, or traverse prodigious distances at a bound. The favorite current explanation of this element is that it harks back to a *prelogical* stage of mentality—that is, to a primitive form of thought unfettered by logical limitations, and some scholars have sought an analogy to this stage in dreams.[68] The fallacy of this thesis, is, however, only too apparent, for the fact is that the fantastic element of myths and tales is usually introduced for the express purpose of pointing up the *extraordinary*. It is not *everyone* who changes shape, possesses magic boots, exhibits suprahuman strength or meets prodigious tests. Indeed, if that were the case, there would be no story. These are the qualities of special characters, and they are endowed with them just because they have to be differentiated from the normal run of men and women. In other words, they possess these qualities precisely because they are extraordinary, and what makes them so is that they are able to defy the ordinary laws of logic and the require-

66. Cf. T. M. P. Mahadevan, *PCHR VII* (1951), p. 143.
67. Cf. S. D. F. Salmond's notable article "Hermeneutics," in the 9th ed. of the *Encyclopaedia Britannica*.
68. Cf. esp. G. Jacob, *Märchen und Traum* (Hannover, 1935); K. Abraham, *Traum und Mythus* (Leipzig, 1909).

ments of ordinary categorical thinking.[69] Nor is the analogy of *dreams* by any means so sound as it looks. For the phantasmata of dreams are produced not by an innocence of logic, but by a confusion of it—they are incoherent, but not irrational—and therefore cannot be cited without further proof (which, in the very nature of the case, is impossible) as identical with, or even similar to, the products of the postulated *pre*logical mentality.

29. But it is not only in general fashion that the inherent parallelism of the real and the ideal is brought home in the mythological story. Sometimes it is conveyed also in a more specific manner by the use of words susceptible (through homonymy) of an effective *double entendre*. Excellent examples of this are afforded by the Egyptian Coronation Drama, to which we have already referred. At one stage,[70] for instance, goats and asses trample the grain on the threshing-floor and are subsequently driven off with blows. This purely functional act is at once mythified as the trampling of Osiris by the henchmen of Set and the subsequent repulsion of them by the former's son, Horus. But the mythic meaning is enforced by a pun: when Horus intervenes, he exclaims, "Lo, I command you, thrash my sire no more!" and the point here is that the Egyptian words for "grain" and "sire" are homonymous (viz. *i t*). Similarly, when, in the cultic performance, the pharaoh is invested with the royal corselet, this is said to represent Horus' embracing the corpse of Osiris, the Egyptian words for "corselet" and "embrace" sounding alike (viz. *ḳ n i*).[71] Indeed, in the 138 lines of the extant text, there are close upon twenty such plays on words—some of them direct homonyms; others, more or less tortured puns.

The same device likewise characterizes the Ugaritic *Poem of the Gracious Gods*. One element of it, for instance, is the following "work-song" or chanty sung by a group of men engaged in trimming vines:

> As lord and master has he been sitting enthroned,
> With a sceptre of bereavement in his one hand,
> And a sceptre of widowhood in his other;
> Yet, lo, they that trim the vine now trim him,
> They that beat the vine now beat him,
> They tear up the ground from beneath him
> As when men prepare a vine.[72]

---

69. Quoted from the present writer's article, "Errors of Method in the Study of Religion," in *Freedom and Reason: Studies . . . in memory of Morris Raphael Cohen* (New York, 1951), p. 381.

70. Lines 29–33; *Thespis*, p. 388.

71. Lines 101–3; *Thespis*, p. 398.

72. Lines 8–11: *mt wšr yṯb / bdh ḫṭ ṯkl / bdh ḫṭ ulmn / yzbrnn zbrm g p n / yṣmdnn ṣmdm g p n / yšql šdmth km g p n. Thespis*, pp. 241–42; J. Finkel, *Joshua Starr Memorial Volume* (New York, 1953), pp. 29–58.

Here, by means of a sustained *double entendre*, a simple viticultural operation is at once mythified as the discomfiture and emasculation of an indwelling demon of infertility. The word rendered "sceptre" also means "(vine-)shoot";[73] that rendered "bereavement" is homonymous with one denoting "grape-cluster";[74] while the reference to "widowhood" instantly suggests the common idiom (familiar especially from Latin *vitis vidua*) whereby an untrained vine is described as "widowed."[75] Furthermore, the word rendered "trim" also means "castrate,"[76] and the expression "they tear up the ground from beneath him" refers, in a literal sense, to a technique used in planting vines.[77]

What is involved in this use of puns is not merely a verbal or artistic conceit. The device is based on the primitive idea that the name is an integral part of the identity. Accordingly, if a name possesses a double meaning, this implies *ipso facto* that what is so designated possesses a double aspect. In the present case, that double aspect consists in the intrinsic parallelism between the real and the ideal.

30. On the other hand, this intrinsic parallelism suffers the same sort of attenuation when it is articulated in story as it does when it is articulated by the other media we have discussed. The principal token of this is a reduction of preterpunctuality to the level of mere antiquity. What really transpires concurrently on another plane is represented as something that occurred "once upon a time" on the same plane. Retrojected thus into the remote past, the mythological story ceases to be the ideal concomitant of a present situation and assumes the character of its archetype or primordial model. The god, so to speak, is no longer conceived as slaying the dragon "ideally" at the very moment when the king slays him "really"; he merely slew him "of old," and the ritual action is simply a mimetic reproduction of that event.

Fundamentally, however, this is simply a concession to the exigencies of empirical articulation, and it should not delude us—as it has deluded some modern students of the subject (e.g. Malinowski and Eliade)[78]—into supposing that the primary function of Myth is to vali-

---

73. The Ugaritic word is *ḫṭ*. Cf. the cognate Hebrew *ḥôṭer*, Isa. 2:1. Analogous is the use of Greek ῥάβδος.

74. The Ugaritic word is *ṯkl*, which sounds like Hebrew *eshkôl*, "grape-cluster."

75. Cf. Catullus 52.49; Horace *Epodes* 3.9–10. Cf. also Shakespeare, *The Comedy of Errors*, act 2, sc. 2, lines 173 ff.: "Thou art an elm, my husband,—I a vine / Whose weakness, married to thy stronger state, / Makes me with thy strength to communicate."

76. The Ugaritic word is *zbr*, which is the Arabic z-b-r and the Hebrew z-m-r. For the latter in the sense of "castrate," cf. Haupt, *American Journal of Semitic Languages and Literature* 26, 1. Similarly, Latin *castrare* is also used of trimming vines (Cato *De re rustica* 32.2; Vitruvius 2.9).

77. The precise meaning of the Ugaritic *yšql šdmth* is disputed; see Finkel, *Joshua Starr Memorial Volume*, pp. 55 f. We equate it (through Syriac *s-q-l*, "remove") with the Accadian *eqla tabālu*, lit. "remove a field," in the sense of "clear the ground."

78. Thus, Malinowski (as cited in n. 2) writes: "The function of myth, briefly, is to

date a traditional usage by representing it as the repetition of a pri-
mordially efficacious act. To maintain this is, once again, to miss the
essential point that Myth and Ritual run *parallel* and do not stand in
lineal or genealogical relationship to each other.

The "Truth" of Myth

31. In what sense can Myth be described as "true"?

To the older investigators, this question scarcely posed a problem.
To them, truth, in this context, was simply the opposite of fiction; a
myth was true if what it related was historical and veracious. If, however, we now define Myth *functionally*, i.e., as a cultic rather than a
purely literary phenomenon, it is obvious that this answer will no
longer do.

In a recent study,[79] Pettazzoni has ventured an alternative formulation:

> Myth [he says] is true story because it is sacred story, not only by vir-
> tue of its content, but also by virtue of the concrete sacral forces which it
> sets in operation. The recitation of myths of origin is incorporated into
> cult because of itself it conduces to the ends for which the cult is per-
> formed, namely, those of conserving and increasing life. . . . To relate the
> story of the creation of the world helps to conserve the world; to recount
> the origins of the human race serves to keep humanity alive, i.e., to per-
> petuate the community or social group; to tell the tale of how initiation
> rites or shamanistic practises were first instituted serves to ensure their
> efficacy and continuance. . . .
> Viewed in this light, myths *must* of necessity be true; they cannot be
> false. Their truth is not of a logical kind, nor of an historical. It is, above

---

strengthen tradition and endow it with a greater value and prestige by tracing it back to
a higher, better, more supernatural reality of initial events. . . . Myth, as a statement of
primeval reality which still lives in present-day life and as a justification by precedent,
supplies a retrospective pattern of moral values, sociological (social?) order, and magical
belief." Similar is the statement of Pettazzoni, *PCHR VII* (1951), p. 72: "Il ne s'agit pas tant
de savoir comment le monde a eu un commencement, que d'en garantir l'existence et la
durée. C'est pourquoi tel mythe de la création est récité au cours d'une célébration
rituelle (par exemple, l'*Enuma eliš* dans l'*akîtu* babylonien), car l'on est convaincu qu'en
racontant des grands événements cosmiques et en proclamant la puissance du Créa-
teur, l'on parvient à assurer la stabilité du monde et à obtenir la protection de Dieu."
Closer to our own position, but still influenced by the notion that a myth is an archetype, is Eliade's formulation in his *Traité d'histoire des religions*, p. 366: "Tout mythe,
indépendamment de sa nature, énonce un événement qui a eu lieu *in illo tempore* et
constitue, de ce fait, un précédent exemplaire pour toutes les actions et 'situations' qui,
par la suite, répéteront cet événement. Tout rituel, toute action pourvue de sens, ex-
écutés par l'homme, répètent un archétype mythique; or . . . la répétition entraîne l'abo-
lition du temps à voir avec la durée proprement dite, mais constitue cet 'éternel présent'
du temps mythique."

79. *Studi e materiali di storia della religioni* 21 (1947–48), 104–16.

all, of a religious kind, and more especially of a magical kind. The efficacy of myth for the aims of cult, *i.e.*, for the preservation of the world
and of the life within it, lies essentially in the magic of the word, in the
evocative power of it, in *mythos* or *fabula*, not in the sense of "fictitious
discourse" but in that of a mysterious and powerful force allied—as the
very etymology implies—to the *fa-tum*.

To this view, however, there is an obvious objection: it confuses
truth with *efficacy*. What it explains—brilliantly and incontrovertibly,
to be sure—is the validity of mythological recitations or performances,
but the "truth" of Myth is something that must inhere rather in the
basic Mythic Idea, and not issue merely out of the mechanics of its
articulate forms. In other words, it is an essentially metaphysical concept and consists, we would submit, in the incontrovertibility of the
basic premise that the real and punctual runs parallel with the ideal
and transcendental. This is the irreducible datum—the axiomatic ver-
ity—on which the entire structure is reared.

32. In support of his thesis, Pettazzoni points out that among several North American Indian tribes (e.g., the Pawnee, the Wichita, the
Oglala Dakota and the Cherokees), as well as among the Karadjeris
of N. W. Australia and the Hereros of S. W. Africa, a distinction is in
fact drawn between "true" and "false" stories, cosmogonies and ancestral histories being assigned to the former category and mere "make-
believe" narratives to the latter. This observation is of extreme significance for our own position, for it attests the actual recognition in the
primitive mind of the two categories of story which we have here suggested, viz. *myths* which are *used in cult*, and *tales* which are *told* for
entertainment. At the same time, it is difficult to see what bearing this
has on the "truth" of Myth *per se*, for it would seem to relate only to
the credence that happens to be attached to particular stories. And
even then, important qualifications are in order.

Before any general deductions can be drawn, it would seem necessary to determine exactly the meaning and frame of reference of the
native terms rendered "true" and "false." Does "true" mean, in this context, accurate, or historical, or real, or valid, or authenticated? Conversely, does "false" mean untrustworthy, or unhistorical, or unreal (fictitious), or futile, or spurious? A story might, for example, be valid
functionally—that is, fully serve a ritual purpose—yet be invalid historically, or it might be valid historically, yet futile and inefficacious as
a cultic recitation. Again, it might be a genuine tradition, yet in itself
fictitious, or, conversely, it might relate an actual, historical fact, yet be
a modern product and no genuinely traditional composition.

Consider, indeed, the various senses of the term "true" in modern parlance. A patent medicine may claim to provide a *true* cure. Here, *true* means simply, certainly efficacious. A custom may claim to be a *true* tradition. Here the word means simply, authentic. A report may be said to be *true*. Here no more is meant than that it relates a fact. The transcript of a document may be described as a *true* copy, where what is implied is that it is accurate. Obviously, then, until we know precisely what words the primitive employs,[80] and in what sense he employs them, it is precarious to deduce from his distinction between "true" and "false" stories anything concerning the fundamental "truth" of Myth.[81]

Some Objections Answered

33. If our basic approach to Myth is sound, the task of the mythologist, when he deals with *stories*, will be to look for elements which reflect or ascend to ritual situations, and by that criterion to determine whether what lies before him is a *myth* (in however attenuated a form) or merely a *tale*. In this pursuit, however, certain fundamental principles must be clearly apprehended.

First, the correspondence need not be strictly and precisely between word and rite, but simply between the concept underlying the former and that which inspires the latter. For what we are really seeking is not a *reproduction* of the one in the other, but rather a *parallelism of expression* through two concurrent media.

Secondly, it must be firmly understood that what is involved is not the specific origin of particular compositions, but the generic origin of certain literary forms. To say that Myth *per se* is the counterpart of Ritual *per se* does not imply that every mythological story is (or once was) the actual libretto of a cultic act or series of acts. In order, for example, to characterize the Ugaritic Poem of Baal as a *myth* rather than a mere *tale*, it is not necessary to assume or to prove that it was actually recited as the concomitant of a sacred pantomime;[82] it is sufficient

80. Compare, for example, the distinction between ἀλήθεια and νημέρτεια in Greek and between *emeth* and *qôsht* in Hebrew.

81. [Logically, the "truth" of a myth and its "efficacy" are not the same, admittedly; but this distinction is made by us. For a primitive thinker, the truth of the myth, consisting as it does in the correspondence between the momentary and the permanent, the real and the ideal, is also the necessary and sufficient condition of the myth's efficacy, that is of its ability, when recited in due form, to guarantee the permanency of the world, the duration of life, the capture of game, abundance of harvest and so on. Therefore, in practice, ideal truth and functional efficacy coincide. It is to be understood that a linguistic and lexicographical research into the terms "true" and "false" in primitive languages would be of fundamental importance—Editor, *Numen.*]

82. When, for instance, H. J. Rose asserts (*PCHR VII* [1951], pp. 118 ff.) that in ancient Greece "we find no clear evidence that there ever was an intimate connection between

if we can find in its content and structure the same pattern as underlies the program of cultic performances.

This is a point which it would be difficult to overemphasize. In 1950,
when the present writer sought, in his work *Thespis*, to apply this approach to the analysis of certain ancient Near Eastern texts, a number
of Orientalists promptly objected that—with one or two exceptions—
there was no conclusive evidence to show that those texts had in fact
ever been acted out dramatically. Such an objection rests, however, on
a basic and crucial misapprehension. The argument is in fact on quite
a different level. What it asserts is that a certain type of story is *au fond*
a literary (or, more neutrally, a verbal) expression of the same situation
as is expressed "behavioristically" in ritual, and that the two things
therefore run parallel, the sequence of incidents in the one finding its
counterpart in the order of actions in the other. In short, what we are
discussing is a parallelism not between an actual *recitation* and an actual *performance*, but between a *pattern* of narrative and a pattern of
ritual, or—to put it more broadly—the ultimate relation of a *genre* of
literature to a *genre* of ceremony.

34. It has been objected also that the assumed parallelism of myth
and seasonal ritual in the ancient Near East rests on the preliminary
construction of a general cultic "pattern" which is, in fact, a mere
eclectic concoction—an arbitrary *potpourri* of elements drawn from
divers and different cultures, lacking any genetic or historical connection with one another. Indeed, Frankfort has gone so far as to object to
this whole line of argument on the grounds that it postulates a radical
unity of cultures which is entirely fictitious and which obscures their
essential and more important differences. It is therefore very necessary to point out that when the present writer uses the term "ritual (or
seasonal) pattern" he most emphatically does *not* mean what it has
come to mean in the hands of the Uppsala school or of such scholars
as I. Engnell or S. H. Hooke. To be quite explicit, he does not assume
any such uniformity of cultic procedures or any such historical connection between the seasonal ceremonies of one and another area as

---

myth and ritual" because "there is, e.g., nothing to prove that myths concerning any god
were exclusively or commonly recited at that god's festivals," he commits this crucial
error, besides confusing Myth per se with mythological story—and, it would seem, with
highly sophisticated and literary forms of the latter to boot.

Similarly, when A. Goetze objects (*Journal of Cuneiform Studies* 6 [1952], 99) to the
present writer's contention that certain ancient Near Eastern stories reflect ritual, by asserting blithely, "The simple fact is that we possess the myth," he merely begs the question. The simple fact is that we possess a *text* or *story*. The very thing that we have to
determine is whether it *is* a myth, or merely a tale; and it is difficult to see how it can be
characterized as the former, if at the same time it is denied that it reflects or ascends to
ritual.

Frankfort justly questions. The comparison is of quite a different order: psychological, not historical. When the present writer speaks of a "seasonal pattern," he means a broad sequence of mortification, purgation, invigoration and jubilation such as indeed characterizes seasonal rites in most parts of the world, and the evidence for which can scarcely be gainsaid by anyone who troubles to collect the data. But he also means something more. He means to imply by this expression that there are indeed certain basic notions which are common to almost all peoples and which find expression not only in folktale but also in folk custom. Such ideas and institutions—one might call them "isologues"—would include, for instance: circumambulation of territory as a means of asserting ownership of it; drenching a human being or a puppet as a means of procuring rain; lighting fires at solstices and equinoxes; assuming that the dead ascend a mountain, and that they return at seasonal festivals. The writer claims that the recognition of such ideas in mythological stories affords useful evidence of their parallelism with ritual practise and hence establishes a criterion for characterizing such stories as myths. It must be observed, however, that when such comparisons are instituted, no *historical* connection between one custom and another is necessarily assumed.

The procedure may be illustrated—and justified—from the analogy of language. Both the Semitic and the Classical tongues, for example, speak of the source of a river as its "head," but when a semanticist refers to these parallels in order to illustrate a mode of thinking, no one dreams of assuming that he is trying to postulate a philological relationship between (say) Hebrew *ro'sh* and Latin *caput*! By the same token, when an anthropologist or a student of comparative mythology compares the customs of divers regions, he is not assuming a direct connection between them, but merely a unity of basic concepts, and from this point of view, the more diversified the evidence, the more effective is his illustration.

Speculation about the nature and origin of Myth will probably never end, but if the approach suggested in this paper be sound, we may perhaps obtain a better insight into its relevance and significance. And it would seem that we would not be going far wrong to suggest that what memory is to the past, and hope to the future, that is Myth to the present.

Cosmogonic Myth and "Sacred History"

MIRCEA ELIADE

*One of the most prolific twentieth-century writers on myth is Mircea Eliade, pro-
fessor of the history of religion at the University of Chicago. He is especially interested in mythic patterns. See his* Cosmos and History: The Myth of the Eternal
Return *(New York, 1959);* Patterns in Comparative Religion *(New York, 1963); and*
Myth and Reality *(New York, 1968). Professor Eliade, considerably influenced by
myth-ritual theory as well as by the alleged universalism of Jungian archetypes,
sees myth as a vehicle for the representation of sacred time and space on earth. In
contrast to scholars who perceive a fundamental opposition between myth (of the
ancient, archetypal, prehistoric past) and history (of the mundane present), Eliade
sees a direct and important linkage between myth and contemporary life. For
Eliade, the sacred history recorded in myths provides a critical blueprint for the
conduct of everyday life.*

*For a helpful summary of Eliade's approach to myth, see Wilson M. Hudson,
"Eliade's Contributions to the Study of Myth," in* Tire Shrinker to Dragster *(Austin,
1968), pp. 218–41. For a partial critique, see I. Strenski, "Mircea Eliade: Some Theoretical Problems," in A. Cunningham, ed.,* The Theory of Myth *(London, 1973),
pp. 40–78. For an entrée to Eliade's works and the more than 300 articles written
about them, see Douglas Allen and Dennis Doeing,* Mircea Eliade: An Annotated
Bibliography *(New York, 1980). For Eliade's own overview of contemporary myth
scholarship, see his "Myth in the Nineteenth and Twentieth Centuries," in Philip P.
Wiener, ed.,* Dictionary of the History of Ideas, *vol. 3 (New York, 1973), pp. 307–18.*

THE LIVING MYTH AND THE HISTORIAN OF RELIGIONS

It is not without fear and trembling that a historian of religion approaches the problem of myth. This is not only because of that prelim-

Reprinted from Mircea Eliade, *The Quest: History and Meaning in Religion* (Chicago,
1969), pp. 72–87, by permission of the author and the University of Chicago Press.
© 1969 by the University of Chicago. This essay is a revised and expanded version of an
article first published in *Religious Studies* 2 (1967), 171–83, an article which was a
slightly modified translation of a public lecture given at the XIII Congress of the "Sociétés
de Philosophie de Langue Française," Geneva, September 2–6, 1966, which accounts for
the oral style in the essay.

inary embarrassing question: what is intended by myth? It is also because the answers given depend for the most part on the documents selected by the scholar. From Plato and Fontenelle to Schelling and Bultmann, philosophers and theologians have proposed innumerable definitions of myth. But all of these have one thing in common: they are based on the analysis of Greek mythology. Now, for a historian of religions this choice is not a very happy one. It is true that only in Greece did myth inspire and guide epic poetry, tragedy, and comedy, as well as the plastic arts, but it is no less true that it is especially in Greek culture that myth was submitted to a long and penetrating analysis, from which it emerged radically "demythicized." If in every European language the word "myth" denotes a "fiction," it is because the Greeks proclaimed it to be such twenty-five centuries ago. What is even more serious for an historian of religion: we do not know a single Greek myth within its ritual context. Of course this is not the case with the paleo-oriental and Asiatic religions; it is especially not the case with the so-called primitive religions. As is well known, a *living myth* is always connected with a cult, inspiring and justifying a religious behavior. None of this of course means that Greek myth should not figure in an investigation of the mythical phenomenon. But it would seem unwise to begin our kind of inquiry by the study of Greek documents, and even more so to restrict it to such documents. The mythology which informs Homer, Hesiod, and the tragic poets represents already a selection and an interpretation of archaic materials, some of which had become almost unintelligible. In short, our best chance of understanding the structure of mythical thought is to study cultures where myth is a "living thing," where it constitutes the very ground of the religious life; in other words, where myth, far from indicating a *fiction*, is considered to reveal the *truth par excellence*.

This is what anthropologists have done, for more than half a century, concentrating on "primitive" societies. We cannot here review the contributions of Andrew Lang, Frazer, Lévy-Bruhl, Malinowski, Leenhardt, or Lévi-Strauss. Some results of ethnological research will have our attention later on. We have to add, however, that the historian of religions is not always happy with the approach of the anthropologists nor with their general conclusions. Reacting against an excessive concern with comparison, most of the authors have neglected to supplement their anthropological research with a rigorous study of other mythologies, for example those of the ancient Near East, in the first place of Mesopotamia and Egypt, those of the Indo-Europeans—especially the grandiose, exuberant mythologies of ancient and medieval India—and those, finally, of the Turco-Mongols, the Tibetans, and the peoples of Southeast Asia. A restriction of the inquiry to "primitive" mythologies risks giving the impression that there is no continuity between archaic thought and the thought of the peoples who played an important role in ancient history. Now, such a solution of continuity does not exist. Moreover, by limiting the research to primitive societies, we are left with no measure of the role of myths in complex and highly developed religions, like those of the ancient Near East and India. To give only one example, it is impossible to understand the religion and, in general, the style of Mesopotamian culture if we ignore the cosmogonic myth and the origin myths preserved in *Enuma elish* and in the Gilgamesh Epic. At every New Year the fabulous events related in *Enuma elish* were ritually reenacted; every New Year the world needed to be re-created—and this necessity reveals a profound dimension of Mesopotamian thought. Moreover, the myth of the origin of man illuminates, at least in part, the tragic world-view and pessimism characteristic of Mesopotamian culture: for man has been molded by Marduk from clay, that is, from the very body of the primordial monster Tiamat, and from the blood of the arch-demon Kingu. And the myth clearly indicates that man has been created by Marduk in order that the gods may be nourished by human labor. Finally, the Gilgamesh Epic presents an equally pessimistic vision by explaining why man did not, and could not, obtain immortality.

This is the reason why the historians of religions prefer the approach of their colleagues—a Raffaelle Pettazzoni or a Gerardus van der Leeuw—or even the approach of certain scholars in the field of comparative anthropology, like Adolf Jensen or H. Baumann, who deal with all categories of mythological creativity, those of the "primitives" as well as of the peoples of high cultures. While one may not always agree with the results of their researches, one is at least certain that their documentation is sufficiently broad to permit valid generalizations.

But the divergences resulting from an incomplete documentation do not constitute the only difficulty in the dialogue between the historian of religions and his colleagues from other disciplines. It is his very approach which separates him, for instance, from the anthropologist or the psychologist. The historian of religions is too conscious of the axiological difference of his documents to marshal them on the same level. Aware of nuances and distinctions, he cannot ignore the fact that there exist great myths and myths of less importance, myths which dominate and characterize a religion, and secondary myths, repetitious and parasitical. *Enuma elish*, for example, cannot figure on the same plane with the mythology of the female demon Lamashtu; the Polynesian cosmogonic myth has not the same weight as the myth of the origin of a plant, for it precedes it and serves as a model for it. Such differences may not be important for an anthropologist or a psychologist. For instance, a sociologist concerned to study the French novel in the nineteenth century or a psychologist interested in literary imagination might discuss Balzac and Eugène Sue, Stendhal or Jules Sandeau indifferently, irrespective of the quality of their art. But for a literary critic such conflation is simply unthinkable, for it annihilates his own hermeneutical principles.

When, in one or two generations, perhaps even earlier, we have historians of religions who are descended from Australian, African, or Melanesian tribal societies, I do not doubt that, among other things, they will reproach Western scholars for their indifference to the scale of values *indigenous* to these societies. Let us imagine a history of Greek culture in which Homer, the tragic poets, and Plato are passed by silently while the *Book of Dreams* of Artemidorus and the novel of Heliodorus from Emessa are laboriously commented on, under the pretext that such works better illuminate the specific traits of the Greek genius and help us to understand its destiny. To come back to our theme, I do not think that we can grasp the structure and function of mythical thought in a society which has myth as its foundation if we do not take into account the *mythology in its totality* and, at the same time, the *scale of values* which such mythology implicitly or explicitly proclaims.

Now in every case where we have access to a still living tradition, and not to an acculturated one, one thing strikes us from the very beginning: the mythology not only constitutes, as it were, the "sacred history" of the tribe, not only does it explain the total reality and justify its contradictions, but it equally reveals a hierarchy in the series of fabulous events that it reports. In general, one can say that any myth tells how something came into being, the world, or man, or an animal species, or a social institution, and so on. But by the very fact that the creation of the world precedes everything else, the cosmogony enjoys a special prestige. In fact, as I have tried to show elsewhere,[1] the cosmogonic myth furnishes the model for all myths of origin. The creation of animals, plants, or man presupposes the existence of a world.

Certainly, the myth of the creation of the world does not always look like a cosmogonic myth *stricto sensu*, like the Indian or Polynesian myth, or the one narrated in *Enuma elish*. In a great part of Australia, for example, such cosmogonic myths are unknown. But there is always a central myth which describes the beginnings of the world, that

---

1. See especially *The Myth of the Eternal Return*, trans. from the French by Willard R. Trask (New York and London, 1954); *Myth and Reality* (New York and London, 1963).

is, what happened before the world became as it is today. Thus, there is always a *primordial history* and this history has a *beginning*: a cosmogonic myth proper, or a myth that describes the first, germinal stage of the world. This beginning is always implied in the sequence of myths which recounts the fabulous events that took place after the creation or the coming into being of the universe, namely, the myths of the origin of plants, animals, and man, or of the origin of marriage, family, and death, etc. Taken all together, these myths of origin constitute a fairly coherent history. They reveal how the cosmos was shaped and changed, how man became mortal, sexually diversified, and compelled to work in order to live; they equally reveal what the supernatural beings and the mythical ancestors did, and how and why they abandoned the earth and disappeared. We can also say that any mythology that is still accessible in an appropriate form contains not only a beginning but also an end, determined by the last manifestation of the supernatural beings, the cultural heroes, or the ancestors.

Now this primordial, sacred history, brought together by the totality of significant myths, is fundamental because it explains, and by the same token justifies, the existence of the world, of man and of society. This is the reason that a mythology is considered at once a *true history*: it relates how things came into being, providing the exemplary model and also the justifications of man's activities. One understands what one is—mortal and of a certain sex—and how that came about, because the myths tell how death and sexuality made their appearance. One engages in a certain type of hunting or agriculture because the myths report how the cultural heroes taught these techniques to the ancestors. I have insisted on this paradigmatic function of myth in other publications, and consequently I do not need to repeat the point again.

I would like, however, to amplify and complete what I have said, having regard mainly to what I called the sacred history preserved in the great myths. This is easier said than done. The first difficulty which confronts us is a material one. To analyze and interpret a mythology or a mythological theme conveniently, one has to take into consideration all the available documents. But this is impossible in a lecture, or even in a short monograph. Claude Lévi-Strauss has devoted more than 300 pages to the analysis of a group of South American myths, and he had to leave aside the mythologies of the Fuegians and other neighboring peoples in order to concentrate primarily on the origin myths of the Amazonians. I must therefore limit myself to one or two characteristic examples. I will examine primarily those elements that seem essential to the myths of aborigines. Of course even such résumés might appear too long. But since I am dealing with rather unfamiliar mythologies, I cannot be content with mere allusions to them, as I could in the case of *Enuma elish* or the Greek, and even Indian, myths. Moreover, any exegesis is grounded in a philology. It would be pointless to propose an interpretation of the myths I have in mind without providing at least a minimum of documentation.

MEANING AND FUNCTION OF A COSMOGONIC MYTH

My first example is the mythology of the Ngadju Dayak of Borneo. I have chosen it because there is available a work about it which deserves to become a classic: *Die Gottesidee der Ngadju Dajak in Süd-Borneo* (Leiden, 1946) by Hans Schärer.[2] The author, who unfortunately died prematurely, studied these people for many years. The mythological documents which he collected, if ever printed, would cover 12,000 pages. Hans Schärer not only mastered the language of these people and thoroughly knew their customs, but he also understood the structure of mythology and its role in the life of the Dayak. As for many other archaic peoples, for the Dayak the cosmogonic myth discloses the eventful creation of the world and of man and, at the same time, the principles which govern the cosmic process and human existence. One must read this book to realize how much everything attains consistency in the life of an archaic people, how the myths succeed each other and articulate themselves into a sacred history which is continuously recovered in the life of the community as well as in the existence of each individual. Through the cosmogonic myth and its sequel, the Dayak progressively unveils the structures of reality and of his own proper mode of being. What happened in the beginning describes at once both the original perfection and the destiny of each individual.

At the beginning, so the myth goes, the cosmic totality was still undivided in the mouth of the coiled watersnake. Eventually two mountains arise and from their repeated clashes the cosmic reality comes progressively into existence: the clouds, the hills, the sun and the moon, and so on. The mountains are the seats of the two supreme deities, and they are also these deities themselves. They reveal their human forms, however, only at the end of the first part of the creation. In their anthropomorphic form, the two supreme deities, Mahatala and his wife Putir, pursue the cosmogonic work and create the upperworld and the underworld. But there is still lacking an intermediary world, and mankind to inhabit it. The third phase of the creation is carried

2. The book has recently been translated into English by Rodney Needham, *Ngaju Religion: The Conception of God Among a South Borneo People* (The Hague, 1963).

out by two hornbills, male and female, who are actually identical with the two supreme deities. Mahatala raises the tree of life in the "Center," the two hornbills fly over toward it, and eventually meet each other in its branches. A furious fight breaks out between the two birds, and as a result the tree of life is extensively damaged. From the knotty excrescences of the tree and from the moss falling out from the throat of the female hornbill, a maiden and a young man come forth, the ancestors of the Dayak. The tree of life is finally destroyed and the two birds end by killing each other.

In sum, during the work of creation the deities reveal themselves under three different forms: cosmic (the two mountains), anthropomorphic (Mahatala and Putir), theriomorphic (the two hornbills). But these polar manifestations represent only one aspect of the divinity. Not less important are the godhead's manifestations as a *totality*: the primordial watersnake, for instance, or the tree of life. This totality—which Schärer calls divine/ambivalent totality—constitutes the fundamental principle of the religious life of the Dayak, and it is proclaimed again and again in different contexts. One can say that, for the Dayaks, every divine form contains its opposite in the same measure as itself: Mahatala is also his own wife and *vice versa*, and the watersnake is also the hornbill and *vice versa*.

The cosmogonic myth enables us to understand the religious life of the Dayaks as well as their culture and their social organization. The world is the result of a combat between two polar principles, during which the tree of life—i.e., their own embodiment—is annihilated. "But from destruction and death spring the cosmos and a new life. The new creation originates in the death of the total godhead."[3] In the most important religious ceremonies—birth, initiation, marriage, death—this creative clash is tirelessly reiterated. As a matter of fact, everything which is significant in the eyes of a Dayak is an imitation of exemplary models and a repetition of the events narrated in the cosmogonic myth. The village as well as the house represent the universe and are supposed to be situated at the Center of the World. The exemplary house is an *imago mundi*: it is erected on the back of the watersnake, its steep roof symbolizes the primeval mountain on which Mahatala is enthroned, and an umbrella represents the tree of life on whose branches one can see the two birds.

During the ceremonies of marriage, the couple return to the mythical primeval time. Such a return is indicated by a replica of the tree of life that is clasped by the bridal pair. Schärer was told that clasping the

3. Schärer, *Ngaju Religion*, p. 34.

tree of life means to form a unity with it. "The wedding is the reenactment of the creation, and the reenactment of the creation is the creation of the first human couple from the Tree of Life."⁴ Birth also is
related to the original time. The room in which the child is born is
symbolically situated in the primeval waters. Likewise, the room
where the young girls are enclosed during initiation ceremonies is
imagined to be located in the primordial ocean. The young girl descends to the underworld and after some time assumes the form of a
watersnake. She comes back to earth as a new person and begins a new
life, both socially and religiously.⁵ Death is equally conceived as a passage to a new and richer life. The deceased person returns to the primeval era, his mystical voyage indicated by the form and decorations
of his coffin. In fact, the coffin has the shape of a boat, and on its sides
are painted the watersnake, the tree of life, the primordial mountains,
that is to say the cosmic/divine totality. In other words, the dead man
returns to the divine totality which existed at the beginning.

On the occasion of each decisive crisis and each *rite de passage*,
man takes up again *ab initio* the world's drama. The operation is carried out in two times: (1) the return to the primordial totality, and (2)
the repetition of the cosmogony, that is to say, the breaking up of the
primitive unity. The same operation takes place again during the collective annual ceremonies. Schärer points out that the end of the year
signifies the end of an era and also of a world;⁶ the ceremonies clearly
indicate that there is a return to the precosmic time, the time of the
sacred totality embodied in the watersnake and in the tree of life. In
fact, during this period, sacred *par excellence*, which is called *helat
nyelo*, "the time between the years," a replica of the tree of life is erected in the village and all the population returns to the primeval (i.e.,
precosmogonic) age. Rules and interdictions are suspended since the
world has ceased to exist. While waiting for a new creation the community lives near the godhead, more exactly lives *in* the total primeval
godhead. The orgiastic character of the interval between the years
ought not to obscure its sacrality. As Schärer puts it, "there is no question of disorder (even if it may appear so to us) but of another order."⁷
The orgy takes place in accordance with the divine commandments,
and those who participate in it recover in themselves the total godhead. As is well known, in many other religions, primitive as well
as historical, the periodical orgy is considered to be the instrument
par excellence to achieve the perfect totality. It is from such a totality
that a new creation will take place—for the Dayaks as well as for the
Mesopotamians.

4. Ibid., p. 85.   5. Ibid., p. 87.   6. Ibid., pp. 94 ff.   7. Ibid., p. 97.

PRIMORDIALITY AND TOTALITY

Even this imperfect résumé of an immense amount of material has enabled us to grasp the considerable role that the cosmogonic myth plays in an archaic society. The myth unveils the religious thought of the Dayaks in all its depth and complexity. As we have just seen it, the individual and collective life has a cosmological structure: every life constitutes a cycle, whose model is the sempiternal creation, destruction, and re-creation of the world. Such a conception is not restricted to the Dayak, or even to peoples having their type of culture. In other words, the Dayak myth reveals to us a meaning which transcends its ethnographic frontiers. Now, what is striking in this mythology is the great importance bestowed upon the *primordial totality*. One may almost say that the Dayaks are obsessed by two aspects of the sacred: the *primordiality* and the *totality*. This does not mean that they belittle the work of creation. There is nothing of the Indian or gnostic pessimism in the Dayak conception of the cosmos and of life. The world is good and significant because it is sacred, since it came out from the tree of life, that is to say from the total godhead. But only the primordial total godhead is perfect. If the cosmos must be periodically abolished and re-created, it is not because the first creation did not succeed, but because it is only that stage which precedes the creation which represents a plenitude and a beatitude otherwise inaccessible in the created world. On the other hand, the myth points out the necessity of creation, that is, of the breaking up of the primeval unity. The original perfection is periodically reintegrated, but such perfection is always transitory. The Dayak myth proclaims that the creation—with all that it made possible: human existence, society, culture—cannot be definitively abolished. In other words, a "sacred history" has taken place, and this history must be perpetuated by periodical reiteration. It is impossible to freeze the reality in its germinal modality, such as it was in the beginning, immersed as it were in the primordial divine totality.

Now, it is this exceptional value conferred upon the "sacred history," ground and model of all human history, that is significant. Such attribution of value is recognizable in many other primitive mythologies, but it becomes particularly important in the mythologies of the ancient Near East and of Asia. If we examine a mythology in its totality we learn the judgment of the particular people upon its own sacred history. Every mythology presents a successive and coherent series of primordial events, but different peoples judge these fabulous acts in different ways, underlining the importance of some of them, casting aside, or even completely neglecting, others. If we analyze the context of what may be called the myth of the estrangement of the creator god and his progressive transformation into a *deus otiosus*, we notice a similar process, involving an analogous choice and judgment: out of a series of primordial creative events, only some of them are exalted, those in particular which are of consequence for human life. In other words, the coherent series of events which constitute the *sacred history* is incessantly remembered and extolled, while the previous stage, everything which existed *before* that sacred history—first and above all, the majestic and solitary presence of the creator God—fades away. If the High God is still remembered, he is known to have created the world and man, but this is almost all. Such a Supreme God seems to have ended his role by achieving the work of creation. He plays almost no role in the cult, his myths are few and rather banal, and, when he is not completely forgotten, he is invoked only in cases of extreme distress, when all other divine beings have proved utterly ineffectual.

THE "GREAT FATHER" AND THE MYTHICAL ANCESTORS

This lesson of the primitive myths is particularly revealing. It not only shows us that man, turning toward the divinities of life and fecundity, became as it were more and more incarnated. It also shows that early man assumes already, in his way, a history of which he is at once both the center and the victim. What happened to his mythical ancestors became, for him, more important than what happened *before* their appearance. One can illustrate this process with innumerable examples. I have discussed a number of such myths in previous works.[8] But I would like to examine now the mythical traditions of a people who for more than half a century have enjoyed a considerable vogue among anthropologists, sociologists, and psychologists, namely the Aranda tribes of Central Australia. I will draw exclusively from the materials collected by T. G. H. Strehlow,[9] the son of the famous missionary Carl Strehlow, whose writings gave rise to heated controversies in Durkheim's time. I think I choose the best living authority, for Aranda was the first language spoken by T. G. H. Strehlow, and he studied these tribes intensely for more than thirty years.

8. See particularly Eliade, *Myth and Reality*, pp. 92 ff.
9. Especially his *Aranda Traditions* (Melbourne, 1947) and his recent article "Personal Monototemism in a Polytotemic Community," in *Festschrift für Ad. E. Jensen* (Munich, 1964), pp. 723–54; cf. also "La Gémellité de l'âme humaine," in *La Tour Saint-Jacques* (Paris, 1957), nos. 11–12, pp. 14–23. See also Mircea Eliade, "Australian Religion: An Introduction, Part II," *History of Religions* 6 (1967), 208–35, especially pp. 209 ff.

According to the Aranda, the sky and the earth have always existed and have always been inhabited by supernatural beings. In the sky there is an emu-footed personage, having emu-footed wives and children: it is the Great Father (*knaritja*), called also the Eternal Youth (*alt-jira nditja*). All these supernatural beings live in a perpetually green land, rich in flowers and fruits, traversed by the Milky Way. All of them are eternally young, the Great Father being in appearance as young as his children. And all of them are as immortal as the stars themselves, for death cannot enter their home.

Strehlow thinks that it would be impossible to regard this emu-footed Great Father as a supernatural being analogous to certain celestial gods of Southeast Australia. Indeed, he did not create or shape the earth, nor did he bring into existence either plants, animals, man, or the totemic ancestors, nor did he inspire or control the ancestors' activities. The Great Father and the other inhabitants of heaven were never interested in what happened on the earth. Evil-doers had to fear not the celestial Great Father but the wrath of the totemic ancestors and the punishment of the tribal authorities. For, as we shall see in a moment, all the creative and meaningful acts were effected by the earth-born totemic ancestors. In sum, one can see here a drastic transformation of a celestial being into a *deus otiosus*. The next step could only be his falling into total oblivion. This probably did happen outside of the western Aranda territory, where Strehlow could not find any comparable beliefs in sky beings.

Nevertheless, there are some characteristic traits which allow this otiose and transcendent Great Father and Eternal Youth a place in the category of supreme beings. There is, first, his immortality, his youth, and his beatific existence; there is then his ontological anteriority with regard to the totemic heroes; indeed, he had been up there, in the sky, for a long time before the emergence of the totemic ancestors from under the earth. Finally, the religious importance of the sky is repeatedly proclaimed: for example, in the myths of certain heroes who conquered immortality by ascending to heaven, in the mythical traditions of trees or ladders connecting heaven and earth, and especially in the widespread Aranda beliefs that death came into being because the communications with heaven had been violently interrupted. Strehlow recalls the traditions concerning a ladder joining the earth to heaven, and describes the sites where, according to the legend, there grew gigantic trees which certain mythical ancestors were able to climb to heaven. Similar beliefs are to be found in many other archaic traditions, particularly in myths relating that after the interruption of the communications between heaven and earth, the gods retired to the highest sky and became more or less *dii otiosi*. From that moment on, only a few privileged personages—heroes, shamans, medicine men—have been able to ascend to heaven. We do not know how much of this mythical theme was familiar to the Aranda. But the fact is that, despite the reciprocal indifference between the Aranda and the celestial beings, the religious prestige of heaven continues to survive along with the haunting memory of a conquest of immortality by an ascension to heaven. One is tempted to read in these mythical fragments a certain nostalgia for a primordial situation irretrievably lost.

In any case the *primordium* represented by the celestial Great Father does not have any immediate significance for the Aranda. On the contrary, the Aranda seem to be interested exclusively in what happened at a certain moment *on the earth*. Such happenings are supremely significant; that is to say, in our terminology, they have a religious value. Indeed, the events that took place in the mythical times, in the "Dream Time," are religious in the sense that they constitute a paradigmatic history which man has to follow and repeat in order to assure the continuity of the world, of life and society.

While the Great Father and his family lived a sort of paradisiacal existence in the sky, without any responsibility, on the surface of earth there existed even from time immemorial amorphous, semiembryonic masses of half-developed infants. They could not develop into individual men and women, but neither could they grow old or die. Indeed, neither life nor death was known on earth. Life existed fully *below* the surface of the earth, in the form of thousands of slumbering supernatural beings. They also were uncreated (as a matter of fact they are called "born out of their own eternity," *altijirana nambakala*). Finally they awoke from their sleep and broke through the surface of the earth. Their birthplaces are impregnated with their life and power. One of these supernatural beings is the sun, and when he emerged out of the ground the earth was flooded with light.

The forms of these chthonian beings were varied; some emerged in animal forms, others as men and women. But all of them had something in common: the theriomorphic ones acted and thought like humans, and those in human forms could change at will into a particular species of animal. These chthonian beings, commonly designated totemic ancestors, began to wander on the surface of the earth and to modify the land, giving the Central Australian landscape its actual physical features. Such works constitute properly speaking a cosmogony; the ancestors did not create the earth, but they gave form to a preexistent *materia prima*. And the anthropogony repeats the cosmogony. Some of the totemic ancestors took on the roles of culture heroes, slicing apart the semiembryonic aggregate, then shaping each individual infant by slitting the webs between his fingers and toes and cutting open his ears, eyes, and mouth. Other culture heroes taught men how to make tools and fire and to cook food, and they also revealed social and religious institutions to them.

As a result of all these labors, an extreme fatigue overpowered the ancestors, and they sank into the ground or turned into rocks, trees, or ritual objects (*tjurunga*). The sites which marked their final resting places are, like their birth places, regarded as important sacred centers, and are called by the same name, *pmara kutata*. But the disappearance of the ancestors, which put an end to the primordial age, is not final. Though reimmersed in their initial slumber under the surface of the earth, they watch over the behavior of men. Moreover, the ancestors reincarnate themselves perpetually; as Strehlow has shown,[10] the immortal soul of each individual represents a particle of an ancestor's life.

This fabulous epoch when the ancestors were roaming about the land is for the Aranda tantamount to a paradisiacal age. Not only do they imagine the freshly formed earth as a paradise, where the different animals allowed themselves to be easily captured and water and fruits were in abundance, but the ancestors were free from the multitude of inhibitions and frustrations that inevitably obstruct all human beings who are living together in organized communities.[11] This primordial paradise still haunts the Aranda. In a certain sense, one can interpret the brief intervals of ritual orgy, when all the interdictions are suspended, as ephemeral returns to the freedom and beatitude of the ancestors.

Such a terrestrial and paradisiacal primordiality—which constitutes both a history and a propaedeutic—is the one that interests the Aranda. In this mythical time man became what he is today, not only because he was then shaped and instructed by the ancestors, but also because he has to repeat continuously everything that the ancestors did *in illo tempore*. The myths disclose this sacred and creative history. Moreover, through initiation, every young Aranda not only learns what happened *in principio*, but ultimately discovers *that he was already there*, that somehow he participated in those glorious events. The initiation brings about an *anamnesis*. At the end of the ceremony, the novice finds out that the hero of the myths just communicated to him is himself. He is shown a sacred and well-guarded ritual object, a

10. Cf. Strehlow, "Personal Monototemism in a Polytotemic Community," p. 730.
11. Ibid., p. 729. Cf. also *Aranda Traditions*, pp. 36 ff. on the "Golden Age" of the totemic ancestors.

tjurunga, and one old man tells him: This is your own body!—for that
tjurunga represents the body of one of the ancestors. This dramatic
revelation of the identity between the eternal ancestor and the individual in which he is reincarnated can be compared with *tat tvam asi* of
the Upanishads. These beliefs are not exclusively Aranda. In Northeast
Australia, for instance, when an Unambal proceeds to repaint the image of a Wondjina on the rock wall (the Wondjina are the equivalent of
the Central Australian totemic ancestors), he says: "I am going now to
refresh and invigorate myself; I paint myself anew, so that the rain can
come." [12]

To the irrevocability of death, as a result of the brutal interruption of
the communications between earth and heaven, the Aranda replied
with a theory of transmigration thanks to which the ancestors—that is
to say, they themselves—are supposed to return perpetually to life.
One can distinguish, then, two sorts of *primordiality*, to which two
types of nostalgia correspond: (1) the *primordium* represented by the
celestial Great Father and by the celestial immortality that is inaccessible to ordinary human beings; (2) the fabulous epoch of the ancestors,
when life in general and human life in particular was brought about.
The Aranda yearn above all for the terrestrial paradise represented by
this second *primordium*.

TWO TYPES OF PRIMORDIALITY

Such a process is also known in other religions, even in the most complex ones. We may refer, for example, to the primordiality of Tiamat
and the passage to the creative primordial epoch represented by the
victory of Marduk, along with the cosmogony, anthropogony, and the
founding of a new divine hierarchy. Or we might compare the primordiality of Ouranos with the establishment of Zeus's supremacy, or
point the passage from the almost forgotten Dyaus to Varuna, and later
still to the consecutive supremacies of Indra, Shiva, and Vishnu. In all
these cases one may say that the creation of a new world is implied,
even when there is no question of a cosmogony properly speaking. But
it is always the emergence of a new religious world that appears to be
in a more direct relation with the human condition.

What is significant in this substitution of an existential primordiality
for a rather speculative one is that this process represents a more radical incarnation of the *sacred* in *life* and in *human existence* as such. Of

12. See Eliade, "Australian Religions: An Introduction, Part II," p. 227.

course, this process is fairly common in the history of religions, and it is not completely foreign to the Judeo-Christian tradition. One may say that we have in Bonhoeffer the most recent example of the incarnation of the sacred in the profane existence of historical man; one may also identify in the most recent American theology, the god-is-dead theology, yet another variant, drastically secularized, of the myth of *deus otiosus*.

Thus, we can distinguish two types of primordialities: (1) a precosmic, unhistorical primordiality, and (2) a cosmogonic or historical one. In effect, the cosmogonic myth opens the *sacred history*; it is an *historical myth*, though not in the Judeo-Christian sense of the word, for the cosmogonic myth has the function of an exemplary model and as such it is periodically reactualized. We can distinguish also two species of *religious nostalgias*: (1) the longing to reintegrate the primordial totality that existed before the creation (the Dayak type of religious nostalgia), and (2) the longing to recover the primordial epoch that began immediately *after* the creation (the Aranda type). In this latter case the nostalgia yearns for the *sacred history* of the tribe. It is with such *myths of the sacred history*—still alive in many traditional societies—that the Judeo-Christian idea of history has to vie.

An Ideological Dichotomy: Myths and Folk Beliefs Among the Shoshoni

ÅKE HULTKRANTZ

By far the majority of myth-ritualists and students of the history of religion are library scholars who propose hypotheses about myth on the basis of data gathered by others. The test of any theory of myth ought to be whether or not it illuminates our understanding of how myths function in their cultural contexts. Only by observing actual recitations in the field and by interviewing the tellers and the audience at such events can the scholar verify or modify given theories.

Åke Hultkrantz, professor of comparative religion at the University of Stockholm, who carried out extensive fieldwork among the Wind River Shoshoni Indians, attempts to determine if the myth-ritual theory is applicable to the myth corpus of the Shoshoni.

Readers interested in more of Professor Hultkrantz's thoughts on American Indian myth and religion may consult The North American Indian Orpheus Tradition *(Stockholm, 1957) and a chapter, "The World Picture and the Deities of Cosmogonic Myths," in his survey* The Religions of the American Indians *(Berkeley and Los Angeles, 1979), pp. 27–43.*

I

What a myth is, and how its function shall be determined, are questions which have been discussed for more than 100 years by representatives of different disciplines—scholars of religion, philologists and anthropologists, folklorists, and historians of literature, philosophers and psychologists. The strange thing is that they have learned so little from each other. The scholars of each discipline represent, apparently,

Reprinted from *History of Religions* 11 (1972), 339–53, by permission of the author and the University of Chicago Press. © 1972 by the University of Chicago. This essay was read as a lecture at a colloquium on mythology arranged by Clare Hall, Cambridge University, in April 1971.

a more or less closed dogmatic system which has been formed within the discipline and has very little in common with the teachings of other disciplines. And if to this is added the circumstance that paths of interest within different areas of research are so diverging, then it is easy to understand that today the idea of myth changes radically from camp to camp: specialists of the Near East talk about cult-myths and ritual myths; folklorists emphasize the entertainment value of myths and their diffusion; historians of literature dwell upon the literary quality of myths; philosophers, upon their truth; and so forth. It is obvious that the term "myth" does not mean the same for all these categories of scholars.

Above all, we can differentiate between the scholars who give the myth a religious meaning and those who designate it as only being of aesthetic and literary value. On the borders of both these categories we find a scientist like Lévi-Strauss, to whom the myth reveals a characteristic way of thought for primitive societies.

To numerous anthropologists, folklorists, and scholars of literature, the myth is an aesthetic and literary creation. This interpretation is especially common in these professional circles in the United States. Here, moreover, myth is used in a manner similar to the way the original Greek term was used, almost as a synonym to "folktale," at the same time that the grading of popular narratives according to belief categories in the style of Herder and Grimm, so common in Europe, is mostly missing—a noticeable exception is William Bascom's program article from 1965, in which he tries to link up with the category schedule of the European folklorists.[1] The scholar of literature Richard Chase writes: "The word 'myth' means story: a myth is a tale, a narrative, or a poem; myth is literature and must be considered as an aesthetic creation of the human imagination."[2] Chase means that the myth does not need to be more philosophical than any other form of literature. A folklorist like A. B. Rooth regards the myth in the same way—predominantly as a literary creation.[3] Certainly this is so—in many cases to a very high degree—but is it the whole truth?

Some anthropologists and philologists, and quite naturally above all the scholars of religion, regard the myth as a religious document, or at least as a preponderantly religious document. Some even go so far as to state that the myth expresses the quintessence, not only of religion,

1. W. Bascom, "The Forms of Folklore: Prose Narratives," *Journal of American Folklore* 78 (1965), 3 ff.
2. R. Chase, *Quest for Myth* (Baton Rouge, La., 1949), p. 73.
3. A. B. Rooth, "Scholarly Tradition in Folktale Research," *Fabula* 1 (1957), 195–96.

but also of culture. The German Frobenius school, with the late A. E. Jensen at its head, launched such an interpretation.[4] A popular writer on religion like Joseph Campbell allows somewhat arbitrarily different religious expressions to pass under the term myth.[5] To these and other scholars—for example, many of those who cooperated in the great corpus, *Mythology of All Races*—the boundaries between myth, conception, and rite are diffuse, and they have filled in religious data with data from mythology without restraint.

Most scholars of religion are, however, clearly conscious that the myth certainly fills a religious function but, at the same time, is a genre of its own with defined qualities and defined functions. Crudely, we can discern the following general opinions:

1. The myth intermediates a philosophic way of looking at things, serving as an interpretation of the surrounding reality or of things above us. During 150 years, comparative religion has seen many such myth theories: Creutzer's allegorical and Max Müller's "meteorological" interpretations of myths have been succeeded by the conviction of Tylor and other evolutionists that myth includes primitive philosophy. In this connection, one can mention above all the so-called etiological or explanatory myths, many of which T. T. Waterman exposed as being secondary myths or myths with extended etiological conclusions.[6]

2. In a graphic form the myth intermediates a content of belief which is difficult to define. As has been maintained, "those circumstances, events, and episodes which the myth narrates, are, to a very great extent at least, true expressions of what he [the mythopoeic man] thinks and believes in these matters."[7] In the myth, however, many elements constitutive of the belief fall away, for example, the mysterious character of miracles. This aspect of the myth has been especially stressed by the Swedes M. P. Nilsson, Arbman, and Ehnmark.

3. The myth constitutes a ritual text, or is in another way connected with the cult. This interpretation has been energetically maintained by the myth and ritual school, first, by the Cambridge scholar Jane Ellen Harrison in her work *Themis* (1912), then by Hocart, Cook, Hooke, Widengren, Engnell, Kérényi, Preuss, de Vries, and others. Some of these scholars have meant that the myth arose as an explanation of the

4. A. E. Jensen, *Myth and Cult Among Primitive Peoples* (Chicago, 1963), pp. 39 ff.

5. J. Campbell, *The Masks of God: Primitive Mythology* (New York, 1959), passim.

6. T. T. Waterman, "The Explanatory Element in the Folk-Tales of the North American Indians," *Journal of American Folklore* 27 (1914), 1 ff.

7. E. Arbman, "Mythic and Religious Thought," in *Dragma, M. P. Nilsson . . . Dedicatum* (Lund, 1939), p. 22.

rite (e.g., Harrison)[8] or as a sanction of the rite (e.g., Hyman).[9] However, other scholars, such as Kluckhohn, have objected to the assumption that in all situations the myth is a cult-myth.[10]

4. The myth sanctions cosmic and natural conditions as well as profane and religious institutions of culture. This theory has mainly been put forward by Malinowski.[11] Later social anthropologists, legion in our own time, have found that the myth forms a model for society. The myth's description of the divine society "pictures" the human society.

There is no doubt that all these interpretations of myth are dependent upon the fact that each scholar in his field of work is confronted with a certain type of mythology which, against the background of his own discipline's traditions, determines his view of the genre. Unfortunately, research on religion is full of examples of such "scholarly blindness." Our only possibility of correcting our judgment of the function and essence of the myth is to study myths from the most varying cultural and religious settings and then put together the results. In this research, we must concentrate on the place of myth within the cultural structure, on its typology and meaning, as well as on its function in relation to distinct belief complexes.

In the following, the function of myth is explored in a little-known field, the traditional tribal religion of the Shoshoni Indians as it has been developed among the Plains Shoshoni of Wyoming. I investigated this religion during a period of years in the 1940s and 1950s when its most vital characteristics still persisted. The aim of my presentation is to show that the place of myth in culture and religion is more varied than shown in most anthropological records.

The minimal definition of myth which is suggested here should be acceptable to scholars of differing disciplines (even if, at the same time, many of them would judge it insufficient): the myth is an epic tradition about gods, whose pattern of actions is located in a higher world— usually a distant, prototype-forming primeval age (Eliade, "*in illo tempore*")—and whose character of true narrative is taken for granted. In comparison with the myth the so-called legend is bound to (presumed or real) events in historical time with both supernatural beings and human beings as participants. It is understood as being true,

---

8. J. E. Harrison, *Themis* (Cambridge, 1912), p. 13.

9. S. E. Hyman, "The Ritual View of Myth and the Mythic," in *Myth: A Symposium*, ed. Th. A. Sebeok (Bloomington, Ind., 1958), p. 90.

10. C. Kluckhohn, "Myths and Rituals: A General Theory," *Harvard Theological Review* 35, no. 1 (1942), 45 ff.

11. B. Malinowki, *Magic, Science and Religion and Other Essays* (Garden City, N.Y., 1954), pp. 96 ff.

while the fictional tale (or story) cannot make any claim at being plausible even if gods and spirits appear in its gallery of stories.

II

First, I will sketch the culture in which the Shoshoni mythology has its function.[12]

The Shoshoni Indians of Wyoming, even called Wind River Shoshoni after their reservation, constitute a branch of the great Shoshonean language group belonging above all to the Great Basin (hereafter called the basin area), but in its entirety extended over an area stretching from the Rocky Mountains to the Pacific Ocean. The culture which was maintained by the Basin Shoshoni—primitive, gathering economy tied up with loose social organization—has, at least in a distant prehistoric age (3000 B.C. to A.D. 500), characterized the Shoshoni of Wyoming.[13] More important for our predisposed points of view here, however, is the fact that these Shoshoni have, up until very recent times, shared the spiritual heritage of the Basin Shoshoni, a simple, rather undifferentiated religious pattern and a narrative cycle dominated by supernatural beings in animal guise. Through documents, we can follow the religiohistorical development right from the first decades of the nineteenth century, when the Sun Dance was introduced (with the result that the whole religious pattern received a more eastern, Plains Indian stamp) and through the whole series of innovations brought about by contact with Christianity, prophet movements, missionary activity, Ghost Dance, Peyote Cult, and reformed Sun Dance.[14]

At the time of the disjunction of the old independent Indian society, in approximately 1875, the culture of the Wyoming Shoshoni had, in the main, the following profile. The foundation of the culture formation was the ecological situation of the Shoshoni between the plains in the east and the mountains and semidesert areas in the west. It showed itself in an extensive sustenance system with seasonal variations in hunting, fishing, and gathering and storing activities (of berries, roots, etc.), and it added to the culture elements from the more specialized bordering cultures: conical tents ("tipis") and deerskin

12. See the comprehensive presentation in Hultkrantz, "Kulturbildningen des Wyomings Shoshoni-indianer," *Ymer* 69 no. 2 (1949), 134 ff.

13. Hultkrantz, "Shoshoni Indians on the Plains: An Appraisal of the Documentary Evidence," *Zeitschrift für Ethnologie* 93, nos. 1–2 (1968), 57 ff.

14. Hultkrantz, "Pagan and Christian Elements in the Religious Syncretism Among the Shoshoni Indians of Wyoming," in *Syncretism*, ed. S. S. Hartman, Scripta Instituti Donneriani Aboensis, vol. 3 (Åbo, 1969), pp. 15 ff.

clothes from the plains, fishing tackle and methods of angling from the plateau area, plaited seed winnowers and mortars from the basin. The social structure was relatively uncomplicated. The tribe upheld a loose and fluctuating band organization which had its nucleus in the family units. There were no clans, kinship structure was bilateral, and pseudo-cross-cousin marriages were common. In the same way, a class system was missing, but certain people gained more prestige than others, for example, chiefs, medicine men, Sun Dance leaders, storytellers, and warriors (and especially members of the military club). During the nineteenth century, two chiefs, both of whom had strong personalities, succeeded in upholding a periodically very strong central authority.

Religion was completely dominated by the so-called vision or guardian-spirit complex, well known in its basic traits over practically the whole of North America, and by the Sun Dance, which had been imported from the Plains Indians in the east. As for the vision quest, it was formed in the same way as in the basin area, but, due to influence from the plains culture, it had partly changed so that it even contained values such as success in war, bravery in fighting, etc. The negative appraisal of the vision sought under ritual forms (which was experienced at isolated rock carvings) and the positive appraisal of the inspirational, unsought-for vision was, however, an inheritance from older times. The visionary *par préférence* was the medicine man, who had much greater supernatural power than other people and who could cure the sick, usually by blowing, touching with the hand, or sucking the ailing part. The Sun Dance was a ceremony which lasted for three to four days, in which the participants expressed their gratitude to the Supreme Being, but it was also a sacrificial dance, a prayer to be delivered from illnesses (at least this was so in later times), and a prayer to be blessed with food and good health during the year to come. Thus, the Sun Dance was, among other things, a "new year's ritual." The Supreme Being, "our father," was the foremost deity, connected with heaven, sun, and moon. Mother Earth was called upon in the Sun Dance. A long line of spiritual beings in animal form and spirits who were in some other way tied to nature intervened more closely in the existence of human beings. Conceptions about life hereafter were, as is mostly the case, modeled according to life in this world.

It was into this cultural and religious setting that the mythology was fitted, a partly autonomous belief system which, as noted before, was common for nearly all the Shoshoni and also appeared in its fundamental traits among the Indians on the so-called plateau (around the Columbia River) and on the northwestern plains, among the Salish

and Crow Indians. The mythology of the Wind River Shoshoni has
stood its ground both to its form and function almost up to present
time, even if continuous secularization has enforced certain changes
which are revealed in the following.

III

In mythology, by which I mean here the world of the mythological
stories, the roles are played by well-known animals attributed with
human qualities and language capabilities. These beings are the prototypes of the present-day animals, and the events which they experience in the stories bind their successors to their way of life for all time.
How the animal beings came to be changed into animals of our time is
unknown to us, but the Shoshoni are, like other Indian peoples, completely convinced that at some occasion in the distant past this change
took place.

It is these fable-type animal beings who supply the material for the
native differentiation among the mythological stories, the so-called
nareguyap.[15] No other differentiation is made among the epic narratives than that which refers to the individuality of the participating beings; all stories are nareguyap, irrespective of their truth value, irrespective of whether to us they represent myths, legends, or fictional
tales. Since the stories are grouped around leading mythological personages, we obtain a certain classification of them, although one less
functional from a scientific point of view: tïndzo :anareguyap concern
forest and mountain trolls who have cannibalistic tendencies; haivona-
reguyap, the turtle dove; kucunareguyap, buffaloes; and tïanareguyap,
horses and horse thieving. The trickster and culture-hero cycle so well
known all over North America passes under the title ïžapönareguyap,
"stories about the coyote (prairie wolf)." All the newly introduced European stories fall under the category "white man's tales," taivonaregu-
yap, where, thus, the main participants no longer mark the differentiating principle.

This is a hunting people's natural way of grouping together narrative material. The value of the stories and their importance depends
upon the individuality of the zoomorphic beings. Because of this,
among other things, modern anthropologists have been led to judge
the mythological stories of the North American Indians as primarily

15. For the following, see Hultkrantz, "Religious Aspects of the Wind River Shoshoni
Folk Literature," in *Culture in History: Essays in Honor of Paul Radin*, ed. S. Diamond
(New York, 1960), p. 554.

entertaining narratives. And certainly narratives such as the trickster stories, which comprise half of the Shoshoni treasure trove of myths, are most entertaining. They appeal to our sense of the ridiculous and obscene in the same way as the stories of the cannibal monsters provide an outlet for our attraction to the scary and the uncanny. Or, perhaps more appropriately, one should talk about the reaction of the Shoshoni rather than our reaction, since it is their psychic makeup which has put its mark on these stories. It would be premature, however, to believe that the Shoshoni stories are only valuable because of their powers of entertainment. When one asks a Shoshoni who knows his mythology about this, he arranges the myths in a chronological order which provides totally different associations: creation stories, coyote stories, stories concerning other mythic animal beings, stories about cannibal monsters, and white men's stories.[16] In principle, all these groups, with the exception of the last-named one, belong to the category of myths, since their action takes place in the mythic primeval times and they are believed to be true descriptions of the past. Naturally we can doubt whether the mythical animal beings deserve to be designated as gods, although certainly they can be counted among the supernatural beings which existed in the early hours of the creation.

Some *nareguyap* in which supernatural beings play a role have their action taking place in modern time and tell about meetings between human beings and representatives of the spirit world. These can suitably be put under the heading of legends. They are presented as *nareguyap* but are only occasionally mentioned together with the other above-mentioned types of narratives, a fact which by itself can justify their having a specific position in our classification. There are also fictional tales, stories which are only of value as entertainment. These also pass as *nareguyap*, although reaction toward them reveals that they are not credited with the same standard of truth as the other *nareguyap*. Partly they are made up of the majority of the white men's stories, partly they may be designated as products of degeneration (inherited stories which have lost their cultural and religious foundation). Through the present process of secularization, more and more myths and legends are changing to fictional tales.

From the point of view of comparative religion, it is possible to discern the following myth categories (which do not have any comparison in the Shoshoni terminology or in their conscious model of the *nareguyap*):[17]

16. Ibid., p. 556.
17. Ibid., pp. 564 ff.

1. Origin myths without cultic or ritual reference. Most of these origin myths—which represent the most common type of myth—belong to the trickster cycle but differ from the other humoristically formed trickster stories by the serious themes they deal with: the creation of humans and animals, the change of the animals from human beings in animal guise to real animals, the spread of the animals throughout the country, how the seasons were determined, the arrival of the medicine men, the introduction of childbirth, and the origin of death. As an example of this myth cycle, the myth of the origin of death will be recounted here. There are several versions, of which I shall present the most common:[18]

> In bygone days, long, long ago, the animals were human beings. Wolf and Coyote were the most important. The Wolf—creator—and the Coyote were such that Wolf was amenable whilst Coyote always tried to do the opposite [of what Wolf did]. Wolf pronounced that when a human being died one could bring him to life again by shooting an arrow under him. But Coyote was of another opinion: "That would not be good, then there would be too many people here, and there is not room for them all. No [he said], let the human being die, his flesh rot and his spirit [mugwa] fly away with the wind, so that all that is left is just a pile of dry bones." The amenable Wolf gave in. But in his heart he decided to let Coyote's son be the first to die. In this way Wolf wished that the boy would die, and just because of his wish it came true. Coyote soon came to Wolf and told him that his son had died. He reminded Wolf of how the latter had said that one could bring a person to life again by shooting an arrow underneath. But Wolf reminded Coyote of how he himself had decided that a person should die for all time.—That is why it turned out that way.

This story is heard, just as other origin myths, with greater seriousness and afterthought than other stories in the trickster cycle. It is regarded as being true, and it constitutes a motivation and sanction for the introduction of death into the lives of human beings. The origin myths have, on the whole, the function of giving sanction to prevailing conditions and institutions.

It is hazardous to decide where the rest of the stories in the trickster cycle and the majority of "animal myths" should be placed. The literary and artistic qualities of these myths have, with time, placed them rather close to the fictional tale.[19]

18. Cf. Hultkrantz, "The Origin of Death Myth as Found Among the Wind River Shoshoni Indians," Ethnos 20, nos. 2–3 (1955), 129.

19. As will be shown more explicitly in a work which I am now in the process of writing, we may suitably (roughly estimated) divide the myths in four categories: cosmological myths, institutional myths, ritual myths, and literary myths. The literary

2. Astral myths, or rather myths with "astral" conclusions. Here, it is mostly a question of loosely attached etiological motifs at the end of certain stories. Their meaning is uncertain. In one myth, for instance, it is told how Coyote seduces his mother-in-law and how his daughters then desert him to become stars in the constellation of the Great Bear. Possibly this myth was initially an origin myth (concerning the Great Bear) which has, after being embroidered upon, changed character.

There is a long line of other etiologically oriented myths which do not have a serious enough aim to enable them to come under the heading of origin myths and whose entertainment value appears to be—at least nowadays—rather dominating.

One myth category is very obviously missing, namely, the solemnly recited sacred myths which, in other religions, take up the first place in mythology, and which often occur as cult- and ritual myths (according to Hooke's definition).[20] It is possible that in ancient times, for instance, the origin-of-death myth had such a serious framework that it deserved the designation "sacred myth," but this cannot be proven. The cult-myth is missing completely among the Shoshoni in Wyoming, nor is it to be found among their tribal relatives in the Great Basin, where possibly the unstable nomadic existence, lack of edible food, and want of a strict social organization hindered a developed cultic activity.[21] Conditions must have been somewhat different in Wyoming before the age of the mounted plains culture (among other things, the access to easily hunted game had been good), but the traces of older cults are rather vague. The introduction of the Sun Dance indicates a change. Surprisingly enough, there is no cult-myth attached to the Sun Dance. A story circulates, however, about the origin of the Sun Dance, according to which this ceremony was instituted as a gift presented by a spirit in a vision—in some variants by the Supreme Being himself. This story, the action of which takes place in a not too distant time, can most adequately be regarded as a cult-legend. It is quite

---

myths—which most of all are marked by the characteristics adduced by Arbman as being typical of myths (see above, and n. 7 above) should represent the transition stage between real myths and fictional tales. The majority of Shoshoni animal tales may be designated as literary myths.

20. See, e.g., S. H. Hooke, *Middle Eastern Mythology* (Harmondsworth, 1963), pp. 11 ff. The distinction between cult-myths and ritual myths is not fully clear. It would be more adequate to talk about cult-foundation myths and ritual myths and, if one so desires, to place both these categories together under the heading cult-myths. According to the division proposed in the previous note, however, the cult-foundation myth is an institutional myth.

21. Among these Shoshoni there existed, however, an annual rite of elementary character.

probable that a ceremony which, in historical times, was taken over from another plains group, Comanche or Kiowa Indians, would receive its fundamentals in an origin story where the pattern of action is supposed to have occurred in historical times. The Shoshoni credit Yellow Hand, the famous chief from the early nineteenth century, with being the man who experienced the initiating vision of the Sun Dance.[22]

IV

The function of myth in Shoshoni culture is not exhausted with the classification of myth genres. It also has a function in relation to religion understood as a system of belief complexes, and it operates thereby in such a way that there appears a difference between religion and mythology as separate conceptual systems. It is possible to discern three to four religious segments, or belief configurations, which become actualized in given situations, and which eliminate each other in practice:[23]

1. The guardian-spirit belief complex, which is based on the individualistic hunting way of life, and which constitutes the religious resource from which a human being can draw in many everyday occurrences, especially outside the sheltered camp atmosphere.

2. The Sun Dance complex, which not only includes the Sun Dance ceremony during the summer season but also religious conceptions which are connected with this cult, such as the conception of an active and intervening Supreme Being. In social situations such as the buffalo hunt and the organized tribal meetings, this cult and its blessings were experienced as being of central religious importance. In our day, the Sun Dance provides a stabilizing factor for tradition and ethnic unity.

3. The mythology, combined with storytelling during winter evenings.

4. Christian religious ideas, particularly in connection with the attendance of church on Sundays. As the missions did not start appearing until 1883, the Christian configuration of belief did not have an effect until after the breakdown of the old tribal autonomy. For many Shoshoni, this configuration is of no consequence.

22. Hultkrantz, "Yellow Hand, Chief and Medicine-Man Among the Eastern Shoshoni," in *Verhandlungen des 38. Internationalen Amerikanistenkongresses*, vol. 2 (Munich, 1970), pp. 293 ff.
23. Hultkrantz, "Configurations of Religious Belief Among the Wind River Shoshoni," *Ethnos* 21, nos. 3–4 (1956), 194 ff.

Each one of these religious complexes contains a closed belief system, with conceptions which correspond to each other at the same time that they depart from the conceptions which appear in the other systems. For example, we find that the Supreme Being, *Tam Apö* ("our Father"), does not actively appear in the guardian-spirit beliefs, that he dominates within the Sun Dance complex, that in mythology he is replaced by a principally theriomorphic creator figure, Wolf, and that in Christian contexts he is identified with the Christian God. In particular, there is no exchange between the mythology and the other religious configurations. Thus, the series *Tam Apö*, Mother Earth, and the buffalo god of the Sun Dance religion is replaced by the series Wolf, Coyote, and the primeval animals of the mythology.

In the old hunting society, the mythological stories supplied the dominant conceptional material during the sedentary life of the wintertime. The entertainment which they provided corresponded in a way to the dances and ceremonies of the summertime. The narratives were told by old men and women who held the reputation of being good storytellers—and, not least essential, good imitators and humorists. The stories describe a primeval Shoshoni society where Wolf is the chief and Coyote is his assistant, the camp crier. Coyote is above all the irresponsible and amoral trickster, a blackguard who recklessly seduces both his mother-in-law and his daughters. Sometimes even Wolf appears as a trickster, but as such he is less gifted than Coyote. It may appear strange to a European, but both these figures in reality comprise a mythological schedule, the twin myth, known from Europe, Asia, and America.[24] In the Shoshoni version of this myth, the divine pair is thus the Supreme Being and his less-successful assistant. It is the latter's lack of efficiency and his imperfectness which make him into a ridiculous being and thus pave the way for his thorough trickster character in the myth (at the same time as the myth, we may suppose, receives a literary form which is ever increasingly embroidered upon). The Shoshoni rather evade the question when one asks them about the divinity of their foremost mythological character, Wolf, but most of them do not seem to doubt it.[25] Wolf's connection with *Tam Apö*, however, causes them to be puzzled when it is brought up by an inquisitive foreigner. Those animals which in our days physically resemble Wolf, Coyote, and the other zoomorphic mythological beings lack importance as guardian spirits, and they are not to be found in the belief complex of the Sun Dance lodge.

24. Concerning the twin myth in America, see Hultkrantz, *Les Religions des Indiens primitifs de l'Amérique: Essai d'une synthèse typologique et historique*, Stockholm Studies in Comparative Religion, vol. 4 (Stockholm, 1963), pp. 41 ff.

25. Hultkrantz, "Religious Aspects" (n. 15 above), pp. 560–61.

V

This short sketch of the mythology of the Wyoming Shoshoni should have shown that the myths of these Indians do not have any cultic function at all. Their aim is, and has been, to supply prototypes or original descriptions of cosmos, the kingdom of Nature, or cultural and religious institutions. The myths provide, as Eliade pointedly says, a "sacred history," [26] and they give sanction to the prevailing conditions.

The deficient cultic integration of the mythological stories is, of course, intimately connected with the isolation of the mythology from the rest of the religion. The mythology replaces the religion; it does not complement it (an exception is, however, the eschatology where religion and mythology cooperate to form the picture). Among the Shoshoni in the Great Basin, religion and mythology are somewhat closer together; in Wyoming, however, the connections between them have been broken through the intervention of the plains culture into the religious system of the Shoshoni. [27] Neither there nor in the Great Basin, however, does the mythology seem to have had a cultic foundation. Among the Plains Shoshoni, it is only the legends connected with the relatively recently imported Sun Dance which occur as cultic narratives. The myths have no such function.

Is it not then probable that the mythology was written down when the myths had passed into a degenerated form? It has been previously mentioned that by all accounts the myths have undergone a recurring literary change as they have been handed down, whereby their religious character has been reduced. Without a doubt, this is an important point. In a shocking manner, my investigations revealed how one and the same myth can be retold in different versions by one and the same informant after short intervals of time. [28] It must be pointed out, though, that the conceptions and motifs mostly remain constant. The epic framework varies, however, especially details which can be represented in a mimic and dramatic way. As mentioned before, the Shoshoni do not have the category "sacred myths" which, as we know, are usually handed down very precisely; on the contrary, the storyteller's changing influence upon the text is sanctioned here. That the mythology of the Plains Shoshoni has not degenerated from a supposed older cultic mythology is clearly shown by, among other things, the

26. M. Eliade, *Aspects du mythe* (Paris, 1963), pp. 23 ff.
27. Hultkrantz, "Religion und Mythologie der Prärie-Schoschonen," *Akten des 34. Internationalen Amerikanistenkongresses* (Vienna, 1963), p. 554.
28. Among the Navajo Indians, even the creation myths change their form according to the raconteur; see J. Chandler, "Navaho Mythmakers," *Folklore Annual of the University Folklore Association*, no. 1 (Austin, Tex., 1969), pp. 20 ff.

fact that the same type of mythology predominates among Shoshonean groups in the deserts, mountains, and plateaus west of the Rocky
Mountains. The Shoshoni in these areas have lived isolated from each
other and have existed under different conditions. But their mythology
shows everywhere the same pattern and, to a great extent, the same
content.

Our conclusion, therefore, must be that in certain cultures myths
can form a field which is quite independent of the other parts of the
religion. This is in itself a valuable result of our investigation and brings
to the fore the question as to what degree similar discrepancies between mythology and religion have occurred within the better-known
religions in ancient and modern times. Up to now, the majority of anthropologists and historians of religion have more or less taken for
granted that both belief complexes, in as much as they may at all
be separated, support each other. An important problem which still
needs to be dealt with is: under what conditions does a dichotomy
such as the one we have observed among the Shoshoni originate?
Should one allege ecological adaptation, social structure, or simply deficient integration between myth and cult?

Our investigation shows, in any case, that myths cannot be confined
to embracing only the category of cult-myths. Neither may one un-
questioningly deduce all myths from cult-myths. The Shoshoni material evinces, in the same way as the myth material from other so-called
primitive peoples, that the main function of the myth is to sanction
the establishment and condition of the world and its institutions,
thereby safeguarding the existence of people and society. In many
cases, the very recitation of the myth is so filled with power that it influences—or is thought to influence—the course of actual events. The
ritual may strengthen this effect by copying the myth, but it certainly
does not follow that everywhere a myth is followed up by a ritual. Neither is every ritual connected with a myth, as examples from ancient
Rome can teach us. The fixed ties between myth and rite appear
to have been most common within strictly organized high cultures
where the division and stratification of professions had paved the way
for ecclesiastical hierarchy and clerical theology and where a sacred
kingship had arisen. Comparative religion has good examples thereof
from the Near East, far too well known to be mentioned in this connection, and from Mexico, where many years ago Preuss called attention
to the affiliation between myth and rite.[29] From these cultures, one has,
in my opinion, concise evidence of how the function of myth closely
reflects the social structure.

29. K. Th. Preuss, *Der religiöse Gestalt der Mythen* (Tübingen, 1933), pp. 14 ff.

The Creation Myths of
the North American Indians

ANNA BIRGITTA ROOTH

One of the consequences of the development of the comparative method in my-
thology was a refinement of typology. From all the data available, it was determined
that there were identifiable myth types, cognates of which could be found in diverse
cultural contexts and which could even be plotted on maps. Assisted by the visual
display afforded by myth mapping, folklorists could get some idea of the geographic
distribution of a given myth. The more widely diffused a myth was, the older it was
assumed to be. Knowledge of the distribution of a myth made it possible to specu-
late about possible paths of migration of the narrative. If peoples moved to North
and South America from Asia, then it was reasonable to assume that they brought
their myths with them. So it is not surprising to learn that a number of studies
have documented the parallels between Asian and American Indian myths.

Comparative, typological studies of myths are not always worldwide. Sometimes
they are limited to one language family or to one continent. See, for example, Mar-
garet W. Fisher, "The Mythology of the Northern and Northeastern Algonkians in
reference to Algonkian Mythology as a Whole," in Man in Northeastern North
America, *ed. Frederick Johnson,* Papers of the Robert S. Peabody Foundation for
Archaeology *no. 3 (1946), 226–62, or Ernst A. Zbinden, "Nördliche und südliche*
Elemente im Kulturheroenmythus der Südathapasken," Anthropos 55 (1960),
689–733.

Comparative, typological studies of myth require enormous bibliographical ex-
pertise, as one must search through numerous published sources to locate ver-
sions of the myths being investigated. The emphasis in typological studies is defi-
nitely on the text of the myth. Whereas myth-ritualists and students of comparative
religion are primarily concerned with the interrelationship between myth and other
elements of culture, e.g., ritual, cult, or religion, the scholar concerned with typol-
ogy is more interested in the myth per se and in its relationship to cognates in
other cultures. In the following essay by Anna Birgitta Rooth, professor of ethnol-
ogy at the University of Uppsala, we can see that among some 300 American Indian
creation myths, there are only eight principal myth-types.

Professor Rooth has studied European folklore. See her comparative studies of
Cinderella *and* Loki, The Cinderella Cycle *(Lund, 1951) and* Loki in Scandinavian
Mythology *(Lund, 1961). Her analysis of* Cinderella *consisted in part of a delinea-*
tion of different types of the folktale. Professor Rooth has also done fieldwork in

Reprinted from *Anthropos* 52 (1957), 497–508, by permission of the author and the
Anthropos-Institut.

mythology in Alaska. See The Alaskan Expedition 1966: Myths, Customs and Beliefs Among the Athabascan Indians and the Eskimos of Northern Alaska *(Lund, 1971);* The Importance of Storytelling *(Uppsala, 1976); and* The Alaska Seminar *(Uppsala, 1980), which contains her essays on "The Wolverine's Trap" (pp. 5–38) and on "The Giants' Wrestling" (pp. 39–83). One of her most extensive comparative studies is* The Raven and the Carcass: An Investigation of a Motif in the Deluge Myth in Europe, Asia and North America, *Folklore Fellows Communications no. 186 (Helsinki, 1962).*

For an introduction to the scholarship on American Indian myth, see Alan Dundes, "North American Indian Folklore Studies," Journal de la Société des Américanistes *56 (1967), 53–79. For considerations of Asian-American Indian myth parallels, see Gudmund Hatt,* Asiatic Influences in American Folklore *(Copenhagen, 1949) and Francis Lee Utley, "The Migration of Folktales: Four Channels to the Americas,"* Current Anthropology *15 (1974), 5–27.*

I have excerpted all creation myths, i.e., all the myths about the beginning, creation, or formation of the world or earth that are found in North American Indian literature.[1] These number about 300 versions or myths in all. Of course, there is still much literature from which to draw and many creation myths to add which could be of importance for the mapping of the detail-motifs, but the material already compiled must be considered sufficient for the present study and for a comparison of the types.

My intention was to compile—if possible—a comparable number of creation myths from each of the different areas of American Indian settlement north of Mexico, and I would still like to complete the material from some of the areas where the material is scarcely known. I did not wish to concentrate only upon a single type of creation myth but upon all variations of the common theme: the creation or beginning of the world.

I have thus compiled 300 creation myths. Of these 17 percent are fragmentary and (or) not classified, but the other 83 percent (about 250 myths) can all be referred to one or the other of eight different types.

1. This is a preliminary report, delivered in 1956 to the Wenner-Gren Foundation for Anthropological Research, which sponsored my studies at a number of universities and libraries in the United States, from January to June, 1955. The bibliography will be published later, in connection with a larger work on the creation myths of the North American Indians. Therein I am comparing these myths with the various types of creation myths found in Eurasia, and studying their geographical distribution in an effort to learn more about cultural areas and contacts. The findings in the present report are founded on versions of creation myths which have been excerpted from about 230 books and papers dealing with the American Indians north of Mexico. Most of this material was compiled in the Library of the Peabody Museum, Cambridge, Massachusetts.

This shows that we have in North American Indian tradition eight traditional myth-types on the theme of the beginning or creation of the world.

I am not ready with the definite investigations of the last four types, therefore I shall have to defer comment upon them until later. Further, I shall not comment at this time upon a series of interesting detail-motifs appearing especially on the Northwest Coast and in California, which show parallels to the myths of East and North Asia. Neither shall I discuss here the interesting congruence in detail-motifs between eastern and western America, on both sides of the Plains. These detail-motifs show the relationship between the East and West, but at the same time reveal an incongruence with the traditions of the Plains. These last, in many cases, seem more closely related to the Meso-American tradition-area.

Some detail-motifs will be found in the Meso-American tradition-area (including Peru in the South and Arizona, New Mexico, and southern California in the North) which will also be found in the Pacific Islands and in Eurasia. I shall also later comment upon some intricate detail-motifs in Popol Vuh and Chilam Balam.

The eight different types to which the creation myths can be referred are these:

1. The Earth-Diver myth
2. The World-Parent myth
3. The Emergence myth
4. The Spider myth
5. The Fighting or Robbery type
6. The Ymir myth
7. The Two Creators and their contests
8. The Blind Brother myth

THE MYTH-TYPES

1. The Earth-Diver

Distribution

This type is found all over the North American continent with the exception of Arizona and New Mexico. No versions are known to me from Alaska, but that holds true for all types of creation myths. As far as the creation myth is concerned, Alaska is a blank (see Map 2).

> The myth relates how some being dives to the bottom of the sole existing ocean, to get sand from which the earth will be created. The usual points are: the diver (animal, god, or man) gets only an extremely small amount of sand or mud under his nail or claw; he is away for a very long time; he is dead or half-dead when he reappears. From the little grain of sand the earth is created by the god (or animal). Sometimes the earth is mixed with seeds or something else. It must be kneaded or stretched and placed upon the waters, and it grows until it reaches its present size. Sometimes it is weak and shaky, and must be strengthened or fastened with pillars or stones in the four quarters of the world. While the earth is growing, the creator sends out an animal to run around the newly created world in order to find out its size, or the creator himself goes around the earth to inspect it. The animal so dispatched (coyote, raven, or buzzard) stops to eat or flaps its wings (thus creating the mountains)—all contrary to the god's order; it is punished by the creator; the white raven becomes black, or is condemned to live on dead corpses.

These are the general outlines of the variations of this myth. Sometimes it is secondarily linked to the deluge, which offers the same situation as the primeval waters. In the Earth-Diver myth, the interest of the audience is directed to the creation itself. In the usual deluge myths, interest is directed to the problem of saving the men or animals, the disaster itself, and the repeopling of the world.

Interesting is the distribution of the Earth-Diver myth in Eurasia, viz., from northern Asia to eastern and southeastern Europe, as far west as the Slavonic area in Germany.

Comments

This myth-type, although not found in Alaska, the blank spot of mythology as well as of most oral tradition, is closely connected with the tradition of the Earth-Diver of the Kolyma Peninsula and also with Wogul and Magyar traditions. B. Munkácsi gives this example from the Woguls:

> The old man and the old woman of the tundra-mound lived surrounded by the primeval waters. To their astonishment, earth begins to grow around their mound, after three "diver birds" from heaven have successively tried to bring up mud from the bottom of the sea. The old couple send out a white raven to learn the size of the earth. The first and

second day he is away for a short time; on the third day he does not
return until late in the evening—so much has the earth grown—but he
is all black because he has eaten from a corpse.

We recognize this motif from the North American Indian tradition;
it is found as far west as the East Baltic states. Another version of the
Earth-Diver myth gives us this motif: the world shakes and the Ural
Mountains are intended to strengthen it. The motif of the tiny amount
of sand (often under the nails) is found in Eurasia as well as in North
America. This is also true of the motif of the creator going around the
world after the creation, whereas that of the animal running around
the world seems to be limited to North America.

1. The distribution of the Earth-Diver myth in the Kolyma Peninsula
among Chuckchis and Yukaghirs, as well as among Burjats, Turko-
Tatarian and Finno-Ugrian peoples, and the correspondence of the
detail-motifs typical of the Earth-Diver myths, both in North America
and Eurasia, indicate that the myth-types are genetically related and
not individually developed on the different continents.

2. The limitation of the Earth-Diver myths to northern Asia (with exceptional offshoots in eastern and southern Asia) and eastern and
southeastern Europe demonstrates that this myth within Eurasia has
its own special distribution showing a geographical continuation. This
supports the probability of a common origin for the Eurasian versions,
and at the same time for the North American ones.

3. We must mention as a curious sidelight that the conception of the
primeval water, i.e., the ocean as the original element from which the
earth grows, seems to be uncalled for in the central areas of the large
continents. Certainly, it has been pointed out that the existence of
shells, etc., in mountains now high above sea level gave rise to this
idea. But the conception of primeval water could hardly have sprung
from these observations. That is shown by the traditional style and
form which is common to all the versions and indicates a common
origin for them. The observations however might have stimulated the
telling of the myths, and could also have been used as a "proof" for the
truth of the myth.

It is logical to seek the origin of the conception of the primeval
ocean in a coastal or island area, where it would seem natural. We may
draw the following conclusion from this reflection: this myth seems to
have originated in the eastern Asiatic coastal area, from whence it
spread westward across Siberia and eastward across the North American continent.

2. The World-Parents
(Sky-Father and Earth-Mother)

The World-Parents type (i.e., the Sky-Father and the Earth-Mother) is limited in North America to southern California, Arizona, and New Mexico. It is the same type of creation myth as we find in the Japanese

Map 1

● The World-Parents Myth. ○ Ib. Related Versions. ◑ Ib. Fragmentary Versions. ▲ The Blind Brother Myth. △ Ib. Fragmentary Versions.

epics Nihongi and Kojiki, and the same as found in the oral tradition of China and Polynesia.

I will give the motifs of both the Japanese and Californian traditions:

Nihongi and Kojiki

The god and goddess of Heaven dip the heavenly jewel-spear in the ocean, causing earth to appear. They descend to the island, erect the jewel-spear as the pillar of heaven, the centre of the land, or the pillar of their home.

The god goes to the left, the goddess to the right around the pillar, exclaiming as they meet: What a lovely youth! Because of the goddess's mistake of speaking first (causing the ceremony to be repeated) her first-born was a failure. They are united as husband and wife. The wife then gives birth to the different islands of Japan, to mountains, streams, and vegetation, to the sun goddess, etc. In one version the sun is created when the god holds a mirror in his left hand and the moon when he holds a mirror in his right hand. Further it is related that when the sun hides from the world, the other gods play this trick: they laugh outside the door of her hidingplace. When she becomes curious to know what the noise is about, they tell her that they have found a new sun. As she opens the door to peep out, the assembled gods are holding a mirror outside. Seeing her own reflection outside, she is so astonished that she goes out to look and then the gods quickly slam the door behind her.

South Californian

Heaven and earth are created as man and woman. They recognize each other in the darkness; they talk.

The earth gives birth to the sacred pointed stones of chipped flint, which are placed for inspection in the end of the sword-shaped staff in the religious ceremonials (var. the staff is erected as a world pillar). Further, she gives birth to stone mortars for ceremonies, to people, animals, trees, mountains, streams. All things were people at that time. The first-born is lost before its birth or the first-born children are heavy and cannot move about. The sun is born, but its light is too intense and burning and it is hidden. Then she gives birth to *Chung-itch-nisch*, the first being who could speak, and to the rattle-snake: both are hidden at first. Later the sun is taken out from its place of concealment, and the people instructed to adore *Chung-itch-nisch*.

In one myth of another type from this area we find the sun going only half way toward a mirror placed in the middle of the heaven.

The goddess of earth giving birth to all things, the mention of the staff with a special point, the erection of the staff, the talk between god and goddess, the failure of the first-born, the birth of the sun, the hiding of the sun—these comprise a series of detail-motifs typical of the World-Parents myth with its limited distribution in southern California, Arizona, and New Mexico, but are not found in the other myth-types of North America. In some of the World-Parents myths, mention is made of the children crouching between the two parents, just as in the motif of the children of Papa and Rangi in Polynesian tradition.

1. The World-Parents type in North America is limited to a narrow area which indicates a relationship of the different versions of this type (Map 1).

2. The World-Parents myth has a series of detail-motifs which are not essential to the myth. T' 'y could belong to even other myth-types, but they do not. They are re. .ed to each other only in this type, which shows that this is a special type with its special detail-motifs.

3. These detail-motifs typical of the World-Parents myth are also found in the Pacific Islands tradition (Japan and Polynesia) and in China, which indicates a genetic relationship with the tradition of the Pacific Islands.

4. The World-Parents type seems to be limited in Eurasia to southeastern and southern Asia, as far west as the eastern Mediterranean area. Because of the distribution of this type in southern North America and because of the relationship of the tradition of this area with that of the Pacific Islands, I draw the conclusion that the World-Parents type came by way of the Pacific Islands to southern California—or rather to the Meso-American tradition-area, whose northern part includes southern North America.

3. The Emergence Myth

Content and Distribution

The Emergence myth is limited in North America to the Southwest (see Map 2), with offshoots in the Plains area. In this myth a conception of an existence of the different worlds is expressed.

> Men, animals, and vegetation live in a cave in the earth. When the earth is ready for people they are instructed in all ceremonies, customs, and crafts; they can now emerge to the surface and begin their wanderings to their present sites. The corn-mother, the sun twins, or a hero is sent to lead them out into the sun from the dark, narrow cave where they have lived in misery. Sometimes the wandering is pictured as a climbing of a tree or a vine which, reaching up to the roof of the cave, pierces a

Map 2
● The Emergence Myth. ○ Ib. Fragmentary Versions. ▲ The Earth-Diver
Myth. △ Ib. Fragmentary Versions.

crevice in the stone; thus men are led into the sun. Sometimes animals
are sent to dig a hole in the "heaven" or the roof: the sunlight destroys
forever the eyes of the mole, or the badger is still marked from his digging. Sometimes this climbing or digging is pictured as a flight from the
deluge; men and animals save themselves in this way, by taking refuge in
another world. Sometimes we hear that people took refuge under the
earth in a cave to escape the deluge, and this is the reason for their subsequent emergence.

Comments

1. It is interesting to note that in a refined version of the Mexican myth we hear about a vine sprung from a crevice in a stone altar and animals on the vine—the same detail-motifs as found in the popular myth.

2. The geographical distribution and the presence of this myth-type and its detail-motifs in the Maya and Quiche epics show that this myth-type belongs to the Meso-American tradition-area.

3. The Emergence myth seems to be peculiar to this area in the American tradition. Whether or not there is a relationship with a similar myth-type in East Asia I cannot yet say. So far I have seen no significant detail-motifs common to the two types with the exception of the Trobriand Islanders' Emergence myth.

4. The Spider as Creator or First Being

In some creation myths of southern California, Arizona, and New Mexico, the Spider takes an active part in the creation. The Spider weaves an umbrella-like foundation for the earth, or he fastens with his web or thread the rushes which will be the earth. This motif is interwoven in a secondary manner in the deluge myths where the Spider weaves not the earth but the scaffold which saves people from drowning. In some versions Spiders of different colours fasten down the world at the four world corners (cf. the "bacabs," which are sometimes associated with spiders). See Map 3.

The conception of the Spider as the first being is found in some myths where the Spider praises his ability to stand on the water or float in the air as he did in the beginning of the world. In a contest with other boasting competitors the Spider wins (see Map 3).

1. These Spider-creation myths are limited to the southern parts of North America (see the Map). Some of the other Spider myths extend a considerable distance north into the Plains area.

2. The centre of this type, however, is in the southern part, as the connection with the Mexican tradition indicates.

3. In Eurasia we find parallels to this Spider myth in the Pacific Islands, in East Asia, and in India.

4. This myth-type also shows special detail-motifs common to Chinese and southern Californian traditions, which are too intricate to be explained as having been individually developed on both sides of the Pacific Ocean. In both the North American Indian and the Asiatic tradition it is pointed out that the Spider fastens the world with his

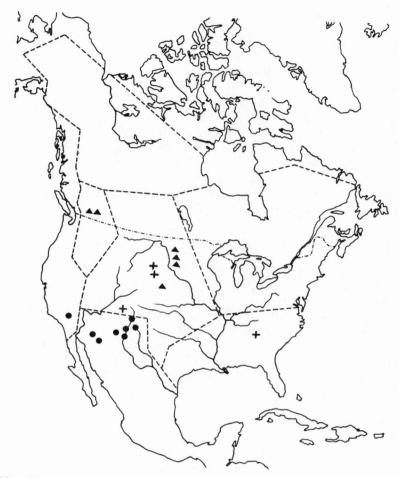

Map 3

The Spider Myths. ● The Spider as Creator. + The Spider's Ability to Stand on Water (Primeval Water). ▲ The Spider as the First Being.

thread. Further, the Spider, both in China and in southern North America, is connected with the colour-directions.

5. Because of the special combination of detail-motifs, these myth-types must be considered to have had a common origin, and because of the geographical distribution of this myth-type in southern North America, the Pacific Islands must be considered the transmitting area.

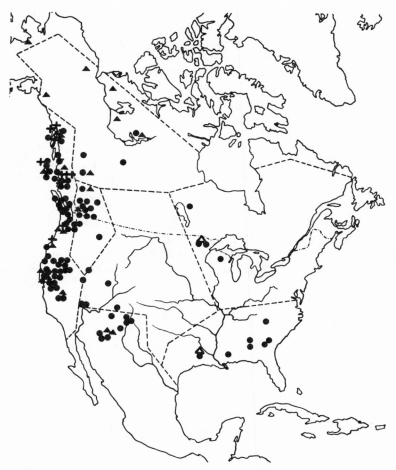

Map 4
The Robbery Myths. ● The Theft of Fire. ▲ The Theft of the Sun (or Light).
△ Ib. Fragmentary Versions. + The Theft of the Water.

5. The Creation or Formation of the World Through Struggle and Robbery

One group of "creation" myths of a more indeterminable type is found in the western area as far south as California. One trait characterizes them all, viz., the "creator" (often in scholarly tradition called trans-former, sometimes traveller) shapes the world and gives it its character by Theft or Robbery of the sun, fire, or water; or he struggles with these "giants" or keepers of fish or of weather.[2] The myths are not concerned with the original owners of these things, so necessary to mankind, but only with the acquiring of them by god or hero.

There are interesting creation myths on the Northwest Coast, e.g., that of the Raven who for ages keeps flying, separating light and darkness with his wings until darkness is compressed to a material substance, i.e., the earth. This myth-type is also found among the Ainus; the bird keeps parting the chaotic mass of earth and water with his wings and tail until they are separated and the earth trampled to a solid substance. Here again is a relationship between the myth tradition of northeastern Asia and of the Northwest Coast, of which many cases have already been pointed out by Franz Boas, Waldemar Bogoras, and Waldemar Jochelson.

The Theft or Robbery myths which seem so popular in the northwestern and western parts of the American continent are interesting as parallels to the same kind of Robbery and Struggle myths in Eurasia, especially in the North Asiatic tradition and Old Scandinavian poetry (see Map 4).

6. The Ymir Type

In some versions in North America the world is created from the corpse of a dead giant or a dead man or woman (see Map 5). We have interesting parallels also for this myth in Eurasia, and I should not be surprised if we find a geographical continuity of this myth-type also in Siberia, connecting the East with the Old Scandinavian creation myth

2. The myths of the theft of the sun (or light) can be further completed. Cf. S. Thompson, *Tales of the North American Indians* (Cambridge, Mass., 1929), p. 281, n. 42. Here, too, the geographical distribution shows that the proper distribution area of the type in America is the western and northwestern Pacific Coast. The versions cited by Thompson from the Menomini, Onondaga, and Seneca are, however, not versions of the sun-theft myth. The Menomini version is a mixture of the sun-snarer, the theft of the sun, and the theft of fire. Swanton, however, reports one version from the southeastern area which seems to belong to the myth of the theft of the sun.

To the myths of the theft of fire which I compiled in connection with the creation myths I have added further versions from Thompson, *Tales*, p. 289, n. 63. It is remarkable that, in this supplementary material, several of these fire-theft myths appear as independent tales. The detail-motifs of the fire-theft myth are of great interest as they show a geographical continuity in their distribution. I shall return to the maps of the detail-motifs in a later work.

As to the theft of the fresh water, I have not included the specific type which is particularly common in northeastern America and also has a parallel in the Plateau area, viz., the Monster (frog) that drank up or stole all the water from mankind; the hero later lets this water out again.

Map 5

● The Ymir Myth. ▲ The Two Creators.

of Ymir. At present, I only know of its existence in China, Tibet, East Asia, the Pacific Islands, and Scandinavia!

However, it shows a connection with another type which has already been pointed out by O. Dähnhardt, viz., the creation of Adam or the first man.

In the Ymir type, the skull is made into the sky, the bones become the stones, the hair becomes the vegetation, the blood becomes the water, etc. One finds just the opposite in the creation of Adam, where stone, water, clouds (for the brain), and vegetation supply the material from which the first man is created.

7. The Two Creators

There is one type of creation myth found all over North America (see Map 5) which emphatically asserts that there were Two Creators, or rather one creator and a companion. Usually this myth or rather episode is combined with other myth-types as a part of them.

Sometimes the Two Creators are pictured as brothers (or sisters), or as belonging to different generations, e.g., father and son or uncle and nephew. Sometimes they are pictured as two gods or godlike beings meeting accidentally and testing each other's strength. It may be a competition of knowledge about the beginning of the world, similar to what we find in Old Scandinavian poetry, to show who is the oldest and the wisest, who is god and who is man.

It may be a competition of abilities, to show who can create the best things and explain why they are best, or who can endure longer the phases of death, lying as if dead, even withering away till only grass covers the bones—and then standing up victorious years later. It may also be a fight in which the gods use their special attributes as weapons, the good god eventually triumphing over the evil one.

As said above, this motif-complex in its different variations appears in different parts of the American continent (which will be shown later on a map, together with the Eurasian parallels).

We have a special form of this motif-complex in a myth which I have called the Blind Brother.

8. The Blind Brother

This myth-type is found only in southern California and Arizona (see Map 1).

> Two brothers come up from the depths of the ocean. The older brother says that he has his eyes open, thus tricking the younger brother into opening his eyes and having them destroyed by salt water. The blind brother cannot create people as well as the other can. In anger he tries to destroy the latter's work, causing a terrible earthquake. He himself goes back to the ocean with his people.

This myth-type is limited to the southern part of North America, and in its detail-motifs it shows a relationship with the Mexican and Meso-American tradition.

This seems to be a type peculiar to the American continent, since so far I have seen no parallels in Asia.

General Conclusions

1. The very small number of myth-types under which the 300 versions can be classified, the fixed geographical areas to which these types belong, and the congruence of the types in detail-motifs show that these types are traditional forms of fiction with geographical boundaries, just like any other form of culture. These facts should be taken into account by those scholars who regard oral literature or traditional fiction as a spontaneous art whose expression can take any form anywhere at any time, and who, without any further investigation, regard the resemblances between myths as the result of *Elementargedanken* or *archetypes* in the ancestral memory.

2. The very small number of myth-types of a global and popular theme (about eight myth-types in all of North America; seven of these also in Eurasia) as well as the congruence of detail-motifs in Asia and America, taken together, show that there is a relationship between the Asiatic and American creation myths.

3. Four of the creation myths in North America, viz., the World-Parents, Emergence, Spider, and Blind Brother types, are limited to the southern part of the continent, thus forming the northern part of the Meso-American tradition-area, which shows a relationship with the Pacific Islands and with East and South Asia. (To this group could be added the World-Egg myth, which is known in Peru, the Pacific Islands, and East and South Asia.[3] As I have not found it in America north of Mexico, it is not included in this investigation. The distribution is only mentioned here as a parallel to these others.)[4]

4. The Earth-Diver, Ymir, Robbery, and Two Creators myths can be characterized as North American in distinction to those myth-types characterized as Meso-American; they indicate their relationship with North and East Asia.

5. The material submitted in this preliminary report proves that there is a relationship between the Meso-American tradition-area and the Pacific Islands, East and South Asia on the one hand, and between North America and East and North Asia on the other, thus showing two channels of cultural contact between Eurasia and America.

3. See M. Haavio, *Väinämöinen*, Folklore Fellows Communications no. 144 (Helsinki, 1952), p. 61.

4. The Meso-American tradition-area includes the southern part of North America, i.e., southern California, Arizona, New Mexico and Texas, with some offshoots in the Plains.

The Cultural-Historical Background of Myths on the Separation of Sky and Earth

K. NUMAZAWA

Each myth-type has its own individual history and area of geographic dispersion. Folklorists often refer to myth-types by a motif number from Stith Thompson's valuable compilation, the six-volume Motif-Index of Folk Literature, *the first edition of which appeared from 1932–36 (2nd ed., 1955–58). In this work, different letters of the alphabet serve as prefixes indicating various thematic classifications. A motifs are "Mythological Motifs." Motifs with a B prefix refer to "Animals," C "Tabu," D "Magic," E "The Dead," F "Marvels," G "Ogres," etc. The Motif-Index, whose subtitle is "A Classification of Narrative Elements in Folktales, Ballads, Myths, Fables, Mediaeval Romances, Exempla, Fabliaux, Jest-Books and Local Legends," is worldwide in coverage, and so a user can discover at a glance something about a given motif's distribution. To be sure, not all the references following a motif heading are necessarily cognate, that is, genetically related. Thus any narrative describing the "Creation of the Sun" would qualify as motif A 710, or any of the stories accounting for the "Origin of Death" would fall under the general rubric of motif A 1335. Readers must locate all the references given at the end of the motif description to determine whether or not the same story was found in all of the cultures listed.*

Scholars outside the discipline of folklore seldom employ the Motif-Index, but they should. It offers the student of myth a place to begin comparative research. All the major myths of the world are contained in the A section of the Index. So the second of Professor Rooth's eight American Indian myth-types, the world-parents, is an example of motif A 625, World parents: sky-father and earth-mother as parents of the universe. (Incidentally, those who automatically assume that the sky is always the father, the earth always the mother, might profit from knowing about motif A 625.1, Heaven-mother—earth-father!) The Motif-Index indicates that A 625, World parents, sky-father and earth-mother, is found in ancient Greece, India, eastern Indonesia, in Tahiti, in Africa, and in native North and South America. Often the Motif-Index gives bibliographical references to books or articles written about a particular motif. In this particular instance, there is no indication of the numerous

The editor wishes to thank *Scientia: International Review of Scientific Synthesis,* via Guastalla 9, Milano, Italy, for permission to reproduce the above article by K. Numazawa, "Background of Myths on the Separation of Sky and Earth from the Point of View of Cultural History," which first appeared in *Scientia* 1 (1953): 28–35.

182

studies of this important narrative. A sample of the scholarship on this myth would include: Henri Théodore Fischer, Het heilig huwelijk van Hemel en Aarde (Utrecht, 1929); Willibald Staudacher, Die Trennung von Himmel und Erde (Tübingen, 1942); K. Marot, "Die Trennung von Himmel und Erde," Acta Antiqua 1 (1951), 35–63; Raffaele Pettazzoni, "Io and Rangi," in Essays on the History of Religions (Leiden, 1954), pp. 37–42. For a Jungian interpretation, see Erich Neumann, "The Separation of the World Parents: The Principle of Opposites," in The Origins and History of Consciousness *(New York, 1954), pp. 102–27; A. Seidenberg, "The Separation of Sky and Earth at Creation,"* Folklore 70 *(1959), 477–82; 80 (1969), 188–96; 94 (1983), 192–200; and G. Komoróczy, "The Separation of Sky and Earth: The Cycle of Kumarbi and the Myths of Cosmogony in Mesopotamia,"* Acta Antiqua 21 *(1973), 21–45.*

In the following essay, K. Numazawa of Nanzan University of Nagoya, Japan, offers a novel explanation of the world-parents myth. He also seeks to interpret an often associated motif, A 625.2, Raising of the sky. While a Freudian might propose an Oedipal explanation of why the (male) offspring of world-parents would want to separate his parents by pushing the sky-father up off the earth-mother, Numazawa prefers to find the myth's origin in an alleged "visit-marriage" custom that he suggests may stem from a time of matriarchy. According to one nineteenth-century theory of the evolution of social organization, primitive matriarchy was eventually replaced by patriarchy, a theory that has enjoyed a renascence in some feminist writings. The matriarchy theory is most commonly associated with the name of the Swiss scholar Johann Jacob Bachofen (1815–87). See Myth, Religion, and Mother Right: Selected Writings of J. J. Bachofen *(Princeton, 1967). For a popular utilization of the theory, see Elizabeth Gould David,* The First Sex *(Baltimore, 1972). For more scholarly considerations of the theory, one may consult Joan Bamberger, "The Myth of Matriarchy," in Michelle Rosaldo and Louise Lamphere, eds.,* Women, Culture and Society *(Stanford, 1974), pp. 213–30; Paula Webster, "Matriarchy: A Vision of Power," in Rayna R. Reiter, ed.,* Toward an Anthropology of Women *(New York, 1975), pp. 141–56; and Sarah B. Pomeroy, "A Classical Scholar's Perspective on Matriarchy," in Berenice A. Carroll, ed.,* Liberating Women's History: Theoretical and Critical Essays *(Urbana, Ill., 1976), pp. 217–33.*

PREFACE

There are different types of myths having the common motif of the separation of the sky and earth, varying considerably in form and content. They can be classified roughly into four categories: (1) Chaos myths, primitive water myths, myths of the Cosmic Egg; (2) Paradise myths; (3) Myths concerning the banishment of heaven; (4) Universal parent myths. It is to be noted that in spite of varying geographical and cultural bases, these myths have a common basic ideology and a common background of cultural history. My purpose is here to explain this common background by citing some typical examples. The full exposition with all details has been given in my work *Die Weltanfänge in der japanischen Mythologie* (Paris-Lucerne, 1946).

OUTLINE

I. BEFORE THE SEPARATION OF SKY AND EARTH

A. Mutual Relation Between Sky and Earth (Four Categories)

Ideas concerning the primitive condition of the universe prior to the separation of the sky and earth can be classified roughly into two groups. In the first group may be included those ideas according to which the sky and earth were combined in a single chaos. And in the second, those ideas according to which the sky and earth existed as such from the beginning, only so close to each other that one practically lay on the other.

1. Sky and Earth in Combination

Among those myths belonging to the first of the two groups mentioned above, there are some which claim that water alone existed in the beginning and others which explain the primitive condition of the universe as being a chaos or an egg. Such myths can be found among practically all peoples. According to these myths, a formless chaotic substance existed in the beginning, covered with utter darkness. This substance, as well as the primitive darkness covering it, was supposed to have existed since the beginning of eternity and later separated into the earth and sky, thus bringing about the beginning of the universe. Light, too, came into existence at the same time. In such myths the separation of the sky from the earth means the beginning of the universe itself. I consider these myths as belonging to the first category.

2. Sky and Earth Lying One Over the Other

According to the second group of ideas, the sky and earth existed from the very beginning as separate entities, but the one lay close over the other. According to some of the myths in this group, the sky and earth are purely physical natural phenomena, while according to others in the same group they are personal entities. In the so-called Paradise myths, which belong to the second of the categories mentioned above, the sky and earth are in most cases purely natural phenomena. In some of the myths concerning the banishment of heaven—and these belong to the third category—the sky and earth are natural phenomena, but in most of them they are personified. In the universal parent myths, which constitute the fourth category, the sky and earth are, of course, always personified.

(a) *Sky and earth as natural phenomena* A typical example of those myths which regard the sky and earth, the one lying over the other, as purely natural phenomena is that found among the Khasi. According to one of their myths, in the primitive ages when no sin or crime existed the sky was close to the earth, and men were able to associate with the gods. When men committed sin, the sky was separated from the earth as a consequence of their wicked deeds, and the state of Paradise came to an end.

The Poso-Todjo-Toradja calls the primitive state before the separation of the sky and earth the golden age. The people of that age did not have to work at all in order to live.

According to the myths of the Riungers of Flores, in the primitive age the sky and earth were bound to each other by Balangliana. The Liana was used by the people to travel between the sky and earth, and a state of Paradise prevailed. Similar Paradise myths are widely spread among many peoples.

According to the Paradise myths, the primitive state in which the sky and earth lay close together, the one over the other, was naturally advantageous to mankind. On the contrary, there are myths widely spread among different peoples which, though similar to the Paradise myths in that they regard the sky and earth as natural phenomena, differ in considering the same condition disadvantageous to mankind. A typical example of this kind is found among the Tai. According to their mythology, in the primitive ages the sky hung so low over the face of the earth that women could not move their pestles freely when they pounded rice, nor could they move their spindles freely when they wanted to spin. Cows and pigs were hindered from walking freely on the surface of the earth because their backs came in contact with the sky. Similar myths are widely spread among many races, chiefly in Indo-China and Indonesia.

The sky hanging low over the earth was disadvantageous to mankind in various ways; hence men tried to drive the sky away from above the earth. I call such myths those of the banishment of heaven, and put them in the third category. Many Paradise myths have such a motif of the banishment of heaven at the same time. In most myths concerning the banishment of heaven the sky and earth are not considered natural phenomena but are personified.

(b) *Sky and earth as man and woman respectively* According to a myth of the Khasi, in ancient times the sky and earth lay close together, the one over the other, and the sky held itself close to the earth by means of its navel-string. This myth regards the sky as being an offspring of the earth. In many other myths, the sky and earth are personified and are regarded as being respectively a man and a woman.

According to a myth of the To Bada, in the beginning the sky said to the earth: "Spread yourself, and I will spread myself over you." The earth answered and said: "If I spread myself first, you would not be able to cover me entirely." But as the sky would not listen to the earth, the earth spread herself as the sky had requested. Then the sky tried to cover the earth, but was not big enough to do so. Thereupon the earth contracted herself, which caused the formation of mountains and valleys. The sun and the moon were born of the union of the sky and earth.

According to a myth of the Rangi-Papa of Polynesia, the sky lay over the earth in the beginning, and all creation lived in utter darkness. The sky and earth embraced each other firmly, and their offspring were caught in the narrow space between their parents' bosoms. Thus embracing each other, the parents still continued to produce offspring.

Similar myths are found among a few Indian peoples (Yuma, Zuni), the Yoruba of Africa, the Egyptians, the Greeks, and the Gipsies. I have classified all such myths as "Welternmythen" (universal-parent myths), and have put them in the fourth category. They are a variation of the myths concerning the banishment of heaven.

B. Primitive Condition on Earth (Reasons for the Separation of Sky and Earth)

One element common to nearly every myth, except genuine Paradise myths, is the idea that in the primitive condition before the separation of the sky and earth the world was covered with utter darkness, and as no sunlight reached the earth the soil was barren and there were many other inconveniences. According to a myth of the Garo, a huge deep pot covered the whole world, and the earth was like waste land, without light or life, utterly unsuitable for human habitation. Many myths refer to similar inconveniences and disadvantages, the most interesting of which being the idea that the sky was so low that women were unable to pound rice freely and that animals were hindered from moving about. The principal animals that appear in this connection are cows and pigs, and though dogs and hens also appear in some rare cases the horse is never mentioned in any of the myths.

The sky hanging low over the earth is generally considered to be disadvantageous, and those who feel the disadvantages most are chiefly the agricultural peoples, particularly the women of those peoples. The fact will be referred to again later when I speak of the nature of the separator of the sky and earth.

II. SEPARATION OF SKY AND EARTH

A. Method of Separation (Banishment of Heaven)

According to the myths belonging to the first category, the universe came into being with the separation of the sky and earth out of a single chaotic substance. Such an idea of the separation merely concerns the theory of cosmogony and has no other remarkable significance. On the contrary, in most of the myths belonging to the other categories, except genuine Paradise myths, the separation of the sky and earth was occasioned by the sky being driven away from above the earth. According to a myth of the Tai, a woman took a knife and cut off the string that bound the sky to the earth, whereupon the sky rose high up, leaving the earth below. According to a myth of the Philippines, a

woman ordered the sky to rise high up. According to another Philippine myth, a woman drove the sky up by striking it with a pestle used
in pounding rice. According to a myth of the Rangi-Papa, the children
caught between the bosoms of the parents consulted with one another
as to how their parents might be separated. Tane, the god of the woods,
said: "We must separate our parents. Let us drive one away upwards
and make him a stranger to us, but keep the other and make her our
mother." And it was Tane who played the role of separator by holding
his mother down with his back and kicking his father up with his foot.

According to a myth of the Akwapim of Africa, in the primitive ages
a person who wanted fish had merely to poke at the sky with a stick
and fish poured down on earth like rain. But one day a woman who
was pounding Fufu in a mortar, finding the sky an obstacle to her
movements, said to the sky: "Rise a little higher. I cannot even move my
pestle freely." The sky obeyed and rose high up.

In Greek mythology, Uranos hid all his children in the bowels of
Gaia and would not even let them see the light of the sun. This made
Gaia so indignant that she schemed to drive the sky away. She made a
huge scythe and then revealed her scheme to her children. Kronos answered his mother and said: "I feel no respect for the sky, who is not
qualified to be our father, for he was the first to wrong us." Gaia handed
the scythe to Kronos and made him lie in ambush to attack his father.
When night came, Uranos descended to cover Gaia. Kronos came out
of his hiding-place and mutilated his father with the scythe.

In myths in which the universe is formed by the separation of the
sky and earth out of chaos, both the sky and earth take part in the
process of separation. In most other myths, however, the separation is
brought about by the sky alone, which moves up. There is no mention
of the earth ever moving downward. This, of course, is in accordance
with the primitive idea that the earth was immovable and the sky
alone able to move. In many myths having the idea of the sky hanging
low over the earth in the beginning, however, we can see not only a
theory of cosmology but a hidden objective, and this objective we see
clearly in the motif of the sky alone being removed in the separation of
the sky and earth. For in the case of the sky rising up while the earth
remains below, the separation is realized either by the sky moving up,
abandoning the earth, or by the earth driving the sky away. According
to the Paradise myths, the sky abandoned the earth and withdrew upwards because of the anger it felt at the sins committed by human
beings. But according to certain Paradise myths, the human beings
themselves, intending to banish the sky, committed sins on purpose.
We find examples of such hidden objectives in the myths of the Tai

and Lao. Myths chiefly concerning the banishment of heaven are widely spread among many other peoples. According to a myth of the Khasi, the reason why the navel-string binding the sky and earth together was cut was that the people wanted to escape the damage caused by the low-hanging sky and be free. According to such myths, the sky did not move away from the earth of its own accord but was driven away. Such an idea of the separation does not merely contain a cosmological meaning but contains an idea of hatred or enmity towards the sky.

B. Agents of Separation

1. *Woman; A Woman Who Pounds Rice*

In those myths in which the sky and earth are formed out of chaos or water there is no reference made to any separator. In most other myths, however, there are specific separators. One remarkable thing in regard to this point is the fact that the same separator appears repeatedly in most cases. And it is usually a woman who plays that role. Another remarkable feature is that it is not merely a woman but a woman who pounds rice or other grains who acts as the separator. In the myths of the Khasi, Santal, Miao, Garo, Tai, Wotjak, Dajak, Nias, Napu, Toradja, To Mori, Ceram, Rotti, Riungers, Philippines, Manobo, Bagobo, Paiwan (of Formosa), Motu, New Hebrides, Samoa, Tonga, Akwapim, Ashanti, Kassera, Margi, and Marocco, the separator of the sky from the earth is either a woman or a woman who pounds rice or other grains. In some other myths a woman is not the immediate separator but is indirectly the cause of the separation, as for instance in the Greek and Yoruba myths.

It is no easy matter to separate the sky from the earth. If it is to be brought about by human beings one would naturally expect the separator to be a strong man. In fact, in a few myths the separation is accomplished by a giant or a demi-god. But in most myths it is a woman who accomplishes the great task. This idea of a woman being the separator is incomprehensible if we consider it in itself. When we consider, however, the fact that, as I have explained above, it was the women who were chiefly annoyed by the inconveniences caused by the low-hanging sky, we see that it is only natural that they should assume the role of separator. Since the disadvantages caused by the union of the sky and earth have to do with the earth and with women, the separation of the sky from the earth should also have to do with women and the earth.

Viewed from this standpoint, it is significant that in most myths a pestle and a woman who pounds rice with it should be connected with the separation of the sky and earth. If the distance between the sky and earth were equal to the length of a pestle, it would be impossible for a man to shoot an arrow. Although bows and arrows must have been widely used among such peoples, reference is seldom made to them in their myths. We must therefore try to analyze such myths by taking into consideration the fact that they are connected first of all with women. Pounding grains was generally considered one of the important tasks of a woman. Hence that labor has a special significance in these myths.

2. *Sun, Fire, Wood*

Nearly every myth refers to the darkness that covered the whole world before the separation of the sky and earth. The myths belonging to the first category refer to this primitive darkness, and those belonging to the other categories refer to the fact that the darkness that covered the earth before the separation of the sky and earth hindered the growth of crops and caused other damage. Therefore everything on earth longed for the light of the sun.

In many myths it is a result of the separation of the sky and earth that the sun appeared on the earth. According to some other myths, however, the sky is separated from the earth by the sun or fire. According to the myths of Ceram, the Dajak, and the Navaho, living in New Mexico and Arizona, the sun separated the sky from the earth. Marduk, who appears in the Babylonian poem of creation as the separator of the sky from the earth, is a symbol of the rising sun. Vishnu, the god of the sun, is also the separator of the sky from the earth. Likewise, Aditya, who separated the sky from the earth, is the god of the sun, as well as being the sun itself.

Orungan in a myth of the Yoruba of Africa and Maui of Polynesia are also sun gods who separated the sky from the earth. Kronos in Greek mythology has the character of light. In the myths of the Adele, Ewe, and Mossi of Africa, smoke banished heaven from the earth. According to Yao, Wintun, and Rotti, fire separated the sky from the earth.

Myths in which the sun or fire acts as the separator of the sky from the earth, however, exist only here and there among peoples comparatively remote from the center of distribution of the myths under discussion. On the other hand, the motif of the sun or light appearing after the separation of the sky and earth is found in most myths. In other words, the sun and the light are not the cause of the separation of the sky and earth but rather the result.

According to a myth of the Rangi-Papa, Tane, the god of the woods, separated the sky from the earth. Tane symbolizes a huge tree which unites as well as separates the sky and earth. In many Indochinese myths, such as that of the Khasi, a huge tree, or a Liana, thus unites and separates the sky and earth. In some myths, because such trees cover the earth the light of the sun cannot reach the earth, and the growth of crops is hindered. According to myths of this type, the sky means the rain cloud that spreads over the trees. When those trees are cut down, and the sky and earth are separated, it means that the rain clouds have left the earth, and the light of the sun is able to reach the earth again.

These considerations will enable us to see why a huge tree is connected with the separation of the sky and earth. The tree is also the material for kindling fire. In this sense, Tane, the god of the woods, is also connected with fire itself. According to another version of the Rangi-Papa myth, when Rangi is driven away from Papa, Papa rubs together tools for kindling fire, at the same time uttering an incantation. Such an act was generally a part of the formalities of divorce. The tool which is used in making the fire is, of course, wood. In connection with this primitive method of kindling fire, the following may also be noted. The Hindus associate the method of kindling fire by using two pieces of wood with the union of man and woman; that is, the piece of wood held down is the woman, and the other piece of wood which is held against it symbolizes the man. These two pieces are rubbed together to make fire. The production of fire symbolizes the generation of offspring. Similar ideas concerning this method of kindling fire is found among various peoples.

III. CONCLUSION

A. Summary of the General Idea

There is, common to nearly all the myths I have spoken of, the idea that darkness filled the universe before the separation of the sky and earth, and that light appeared for the first time in the universe when the sky and earth had been separated. And with the coming of the light, everything on earth which had been hidden in the darkness appeared for the first time. This is precisely what we see every morning at the break of dawn. The breaking of dawn starts with the union of the sky and earth in the darkness of the night. This union is the union of father sky and mother earth, and all things that appear with the rising of the sun are born of these two. The myths in which father sky leaves mother earth in the morning show clearly traces of the custom of visit marriage (*Besuchsehe*). When morning comes, the man, like Uranos, must leave the woman. Therefore the myths have merely transferred what happens every morning to the first morning of the beginning of the universe—in other words, to the morning of the creation of all things.

B. Product of Matriarchal Cultural Spheres

A principal feature in so many myths, particularly those whose motif is the banishment of heaven, is agriculture, specifically agriculture whose chief product is rice. The central figure in these myths is a woman, and the principal animals are cows and pigs. In the social system one may see the prevalence of visit marriage (*Besuchsehe*), the earliest form of marriage in the matriarchal cultural sphere that developed out of the status that women had acquired economically in the course of social development. From such facts one may conclude that the myths we have been discussing are products of the matriarchal cultural sphere.

C. Cradle of the Idea

Though I cannot specifically identify the cradle of those myths, I have been able to show that elements of matriarchal cultural spheres are found in nearly every one of them as a basic component. The cradle of such spheres is to be found on the eastern slopes of the Himalayas, drained by the Ganges, the Bramaputras, the Irawadi, and other rivers. The district in which our myths are most densely distributed in their most typical forms approximately corresponds to the cradle of the matriarchal cultural spheres. These myths may most probably be connected with the southern Indo-Chinese Language Sphere, which has been influenced by the Austronesian Languages. In concluding, I should like to mention that the Japanese myth of Izanagi and Izanami also belongs, in its fundamental elements, to the same matriarchal cultural sphere.

The Role of Myth in Life

BRONISLAW MALINOWSKI

Anthropologists have contributed to the study of myth by studying it in situ. Through long months of observation and extended interaction with informants in the field, anthropologists began to discover that myths could not be properly understood without reference to the cultural context in which they exist. The shift in theoretical emphasis from that of armchair theorists such as James Frazer (1854– 1941) and Andrew Lang (1844–1912) to that of twentieth-century ethnographic fieldworkers like Franz Boas (1858–1942) and Bronislaw Malinowski (1884–1942) has greatly facilitated advances in the study of myth.

Franz Boas, in many ways the founder of the academic study of anthropology in the United States, had a lifelong interest in mythology. He felt that myth constituted a kind of autobiographical ethnography. Consequently, he made a point of not only collecting myths himself, particularly from the native peoples of the Pacific Northwest Coast, but also encouraging his many students at Columbia University to do likewise. Boas's monumental Tsimshian Mythology *(Washington, D.C., 1916) exemplifies his approach to myth. Boas regarded myths as "cultural reflectors," and he used myths as sources from which he extrapolated ethnographic details about kinship terms, house types, hunting techniques, etc. In* Tsimshian Mythology, *after a brief description of the Tsimshian people (pp. 43–57), we find the myths (pp 58– 392). Then follows a detailed "Description of the Tsimshian, Based on Their Mythology" (pp. 393–564) in which everything from household furniture and utensils to shamanism is treated through data culled from all the myths. Boas next provides a "Comparative Study of Tsimshian Mythology" (pp. 565–871) in which he gives parallels from the myth repertoires of most of the other Pacific Northwest Indian tribes. After a brief conclusion (pp. 872–81), there is an appendix containing Nootka and Bellabella myths (pp. 883–935). Appendix 2 (pp. 936–58) consists of an impressive "Summary of Comparisons." Appendices of place names and glossaries are followed by a final "Index to References" (pp. 980–1037) that not only lists the books consulted but gives the titles of each myth contained in these books with the pages on which they may be found.*

Needless to say, there have been few presentations of myths of the scope of Tsimshian Mythology. *A later work by Boas,* Kwakiutl Culture as Reflected in Mythology *(New York, 1935), similarly gleaned an ethnographic account of the Kwakiutl from mythological texts. The only innovation was that Boas compared the images of the Tsimshian and the Kwakiutl based on their respective myths. Boas's literal approach was eventually challenged by several of his students. Ruth Benedict,* Zuni Mythology, *2 vols. (New York, 1935); Melville J. Herskovits and Frances S.*

Reprinted from *Psyche* 24 (1926), 29–39, by permission of the Orthological Institute, Westminster, London SW1H 9LG.

Herskovits, Dahomean Narrative *(Evanston, Ill., 1958); and Melville Jacobs,* The Content and Style of an Oral Literature *(Chicago, 1959) realized that there was more to myth than a literal reflection of ethnographic facts. Some events like incest that occurred in myth texts did not correspond to everyday reality. But Boas at least drew attention to the value of recording full texts of myths, preferably in the native languages, and of trying to relate them to the culture as a whole.*

Bronislaw Malinowski was one of the pioneers of what is called functionalism in anthropology. He helped stimulate a change from the nineteenth-century interest in the origin of myth to a more practical concern with how myth functions in a living society. He felt strongly that anthropologists should live among the people they study and not visit them occasionally through periodic sorties from the sanctuary of missionary quarters or nearby resort hotels, if such were available. This technique he termed participant observation. Malinowski was especially critical of literary students of myth, claiming that they based their theories and methods on mutilated bits of reality. Like Boas, Malinowski formulated his approach to myth from myth texts he collected himself in the field.

Malinowski's major consideration of myth was presented as a lecture delivered in honor of Sir James Frazer at the University of Liverpool in November 1925. It was published in 1926 under the title Myth in Primitive Psychology *and was eventually reprinted in* Magic, Science and Religion and Other Essays *(Garden City, N.Y., 1954). The first portion of this important essay was published also in the journal* Psyche *in April 1926 and is reprinted in this volume. It does not include all of Malinowski's pronouncements on the nature of myth, e.g., "Myth, as a statement of primeval reality which still lives in present-day life and as a justification by precedent, supplies a retrospective pattern of moral values, sociological order, and magical belief. It is, therefore, neither a mere narrative, nor a form of science, nor a branch of art or history, nor an explanatory tale. It fulfills a function sui generis closely connected with the nature of tradition, and the continuity of culture, with the relation between age and youth, and with the human attitude towards the past. The function of myth, briefly, is to strengthen tradition and endow it with a greater value and prestige by tracing it back to a higher, better, more supernatural reality of initial events" (*Magic, Science and Religion, *p. 146). However, it does articulate most of what Malinowski meant when he termed myth a "sociological charter" for belief. The reader may also wish to consult the chapter devoted to mythology in Malinowski's classic ethnographic document,* Argonauts of the Western Pacific *(New York, 1961), pp. 290–333 (first published in 1922).*

For all Malinowski's contribution to the culturally relative study of myth in context, he shared with Boas a deep-seated antipathy to the idea that myth could be symbolic. Just as Boas favored a literal one-to-one "myth reflects culture" approach, Malinowski went so far as to say, "Studied alive, myth, as we shall see, is not symbolic but a direct expression of its subject matter." This literal, anti-symbolic bias has continued to prevail among many anthropologists interested in myth. Malinowski was sufficiently exercised against what he considered to be the excesses of the psychoanalytic approach as to engage in a spirited debate with the fervent Freudian disciple in England, Ernest Jones, on the question of whether or not the Oedipus Complex was universal. Malinowski claimed that matrilineal societies (such as the one he studied in the Trobriand Islands) did not have an Oedipus Complex, but rather had an avuncular complex instead. In such matrilineal societies, he argued, it is the mother's brother, not the father, who possesses the wealth to be inherited and who disciplines his nephews. In rebuttal Ernest Jones

and Géza Róheim pointed out that a boy's uncle did not constitute a sexual rival for
the affections of the boy's mother. That rival was the boy's father. In Malinowski's
own published field data, one can find myths in which a boy slays a threatening
monster who has a separate identity from the boy's maternal uncle. For a discussion of Oedipal myths collected by but not recognized by Malinowski, see John
Ingham, "Malinowski: Epistemology and Oedipus," Papers of the Kroeber Anthropological Society 29 (1963), 1–14, or for more detail on this issue, see Melford E.
Spiro, Oedipus in the Trobriands (Chicago, 1982). For a valuable overview of Malinowski's approach to myth as well as other genres of folklore, see William
Bascom, "Malinowski's Contributions to the Study of Folklore," Folklore 94 (1983),
163–172.

By the examination of a typical Melanesian culture and by a survey of
the opinions, traditions, and behaviour of these natives, I propose to
show how deeply the sacred tradition, the myth, enters into human
pursuits, and how strongly it controls their moral and social behaviour. In other words, the thesis of the present work is that an intimate
connection exists between the word, the mythos, the sacred tales of a
tribe on the one hand and their ritual acts, their moral deeds, their
social organization, and even their practical activities on the other.

In order to gain a background for our description of the Melanesian
facts, I shall briefly summarize the present state of the science of mythology. Even a superficial survey of the literature would reveal that
there is no monotony to complain of as regards the variety of opinions
or the acrimony of polemics. To take only the recent up-to-date theories
advanced in explanation of the nature of myth, legend, and fairy-tale,
we should have to head the list, at least as regards output and self-
assertion, by the so-called school of Nature-mythology which flour-
ishes mainly in Germany. The writers of this school maintain that
primitive man is highly interested in natural phenomena, and that his
interest is predominantly of a theoretical, contemplative, and poetical
character. In trying to express and interpret the phases of the moon, or
the regular and yet changing path of the sun across the skies, primitive
man constructs symbolic personified rhapsodies. To writers of this
school every myth possesses as its kernel or ultimate reality some
natural phenomenon or other, elaborately woven into a tale to an extent which sometimes almost masks and obliterates it. There is not
much agreement among these students as to what type of natural phenomenon lies at the bottom of most mythological productions. There
are extreme lunar mythologists so completely moonstruck with their
idea that they will not admit that any other phenomenon could lend
itself to a savage rhapsodic interpretation except that of earth's noctur-

nal satellite. The Society for the Comparative Study of Myth founded in Berlin in 1906, and counting among its supporters such famous scholars as Ehrenreich, Siecke, Winckler, and many others, carried on their business under the sign of the moon. Others, like Frobenius for instance, regard the sun as the only subject around which primitive man has spun his symbolic tales. Then there is the school of meteorological interpreters who regard wind, weather, the colours of the skies as the essence of myth. To this belonged such well-known writers of the older generation as Max Müller and Kuhn. Some of these departmental mythologists fight fiercely for their heavenly body or principle, others have a more catholic taste and prepare to agree that primeval man has made his mythological brew from all the heavenly bodies taken together.

I have tried to state fairly and plausibly this naturalistic interpretation of myths, but as a matter of fact this theory seems to me to be one of the most extravagant views ever advanced by an anthropologist or humanist—and that means a great deal. It has received an absolutely destructive criticism from the great psychologist Wundt, and appears absolutely untenable in the light of any of Sir James Frazer's writings. From my own study of living myths among savages I should say that primitive man has to a very limited extent the purely artistic or scientific interest in nature; there is but little room for symbolism in his ideas and tales; and myth, in fact, is not an idle rhapsody, not an aimless outpouring of vain imaginings, but a hard-working, extremely important cultural force. Besides ignoring the cultural function of myth, this theory imputes to primitive man a number of imaginary interests and it confuses several clearly distinguishable types of story, the fairy tale, the legend, the saga, and the sacred tale or myth.

In strong contrast to this theory which makes myth naturalistic, symbolic, and imaginary, stands the theory which regards a sacred tale as a true historical record of the past. This view, recently supported by the so-called Historical School in Germany and America, and represented in England by Dr. Rivers, covers but part of the truth. There is no denying that history as well as natural environment must have left a profound imprint on all cultural achievements, hence also on myths. But to take all mythology as mere chronicle is as incorrect as to regard it as the primitive naturalist's musings. It also endows primitive man with a sort of scientific impulse and desire for knowledge. Although the savage has something of the antiquarian as well as of the naturalist in his composition, he is, above all, actively engaged in a number of practical pursuits, and has to struggle with various difficulties; all his interests are tuned up to this general pragmatic outlook.

Mythology, the sacred lore of the tribe, is, as we shall see, a powerful means of assisting primitive man, of allowing him to make the two ends of his cultural patrimony meet. We shall see, moreover, that the immense services to primitive culture performed by myth are done in connection with religious ritual, moral influence, and sociological principle. Now religion and morals draw only to a very limited extent upon an interest in science or in past history, and myth is thus based upon an entirely different mental attitude.

The close connection between religion and myth which has been overlooked by many students has been recognized by others. Psychologists like Wundt, sociologists like Durkheim, Hubert, and Mauss, anthropologists like Crawley, classical scholars like Miss Jane Harrison have all understood the intimate association between myth and ritual, between sacred tradition and the norms of social structure. All of these writers have been to a greater or lesser extent influenced by the work of Sir James Frazer. In spite of the fact that the great British anthropologist as well as most of his followers have a clear vision of the sociological and ritual importance of myth, the facts which I shall present will allow us to clarify and formulate more precisely the main principles of a sociological theory of myth.

I might present an even more extensive survey of the opinions, divisions, and controversies of learned mythologists. The science of mythology has been the meeting-point of various scholarships: the classical humanist must decide for himself whether Zeus is the moon, or the sun, or a strictly historical personality; and whether his ox-eyed spouse is the morning star, or a cow, or a personification of the wind— the loquacity of wives being proverbial. Then all these questions have to be re-discussed upon the stage of mythology by the various tribes of archaeologists, Chaldean and Egyptian, Indian and Chinese, Peruvian and Mayan. The historian and the sociologist, the student of literature, the grammarian, the Germanist and the Romanist, the Celtic scholar and the Slavist discuss, each little crowd among themselves. Nor is mythology quite safe from logicians and psychologists, from the metaphysician and the epistemologist—to say nothing of such visitors as the theosophist, the modern astrologist, and the Christian Scientist. Finally we have the psychoanalyst who has come at last to teach us that the myth is a day-dream of the race and that we can only explain it by turning our back upon nature, history, and culture, and diving deep into the dark pools of the sub-conscious, where at the bottom there lie the usual paraphernalia and symbols of psychoanalytic exegesis. So that when at last the poor anthropologist and student of folk lore come to the feast, there are hardly any crumbs left for them!

If I have conveyed an impression of chaos and confusion, if I have inspired a sinking feeling towards the incredible mythological controversy with all the dust and din which it raises, I have achieved exactly what I wanted. For I shall invite my readers to step outside the closed study of the theorist into the open air of the anthropological field, and to follow me in my mental flight back to the years which I spent among a Melanesian tribe of New Guinea. There, paddling on the lagoon, watching the natives under the blazing sun at their garden-work, following them through the patches of jungle, and on the winding beaches and reefs, we shall learn about their life. And again, observing their ceremonies in the cool of the afternoon or in the shadows of the evening, sharing their meals round their fires, we shall be able to listen to their stories.

For the anthropologist—one and only among the many participants in the mythological contest—has the unique advantage of being able to step back behind the savage whenever he feels that his theories become involved and the flow of his argumentative eloquence runs dry. The anthropologist is not bound to the scanty remnants of culture, broken tablets, tarnished texts, or fragmentary inscriptions. He need not fill out immense gaps with voluminous but conjectural comments. The anthropologist has the myth-maker at his elbow. Not only can he take down as full a text as exists with all its variations, and control it over and over; he has also a host of authentic commentators to draw upon; still more he has the fulness of life itself from which the myth has been born. And as we shall see, in this live context there is as much to be learned about the myth as in the narrative itself.

Myth as it exists in a savage community, that is in its living primitive form, is not merely a story told but a reality lived. It is not of the nature of fiction, such as we read to-day in a novel, but it is a living reality, believed to have once happened in primeval times, and continuing ever since to influence the world and human destinies. This myth is to the savage what, to a fully believing Christian, is the Biblical story of Creation, of the Fall, of the Redemption by Christ's sacrifice on the Cross. As our sacred story lives in our ritual, in our morality, as it governs our faith and controls our conduct, even so does his myth for the savage.

The limitation of the study of myth to the mere examination of texts has been fatal to a proper understanding of its nature. The forms of myth which come to us from classical antiquity and from the ancient sacred books of the East and other similar sources have come down to us without the context of living faith, without the possibility of obtaining comments from true believers, without the concomitant knowledge of their social organization, their practised morals, and their popular custom, at least without the full information which the modern fieldworker can easily obtain. Moreover, there is no doubt that in their present literary form these tales have suffered a very considerable transformation at the hands of scribes, commentators, learned priests, and theologians. It is necessary to go back to primitive mythology in order to learn the secret of its life in the study of a myth which is still alive—before, mummified in priestly wisdom, it has been enshrined in the indestructible but lifeless repository of dead religions.

Studied alive, myth, as we shall see, is not symbolic but a direct expression of its subject-matter; it is not an explanation in satisfaction of a scientific interest, but a narrative resurrection of a primeval reality, told in satisfaction of deep religious wants, moral cravings, social submissions, assertions, even practical requirements. Myth fulfils in primitive culture an indispensable function: it expresses, enhances, and codifies belief; it safeguards and enforces morality; it vouches for the efficiency of ritual and contains practical rules for the guidance of man. Myth is thus a vital ingredient of human civilization; it is not an idle tale but a hard-worked active force; it is not an intellectual explanation or an artistic imagery, but a pragmatic charter of primitive faith and moral wisdom.

I shall try to prove all these contentions; and to make our analysis conclusive it will be necessary to give an account not merely of myth, but also of fairy tale, legend, and historical record.

Let us then float over in spirit to the shores of a Trobriand lagoon, and penetrate into the life of the natives—see them at work, see them at play, and listen to their stories.[1] Late in November the wet weather is setting in. There is little to do in the gardens, the fishing season is not in full swing as yet, overseas sailing looms ahead in the future, while the festive mood still lingers after the harvest dancing and feasting. Sociability is in the air, time lies on their hands, while bad weather keeps them often at home. Could we but step through the twilight of the approaching evening into one of their villages and sit at the fireside,

1. The Trobriand Islands are a coral archipelago lying to the northeast of New Guinea. The natives belong to the Papuo-Melanesian race, and in their physical appearance, mental equipment, and social organization they show a combination of the Oceanic characteristics mixed with some features of the more backward Papuan culture from the mainland of New Guinea.

For a full account of the Northern Massim, of which the Trobrianders form a section, compare the classical treatise of Professor C. G. Seligman, *Melanesians of British New Guinea* (Cambridge, 1910). This book shows also the relation of the Trobrianders to the other races and cultures on and around New Guinea. A short account will also be found in *Argonauts of the Western Pacific*, by the present author (London, 1922).

where the flickering light draws more and more people as the evening falls and the conversation brightens, sooner or later a man would be asked to tell a story, for this is the season of *fairy tales*. If he is a good reciter, he will soon provoke laughter, rejoinders, and interruptions, and his tale will develop into a regular performance.

At this time of the year folk-tales of a special type called *kukwanebu* are habitually recited in the villages. There is a vague belief, not very seriously taken, that their recital has a beneficial influence on the new crops recently planted in the gardens. In order to produce this effect, a short ditty in which an allusion is made to some very fertile wild plants, the *kasiyena*, must always be recited at the end.

Every story is "owned" by a member of the community. Each story, though known by many, may be recited only by the "owner," who may, however, present it to someone else by teaching that person and authorizing him to retell it. But not all the "owners" know how to thrill and to raise a hearty laugh, which is one of the main ends of such stories. A good raconteur has to change his voice in the dialogue, chant the ditties with due temperament, gesticulate, and in general play to the gallery. Some of these tales are certainly "smoking-room" stories, of others I will give one or two examples.

Thus there is the maiden in distress and the heroic rescue. Two women go out in search of birds' eggs. One discovers a nest under a tree, the other warns her, "These are eggs of a snake, don't touch them." "Oh, no! They are eggs of a bird," she replies and carries them away. The mother snake comes back and finding the nest empty starts in search of the eggs. She enters the nearest village and sings a ditty,

> I wend my way as I wriggle along,
> The eggs of a bird it is licit to eat;
> The eggs of a friend are forbidden to touch.

This journey lasts long, for the snake is traced from one village to the other and everywhere has to sing her ditty. Finally, entering the village of the two women, she sees the culprit roasting the eggs, coils around her, and enters her body. The victim is laid down helpless and ailing. But the hero is nigh; a man from a neighbouring village dreams of the dramatic situation, arrives on the spot, pulls out the snake, cuts it to pieces, and marries both women, thus carrying off a double prize for his prowess.

In another story we learn of a happy family, a father and two daughters, who sail from their home in the northern coral archipelagoes and run to the south-west till they come to the wild steep slopes of the rock island Gumasila. The father lies down on a platform and falls asleep. An ogre comes out of the jungle, eats the father, captures and ravishes one of the daughters while the other succeeds in escaping. The sister from the woods supplies the captive one with a piece of lawyer-cane, and when the ogre lies down and falls asleep they cut him in half and escape.

A woman lives in the village of Okopukopu at the head of a creek with her five children. A monstrously big stingaree paddles up the creek, flops across the village, enters the hut, and to the tune of a ditty cuts off the woman's finger. One son tries to kill the monster and fails. Every day the same performance is repeated till on the fifth day the youngest son succeeds in killing the giant fish.

A louse and a butterfly embark on a bit of aviation, the louse as a passenger, the butterfly as aeroplane and pilot. In the middle of the performance while flying over-seas just between the beach of Wawela and the island of Kitava, the louse emits a loud shriek, the butterfly is shaken, and the louse falls off and is drowned.

A man whose mother-in-law is a cannibal is sufficiently careless to go away and leave her in charge of his three children. Naturally she tries to eat them; they escape in time, however, climb a palm, and keep her (through a somewhat lengthy story) at bay, until the father arrives and kills her. There is another story about a visit to the Sun, another about an ogre devastating gardens, another about a woman who was so greedy that she stole all food at funeral distributions, and many similar ones.

In this place, however, we are not so much concentrating our attention on the text of narratives, as on their sociological reference. The text, of course, is extremely important, but without the context it remains lifeless. As we have seen, the interest of the story is vastly enhanced and it is given its proper character by the manner in which it is told. The whole nature of the performance, the voice and the mimicry, the stimulus and the response of the audience mean as much to the natives as the text; and the sociologist should take his cue from the native. The performance again has to be placed in its proper time-setting: the hour of the day, and the season with the background of the sprouting gardens awaiting future work and slightly influenced by the magic of the fairy tales. We must also bear in mind the sociological context of private ownership, the sociable function and the cultural rôle of amusing fiction. All these elements are equally relevant; all must be studied as well as the text. The stories live in native life and not on paper, and when a scholar jots them down without being able to evoke the atmosphere in which they flourish he has given us but a mutilated bit of reality.

I pass now to another class of stories. These have no special season, there is no stereotyped way of telling them, and the recital has not the character of a performance, nor has it any magical effect. And yet these tales are more important than the foregoing class; for they are believed to be true and the information which they contain is both more valuable and more relevant than that of the *kukwanebu*. When a party goes on a distant visit or sails on an expedition, the younger members, keenly interested in the landscape, in new communities, in new people, and perhaps even new customs, will express their wonder and make enquiries. The older and more experienced will supply them with information and comment, and this always takes the form of a concrete narrative. An old man will perhaps tell his own experiences about fights and expeditions, about famous magic and extraordinary economic achievements. With this he may mix the reminiscences of his father, hearsay tales and legends, which have passed through many generations. Thus memories of great droughts and devastating famines are conserved for many years, together with the descriptions of the hardships, struggles and crimes of the exasperated population.

A number of stories about sailors driven out of their course and landing among cannibals and hostile tribes are remembered, some of them set to song, others formed into historic legends. A famous subject for song and story is the charm, skill, and performance of famous dancers. There are tales about distant volcanic islands; about hot springs in which once a party of unwary bathers were boiled to death; about mysterious countries inhabited by entirely different men or women; about strange adventures which have happened to sailors in distant seas; monstrous fish and octopi, jumping rocks and disguised sorcerers. Stories again are told, some recent, some ancient, about seers and visitors to the land of the dead, enumerating their most famous and significant exploits. There are also stories associated with natural phenomena; a petrified canoe, a man changed into a rock, and a red patch on the coral rock left by a party who ate too much betel nut.

We have here a variety of tales which might be subdivided into *historical accounts* directly witnessed by the narrator, or at least vouched for by someone within living memory; *legends*, in which the continuity of testimony is broken, but which fall within the range of things ordinarily experienced by the tribesmen; and *hearsay tales* about distant countries and ancient happenings of a time which falls outside the range of present-day culture. To the natives, however, all these classes imperceptibly shade into each other; they are designated by the same name, *libwogwo*; they are all regarded as true; they are not recited as a performance, nor told for amusement at a special season. Their subject-matter also shows a substantial unity. They all refer to subjects intensely stimulating to the natives; they all are connected with activities such as economic pursuits, warfare, adventure, success in dancing and in ceremonial exchange. Moreover, since they record singularly great achievements in all such pursuits they redound to the credit of some individual and his descendants or of a whole community; and hence they are kept alive by the ambition of those whose ancestry they glorify. The stories told in explanation of peculiarities of features of the landscape frequently have a sociological context, that is they enumerate whose clan or family performed the deed. When this is not the case, they are isolated fragmentary comments upon some natural feature, clinging to it as an obvious survival.

In all this it is once more clear that we can neither fully grasp the meaning of the text, nor the sociological nature of the story, nor the natives' attitude towards it and interest in it, if we study the narrative on paper. These tales live in the memory of man, in the way in which they are told, and even more in the complex interest which keeps them alive, which makes the narrator recite with pride or regret, which makes the listener follow eagerly, wistfully, with hopes and ambitions roused. Thus the essence of a *legend* even more than that of a *fairy tale* is not to be found in a mere perusal of the story, but in the combined study of the narrative and its context in the social and cultural life of the natives.

But it is only when we pass to the third and most important class of tales, the *sacred tales* or *myths*, and contrast them with the legends, that the nature of all three classes comes into relief. This third class is called by the natives *liliu*, and I want to emphasize that I am reproducing prima facie the natives' own classification and nomenclature, and limiting myself to a few comments on its accuracy. The third class of stories stands very much apart from the other two. If the first are told for amusement, the second to make a serious statement and satisfy social ambition, the third are regarded, not merely as true, but as venerable and sacred, and they play a highly important cultural part. The *folk-tale* as we know is a seasonal performance and an act of sociability. The *legend*, provoked by contact with unusual reality, opens up past historical vistas. The *myth* comes into play when rite, ceremony, or a social or moral rule demands justification, warrant of antiquity, reality, and sanctity. Take for instance the annual feast of the return of the dead. Elaborate arrangements are made for it, especially an enormous display of food. When this feast approaches, tales are told of how death began to chastise man, and how the power of eternal rejuvenation was lost. It is told why the spirits have to leave the village and do not remain at the fireside, finally why they return once in a year. Again at certain seasons in preparation for an overseas expedition, canoes are overhauled and new ones built to the accompaniment of a special magic. In this there are mythical allusions in the spells, and even the sacred acts contain elements which are only comprehensible when the story of the flying canoe, its ritual and its magic are told. In connection with ceremonial trading, the rules, the magic, even the geographical routes are associated with corresponding mythology. There is no important magic, no ceremony, no ritual without belief; and the belief is spun out into accounts of concrete precedent. The union is very intimate, for myth is not only looked upon as a commentary of additional information, but it is a warrant, a charter, and often even a practical guide to the activities with which it is connected. On the other hand the rituals, ceremonies, customs, and social organizations contain at times direct references to myth and they are regarded as the results of mythical event. The cultural fact is a monument in which the myth is embodied; while the myth is believed to be the real cause which has brought about the moral rule, the social grouping, the rite, or the custom. Thus these stories form an integral part of culture. Their existence and influence not merely transcend the act of telling the narrative, not only do they draw their substance from life and its interests—they govern and control many cultural features, they form the dogmatic backbone of primitive civilization.

This is perhaps the most important point of the thesis which I am urging: I maintain that there exists a special class of stories, regarded as sacred, embodied in ritual, morals, and social organization, and which form an integral and active part of primitive culture. These stories live not by idle interest, not as fictitious, or even as true narratives; but are to the natives a statement of a primeval, greater, and more relevant reality, by which the present life, fates, and activities of mankind are determined, the knowledge of which supplies man with the motive for ritual and moral actions, as well as with indications as to how to perform them.

In order to make the point at issue quite clear, let us once more compare our conclusions with the current views of modern anthropology, not in order idly to criticize other opinions, but so that we may link our results to the present state of knowledge, give due acknowledgment for what we have received, and state where we have to differ clearly and precisely.

It will be best to quote a condensed and authoritative statement, and I shall choose for this purpose the definition and analysis given in

Notes and Queries on Anthropology, by the late Miss C. S. Burne and Professor J. L. Myres. Under the heading "Stories, Sayings, and Songs," we are informed that "this section includes many *intellectual* efforts of peoples . . ." which "represent the earliest attempts to exercise reason, imagination, and memory." With some apprehension we ask where is left the emotion, the interest, and ambition, the social rôle of all the stories, and the deep connection with cultural values of the more serious ones? After a brief classification of stories in the usual manner we read about the sacred tales: "*Myths* are stories which, however marvellous and improbable to us, are nevertheless related in all good faith, because they are intended, or believed by the teller, to explain by means of something concrete and intelligible an abstract idea or such vague and difficult conceptions as Creation, Death, distinctions of race or animal species, the different occupations of men and women; the origins of rites and customs, or striking natural objects or prehistoric monuments; the meaning of the names of persons or places. Such stories are sometimes described as *aetiological*, because their purpose is to explain why something exists or happens."[2]

Here we have in a nutshell all that modern science at its best has to say upon the subject. Would our Melanesians agree, however, with this opinion? Certainly not. They do not want to "explain," to make "intelligible" anything which happens in their myths—above all not an abstract idea. Of that there can be found to my knowledge no instance either in Melanesia or in any other savage community. The few abstract ideas which the natives possess carry their concrete commentary in the very word which expresses them. When being is described by verbs to lie, to sit, to stand, when cause and effect are expressed by words signifying foundation and the past standing upon it, when various concrete nouns tend towards the meaning of space, the word and the relation to concrete reality make the abstract idea sufficiently "intelligible." Nor would a Trobriander or any other native agree with the view that "Creation, Death, distinctions of race or animal species, the different occupations of men and women" are "vague and difficult conceptions." Nothing is more familiar to the native than the different occupations of the male and female sex; there is nothing to be *explained* about it. But though familiar, such differences are at times irksome, unpleasant, or at least limiting, and there is the need to justify them, to vouch for their antiquity and reality, in short to buttress their validity. Death, alas, is not vague, or abstract, or difficult to grasp for any human being. It is only too hauntingly real, too concrete, too easy to compre-

---

2. Quoted from *Notes and Queries on Anthropology*, pp. 210 and 211.

hend for anyone who has an experience affecting his near relatives or a personal foreboding. If it were vague or unreal, man would have no desire so much as to mention it; but the idea of death is fraught with horror, with a desire to remove its threat, with the vague hope that it may be not explained, but rather explained away, made unreal, and actually denied. Myth, warranting the belief in immortality, in eternal youth, in a life beyond the grave, is not an intellectual reaction upon a puzzle, but an explicit act of faith born from the innermost instinctive and emotional reaction to the most formidable and haunting idea. Nor are the stories about "the origins of rites and customs" told in mere explanation of them. They never explain in any sense of the word; they always state a precedent which constitutes an ideal and a warrant for its continuance, and sometimes practical directions for the procedure.

We have, therefore, to disagree on every point with this excellent though concise statement of present-day mythological opinion. This definition would create an imaginary, nonexistent class of narrative, the aetiological myth; corresponding to a nonexistent desire to explain; leading a futile existence as an "intellectual effort"; and remaining outside native culture and social organization with their pragmatic interests. The whole treatment appears to us faulty, because myths are treated as mere stories; because they are regarded as a primitive intellectual arm-chair occupation; because they are torn out of their life-context; studied from what they look like on paper, and not from what they do in life. Thus it is impossible either to see clearly the nature of myth or to reach a satisfactory classification of folk-tales. In fact we would also have to disagree with the definition of legend and of fairy tale given subsequently by the writers in *Notes and Queries on Anthroplogy.*

But above all, this point of view would be fatal to efficient field-work, for it would make the observer satisfied with the mere writing down of narratives. The intellectual nature of a story is exhausted with its text, but the functional, cultural, and pragmatic aspect of any native tale is manifested as much in its enactment, embodiment, and contextual relations as in the text. It is easier to write down the story than to observe the diffuse, complex ways in which it enters into life, or to study its function by the observation of the vast social and cultural realities into which it enters. And this is the reason why we have so many texts and why we know so little about the very nature of myth.

The Plasticity of Myth:
Cases from Tikopia

RAYMOND FIRTH

One of the critical ways in which myth (like all folklore) differs radically from writ-
ten or printed literature concerns variation. There may be as many different ver-
sions of a particular myth as there are tellers of that myth. Even one individual
teller may alter details in his account of a myth over a period of years or a lifetime.
In contrast, the text of a published poem, short story, or novel does not vary at all,
thanks to the fixity of print. Different generations of readers may well interpret a
piece of fiction differently according to their own esthetic bias or worldview, but
the text is stable.

Most folklorists are content simply to record numerous versions of a myth in
the field, or to comment on specific trait variation in the process of undertaking
a comparative study of a narrative. What is rare is any attempt to correlate varia-
tions in the versions of a myth with individual narrators or with other cultural
factors. In the following essay, social anthropologist Raymond Firth, who was in
Malinowski's seminar in the fall of 1924 and who is very much in the Malinowskian
functionalist tradition, demonstrates the significance of myth variation. Even though
the second of his examples would appear to be a legend rather than a myth, the
insightful analysis of the narrative does illustrate the importance of collecting and
analyzing variants in the field.

For more information about the people and culture of Tikopia where Firth car-
ried out his fieldwork, see his ethnography, We, The Tikopia: Kinship in Primitive
Polynesia *(Boston, 1965), first published in 1936.*

The general anthropological view is that myths are an integral part of
religion.[1] They may be very brief, like the Trobriand clan origin myths,
or very elaborate, like the origin tales of Polynesia. They may enunciate
a creed or simply illustrate it. They may outline the character of divinity or may describe only a few of the divine acts. They may justify

Reprinted from *Ethnologica*, n.f. 2 (1960), pp. 181–88, by permission of the author
and E. J. Brill, Leiden.

1. In the preparation of this paper I have been much helped by the facilities afforded
me as a Fellow, in 1959, of the Center for Advanced Study in the Behavioral Sciences at
Stanford. I am indebted for comment and suggestion especially to Professors Fred
Eggan, Meyer Fortes, Kaspar Naegele, and Melford E. Spiro.

and interpret ritual actions, and they may even purport to provide the model for rites. But whatever be the specific forms and functions of myths, in general they are reckoned to embody a system of beliefs common to the society, and to express and support a set of common basic social ideas and values. So much of the modern treatment of myth goes back to the analyses of Durkheim that we may once again adapt his statements on the Warramunga rites and say that the mythology of a group perpetuates traditions which express the way in which society represents man and the world; the myths form a moral system and a cosmology as well as a history.[2]

But while this may be so on the whole, there are some pertinent questions still to answer. Two of these concern the possibility of variation.

The first question has to do with the measure of agreement on the form of a myth that is expected among the members of a group. It is usually assumed for convenience that a "tribe" or a "people" have a basic set of myths, in recognisable specific form or normal version, granted that the anthropologist may have recorded a number of sub-specific forms or idiosyncratic versions of any myth. This assumption may be conceded, since the criteria for recognition of a normal or standard version have usually been carefully considered. But the problems raised by the existence of these sub-specific forms, these idiosyncratic versions, are not often examined. It is ordinarily assumed, however, nowadays, that discrepant versions of what in general can be regarded as the same myth are not simply a result of picturesque invention, but correspond in some way to the differences of interest of the narrators. When myths of origin, for example, are in conflict, the anthropologist understands that what really is at stake is a common principle in competitive terms—that the version of each dissenting party is in effect a claim (conscious or unconscious) by a group to some kind of right or status—as to land, or to priority of title—which is acknowledged to be of basic value to the society as a whole. What each version of the myth does is to assert, apart from particular claims, the general significance of local origin, priority of arrival, control of *sacra*, or whatever may be the point at issue. The problem of "closeness of fit" between versions of myth and group structure of the society is not usually a very refractory one. With individual versions within a single group or sub-group, the general principle is the same, but it is harder to identify the particular elements to which mythic variation should be related. Individual claims, aggressions or resent-

2. E. Durkheim, *The Elementary Forms of the Religious Life*, trans. J. W. Swain (1915), p. 375.

ments along structural lines can occasionally be documented.[3] But at times, as we should expect, aesthetic interest in systematization or in fantasy elaboration seem to be responsible for variation, apart from special domestic or other personal factors.

The second question has to do with the degree of fixity that is expected in a myth. Here the position is less clear. If myths represent the traditional values of the society, including the moral norms, one would expect them to maintain a firm shape, to show very little variation from one generation to another. Taking for granted that over the course of time they have been altered and garbled from their original versions, and even adopting the more extreme standpoint that they cannot be interpreted as an historical source at all, but only as sociological validation of an existing structure, the projection of the present back into the past, there has still been a reluctance to treat them as possibly recent or changing items. Not, I think, that any modern social anthropologist would deny this possibility; merely that perhaps for lack of evidence, myths have been handled with a kind of timeless attitude, or have been credited with a quality of antiquity. One of the few who have recognised the problem and published some details bearing on it is Gregory Bateson,[4] who showed how in a village group of Bali a syncretist myth linking gods as siblings was introduced to provide a ritual basis for a socio-political unity. Evidence on this plasticity of myth is not easy to get, so I present here two Tikopia cases.

The first shows how a Tikopia myth dealing with some of the major gods of the pantheon, and purporting to describe the origination of one of the central sacred objects of the society, a temple, could not have been formulated before about the beginning of the nineteenth century, whereas the period of Tikopia society to which it refers can most plausibly be put at not later than the beginning of the eighteenth century.

The myth concerns the building of Rarofiroki temple, a small thatch hut standing at the north side of the area known as Marae, the religious heart of pagan Tikopia.[5]

I was given the myth in 1929, on two occasions. The first was by my friend Pae Sao, a ritual elder of high status in Tafua clan, who was recognized as having a great deal of knowledge about Tikopia religious

3. I have given an example in my *History and Traditions in Tikopia*, shortly to be published. This work also gives a general classification of Tikopia traditional material of a "mythical" character, and a more extended analysis of its sociological implications.

4. G. Bateson, "An Old Temple and a New Myth," *Djawa* 17 (1937).

5. A plan of Marae, and an account of the rites which used to take place there, are given in my *Work of the Gods in Tikopia*, London School of Economics Monographs on Social Anthropology nos. 1 and 2 (London, 1940).

matters. From discussions about the Work of the Gods, and the nature of Rarofiroki temple, it emerged that the house was conceived to exist on two planes, the material and the spiritual. The actual temple in Marae had its prototype in the Heavens, where it had been built by the gods, a set of siblings known as the Brethren (Fanau). Pae Sao proceeded to tell me the tale about the building of the temple in the Heavens.

"It was built by the Brethren. As it was being built, it was lashed with coconut sinnet cord. But the Great God (senior of the siblings), standing up above, called down to his brothers to pass him up iron (nails). But they would not, they objected, and handed him up only coconut sinnet, and coconut husk and cord. They went on building the house, and when it was finished the Great God came down. He took the iron and went off to the lands of the white men, leaving behind the lands of the black men, in his rear, and he brought the iron to the lands of white men. Then he said to his brothers, 'You objected to giving me iron; I asked you to give me iron to secure the house. So you can stay and secure your houses with coconut sinnet and husk.' Then he went to arrange the valuables in the lands of the white men, while this land had to make do with adzes of any old thing."

As the tale proceeded it soon became clear that what I was listening to was not so much an account of the construction of this sacred temple in the spiritual realm, as an explanation of why white men and not Tikopia came to be endowed with iron tools. This was in fact an aetiological myth of common type, with the usual moral overtones. There was also, as was common with Tikopia stories of this comparative kind, a wry self-deprecatory scorn on the part of the narrator for the Tikopia technology which had to use only relatively soft materials and also scorn for the stupid Tikopia gods who were too obstinate to realise a good thing when they saw it. (The phrase I have rendered as "any old thing" is more literally translated as "foolish things," but the former expression is more idiomatic in English.) The question of how the Brethren happened to have iron available in the first place was of course not answered; it was just there.

At first I wondered if the narrator had not strayed from his theme, and if the text really corresponded to the announced title. But I realised from later talk with him and others that this was all there was, and that making allowance for variants, this was the matter of the spiritual temple-building. Some time later I got another version, even more exotic. This was by Pa Rangifakaino, of the lineage of Tavi, of Kafika clan. According to this the temple of the Brethren was built in England, in a land of the white man. The senior brother mounted the roof and called down *in English* for nails with which to make the roof fast. But his brothers did not hear him aright, in this foreign tongue, and kept handing him up various kind of lashing materials, which he rejected one after another. Finally they handed him up coconut sinnet cord. He drove them away in disgust, and they came to Tikopia in a canoe. Hence iron stayed with white men, and coconut sinnet cord came to Tikopia. To crown the whole story, their senior brother was "God"!

This version of the myth, though in my pursuit of Tikopia pagan religion at the time I considered it somewhat puerile, is in some ways more interesting than the other. Pa Rangifakaino was a pagan, as of course was Pae Sao, and both appeared to believe quite sincerely in the truth of their stories (in which, incidentally, neither had any vested structural interest). But the second version was in a way more "logical" than the first. It accounted for the presence of iron in the situation by locating the building site where iron was known to occur—in England or at least some white man's country. And it attributed the knowledge of the properties of iron, and the wisdom to try and get it used, not to a purely Tikopia god, but to a syncretistic figure—the God of the white men, who was at the same time the senior of the Tikopia Brethren.

Both versions of the myth illustrated the almost obsessional interest which—for good reason—the Tikopia had even in 1929, for iron. But they also indicate that some part at least of this myth must be a relatively recent construct. The actual temple Rarofiroki, as a material building, was stated by the Tikopia to have been erected on the spiritual model in expiation after the expulsion of a section of the population known as Nga Ravenga, at a period which can be put by genealogical evidence as possibly about 1700 A.D.[6] Almost certainly, knowledge of iron did not come to the Tikopia until about a century later. Whatever be one's views about these dates, one or other account is out of place on the time scale—either the real temple was first built much later, when iron was known; or the story of the abstract spiritual temple having an alternative of *iron* fastenings was an afterthought. My guess is that the latter happened. But in either case the plasticity of myth, its adaptive quality, is clear. There is one further point. Both of these stories can be legitimately classed as myth. They dealt with basic figures in the pantheon, they referred to one of the most important Tikopia religious *sacra*, they were told in conditions of some secrecy, they were believed to be true, and they were intended to explain a fact of very great concern to all Tikopia, namely, their lack of iron. How or by whom these versions of the myth were invented I do not know, but

6. Firth, *Work of the Gods*, p. 211.

as to when—it cannot have been much more than a century before I
made the record.

My second case concerns the genesis of myth, or rather myth-
making in operation. It arises in connection with stories about a highly
sacred stone, which was a symbol of the Octopus God, and which was
deemed to be responsible under proper care, for fertility of the crops
and especially for good fortune in fishing. This stone lay in a cycas-leaf
lined bed in the orchard of Takarito, in the district of Faea, and was
known accordingly as Te Atua i Takarito—the Deity of that place. In
tradition, the site had been that of a long-vanished temple, and it was
part of the function of the Ariki Kafika every year to complete a season's rites of the Work of the Gods by a washing of the sacred stone, a
re-lining of its bed, and offerings and libations to the gods and ancestral spirits associated with the temple. In 1929 the rites of Takarito
were in full operation.[7] When I returned to Tikopia in 1952 they had
been abandoned. This had been done at the instance of the Ariki Kafika, probably about 1935. The events concerned with this abandonment illustrate the complexity of Tikopia religious thinking, and also
some of the processes involved in the creation of myth.

With the annual ritual of Takarito was associated a ceremonial levy,
in which members of the ritual party silently but publicly entered
every orchard in the vicinity in turn and took a small amount of produce for offerings and a meal at the temple site. In 1929 this levy,
known as *aru*, was still in operation, though the people of Faea, the
district in which the symbol of the god lay, had by that time all been
Christian for some years and did not support these pagan rites. In
1952 I first heard that the rites of Takarito had been given up when I
was talking with a son of the Ariki Kafika about the use of orchards. He
explained that he himself took food from the orchard as did his brothers too, going in place of the chief who now had got too old to culti-
vate. But the *kava* ritual there had been abandoned since folk objected
to the levy of the *aru*, this licensed raid on their cultivations. They
were said to have scolded the chief for it, so the old man replied, "Give
it up, and the *kava* there too." When I asked the chief's son if it were
good or bad for folk thus to object, he replied, "It is bad—it is good and
yet bad," meaning that they were within their rights to protest but that
they should not have proceeded against ancient custom.

A little later I was talking about the Work of the Gods with Pa Fatumaru, one of the Taumako pagan elders. I again asked the reason for
the abandonment of the Takarito rites. He answered that Mission

7. Ibid., chap. 10.

teachers had removed the stone from its resting place. His story was that some time after I had left Tikopia the "missionaries," i.e., some local Mission teachers, had taken the sacred stone away and hidden it in the bushes. Then, he said, they waited to see the result—and it got back again in position by itself! So then they took it out to sea and threw it overboard from a canoe. Soon they observed that it was back in position! Then they took it and used it as an oven stone in the earth oven for cooking sago. (The notion here was to degrade the symbol of the god by using it for the menial task of cooking food; perhaps they hoped also that the fierce heat would split the stone.) But the result of this maneuver was that through the power of the stone the food remained raw! (Laughter arose at this point from the assembled family, who were listening with me to the story.) So then the Ariki Kafika abandoned the rites.

I asked where was the stone now. The answer was, "We don't know whether it is back in position or still in the sago oven." Then the ritual elder added that afterwards a son of the Mission priest died. He and a friend were going to voyage overseas. They went out on the reef in their canoe, and he was attacked by a shark. The god had entered into the shark and the young man was so bitten that he died. He said also that after the chief had abandoned the rites fish became scarce off Tikopia—both for men's fishing at sea and for women's fishing on the reef. This accorded with the pagan view that one of the objects of the Takarito ritual had been increase of fish.

Some weeks later I discussed this matter again with the same man. He told me that the Mission teacher who probably had interfered with the stone had been one of the younger sons of the Mission priest. I commented that nothing had happened to the offender himself. "Oh, it struck his brother," replied the elder's wife (herself a baptised Christian). Her husband added that the teacher actually concerned had in fact slipped and fallen one day on the hillside, had injured himself and had never been the same since. (It was true that his body did not look well nourished.) Curiously neither of my informants mentioned the recent death of a baby son of the Mission teacher. So I enquired if this also was to be put down to the sacrilegious act? "No; when it died the casting away of the stone had ended—this is different," was the reply. They confirmed, however, a story I had heard in the meantime that the priest himself had been opposed to interference with the Takarito stone. According to a report he had said, "The original things of a land, they are present in all lands; do not go and interfere with them." If this was true it may not have been due to respect but to fear, for the priest was not free from all such "superstitions."

Later, on several occasions, I heard from other men (including Christians and a lapsed Christian) the same story—though one gave the order of incidents in reverse. It was generally taken as a joke that the Mission teacher had so much trouble to get rid of the stone yet all in vain.
There seemed to be some difference of view as to whether the stone
was now back in its bed, whether the bed was empty or whether it was
occupied by another stone. However, by those most closely concerned,
it was regarded as common knowledge that the stone was now back in
its old place. The ritual elder told me that one of the younger Tikopia
leaders, John Fararava, prominent Christian as he was but still a member of the chiefly house of Kafika, had reported that the deity was in
truth there. He owned a share in the Takarito orchard, and it was reported that he had cut cycas fronds and relined the stone's bed in the
ground, making a "house" for it as in the traditional rites. A month or
so later an elderly man of the same family, Fararava's father's brother,
and also a Christian, told me personally that he had observed the deity
there—the same one, not a different stone. It was in his mind, he said,
also to cut cycas fronds and reline the bed some morning. I then asked
the Ariki Kafika himself about it. He told me the story of the throwing
away of the stone, that it had disappeared either in the ocean or in the
oven, but that it had reappeared of itself in its home. He said that John
Fararava (who was a classificatory grandson of his) saw it and came
and reported to him, "Grandfather! The god has come and is there,
what is to be done?" Fararava then asked if the rites of Takarito would
be resumed forthwith. But the old chief had replied, "Oh, they won't
be resumed. The missionaries have persisted in making sport of it. The
god has returned to dwell in his dwelling-place, but nothing more will
be performed, that there is his ground." By this he meant that the deity
had come back and that was enough; the land was under his jurisdic-
tion but no more rites would take place since the Christians had consistently attempted to interfere. He said too, that he had observed the
loss of the stone the last time he went over to carry out the ritual. He
saw cycas fronds in the bed but they were empty—no deity. He
searched and searched, but the stone was missing. He and his party
then carried on with the rites, but they did not have any ceremonial
levy as was customary. It was after this, he said, that the stone returned.

It was impossible to get an accurate idea of what finally happened
in this case, and it was inadvisable for me to try and check by personal
observation whether or not the stone was still there. It seemed clear
that the stone had been removed from its bed by one or more Mission
teachers associated with the family of the priest. It seemed likely also
that the stone had since been returned—but whether by one of the

delinquents fearing further disorder to his family, or by a junior member of Kafika who did not like to tell the chief that he had actually handled the sacred stone, one cannot say.

What was clear, however, was the sense of triumph rather than of dismay among the pagans—they regarded their god as having vindicated himself. The Christians did not seem to try and contradict this. On the whole, they seemed to have accepted the main incidents in the story. The abandonment of the rites of Takarito was a matter of definite decision by the Ariki Kafika. With this was associated the not unnatural objections of the Christian population of Faea as a whole to the operations of the ceremonial levy, to support a pagan ritual, and a pagan god. The reasons for his decision were as much political as religious. The handling of the stone by unauthorised outsiders was an offence; the repetition of this was an outrage and a nuisance. But the underlying cause of the abandonment was the political pressure that lay behind this action. As some people said, it was "because Christianity has become established in Faea" or "because the missionaries don't want the Ariki Kafika to perform the *kava* in Faea," or as the Ariki Kafika himself said "because of the objections of the priest's family."

As the leader with the prime responsibility for public order for the whole community he did not wish to persist in a course of action which would alienate half the Tikopia population, and make social co-operation with them very difficult.

This seemed to be a situation of crystallization of incipient myth. For in 1928–29 I had been told similar stories of the dire effects of interference with the god of Takarito.[8] When Pa Fatumaru, the ritual elder, told the stories in 1952 he also referred to the earlier cases. Over the years then, a body of putative incidents had been accumulated, referring to the powers of the stone symbol of the god. These could be regarded as contemporary myths. They dealt with the powers and activities of a highly sacred object; though not in any sense secret tales they were told in some privacy as being concerned with this sacred being; they were believed to be quite true; and they supported and justified a range of beliefs and values in the Tikopia traditional scheme. The tales themselves were admittedly quite recent, and there were agreed to be divergent accounts of what had happened. But save for a "hard core" of Christian sceptics, the bulk of the Tikopia population, both Christian and pagan, seemed to be quite convinced that something of the kind described had actually occurred: initial exercise of force by human antagonists countered by super-human power of the

8. Firth, *We, The Tikopia* (1936), p. 49; *Work of the Gods*, p. 292.

threatened deity; ridiculous outcome of an attempt to degrade the deity's symbol; and final punishment of the sacrilegious person.

This illustration of myth in a formative phase indicates an important aspect of its creation. It does not simply arise as a kind of intellectual or imaginative exercise. One type of myth at least arises in response to a situation of challenge, where justification or explanation of event has to be secured if status or more material benefit is not to be lost. In this case, something substantial was lost in the course of the struggle—the right to exact a levy on the cultivations in the name of the god. Yet the situation was rectified to some degree in the eyes of both Christians and pagans, it would seem, by the affirmation of the undiminished powers of the god. The myths of his return, and of his punishment of offenders against his dignity gave some satisfaction and comfort to his pagan adherents. They clearly enjoyed hugely the stories of the god's victory over his opponents. In the upshot, these stories were a gloss on the event; the Christian zealots' attack resulted in a cessation of the rites (and ultimately in a wider context in the conversion of all pagan Tikopia to Christianity). But at least the pagans had some immaterial offset to their material loss. In this situation the creation of contemporary myth had a significant function of compensation.

The Flexibility of Myth

TH. P. VAN BAAREN

The results of anthropological fieldwork by Malinowski, Firth, and others had a considerable impact on the study of myth in other disciplines. Scholars in the history of religion, for example, avidly read ethnographic accounts from all over the world in order to hone their conceptualization of myth. In this sense, they are like the nineteenth-century scholars such as Frazer and Lang who read what was available to them. The difference is in the quality of the ethnographic reporting of myths in context.

In this essay by Th. P. van Baaren, professor of science of religion and Egyptology at the University of Groningen, an essay stimulated in part by Firth's, which preceded this, we find a sophisticated discussion of such questions as whether myth reflects the past or the present, whether myth is a relatively unchanging charter for belief or a vehicle for the expression of culture change, and whether myths are theoretical and explanatory or whether they are practical guides for the attitudes and conduct of everyday life.

It has been often taken for granted that religions in general, and primitive religions in particular, are highly conservative. Without going to the other extreme, it may be stated with some confidence that most religions, including many religions of the non-literate cultures, show a high degree of flexibility. Myth, even if we define it as the supernatural charter on which a society is based, is not at all inflexible, except in theory. In practice it may change and does so, as long as its unchangeability can be upheld in theory. This process of change is, of course, easier in non-literate cultures than in cultures with a written tradition which can be checked for deviations.

Although myth still remains a subject of discussion in science of religions,[1] its flexibility seems to a great extent to have escaped expert attention. This is worth mentioning because in 1960 R. Firth published

Reprinted from *Studies in the History of Religions* 22 (1972), 199–206, by permission of the author and E. J. Brill, Leiden.

1. To mention only three recent articles: C. Colpe, "Mythische und religiöse Aussage ausserhalb und innerhalb des Christentums: Beiträge zur Theorie des neuzeitlichen Christentums," *Festschrift Wolfgang Trillhaas, zum 65. Geburtstag* (Berlin, 1968), pp. 16–

an important article on "The Plasticity of Myth."[2] Although the study of myth still offers many fascinating problems, the present paper is only concerned with its flexibility, not in the sense of degeneration or secularization when a certain myth is in process of losing its function, sometimes followed by complete disappearance, but in the sense of its adaptability to new situations and challenges. The occurrence of changes in a myth as such does not mean that the myth in question is beginning to lose its function and will probably disappear in time; on the contrary, changes in myth occur as a rule to prevent loss of function or total disappearance by changing it in such a way that it can be maintained. By changing it, a myth is adapted to a new situation, armed to withstand a new challenge. To mention one example from our own culture, without discussing it further, we are reminded of the way in which various theological schools of the last 150 years have treated the creation myths in the first chapters of Genesis.

To illustrate the flexibility of myth I will give a few examples. Tahiti before the coming of the Europeans was governed by a king belonging to one of the great noble families. However, change of dynasties was not unknown and because the noble houses claimed descent from divine beings, their genealogies were of importance to legitimate the claim to the throne of the reigning one. The myths used to be recited by the priests at important festivals, and it was of the highest importance that this was done without any error being made. A priest who made a mistake in reciting could be executed. In this way the myth was protected against change and we think, of course, of Durkheim, according to whom the maintenance of the tradition was the paramount function of myth. However, when dynasties changed, the problem arose that the existing "traditional" myth was no longer in accordance with the real political situation. To solve this problem the priests made small unobtrusive errors every time they recited the myths, till the text of the myth was wholly adapted to the new situation. Officially the myth was not changed at all. The Polynesian priests could, not only when confronted by this specific problem of the change of dynasty, but also more in general make changes in existing myths. Guiart writes: "L'abondance des personnages aux contours imprécis, aux noms symboliques, permettait d'exciper d'une connaissance ésotérique pour introduire un changement considérable sous couleur de préciser un récit."[3]

36; L. Honko, "Der Mythus in der Religionswissenschaft," *Temenos* 6 (1970), 36–67; K. Rudolph, "Der Beitrag der Religionswissenschaft zum Problem der sogenannten Entmythologisierung," *Kairos* (1970), pp. 183–207.

2. R. Firth, "The Plasticity of Myth," *Ethnologica* 2 (1960), 181–88.

3. J. Guiart, *Les Religions de l'Océanie* (Paris, 1962), p. 100.

My second example I take from Borneo. Among the Dayak there exists (or existed) the custom of bringing a foundation sacrifice when a building was erected. In former times human beings were sacrificed on this occasion. When a large longhouse was to be built, a slave was placed in the hole that was dug for the main pillar on which the house was to rest, and he was killed by stamping with this heavy wooden pole. The then Dutch government, wherever it had effective power, prohibited these sacrifices. This resulted in a small change in the myth of the foundation sacrifice: when this sacrifice in primeval times was to be brought for the first time, the slave who was already brought for this purpose was changed into a water buffalo. This change in the myth made it possible henceforth to sacrifice a water buffalo instead of a human being.[4]

My third example I take from the Anuak, a Nilotic tribe on the Upper Nile. They tell a myth relating the origin of death which is more or less the same as the myths on this theme among the related Dinka and Nuer. But they have a supplementary myth which is unknown among the other tribes. It tells, in short, that God created white men as well as black men. When God falls ill, he asks the black people for a skin to be laid in when he dies. They, however, refuse him this service thinking: why shall we bother if he is going to die? Then God said: "You ugly, bad white people, give me a skin." The white men gave him one and that is the reason why God blessed the white people with power and riches and cursed the black ones that they should remain poor.[5]

It is an interesting question why this myth originated among the Anuak and not among other related tribes, and in this case we are probably able to give an answer. Lienhardt writes that the Anuak "are concerned with anticipating death."[6] For this he gives an explanation: "A preparedness for death is an essential part not only of their philosophy, but also of the system by which inheritance, both of tradition and of material possessions, is assured."[7] The Anuak have the custom of a verbal last will which is highly valued, and they possess valuable goods which they can dispose of because they are held as individual property. Among the related tribes the riches consist mainly of cattle which are not individual property and which can only be transmitted by inheritance according to fixed rules. These data are perhaps not yet sufficient, but when we see how much Anuak culture in general is preoccupied with political power, totally different in this respect from the

4. H. Shärer, "Die Bedeutung des Menschenopfers im dajakischen Totenkult," *Mitteilungsblatt der deutschen Gesellschaft für Volkerkunde* (Hamburg, 1940), p. 25.
5. G. Lienhardt, "The Situation of Death: An Aspect of Anuak Philosophy," in *Witchcraft, Confessions and Accusations*, ed. Mary Douglas (London, 1970), pp. 282–83.
6. Ibid., p. 281.
7. Ibid.

cultures of the Nuer and Dinka, we can understand what has given rise to the supplementary myth on the origin of death.[8]

In many cases, as in our second and third example, myths have been changed owing to outside influences. The Papuans of the Wantoat region in Northeast New Guinea have myths of origin concerning their own tribe and the neighbouring ones in which it is related that they sprang from clumps of bamboo. Every tribe has its own bamboo clump. Since the coming of the white man he also got his own clump of bamboo from which he originated and during the second world war, when they became acquainted with the Japanese, these were also assigned their own clump of bamboo.[9] To return to Africa, Vansina writes: "A number of myths are exclusively aimed at providing an explanation of the world and of society as it exists, and their function is to justify the existing political structure. An eloquent proof of this is provided by myths found in many parts of Africa explaining the arrival of a European administration."[10]

Technological changes too may give rise to changes of myth. Firth relates a myth from Tikopia concerning the building of a temple in which iron nails are mentioned, so that it cannot be earlier than the beginning of the nineteenth century, "whereas the period of Tikopia society to which it refers can most plausibly be put at not later than the beginning of the 18th century."[11] The myth has a double meaning; on the one hand it describes the building of a central sanctuary which is erected on earth and in heaven at one and the same time, but on the other hand it answers the question why white people have iron and the inhabitants of Tikopia lack this valuable material. The great god, the senior god, who is building the temple in heaven, calls down to his brothers on earth, who are building the temple there, to pass him up iron nails, but they handed him only native materials like coconut sennet, with which the poles are fastened to each other. To punish them the great god descends to the earth and takes all iron with him to heaven and gives it to the whites.[12]

The type of occurrence as demonstrated in several of the examples given is often called syncretism, but it is uncertain whether this really touches the specific character of this phenomenon; myths also change

---

8. See for further information in short on this culture: Lucy Mair, *Primitive Government* (Harmondsworth, 1962).

9. C. A. Schmitz, *Wantoat: Art and Religion of the Northeast New Guinea Papuans* (The Hague, 1963), p. 59.

10. J. Vansina, *Oral Tradition: A Study in Historical Methodology* (London, 1965), p. 51.

11. Firth, "Plasticity of Myth," p. 182.

12. Ibid., pp. 183 ff.

without outside influences. Syncretism is only one of the possible reasons, but the cause of this process is, in my opinion, to be found in the character of myth itself.

In non-literate societies changes in myth are comparatively easy to make, because oral traditions are easier to manipulate than those which are fixed in writing. In these cultures it is less of a problem to maintain that nothing has been changed, while at the same time changes are proceeding. What Turner writes about ritual among non-literate peoples with reference to his own experiences among the Ndembu of Rhodesia is, in my opinion, also valid for myth in these cultures: "From my experience . . . I am prepared to assert that no performance of a given cult ritual ever precisely resembles another."[13] Science of religion has suffered much from a kind of optical illusion, further intensified by inexact theoretical presuppositions, that primitive cultures are highly static. As a matter of fact, for many primitive cultures we have only one source, or a few approximately contemporary sources at our disposal. If asked, the answer of the informants as a rule will be that things are as they used to be since immemorial times. This is self-evident, because within their cultural frame this is the only fitting answer. This answer, however, only has value as a statement of principle in the same way as when we say that a Christian loves his neighbours as the Gospel teaches. In this way there resulted an inexact image of primitive cultures as static and stagnant ones. Firth questions "the degree of fixity that is expected in a myth."[14] He concludes rightly that "perhaps for lack of evidence, myths have been handled with a kind of timeless attitude, or have been credited with a quality of antiquity."[15] He also mentions the frequently seen "reluctance to treat them as possibly recent or changing items."[16] It is clear that Firth does not share this opinion, and it is indeed easy to cite examples of changing myths, as we have done already.

One of the reasons for this erroneous conception of myth as unchanging is, in my opinion, the fact that the former generation of scientists of religion have been insufficiently conscious of the great difference which exists between general religious utterances of a more or less theoretical character, even when they really represent a *communis opinio*, and religious behaviour as it actually is. In other words, they have taken the pronouncements of religions literally, although

---

13. V. W. Turner, *Chihamba, the White Spirit: a Ritual Drama of the Ndembu* (Manchester, 1969), p. 3.
14. Firth, "Plasticity of Myth," p. 182.
15. Ibid.
16. Ibid.

they could have known better from an elementary analysis of their own belief and behaviour. A simple but instructive example is given by Marwick. According to general opinion among the Cewa (East Africa), 93 percent of all deaths are due to witchcraft and sorcery and 73 percent of the witches and sorcerers are women. Checking this result by inquiring into concrete cases, he found that 55 percent was attributed to witchcraft and sorcery and that of the persons held responsible 42 percent were women.[17]

I should like to posit that changeability is one of the specific characteristics of myth. Only the study of the changes of myth makes it possible to discover the constant and variable elements of this phenomenon.

Generally speaking we may say that science of religion in the last half-century has thoroughly discussed whether myths are in the first place theoretical and explanatory, or whether, on the contrary, their function is in the first instance a very practical one (Malinowski). It may be said that this opposition is only an imaginary problem. All myths, perhaps without exception, are aetiological myths, i.e., they indicate an *aition*, they tell how and why something came into existence, happened, etc. The first chapters of Genesis are as much aetiological myths as the story of the Solomon Islands which explains why the coast line of the island Buka is partly straight and partly very much otherwise.[18] If we like, we may continue the term aetiological myth for a certain type of myth, but the use of this term must not delude us into thinking that there exist myths which are not aetiological. Eschatological myths simply form a special variation.

It is true, on the other hand, that myths which are an essential part of a religion as a rule have a more or less important practical significance, and it is even true that this last is often far more important than their theoretical function, that is to say, than the element of explanation. But there, I think, an error has crept in which has led to the polarization of myth as explanation and myth as charter. The participants in this discussion failed to see that every explanation forms a nucleus round which authority crystallizes, and, on the other hand, that mythical explanations only are sought and given, because there is a need for an authoritative arrangement of world and life. There is no antithesis but only two aspects of one and the same thing. From every explanation, mythical or not, a certain authority emanates which has consequences for the way in which world and life are considered. That is why every myth is at one and the same time an explanation and a

17. M. Marwick, "Witchcraft as a Social Strain-Gauge," in *Witchcraft and Sorcery*, ed. M. Marwick (Harmondsworth, 1970), pp. 284–85.

18. G. Thomas, "Customs and Beliefs of the Natives of Buka," *Oceania* (1931–32), p. 220.

charter. I may add, perhaps, that the dispute between science and religion is not so much a dispute between science as such and religion as such, but rather a clash between two different kinds of authority.

Myth explains the why and how of the here and now. The explanation given is not only authoritative, because it is given in the form of a myth, it is as true to say that a myth has authority, because it offers an explanation. There are, of course, degrees of authority: an explanation given in the form of a myth contains the authority of the entire community that believes in this myth; private explanations have little or no authority, unless the person who gives them succeeds in forming a new community of his own. Whether he succeeds in this or not depends only partly on the merits of the explanation offered. The theoretical element of explanation and the practical element of authority in myth form no contradistinction; both elements are related and tend to reinforce each other.

To conclude, I should like to enumerate very shortly what the consequences of this view concerning the changeability of myth are:

1. A myth explains the why and how of a given thing.

2. The fact that this explanation is contained in a myth gives it a more than human authority.

3. In virtue of this authority myths function as part of the belief-system of a religion from which the value- and action-system are felt to be derived. Whether the belief-system is really primary is a different question which need not concern us here.

4. Religious behaviour is determined partly by the authority of myth, partly by the force which the real situation exercises on man.

5. If both forces are in harmony then there results a form of behaviour which is meaningful in both directions.

6. If not, there results a form of behaviour which is only meaningful according to one of the constituent forces, and non-sense according to the other: either religious behaviour which is not adapted to the real situation, or an effective form of behaviour taking no account of religion.

7. In this conflict-situation between mythical and worldly reality one force must give in and change, or disappear.

8. The character of myth is opposed to disappearance, but not, in view of what we said about its plasticity, to change.

9. The reality of this world is only rarely open to sufficiently fundamental change; therefore, in case of conflict, as a rule it is the myth which will change.

10. In this situation the invention of writing has wrought havoc, because this invention has made it possible to fix the text of a myth more or less permanently.

11. History of religions teaches us that in this situation the flexibility of myth is transferred to its exegesis. This explains the important function of this branch of theology in all religions based on sacred texts. It is well-known that in primitive religions a large number of versions of one and the same myth exist and that it is not possible to point out one of them as the generally authoritative and original version. In the same way do we encounter in the book-religions a large variety of exegeses of which, *mutatis mutandis*, the same can be said.

The Mythic

ERIC DARDEL

Missionaries have always been fascinated by the myths they encountered among the peoples whom they hoped to convert. In part, the myths represented the "opposition" that had to be overcome in order to succeed in introducing Catholicism or some other form of Christianity in its place. It is no accident that the first myths recorded in the New World were collected by Ramon Pane, a priest left on Hispaniola by Columbus for the purpose of studying the native religion. See Edward Gaylord Bourne, "Columbus, Ramon Pane and the Beginnings of American Anthropology," Proceedings of the American Antiquarian Society *n.s. 17 (1907), 310–48.*

Even in the twentieth century, we find expert linguists working in remote areas under the auspices of the S.I.L. (Summer Institute of Linguistics), whose primary motivation to analyze and provide a written form for exotic tribal languages is to translate the Bible into that language. Some of these linguists have become interested in the language used in the tribal myths because sometimes, e.g., in Meso-America, there are archaic verb forms that are used exclusively to express mythic time in the far distant past and that occur only in myth texts. By using such forms in their Bible translations, these missionary linguists hope to give the native version the same kind of resonance and feeling Euro-Americans get when reading or listening to passages from the Old or New Testaments. See, for example, H. Daniel Shaw, "The Structure of Myth and Bible Translation," Practical Anthropology *19 (1972), 129–32. See also a special issue of this periodical, which serves missionary anthropologists, on the subject of myth. In a six-part essay in that issue by Jacob A. Loewen,* Practical Anthropology *16 (1969), 147–92, the utility of myth for the missionary is discussed in some detail.*

Missionaries often become veritable ethnographers inasmuch as they faithfully record authentic texts of myths. Because they frequently live for extended periods among a people (in contrast to the anthropologist who may limit his or her visit to a year or to a series of occasional visits of a month or so), missionaries may succeed in eliciting fuller and more reliable texts than anthropologists.

The following somewhat poetic and rhapsodic celebration of the mythic was inspired by the work of such a missionary-ethnographer. The full title of the essay is "The Mythic According to the Ethnological Work of Maurice Leenhardt." Written without footnotes for a more popular intellectual audience, the essay nevertheless touches on many critical issues in the study of myth. What is the relationship between logic or rationality and myth? (Are myth and rationality compatible?) Does the concept of myth or the mythic go beyond discrete narratives? Is there an esthetic component of myth?

Reprinted from *Diogenes* 7 (1954), 33–51.

Both Leenhardt and Eric Dardel were especially influenced by philosophical and religious aspects of myth. Earlier writers in this tradition include Ernst Cassirer, Language and Myth (New York, 1946); G. Van der Leeuw, "Die Bedeutung der Mythen," in Festschrift Alfred Bertholet (Tübingen, 1950), pp. 287–93; Konrad Theodor Preuss, Der religiöse Gehalt der Mythen (Tübingen, 1933); and Lucien Lévy-Bruhl, La Mythologie primitive (Paris, 1963). Readers may wish to consult some of Leenhardt's works for themselves rather than relying on Dardel's summary. They should perhaps start with Do Kamo, published in French in 1947 but also available in English translation: Do Kamo: Person and Myth in the Melanesian World (Chicago, 1979). Chapter 12, entitled "Myth" (pp. 170–95), is especially relevant. For a more extensive introduction to Leenhardt's life and work, see James Clifford, Person and Myth: Maurice Leenhardt in the Melanesian World (Berkeley and Los Angeles, 1982). For another essay by Dardel treating myth, see "Magie, Mythe et Histoire," Journal de psychologie normale et pathologique 43 (1950), 193–229 (see especially pp. 204–16). For another essay on myth influenced by Leenhardt, see Jean Poirier, "Sens et rôle du mythe en ethnologie," Journal de la Société des Océanistes 4 (1948), 28–47.

We have learned by now not to see myth as simple entertainment or a babbling. Where the nineteenth-century eye could find only an out-of-date toy left behind by childish peoples or a cultural stage-set for leisured social circles, the human sciences have taught us to recognise an authentic expression of man: myth says with utmost seriousness something that is of essential importance. What is more, it is a way of living in the world, of orienting oneself in the midst of things, of seeking an answer in the quest for the self. We owe this alteration of perspective to a whole group of scholars: Cassirer, Van der Leeuw, Unger, Preuss; we owe it in a quite special way to Maurice Leenhardt and to the original work which his recent death left uncompleted.[1]

1. In the course of a long missionary career in New Caledonia, serving the Paris Society of Evangelical Missions (1902–26), Maurice Leenhardt became interested in the sciences of man, sociology and ethnology. Entrusted with a scientific mission by the National Ministry of Education, he made a research trip to Black Africa, followed some years later by a scientific inquiry in Oceania, at Nouméa (1947). Called to take Marcel Mauss' place at the École des Hautes Études, he was named to his chair in 1940. After a course in Oceanian languages was set up at the École des Langues Orientales, he was called to ensure its instruction (1945). Death (on January 26 last) prevented him from putting a final touch, as he was trying to do, to his scientific work, from making precise some points that seemed to him insufficiently clear and from dispelling some misunderstandings to which studies of this type lend themselves. Nevertheless his scholarly work as it stands is important and original. Scattered through several journals (*Revue philosophique, Revue de metaphysique et de morale, Revue d'histoire et philosophie religieuses, Anthropologie*, etc.), it is especially well-represented by some scientific publications of the Institute of Ethnology: *Notes d'ethnologie néo-Caledonienne* (1930), *Documents néo-caledoniens* (1932), *Vocabulaire et grammaire de la langue de Houailou* (1935), and by two works which are more personal in nature, *Do Kamo* and *Arts d'Océanie*. This body of work, although uncompleted, to

Like Lévy-Bruhl, to whom he often felt himself so close, Maurice Leenhardt had to make his way through pitfalls dug by the last century and its intellectual habits. When the subject of science is man himself, and when the scholar does not want to sacrifice any of his condition as a man, he must avoid the snares of language; and our language, which is so full of abstractions, begins by concealing what it is trying to show. Coming from another base than did Lévy-Bruhl, Maurice Leenhardt also had to engage in the same ceaseless struggle against language to save the experience of the "primitive" from distorted transcription into our vocabulary of terms and notions. Man at the mythic stage sees a relation between stone and ancestor which we try to express by means of an identity: we say that for him the ancestor *is* the stone. But our verb "to be," weakened by centuries of grammar and philosophy, absolutely lacks the living experience of the primitive who senses in the stone a mythic presence, a manifestation of the ancestor's own reality. Terms like identity, participation, consubstantiality are themselves only awkward approximations, dulled by conceptual extensions distorting the truth of the relationship. Myth, like music or poetry, requires us to be transported into the world where it has its being. It is there, for example, that the rock-ancestor identity, which is felt before it is conceived, allows its proper meaning to appear. Understanding of this order is not possible to a Western scholar unless, behind the *Logos* and its logical and spatial objections, something of the primitive *Mythos* survives in him. Maurice Leenhardt found this access to the mythical not in books or theories but in his daily experience as a missionary, hunting for a way to approach the men of Oceania and to communicate with them. That human sympathy, which enabled him to understand the primitive soul from within, gave his scientific work a very individual coloration, perhaps not so compatible with the conception of science cherished in the last century, but surely less foreign to the science of man which our own period seems to be trying to build.

In the opposite direction, Maurice Leenhardt had to protect his ethnological work against the cover-up words and the vague notions that lie in wait for the scholar off the beaten track of the natural sciences. He accordingly avoided, as much as possible, the term "primitive," which forces on the mind an order of succession, accompanied

---

which must be added two important articles in *Histoire des religions* (Quillet, publishers), and *Histoire des Religions* (Bloud & Gay, publishers, 1935), has contributed to the enrichment and renovation of a whole wide sector of the science of man. It is one of those works which sustain new pioneers and open horizons, because there was talent in Maurice Leenhardt for awakening interests and developing vocations.

by an order of evaluation, the "primitive" usually being taken as ante-
rior or inferior to the things we attribute to "antique" or "modern"
man. The mentality imputed to the so-called primitives can be re-
discovered in the heart of the Western mind; inversely, the rational co-
exists with the mythic among less-developed peoples, to whom the
term "archaic" peoples is more appropriate.

Anxious to preserve the rights of clear language, Maurice Leenhardt
rejected the overly-equivocal word "mystic." The Melanesian does not
act under the influence of mysterious or determined forces. On the
contrary, he has a clear view of the relations between the world and
himself; he sees these relations through the myth as through a mirror.
The fog or half-light of the mystic scarcely belong in a world where the
mythic relation appears as an unveiling of the world, as a truth about
being, revealing itself to man. The mythic is not a prelogical, as opposed to a logical, structure of the mind, but rather another reading of
the world, a first coherence put upon things and an attitude that is
complementary to logical behaviour.

I. ESSENCE OF THE MYTHIC

On the evidence of classical mythology and the plastic commentaries
on it which we have had from modern painters in search of picturesque or "poetic" subjects, we have for a long time believed that myths
were nothing but stories about gods, descents into Hell, heroic fights.
Here, it was thought, was a crop of imaginary tales invented by poets,
bare of anything serious or true, which our Western logic ought to look
down upon as mere amusement or child's play.

But the work of ethnologists and sociologists, together with studies
in "depth psychology," have obliged us for a half-century now to revise
this excessively simplified notion. They show us that myths are a language affected with seriousness, often with warmth or tenderness,
corresponding to a certain picture of the world, which is perfectly
valid although it obeys wholly different mental requirements than
does the conduct of reason and of history. Lévy-Bruhl, in his *Primitive
Mythology*, recalled the interest we moderns still take in mythic accounts, which often come down to us in the form of fairy-tales and
legends, although we may have ceased to "believe" in them. He attributed this interest to the sense of relaxed ease we feel when we
plunge into this fairy-tale atmosphere where the connexions and ten-
sions of logical relationships fade from our awareness. But the attraction exercised over us in this way by the mythical does not reduce itself to a simple mental recreation: it has deeper, positive reasons.

Under the legend and the fairy-tale, there is the mythic, and the mythic includes an experience, a reaction to reality. When the "primitive" recognises an ancestor looking at him out of the shark's or the lizard's eye, he is certainly making a reference to reality, but he interprets it mythically; he expresses by this connexion, which for us lacks foundation, the impression he feels, his affective reaction to "things." The myth is neither "true" nor "false"; it is born, beyond our logic's horizon, in that "pang" which comes upon man in the midst of things. In the myth and by means of the mythic image, there is an externalisation of the inner stirring, the emotion of man as he meets the world, his receptivity to impulses coming from "outside," the communality of substance which welds him to the totality of beings.

If the mythic is the language of a man who feels himself thoroughly at one with the world, part of the world, form amid the forms of the universe, it is also the first rupture in his being, the first flight above, which makes the real unreal, and detaches man from his environment, and so a source of all poetry and all culture. It is not impermeable to logic, as we shall see below. But rationality is not a first-level concern for archaic thought: it occupies only a secondary place, the essential thing being to place oneself in the current of the whole world's life. As rationality assumes greater importance, the interpretation which man gives to the world may be seen to pass through three successive stages: a *mythic* stage, to which we shall confine ourselves here, an *epic* stage, and an *historic* stage. The *mythic* stage changes into the *epic* outlook when man bases his conduct and his universe on the repetition of the *model* man, on the cult of the hero: the hero being an archetype after whose qualities and gestures those of his successors are drawn, and in whom human destiny is discovered. Men, drawing back before the audacity of being themselves, have asked for a justification of their existence from the hero. Hercules, Theseus, or Hector are "supermen," who lend authority, by their exemplary value, to the ordinary careers of simple mortals; they are the heirs of virtues and actions which transmit greatness to the daily round of commonplace life. A feeling of being strengthened with this superhuman power was necessary in order to face history. . . . As Ernst Junger has commented, the epic, "dedicated to the spirit of the tombs," made "the introduction to history" out of this pilgrimage to the hero's graves. The historic as such does not fully emerge until men stop turning to this exemplary past, in order to dare to act for themselves, to set themselves human objectives and to adopt human means for their attainment, but above all, when their rational emancipation has set them to seeking a direction in the unfolding of events, in a word, to caring about having a History.

But even in our world, dominated by logical and historical concerns, with our explanations ruled by the principle of causality, we remain sensitive to another colouring of the universe, to that actual and emotional tone which fascinates or disturbs us. The mythic even in myths would remain a closed book to us if it did not awaken some sleeping potentialities within us, an affective and imaginary predisposition always ready to react by way of myths to the world's approaches. It is well to remember once and for all that the mythic, which is closely bound up with the sphere of sentiment and of emotion, shares the universality of the emotional life which renounces reflection, and takes refuge in silence or changes under the impartial eye of the observer. There is in us that vibration of our whole being which shows itself in convictions or in beliefs, in "verities" which we declare to be true. The romantics' myth of Nature, the myth of progress, the myth that the world is absurd—every period declares "its" truth in this way and is warmly attached to it. Our "truth" of the moment is often only a myth that does not know that it is one, and, as M. Jourdain put it, we make myths every day without knowing it. The myth, deep within ourselves, illumines every reality giving it direction and value. The myth is accordingly surely a universal, or fundamental, *phenomenon* which, while keeping profound motives, inexpressible emotions and feelings hidden within the secret of the individual, reveals through surface gestures, forms and words, something of that internality which, without ever growing old, lives on in man's heart century after century.

1. The Mythic Is Not in the Past

"Once upon a time," "in the beginning," "then" . . . ; the folk-tale takes us into the past with its first words. The myth leads back to a remote, primordial past: to events, heroes, and gods who pre-exist everything that is. The opposition between the sun and the moon derives, according to the Melanesians, from an act of unfaithfulness. Customs and rites derive from precedents that institute and justify them. The festivals which consummate group life only repeat certain sanctified rituals. It is for the present generation to actualise these precedents or archetypes in order to validate at the same moment their acts of the present time. Nothing ever begins, nothing is ever new on this horizon where the foundation of the established order also indicates, simultaneously, its origin.

An optical illusion is involved here, however, and it has been kept up in us by developed mythologies. The Melanesian myths go in quite another direction. There is nothing further removed from the historian's scrutinising of the past than the "primitive's" attitude with respect to the mythic happening. The mythic past cannot be dated, it is a past "before time" or, better, outside of time. "Long ago," "one day," "in the beginning," "and then," all this customary vocabulary of the mythic, visibly trifles with historic time. Primordial actions are lost "in the night of time," what happened "once" (nobody knows when) goes on in a floating and many-layered time without temporal location. Myths of causality or origin-myths nevertheless seem to invoke, like the ancient cosmologies, some fixed periods and moments. But we must be careful in handling these elaborated "accounts" from a later stage, where an effort at narration and explanation, on the way toward history, is foreshadowed. Maurice Leenhardt asks us to see a degeneration of the mythic in them, a rationalisation, the awakening of a still poorly emancipated historic awareness. The mythic, stripped of its power, of its perenniality, is found in them relegated to "the beginning."

The mythic is *present*. First, it is present in the sense that the narrator, in his account, is transported and transports the listener into the time of the happening, "in the centre," "down there," "far away." He draws the audience of the story away, but only to make them set themselves at the desired distance. The mythic actualises everything it touches: it makes the narrator an actor in his "story," the listener a witness, the world a present without past or future. The account is made one with what it tells: it is the event itself that is being told, and, in being told, is realised. Even in the fairy-tale, the expression "once upon a time" does not bring the past as such into the case; it evokes it, in the magical sense of the term, it calls it into being.

The mythic is even more deeply present because the original event, by repetition, is once again "presently" produced. "Original" means not so much "earlier" as "permanent." Primordial reality lies close to present reality. Constitutive and fundamental as well as institutive and founding, it is always there, ready to be incarnated. Inversely, it does not exist by itself: to protect its power, it must be reproduced each time. The myth, in its images and narrations, transmits an experience of the perenniality of life, the return of known situations and of affective states sanctified by precedents. The old Canakas, in order to reconstitute the "Lizard myth," express themselves in the present: they point to the hill where the lizard lives, "waiting until the affectionate faithfulness of his loved ones returns." Myth-time is a discontinuous time, a repeated "now," not a duration, but an actualisation which proceeds by leaps from one "now" to another "now." Van der Leeuw chose to speak of the "eternalising" tendency of the myth. It is better to content oneself, like Maurice Leenhardt, with the *perennial* character of mythic time. What we have here, in fact, is a time which has the continuity of life, and not in any sense a time which, lacking as it does any experience of death and any feeling of nothingness, could fit in with our ideas of finitude and of eternity. It is a present which sounds the affective depths of being, ignorant of the abstractions and negatives of our temporality, which awakens warmth, fear, or exaltation, and makes all nature sing in images and symbols derived from all the senses. By way of the myth, man identifies himself and his habitat with the totem, feels himself a contemporary of the totemic life and responsible for the carrying-on of existence. That is why the error *par excellence*, the major unfaithfulness, is sterility, which ruptures the chain of actualisations, or a breaking of the taboos which safeguard the correct transmission of life.

In this undifferentiated time, man may find himself in several times at once. The rock he sees *is*—now—the ancestor he sees no more; it is his "apparition," the visible form at once hiding and revealing the invisible. The same act of awareness envelops the rock which, in its present form, remembers its old state, and the ancestor who, present in the rock, is always watching over the living. Mythic time is made up of these simultaneities, as the New Guinea myth of the man-bird shows: this man, who takes off his fungus-ridden skin to put on wings and become a bird, then slips once more into his diseased skin, moves on the affective and imaginative plane where the simultaneity of two "moments" is translated into a rapid succession of images. By virtue of this mythic time, man feels united to all generations, to all the living: he feels himself in his grandparent as well as in his grandson, in the totemic lizard gliding across his path as well as in the ancestral tree where the past meditates on the present. Deprived of ontological ground, not knowing just "where" his I is, the mythic man cannot distinguish what was from what will be and from what goes to make up the present. His temporality falls like petals into states, into "nows" into which he is transported, unaware of contradictions.

The ritual must be faithful, the narration without omissions, in order that the mythic model may become a presence and a power in the person of the officiating leader or narrator. The myth is not a single story but always a *typical* story: it has an exemplary value, which, however, is concrete and alive. The totem resides in the maternal uncle, waiting for the nephew to receive its lodgment. It is present in the New Caledonian gecko lizard which assumes the colour of the twig; "without any movement other than that of his open eyes, he seems to be the living being that has one body with the forest and indicates life in the inert mass of the world." He inhabits space and sets it in place. He is time as the power of life, as the presence which gathers all the dispersed presences in the world together. He whom the myth proclaims to be the master of the crops and of genetic life is also a revelation that lights up the world, unconscious poetry mixed with every substance and lodged in every form.

2. The Mythic Is Not to Be Confused with the Narrative

Greek, Celtic, and German mythologies are collections of accounts. Besides the *Epic* or epic account and the *Logos* or logical discourse, the myth appears as a special kind of expression. It found its form in the "fable," an account which was without chronological localisation and was of an exemplary character. Whether it be a story of the gods or a fable, the myth necessarily seems to imply a narration, written or oral.

But among archaic peoples, the myth projects far beyond the domain of narrative and even that of language. This is true, first, because "word" in this case goes beyond oral formulations, but also because this "word," even enlarged to the meaning in which these peoples understand it, does not come close to covering the whole extent of the mythic.

Among the Melanesians, the decision which the father reserves to himself before a marriage request is "word"; likewise, the avenging action which enables a man to punish an outrage inflicted on his brother by a third person; likewise, the magical operation, and likewise, thought. "Word" is what has force, what has the solidity of a rock, what manifests being and establishes its lasting existence: tradition is the "lasting word," the Fame that comes down from gods and ancestors, the custom that cements society. More particularly important is the "long-drawn-out word," otherwise the mythic account which is equivalent to the "total life of the clan caught across the ages." The chief's prestige is not attached to emblems or special honours, but to the fact that he is the guardian of this fundamental word: it is for him "to recall . . . all the clan's traditions, alliances, and great hours, all the engagements, all its honour." The chief is the word of the clan. And the word is the man: as in feudal society, it involves the whole person. The word is not a discourse, it is a force: from it issues the power to think, to act, to construct. Through it, man faces the world, exists, and knows.

Word is also what brings the world's answer back to him, what the mountain, the forest, the moon's reflection, the moving script of the sea and the rustling of the leaves have to tell him. Even in our modern universe, as Jean Vogué comments, we still can feel "the dramatic character of purple sunsets, and the serenity of the blue sky," and the poet, according to Martin Buber, still knows afresh, in the presence of the moon, "the emotional image of the lunar fluid that flows through the body." Here is a survival in us, as we stand before the world, of that primitive mythic where things still have the initiative, where animals and plants "talk," where from everywhere the world's voices are heard, those calls that resound in man: diffuse presences from which come signals, orders, refusals. The mythic is that word which, from every-where, calls men together and breaks up the darkness. It is neither al-legory nor fiction, but forms and sounds, patterns and sayings which are also calls, apparitions, meanings: in short, a word.

This eternal dialogue between man and the world gives the myth as word an extreme importance and at the same time an extension which far exceeds the limits of its formulation. New Caledonian plastic art expressed this essential role in a striking way through the symbol of the protruded tongue. Whatever is most fleeting and vain in us, scat-tered in gossip and in official speeches, is there condensed into cre-ative power. The Canaka carver chisels, on the door frame and on the ridge-pole of the huts, those faces of ancestors sticking out their tongues, which we might mistake for disrespectful masks. The tongue, which "carries to the outside the traditional virtues, the manly deci-sions, and all the manifestations of life which the word bears in itself," becomes the symbol of wisdom, vigour, and plenitude. The word which no longer has this power is the formal word—we would say, the *logos*— in which there is a foreshadowing of abstract thought, and this, for the Oceanian, means an empty and powerless formula: for it comes out of the lips, not the deep feelings within.

The mythic, woven into this living and powerful word, clings to man. But its power is softened into an account which lacks warmth and weight, ready for mythology and literature: a decoration which the spirit has abandoned. The authentic myth keeps its vital pith in a world very different from our own, a world that has no equivalent for our verb "to die," where our conception of life is too abstract to be grasped, but where everything that is important or affirmative, all that *is*, is alive, where there are no things, only beings participating in the same life-current—men, animals, plants or stones. The tree of life planted in the hole where the placenta is buried will live as long as the man does and, at his death, will wither. Inversely, man is hardly more than a momentary form of vegetable life. It is through this other, through this co-existence with the tree, through the yam, image of his life, in a word, through the lived and projected myth, that man grasps his existence and knows himself. He sees himself only in the reflection of his being that the world gives back to him, and his life which, by itself, is not justified, finds validity only in the myth, which ties it to universal life, to all the living. It is the secret word, inscribed in sexuality, pronounced over man by ancestors and gods, *fatum*, the Latins called it: "what has been said" about him, and what involves his existence, his destiny. But it is a word that can remain unspoken, bound to the name that is never uttered, or it can simply be read in the silent work of the carver.

The myth traces and avows the existential bond of man with his environment, with his habitat, with his clan, and the principle of his conduct. Instead of seeking, as we do, for a logical and objective relation with the world, in order to know it, break it up and master it, the "Primitive" trusts his myths, lets himself be guided by them and sees himself by way of them. It is useless, if we want to understand his reactions and his thought, to reconstruct his myths "scientifically" or to tell them over again in romantic attitudinising. It is better to follow the poet in his "fantasy," then, or to listen to the musician, ask of the painter, let oneself be inspired, as they are, by those "worlds" in their freshness and brightness. It is better above all to lend an ear to this mythic, underlying our own reason and our knowing, which the work of Jung and his school have brought to light as one of the great realities of our mental life.

The mythic is the common source of morality and of religion, of nature and of society, of the aesthetic and of exchange. It connects the individual to his clan and invests him with his social role, with his dramatic part. Yam or fish, man finds his place in the world, his ontological status, through the myth. From it comes the very strong sense of dependence which he feels with regard to the life he has received as a heritage, and of responsibility towards it. The myth controls the exchange of women by marriage among clans, in such a way as to guarantee "the conveyance of the totemic life." In this mythic view of things, the central place quite naturally goes to the life-myth *par excellence*, the totemic myth. The totemic lizard fertilises the crops. The path he is to follow in descending the mountain is carefully cleared. He is surrounded with respect. It is a grave error to mention him lightly; to call someone by the name of his totem is to take a liberty that hits him in his most intimate being. The totem presides over sexuality and fertility. He follows the maternal line and gives it its priority; it is he whom the young girl, when she marries, brings to her new clan: a holy deposit which nephews take on from their maternal uncles and over which respect for taboos, religious fervour, exercise their care.

And now we are far from the myth-account, from the "stories of the gods," from that colour-drained, peripheral mythic which some take to be nothing but a superstructure of society or simple-heartedness. It is in totemism, mythic time and space, the ancestral scenery, the feast where the clan is exalted, that, outside himself, the "primitive" abides, there that he lives, from there that he will set out to discover himself when the decline of the mythic world liberates the individual. Beyond this horizon, he loses his footing in a foreign world, a world of lonely mountains, of wild expanses where the gusts of anger blow, oceanic immensities out of which the white men come ashore, those phantoms who no longer have human faces. Where the myth has nothing more to tell him, there is nothing any more, except chaos, malediction and hostility.

3. The Mythic and the Aesthetic

Long before it took literary form or became the "story of the gods," the heroic adventure, and the descent into Hell, the myth found its plastic expression. The Oceanian world offers a remarkable and doubtless unique example of societies where art, far from representing a secondary activity or a trimming for life, is at the very centre of existence. The aesthetic there is not, as with us, a limited sector of activity, a luxury that is marginal to essential concerns. It is itself the aspect under which the world presents itself to man, its human face, the form given to the myth. The world, where it is first encountered by way of sensations, emotions, feelings, beliefs, manifests itself as the life of forms, in an aesthetic participation. The carved prow of a boat, some ear-rings, a diadem, everything man seems to add to the world, translate into form that wholly mythic representation and that aesthetic manner of living which dominate Oceanian society.

The aesthetic is an assent to the world: a deep accord with the natural and social environment, with the seasonal rhythm, with the aspects and changes of things, a confiding abandon to the proposals of what is felt, to everything that "affects" and moves men, whether individually or collectively. This aesthetic attitude with respect to the world inclines man to put into his gestures and his speech, into his whole being, that form or liking for the flourish and for elegance which often takes on the validity of custom or even of morals. It has sometimes seemed astonishing to find among these men a harmoniousness, a nobility of attitude, a "style of life" which is very far removed from the reputation for being savages which has quite thoughtlessly been given them. This aesthetic concern is shown not only in the colours, feathers, and painted designs with which the Oceanian loves to get himself up, not only in the decoration of huts, or in the arrangement of tiers and dances at the great feasts, but also in the actions of daily life and in personal behaviour. The meal where the yam, the ancestor's flesh, is consumed, takes place in silence, as becomes the celebration of a communion. The Dyaks of Borneo and the New Caledonians have been accused of crudity and grossness because the Dyak woman always walks several steps behind her husband, or because the Oceanian woman must cross four steps behind her husband if he is accompanied by other men. But to say this is to show ignorance of the fact that custom requires the Dyak to preserve his wife from snakes, scorpions and other dangers on the path, and also to forget the Oceanian woman's tact and subtlety, "her art in intruding, bowing, standing up again, without bringing the least disturbance into the men's conversation while on the contrary having secretly charmed them."

But the aesthetic, the expression of myth, is also a protection which makes man secure against the pressure of his environment. In the disorder and confusion of the primitive world, it is a first order put upon things. The Oceanians "grasp the form of things before analysing things, and they have a sufficient acquaintance with them in this way. . . . Their thought is already ordered according to the aesthetic mode, long before it achieves ordering according to the logical mode." It is perhaps not pointless to recall here that the Greek word *kosmos* and the Latin *mundus* have this aesthetic value, conjointly with their sense of "order," of "universe." The first order attributed to the world was an aesthetic coherence, that arrangement which man first looked for in the aspect of things. The aesthetic slipped the screen of forms between man and things; it was a veil thrown over what was hidden in the depths and over the original chaos of which all causal myths make so much, before the *founding* and the *forming* set and ordered all things. In the shelter of this protective arranging, the "primitive" organised his life and his society, limited but always secured by sounds, colours, and forms, by all that "graining" which unceasingly confirmed to him the presences and the certainties by which he lived.

The world blossoms into living forms. Man himself is one of these. He is a being in a performance, he is a role, a kind of crowd-actor, on the world's scene. His gestures and his words obey tradition, express the myth, "represent" ancestors and gods. Any personal whimsy, by breaking the established aesthetic, would be gravely incorrect, involving outrage on the ancestors' honour and on the bases of society. Not ornamental or arbitrary in any way, these forms are an expression, a mythic language: the bodily array, the beautiful Maori or Guinea canoes, the tall statues on Easter Island, belong to that lexicon of forms through which the Oceanians deciphered the world's meaning. Nature, with a very sure sense of taste, is called in to join the artist in the joy of aesthetic creation: the sun gives their shine to mother-of-pearl and jade; the wind makes the feathers shake and spreads their vivid colours on the breeze; the ocean furnishes foam for the slender canoes and their chiselled prows. Working from instinct and with startling sensitivity, man brought the complicity of light and the hours into his play-acting, in order to enter into communion with the world. Songs and dances, head-dresses and ear-rings, among these people who had neither literature nor philosophy, make up the figurative vocabulary which for them took the place of ideas and of wisdom.

This symbolic activity where the symbol participates in what it represents, and joins the invisible to the visible, will develop, with the progress of logic, towards a more conscious symbolism. We can decipher without difficulty that language in which white is the colour of death, red of life, where the bird suggests the fluidity of the mythic to the imagination. When the myth has lost its force, the symbol will dry away into allegory or formalism. Allegory invaded classical mythology. Mythic images, reduced to their formal value, became themes and sayings for secularised speculation.

II. REGRESSION OF THE MYTHIC

1. "Birth" of the Gods

Maurice Leenhardt, in chapter 12 of *Do Kamo*, traced the process of decomposition of the myth. Nothing is more instructive as a means for understanding the specific traits of the archaic mentality compared to the mentality of advanced peoples. The myth begins to decline when the distance widens between man and the world, when things begin to separate from one another and to be situated at distinct levels.

Mythic perspective is disturbed when art, for example, evolves the third dimension. For the vision of the world which corresponds to the mythic stage spreads everything out in two dimensions. "The myth," Maurice Leenhardt writes in *Arts de l'Océanie*, "has no depth; it does its whole unfolding on one level." We observe the Guinea sculptor chiselling the prow of the canoe as a crocodile with bird's feathers and a human countenance. Then a being appears in whom his mythic vision finds an intelligible expression. In this way is shown "a first discovery and taking possession of space," a sort of bodying-forth and individualisation of the object. At the same stroke the depth of space and the temporality of time are found presented. Rationality insinuates itself into the mythic mentality.

Man finds himself cut off from his environment little by little and acquires awareness of his own person. He begins to allot himself a residence in space, to measure the duration of his life, to take possession of his body. It would be impossible, certainly, to try to date these changes or to fix their causes. One can only note some steps in this penetration of the *logos* into the "primitive" mental universe.

The myths of developed peoples have made us think that "stories of the gods" or the deeds of heroes were indissolubly bound to myths. But that imagery which comes to us from Hesiod and Ovid only brings dead myths into the picture and can only furnish doubtful evidence. Work like that of Maurice Leenhardt does us the service of freeing us from that kind of premature conclusion. The idea of a god is not primitive; it requires an idea of the person to be evolved beforehand, and we must await a rather advanced degree of rationalisation for the person to emerge from the confusion in which it is at first submerged. The gods are only heirs: their "stories" were shaped starting from mythic expressions formed around totems and other beings in whom the power of life declared itself. A certain hardening around the idea of power, a labour of intellection and of explanation precedes the hatching out of the divine into individual gods.

Long before the gods are clothed in a personality, it is around the life-cults, the passionate agitations, gifts and offerings into which affectivity has cast the deep intimacy of man with the world, that the myths, attuned in an aesthetic way, were formed, to regulate, in their turn, social discipline and the conduct of life. The myth pre-exists the gods, and it is in this totemic sphere that the root of mythic creation must be sought. According to Maurice Leenhardt's decisive observation, the legends of the gods and the totemic myths are often intermingled without being confused: the behaviour of archaic man proves that he always distinguishes what depends on the totem from what depends on the gods. He displays an uneasy, respectful interest with respect to totemic reality. He venerates the maternal ancestors, "bearers of the power of life." He strongly feels his dependence and his debt toward that life which emanates from the totem, and which the taboos envelop with sacredness. The totemic element has a strong affective tinge: piety, faithfulness, affection come from that direction; man feels himself bound to it by a relation of communion, and the offering to the totem must be presented with pure hands. Condition for life's perpetuation, the totemic cult confers an extreme importance on woman and on the feminine element, which is surrounded by the extraordinary prestige granted to the sacred principle of life. From this come the heavy responsibilities that fall on the husband, for example, in a case where the wife dies on the point of becoming a mother, even if this death, from our point of view, is only due to natural causes. An ethical value attaches to everything that is totemic; a sort of social and moral aesthetic arises from this mythic of life, and gives those who, like the people of Dobu and of the "Grande Terre," have kept the religious patrimony intact, an astonishing poise, a seriousness combined with ease; on the other hand, among the Trobrianders, mythic regression has brought with it the erosion of social discipline, and libertinism.

The gods took birth in a different mental region. There was once a state of things in which the god, the dead man, the aged, and even the man without rivals, remained undifferentiated. In the Houailou language, the same word *bao* designated them without distinction. Death is a passage to a new mode of existence. The same respectful idea enfolds the old man and the ancestor, the deceased and the soil to which his "virtues" are communicated. The earth where the ancestors are dissolved, the trees in which they survive, the winds that carry their voices, the rocks where they are watching, everything that commands strength and dignity, constitutes the divine, that divine which is scattered through the world, that invisible within the visible.

Much later the corpse will be separated from the habitat, set apart as corpse and singularised. Apart from the habitat, there will be a grave and a cemetery. The dead one will cease to be a *bao*-god in order to become a *bao*-corpse. He grows in dignity, they honour him as deceased. The world is cut up into levels of differing value, into stages. The supraterrestrial is freed from the limitations of the earthly world, at the very moment when space and time are delimited into isolated places and instants. The notion of power is emancipated from fervour and from life. The cult of deified ancestors takes precedence over the totemic taboos and observations, the masculine line over the maternal strain. The rationalisation which fixes this long maturation removes the ancestral female from the myth of life, to set her up as the goddess of fertility. The male ancestor, exalted through hero and chief, grows in power, and becomes a god. A function is assigned to him in some region of the cosmos: he is the force of the solar rays the sun-god, the power of lightning, the thunder-god, the majesty of the sea, the ocean-god. Deluded in his will to power, by the desire to prolong himself and make himself big, the chief has sumptuous tombs and pyramids constructed for himself, and will mark his superiority by the quantity and cost of his offerings, by counting up the sacrifices, the bloody hecatombs which flatter his pride and assure him a vantage point with an eye to life beyond the earth. He will seek, while living, to elevate himself to divinity, to get the gods and the world into his power.

The gods will cash, little by little, the content of reality and of glory which the myths carried in themselves. They will betoken that "other" reality, that supernatural essence, broken free of the common and day-to-day reality of simple mortals. They will be of another world, and reflective thought, "theology," will take them in hand to define their place of being and their role. But, on the social level, grave consequences emanate from this transformation—first of all, a rupture of the equilibrium between, on the one hand, the myth oriented toward the veneration and safeguarding of life, and, on the other hand, the idea of power which exalts strength, quantity, mastery; between fervour and majesty; between the maternal-feminine and the political masculine element. The religious history of humanity is, in large part, the struggle between these two spirits and these two lineages, an antagonism intermingled with exchanges and compromises.

The drawing-back of the mythic before rationality is often accompanied by a degradation of which man himself pays the price. The ground lost by the myth is not always won by reason and freedom. All too often, magic and its formalism invade it. When the iron is defective, the African smith blames the sorcery of a woman who passed while it was being cast. This magical pre-judgment disobliges him from seeking the natural cause, a mistake in its preparation, and robs him of the desire to make corrections, a first condition of any progress. Magical rigidity brings with it stagnation or regression, and such peoples as are called primitive because their behaviour has congealed into magical mechanisms, would be better classed among the retarded, if not the degenerated. The offering falls into formalism, the sacrifice into the bloody massacres where the gods are constrained by the very quantity of the victims. Where, without the mythic horizon, men "fervently believed . . . that the order of the world depended on the norms of their conduct," all was stiffened into a blind *fatum*, into a destiny pronounced for all eternity, in which people rested, to rid themselves of all risk and all initiative.

2. Mythic and Logic

The mythic does not exclude the rational, it does not precede it in time, it does not entirely disappear before its advance. It co-exists with it, and is complementary to it. The Melanesian, without abandoning any of the *no*, of the "word" which proceeds by affective ways and derives from the myth, recognises another realm open to a certain rationality: it is that of the *sa*, of fabrication, of *technique*, where calculation and measurement enter. A logic presides, for example, over the sewing of fibre skirts, in which recourse is had to a wooden measuring stick in order to obtain fibres of equal length. This bit of stick is the object around which the idea of measure and of adjustment is formed. One might be tempted to couple this important piece of evidence with Rudolph Kassner's remark about the Greek world, where the revolution of the mind was accomplished, as he sees it, around the idea of measure, the core of all rational thought. It is a rather abbreviated logic among the Canakas, who still lack the logical materials and the considered experience which would be needed to elevate them, like the Greek world, to the idea of law and of cause; but logic it is all the same, which will gain in firmness as the native is developed. It is thus by the *intelligence of the hands* that the ascent by way of abstraction begins which will lift man to the very summits of conceptual activity.

But this is a groping progression, which a formal shell threatens to enclose at every moment. As long as the technician feels himself inspired by the original word, by revelation, he keeps the dignity and freshness of his work. But when technique is no longer understood as a gift from ancestors and gods, zeal and talent are muddied and the work degenerates. An attempt is still made to keep the form of the act and the phrase that had efficacy. But what remains is nothing but incantations and magic formulas, a technique without soul or an empty vocabulary, and nothing survives of the force that kept social organisation in balance, of the heart that used to be put into cultivating one's country. The feeling of essential intimacy is lost.

In societies where, with the advent of the Logos, nature has come out of her darkness, the myth has been driven back into the shadows. It has become suspect or it has gone underground. But even so it has not disappeared. It subsists, it subsists in the depths and continues to enliven many of the forms of our culture or to externalise many a movement of the soul. It inspires poet, novelist, and orator. It is at the bottom of certain collective sentiments which to us seem as "natural," as "demonstrated" as possible: national feeling, class consciousness, the republican ideal, etc. . . . It sometimes assumes the face of science and the diction of reason: it is called the idea of progress, theory of evolution, or materialism. It explains the impassioned tonality which make certain "verities" vibrate inside us, which ought to remain serene and indifferent to contradiction. The myth is what we can never "see" in ourselves, the secret spring of our vision of the world, of our devotion, of our dearest notions. Whoever calls men to deeds of sacrifice, addresses himself, beyond all that is demonstrable and reasoned, to psychic dispositions and inner movements which can involve the individual and are of the same essence as those that take mythic form among archaic peoples.

Along the line where Lévy-Bruhl had advanced, Maurice Leenhardt completed his thinking and, on some points, went beyond him, with the freedom that direct observation could give him. Method is inseparable here from the objectives it was able to attain. Daily contact with men is the best introduction to the study of the human sciences. In any case, it is this concrete experience and this truly human comprehension that renovate our manner of understanding man in archaic civilisations and, indirectly, by comparison, permit us better to grasp certain traits of the most advanced human societies. A whole part of the human inheritance, a whole structure, as yet not well elucidated, of human reality, is thus placed within our reach, and lastly, we see more clearly into ourselves. Primitive societies are more than a geographical curiosity or a contrast to set off our own high state of culture. What we discover in them is that there may be something of the primitive and the original in the man who has always existed and who we, too, are. In breaking pathways towards this primitivity and these original things, Maurice Leenhardt wrote his name into the line of contemporary thinking, which taken together, appears as a return to the sources. Some, going back beyond the earliest philosophic speculations, ask Greek tragedy or the epic to return to us those human problems, those anxieties, those audacities, that torment of the human being as he faces the things that philosophy has rather fled from than answered. Others dig into philosophy to its very foundations, in order to find solid ground, a last basis, the root of essential questions. Tired of going along from cause to cause without ever finding the end of the chain, never surfeited by explanations which level things rather than throw light upon them, our century is turning by preference towards what is source and foundation, towards what never grows old and cannot be surmounted, and the mythic, to which Maurice Leenhardt consecrated much of his research and his writing, is dominated by precisely this concern about the *archeus*, on which everything already stands and rests, where causes are found in advance in the *raison d'être* of things. The images of fairy-tales, of fantastic narratives, of mythological figures may well seem to us to bear the marks of simplicity. But under their sometimes childish form they translate an interrogation which belongs to all the centuries, since it is man who raises these questions, man in his totality as a being at once organic, psychic, and spiritual, and he raises them in the very fact that he exists and that his life casts him into the midst of the world. At least, the mythic mentality, as Maurice Leenhardt unveiled it to us, corresponds to an attitude which is open, with respect to the world: for Oceanian man, as for ancient man, it is the universe itself that speaks of the beginnings and declares its permanence in the ephemeral, just as does the dawn of each new day, in the shrill dialogue between the real and the unreal.

The Psychology
of the Child Archetype

C. G. JUNG

Among the advocates of a psychological approach to myth, no one has written more on the subject than Carl Jung (1885–1961). Jung believed in the existence of a "collective unconscious" common to all mankind. The notion is reminiscent of the idea of "psychic unity" that was popular in the nineteenth century. From this instinctive and precultural stratum, according to Jung, come "archetypes," which appear in dreams and in myth, among other manifestations. In a somewhat mystical fashion, these archetypes operate independently of man's conscious mind. Since the archetypes exist a priori, man does not invent them but simply inherits or receives them. In his 1957 introduction to a selection of writings Psyche and Symbol (Garden City, N.Y., 1958), Jung offered the following remarks: "Mind is not born as a tabula rasa. Like the body, it has its pre-established individual definiteness; namely, forms of behaviour. They become manifest in the ever-recurring patterns of psychic functioning. . . . The psychological manifestations of the instincts I have termed archetypes. The archetypes are by no means useless archaic survivals or relics. They are living entities, which cause the praeformation of numinous ideas or dominant representations." Jung then discusses the controversial idea of the inherited nature of these allegedly pan-human archetypes. "It is important to bear in mind that my concept of the archetypes has been frequently misunderstood as denoting inherited patterns of thought or as a kind of philosophical speculation. In reality they belong to the realm of the instincts and in that sense they represent inherited forms of psychic behaviour." The reader may judge for himself how well Jung has clarified the inheritance issue.

On the one hand, several of Jung's archetypes are so general—the great mother, the child, the wise old man, etc.—that they probably are very widespread and maybe even universal. It is hard to imagine a culture that has no image of a mother figure. But even if a general mother image were universal, there would be no need to postulate that such an image was part of one's genetic inheritance. That image might be acquired through the mediation of culture. Mother images may look different in different cultures to the extent that mothers look different in different cultures. Certainly the information available in the A section of the Motif-Index of Folk Literature suggests that no myths are universal. Most myths have very definite areas of

---

geographical dispersion: Asian–American Indian, Indo-European and Semitic, African and Afro-American, etc. Since Jung's archetypes are by definition precultural, cultural anthropologists have not been very sympathetic to the Jungian approach to myth. Cultural relativism, the hallmark of most anthropological fieldwork, does not play much of a role in Jungian theory. Jungian theory has had more impact on the study of myth in the humanities. Some literary critics and art historians are intrigued by the possible universal nature of patterns, although most of the Jungian-inspired discussions rarely cite much if any data from non-Western sources. Since the Jungian data are typically drawn from Indo-European traditions (like alchemy), they seem plausible to readers from the same Indo-European world who forget that more than half of the peoples of the world (from aboriginal Australia and New Guinea, from North and South America, from Polynesia, from sub-Saharan Africa) are not represented.

There is unquestionably a mystical, anti-intellectual aspect of Jung's thought. Since the archetypes are part of the collective unconscious, they cannot, Jung maintains, ever be made fully conscious. They are therefore not completely susceptible to rational definition or analysis. As Jung puts it in the following essay, "Contents of an archetypal character are manifestations of processes in the collective unconscious. Hence they do not refer to anything that is or has been conscious, but to something essentially unconscious. In the last analysis, therefore, it is impossible to say what they refer to."

Despite the theoretical problems with the Jungian approach to myth, students of mythology should be familiar with it. For a better understanding, they might profitably consult Wilson M. Hudson, "Jung on Myth and the Mythic," in Wilson M. Hudson and Allen Maxwell, eds., The Sunny Slopes of Long Ago *(Dallas, 1966), pp. 181–97, or they may wish to read some of the many works by Jung's followers, e.g., Erich Neumann,* The Origins and History of Consciousness *(New York, 1954); Neumann,* The Great Mother: An Analysis of the Archetype *(New York, 1972); and Marie-Louise Von Franz,* Patterns of Creativity Mirrored in Creation Myths *(Zurich, 1972).*

---

1. INTRODUCTION

The author of the companion essay on the mythology of the "child" or the child god has asked me for a psychological commentary on the subject of his investigations.[1] I am glad to accede to his request, although the undertaking seems to me no small venture in view of the great significance of the child motif in mythology. Kerényi himself has enlarged upon the occurrence of this motif in Greece and Rome, with parallels drawn from Indian, Finnish, and other sources, thus indicating that the presentation of the theme would allow of yet further extensions. Though a comprehensive description would contribute nothing decisive in principle, it would nevertheless produce an overwhelming impression of the world-wide incidence and frequency of

---

1. C. Kerényi, "The Primordial Child in Primordial Times."

the motif. The customary treatment of mythological motifs so far in separate departments of science, such as philology, ethnology, the history of civilization, and comparative religion, was not exactly a help to us in recognizing their universality; and the psychological problems raised by this universality could easily be shelved by hypotheses of migration. Consequently Adolf Bastian's ideas met with little success in their day.[2] Even then there was sufficient empirical material available to permit far-reaching psychological conclusions, but the necessary premises were lacking. Although the psychological knowledge of that time included myth-formation in its province—witness Wundt's *Völkerpsychologie*—it was not in a position to demonstrate this same process as a living function actually present in the psyche of civilized man, any more than it could understand mythological motifs as structural elements of the psyche. True to its history, when psychology was metaphysics first of all, then the study of the senses and their functions, and then of the conscious mind and *its* functions, psychology identified its proper subject with the conscious psyche and its contents and thus completely overlooked the existence of a nonconscious psyche. Although various philosophers, among them Leibniz, Kant, and Schelling, had already pointed very clearly to the problem of the dark side of the psyche, it was a physician who felt impelled, from his scientific and medical experience, to point to the *unconscious* as the essential basis of the psyche. This was C. G. Carus, the authority whom Eduard von Hartmann followed.[3] In recent times it was, once again, medical psychology that approached the problem of the unconscious without philosophical preconceptions. It became clear from many separate investigations that the psychopathology of the neuroses and of many psychoses cannot dispense with the hypothesis of a dark side of the psyche, i.e., the unconscious. It is the same with the psychology of dreams, which is really the *terra intermedia* between normal and pathological psychology. In the dream, as in the products of psychoses, there are numberless interconnections to which one can find parallels only in mythological associations of ideas (or perhaps in certain poetic creations which are often characterized by a borrowing, not always conscious, from myths). Had thorough investigation shown that in the majority of such cases it was simply a matter of forgotten knowledge, the physician would not have gone to the trouble of making extensive researches into individual and collective parallels. But, in point of fact, typical mythologems were observed among individuals to whom all knowledge of this kind was absolutely out of the question,

2. *Der Mensch in der Geschichte* (1860).
3. *Psyche* (1846).

and where indirect derivation from religious ideas that might have been known to them, or from popular figures of speech, was impossible.[4] Such conclusions forced us to assume that we must be dealing with "autochthonous" revivals independent of all tradition, and, consequently, that "myth-forming" structural elements must be present in the unconscious psyche.[5]

These products are never (or at least very seldom) myths with a definite form, but rather mythological components which, because of their typical nature, we can call "motifs," "primordial images," types or—as I have named them—*archetypes*. The child archetype is an excellent example. Today we can hazard the formula that the archetypes appear in myths and fairytales just as they do in dreams and in the products of psychotic fantasy. The medium in which they are embedded is, in the former case, an ordered and for the most part immediately understandable context, but in the latter case a generally unintelligible, irrational, not to say delirious sequence of images which nonetheless does not lack a certain hidden coherence. In the individual, the archetypes appear as involuntary manifestations of unconscious processes whose existence and meaning can only be inferred, whereas the myth deals with traditional forms of incalculable age. They hark back to a prehistoric world whose spiritual preconceptions and general conditions we can still observe today among existing primitives. Myths on this level are as a rule tribal history handed down from generation to generation by word of mouth. Primitive mentality differs from the civilized chiefly in that the conscious mind is far less developed in scope and intensity. Functions such as thinking, willing, etc., are not yet differentiated; they are pre-conscious, and in the case of thinking, for instance, this shows itself in the circumstance that the primitive does not think *consciously*, but that thoughts *appear*. The primitive cannot assert that he thinks; it is rather that "something thinks in him." The spontaneity of the act of thinking does not lie,

4. A working example in "The Concept of the Collective Unconscious," pars. 105 ff., *Collected Works*, 9.1.

5. Freud, in his *Interpretation of Dreams* (p. 261), paralleled certain aspects of infantile psychology with the Oedipus legend and observed that its "universal validity" was to be explained in terms of the same infantile premise. The real working out of mythological material was then taken up by my pupils: A. Maeder, "Essai d'interprétation de quelques rêves" (1907) and "Die Symbolik in den Legenden, Märchen, Gebräuchen, und Träumen" (1908); F. Riklin, "Über Gefängnispsychosen" (1907) and *Wishfulfillment and Symbolism in Fairy Tales* (orig. 1908); and by K. Abraham, *Dreams and Myths* (orig. 1909). They were succeeded by Otto Rank of the Viennese school, *The Myth of the Birth of the Hero* (orig. 1922). In the *Psychology of the Unconscious* (orig. 1911; revised and expanded as *Symbols of Transformation*), I presented a somewhat more comprehensive examination of psychic and mythological parallels. Cf. also my essay "Concerning the Archetypes, With Special Reference to the Anima Concept."

causally, in his conscious mind, but in his unconscious. Moreover, he is incapable of any conscious effort of will; he must put himself beforehand into the "mood of willing," or let himself be put—hence his *rites d'entrée et de sortie*. His consciousness is menaced by an almighty unconscious: hence his fear of magical influences which may cross his path at any moment; and for this reason, too, he is surrounded by unknown forces and must adjust himself to them as best he can. Owing to the chronic twilight state of his consciousness, it is often next to impossible to find out whether he merely dreamed something or whether he really experienced it. The spontaneous manifestation of the unconscious and its archetypes intrudes everywhere into his conscious mind, and the mythical world of his ancestors—for instance, the *alchera* or *bugari* of the Australian aborigines—is a reality equal if not superior to the material world.[6] It is not the world as we know it that speaks out of his unconscious, but the unknown world of the psyche, of which we know that it mirrors our empirical world only in part, and that, for the other part, it moulds this empirical world in accordance with its own psychic assumptions. The archetype does not proceed from physical facts, but describes how the psyche experiences the physical fact, and in so doing the psyche often behaves so autocratically that it denies tangible reality or makes statements that fly in the face of it.

The primitive mentality does not *invent* myths, it *experiences* them. Myths are original revelations of the preconscious psyche, involuntary statements about unconscious psychic happenings, and anything but allegories of physical processes.[7] Such allegories would be an idle amusement for an unscientific intellect. Myths, on the contrary, have a vital meaning. Not merely do they represent, they *are* the psychic life of the primitive tribe, which immediately falls to pieces and decays when it loses its mythological heritage, like a man who has lost his soul. A tribe's mythology is its living religion, whose loss is always and everywhere, even among the civilized, a moral catastrophe. But religion is a vital link with psychic processes independent of and beyond consciousness, in the dark hinterland of the psyche. Many of these unconscious processes may be indirectly occasioned by consciousness, but never by conscious choice. Others appear to arise spontaneously, that is to say, from no discernible or demonstrable conscious cause.

Modern psychology treats the products of unconscious fantasy-activity as self-portraits of what is going on in the unconscious, or as

6. This fact is well known, and the relevant ethnological literature is too extensive to be mentioned here.

7. Cf. "The Structure of the Psyche," pars. 330 ff.

statements of the unconscious psyche about itself. They fall into two categories. First, fantasies (including dreams) of a personal character, which go back unquestionably to personal experiences, things forgotten or repressed, and can thus be completely explained by individual anamnesis. Second, fantasies (including dreams) of an impersonal character, which cannot be reduced to experiences in the individual's past, and thus cannot be explained as something individually acquired. These fantasy-images undoubtedly have their closest analogues in mythological types. We must therefore assume that they correspond to certain *collective* (and not personal) structural elements of the human psyche in general, and, like the morphological elements of the human body, are *inherited*. Although tradition and transmission by migration certainly play a part, there are, as we have said, very many cases that cannot be accounted for in this way and drive us to the hypothesis of "autochthonous revival." These cases are so numerous that we are obliged to assume the existence of a collective psychic substratum. I have called this the *collective unconscious*.

The products of this second category resemble the types of structures to be met with in myth and fairytale so much that we must regard them as related. It is therefore wholly within the realm of possibility that both, the mythological types as well as the individual types, arise under quite similar conditions. As already mentioned, the fantasy-products of the second category (as also those of the first) arise in a state of reduced intensity of consciousness (in dreams, delirium, reveries, visions, etc.). In all these states the check put upon unconscious contents by the concentration of the conscious mind ceases, so that the hitherto unconscious material streams, as though from opened side-sluices, into the field of consciousness. This mode of origination is the general rule.[8]

Reduced intensity of consciousness and absence of concentration and attention, Janet's *abaissement du niveau mental*, correspond pretty exactly to the primitive state of consciousness in which, we must suppose, myths were originally formed. It is therefore exceedingly probable that the mythological archetypes, too, made their appearance in much the same manner as the manifestations of archetypal structures among individuals today.

The methodological principle in accordance with which psychology treats the products of the unconscious is this: contents of an archetypal character are manifestations of processes in the collective

---

8. Except for certain cases of spontaneous vision, *automatismes téléologiques* (Flournoy), and the processes in the method of "active imagination" which I have described, e.g., in "The Transcendent Function" and *Mysterium coniunctionis*, pars. 706, 753 ff.

unconscious. Hence they do not refer to anything that is or has been conscious, but to something essentially unconscious. In the last analysis, therefore, it is impossible to say what they refer to. Every interpretation necessarily remains an "as-if." The ultimate core of meaning may be circumscribed, but not described. Even so, the bare circumscription denotes an essential step forward in our knowledge of the pre-conscious structure of the psyche, which was already in existence when there was as yet no unity of personality (even today the primitive is not securely possessed of it) and no consciousness at all. We can also observe this pre-conscious state in early childhood, and as a matter of fact it is the dreams of this early period that not infrequently bring extremely remarkable archetypal contents to light.[9]

If, then, we proceed in accordance with the above principle, there is no longer any question whether a myth refers to the sun or the moon, the father or the mother, sexuality of fire or water; all it does is to circumscribe and give an approximate description of an *unconscious core of meaning*. The ultimate meaning of this nucleus was never conscious and never will be. It was, and still is, only interpreted, and every interpretation that comes anywhere near the hidden sense (or, from the point of view of scientific intellect, nonsense, which comes to the same thing) has always, right from the beginning, laid claim not only to absolute truth and validity but to instant reverence and religious devotion. Archetypes were, and still are, living psychic forces that demand to be taken seriously, and they have a strange way of making sure of their effect. Always they were the bringers of protection and salvation, and their violation has as its consequence the "perils of the soul" known to us from the psychology of primitives. Moreover, they are the unfailing causes of neurotic and even psychotic disorders, behaving exactly like neglected or maltreated physical organs or organic functional systems.

An archetypal content expresses itself, first and foremost, in metaphors. If such a content should speak of the sun and identify with it the lion, the king, the hoard of gold guarded by the dragon, or the power that makes for the life and health of man, it is neither the one thing nor the other, but the unknown third thing that finds more or less adequate expression in all these similes, yet—to the perpetual vexation of the intellect—remains unknown and not to be fitted into a formula. For this reason the scientific intellect is always inclined to put on airs of enlightenment in the hope of banishing the spectre once

9. The relevant material can be found in the unpublished reports of the seminars I gave at the Federal Polytechnic Institute (ETH) in Zurich in 1936–39, and in Michael Fordham's book *The Life of Childhood* (London, 1944).

and for all. Whether its endeavours were called euhemerism, or Christian apologetics, or Enlightenment in the narrow sense, or Positivism, there was always a myth hiding behind it, in new and disconcerting garb, which then, following the ancient and venerable pattern, gave itself out as ultimate truth. In reality we can never legitimately cut loose from our archetypal foundations unless we are prepared to pay the price of a neurosis, any more than we can rid ourselves of our body and its organs without committing suicide. If we cannot deny the archetypes or otherwise neutralize them, we are confronted, at every new stage in the differentiation of consciousness to which civilization attains, with the task of finding a new *interpretation* appropriate to this stage, in order to connect the life of the past that still exists in us with the life of the present, which threatens to slip away from it. If this link-up does not take place, a kind of rootless consciousness comes into being no longer oriented to the past, a consciousness which succumbs helplessly to all manner of suggestions and, in practice, is susceptible to psychic epidemics. With the loss of the past, now become "insignificant," devalued, and incapable of revaluation, the saviour is lost too, for the saviour is either the insignificant thing itself or else arises out of it. Over and over again in the "metamorphosis of the gods" he rises up as the prophet or first-born of a new generation and appears unexpectedly in the unlikeliest places (sprung from a stone, tree, furrow, water, etc.) and in ambiguous form (Tom Thumb, dwarf, child, animal, and so on).

This archetype of the "child god" is extremely widespread and intimately bound up with all the other mythological aspects of the child motif. It is hardly necessary to allude to the still living "Christ-child," who, in the legend of Saint Christopher, also has the typical feature of being "smaller than small and bigger than big." In folklore the child motif appears in the guise of the *dwarf* or the *elf* as personifications of the hidden forces of nature. To this sphere also belongs the little metal man of late antiquity, the ἀνθρωπάριον,[10] who, till far into the Middle Ages, on the one hand inhabited the mine-shafts,[11] and on the other represented the alchemical metals,[12] above all Mercurius reborn in perfect form (as the hermaphrodite, *filius sapientiae*, or *infans noster*).[13] Thanks to the religious interpretation of the "child," a fair amount of evidence has come down to us from the Middle Ages showing that

---

10. Berthelot *Alchimistes grecs* 3. 25.
11. Agricola *De animantibus subterraneis* (1549); Kircher *Mundus subterraneus* (1678) 8. 4.
12. Mylius *Philosophia reformata* (1622).
13. "Allegoria super librum Turbae," in *Artis auriferae*, vol. 1 (1572).

the "child" was not merely a traditional figure, but a vision spontaneously experienced (as a so-called "irruption of the unconscious").
I would mention Meister Eckhart's vision of the "naked boy" and the
dream of Brother Eustachius.[14] Interesting accounts of these spontaneous experiences are also to be found in English ghost-stories,
where we read of the vision of a "Radiant Boy" said to have been seen
in a place where there are Roman remains.[15] This apparition was supposed to be of evil omen. It almost looks as though we were dealing
with the figure of a *puer aeternus* who had become inauspicious
through "metamorphosis," or in other words had shared the fate of the
classical and the Germanic gods, who have all become bugbears. The
mystical character of the experience is also confirmed in Part II of
Goethe's *Faust*, where Faust himself is transformed into a boy and ad-
mitted into the "choir of blessed youths," this being the "larval stage" of
Doctor Marianus.[16]

In the strange tale called *Das Reich ohne Raum*, by Bruno Goetz, a
puer aeternus named Fo (= Buddha) appears with whole troops of
"unholy" boys of evil significance. (Contemporary parallels are better
let alone.) I mention this instance only to demonstrate the enduring
vitality of the child archetype.

The child motif not infrequently occurs in the field of psychopathology. The "imaginary" child is common among women with mental disorders and is usually interpreted in a Christian sense. Homun-
culi also appear, as in the famous Schreber case,[17] where they come in
swarms and plague the sufferer. But the clearest and most significant
manifestation of the child motif in the therapy of neuroses is in the
maturation process of personality induced by the analysis of the unconscious, which I have termed the process of *individuation*.[18] Here we
are confronted with preconscious processes which, in the form of more
or less well-formed fantasies, gradually pass over into the conscious
mind, or become conscious as dreams, or, lastly, are made conscious
through the method of active imagination.[19] This material is rich in ar-

14. *Texte aus der deutschen Mystik des 14. und 15. Jahrhunderts*, ed. Spamer, pp.
143, 150.

15. John Henry Ingram, *The Haunted Homes and Family Traditions of Great Britain*
(London, 1890), pp. 43 ff.

16. An old alchemical authority variously named Morienes, Morienus, Marianus ("De
compositione alchemiae," Manget, *Bibliotheca chemica curiosa*, vol. 1, pp. 509 ff.). In
view of the explicitly alchemical character of *Faust* part 2, such a connection would not
be surprising.

17. Daniel Paul Schreber, *Memoirs of My Nervous Illness* (London, 1955).

18. For a general presentation see my "Conscious, Unconscious, and Individuation."
Special phenomena in the following text, also in *Psychology and Alchemy*, part 2.

19. "The Relations between the Ego and the Unconscious," part 2, chap. 3, also "The
Transcendent Function."

chetypal motifs, among them frequently that of the child. Often the child is formed after the Christian model; more often, though, it develops from earlier, altogether non-Christian levels—that is to say, out of chthonic animals such as crocodiles, dragons, serpents, or monkeys. Sometimes the child appears in the cup of a flower, or out of a golden egg, or as the centre of a mandala. In dreams it often appears as the dreamer's son or daughter or as a boy, youth, or young girl; occasionally it seems to be of exotic origin, Indian or Chinese, with a dusky skin, or, appearing more cosmically, surrounded by stars or with a starry coronet; or as the king's son or the witch's child with daemonic attributes. Seen as a special instance of "the treasure hard to attain" motif,[20] the child motif is extremely variable and assumes all manner of shapes, such as the jewel, the pearl, the flower, the chalice, the golden egg, the quaternity, the golden ball, and so on. It can be interchanged with these and similar images almost without limit.

II. THE PSYCHOLOGY OF THE CHILD ARCHETYPE

The Archetype as a Link with the Past

As to the *psychology* of our theme I must point out that every statement going beyond the purely phenomenal aspects of an archetype lays itself open to the criticism we have expressed above. Not for a moment dare we succumb to the illusion that an archetype can be finally explained and disposed of. Even the best attempts at explanation are only more or less successful translations into another metaphorical language. (Indeed, language itself is only an image.) The most we can do is to *dream the myth onwards* and give it a modern dress. And whatever explanation or interpretation does to it, we do to our own souls as well, with corresponding results for our own well-being. The archetype—let us never forget this—is a psychic organ present in all of us. A bad explanation means a correspondingly bad attitude to this organ, which may thus be injured. But the ultimate sufferer is the bad interpreter himself. Hence the "explanation" should always be such that the functional significance of the archetype remains unimpaired, so that an adequate and meaningful connection between the conscious mind and the archetypes is assured. For the archetype is an element of our psychic structure and thus a vital and necessary component in our psychic economy. It represents or personifies certain instinctive data of the dark, primitive psyche, the real but invisible roots

20. *Symbols of Transformation*, index, s.v.

of consciousness. Of what elementary importance the connection with these roots is, we see from the preoccupation of the primitive mentality with certain "magic" factors, which are nothing less than what we would call archetypes. This original form of *religio* ("linking back") is the essence, the working basis of all religious life even today, and always will be, whatever future form this life may take.

There is no "rational" substitute for the archetype any more than there is for the cerebellum or the kidneys. We can examine the physical organs anatomically, histologically, and embryologically. This would correspond to an outline of archetypal phenomenology and its presentation in terms of comparative history. But we only arrive at the *meaning* of a physical organ when we begin to ask teleological questions. Hence the query arises: what is the biological purpose of the archetype? Just as physiology answers such a question for the body, so it is the business of psychology to answer it for the archetype.

Statements like, "The child motif is a vestigial memory of one's own childhood," and similar explanations merely beg the question. But if, giving this proposition a slight twist, we were to say, "The child motif is a picture of certain *forgotten* things in our childhood," we are getting closer to the truth. Since, however, the archetype is always an image belonging to the whole human race and not merely to the individual, we might put it better this way: "The child motif represents the preconscious, childhood aspect of the collective psyche."[21]

We shall not go wrong if we take this statement for the time being *historically*, on the analogy of certain psychological experiences which show that certain phases in an individual's life can become autonomous, can personify themselves to the extent that they result in a *vision of oneself*—for instance, one sees oneself as a child. Visionary experiences of this kind, whether they occur in dreams or in the waking state, are, as we know, conditional on a dissociation having previously taken place between past and present. Such dissociations come about

21. It may not be superfluous to point out that lay prejudice is always inclined to identify the child motif with the concrete experience "child," as though the real child were the cause and pre-condition of the existence of the child motif. In psychological reality, however, the empirical idea "child" is only the means (and not the only one) by which to express a psychic fact that cannot be formulated more exactly. Hence by the same token the mythological idea of the child is emphatically not a copy of the empirical child but a *symbol* clearly recognizable as such: it is a wonder-child, a divine child, begotten, born, and brought up in quite extraordinary circumstances, and not—this is the point—a human child. Its deeds are as miraculous or monstrous as its nature and physical constitution. Only on account of these highly unempirical properties is it necessary to speak of a "child motif" at all. Moreover, the mythological "child" has various forms: now a god, giant, Tom Thumb, animal, etc., and this points to a causality that is anything but rational or concretely human. The same is true of the "father" and "mother" archetypes which, mythologically speaking, are equally irrational symbols.

because of various incompatibilities; for instance, a man's present state may have come into conflict with his childhood state, or he may have violently sundered himself from his original character in the interests of some arbitrary persona more in keeping with his ambitions.[22] He has thus become unchildlike and artificial, and has lost his roots. All this presents a favourable opportunity for an equally vehement confrontation with the primary truth.

In view of the fact that men have not yet ceased to make statements about the child god, we may perhaps extend the individual analogy to the life of mankind and say in conclusion that humanity, too, probably always comes into conflict with its childhood conditions, that is, with its original, unconscious, and instinctive state, and that the danger of the kind of conflict which induces the vision of the "child" actually exists. Religious observances, i.e., the retelling and ritual repetition of the mythical event, consequently serve the purpose of bringing the image of childhood, and everything connected with it, again and again before the eyes of the conscious mind so that the link with the original condition may not be broken.

22. *Psychological Types* (1923 ed.), p. 590; and *Two Essays on Analytical Psychology*, index, s.v. "persona."

Joseph Campbell's Theory of Myth

R O B E R T A. S E G A L

Another prolific writer on myth is Joseph Campbell, a charismatic lecturer on the subject who was formerly on the faculty at Sarah Lawrence College. Campbell's works on myth may be more widely read than any other mythologist's. As in the case of Jung, Campbell's influence is greater in the humanities than in the social sciences. Why don't social scientists like Campbell's approach to myth?

Let us consider one illustration from Campbell's corpus. In The Hero with a Thousand Faces, *which first appeared in 1949, Campbell delineates what he terms a monomyth (the term borrowed from James Joyce's* Finnegans Wake*). The monomyth supposedly refers to a standard cross-cultural hero pattern. Although Campbell does mention Otto Rank's* The Myth of the Birth of the Hero *(1909) in one footnote, he fails to refer to most of the earlier scholarly considerations of the hero pattern, e.g., Johann Georg von Hahn's "Aryan Expulsion and Return Formula," based on the biographies of fourteen heroes (1876), or the important study by Lord Raglan, "The Hero of Tradition," which appeared first as an article in* Folklore *(1934) and shortly thereafter in expanded book form as* The Hero *(1936). Raglan's hero pattern consists of a list of twenty-two stereotypical biographical details occurring in the lives of major Indo-European and Semitic heroes. These details, extrapolated from the careers of some twenty-one heroes (Oedipus, Theseus, Perseus, Moses, Arthur, etc.), include "His mother is a royal virgin," "The circumstances of his conception are unusual," "At birth an attempt is made, often by his father, to kill him," and "Reared by foster parents in a far country." But it is not from bibliographical omissions that Campbell's work suffers.*

Campbell constructs a composite hero pattern, based on bits and pieces from many different myths and legends. No one legend is analyzed in full. For each proclaimed element in the pattern, Campbell adduces several examples. One element in the pattern is entitled by Campbell "The Belly of the Whale." Campbell cites several examples of narrative protagonists being swallowed, e.g., Little Red Riding Hood's being swallowed by a wolf. For one thing, Red Riding Hood would be a heroine, not a hero; her story is a fairy tale, not a myth (as in monomyth); and she is swallowed by a wolf, not a whale. Only two bona fide whale incidents are cited, an Eskimo tale of the Raven trickster and, of course, the Jonah account from the Old Testament. Campbell's four-page discussion of this element of the hero pattern begins, "The idea that the passage of the magic threshold is a transit into a sphere of rebirth is symbolized in the worldwide *[my emphasis] womb image of the belly of the whale."*

Reprinted from the *Journal of the American Academy of Religion* 44, suppl. 1 (March 1978), 97–114, by permission of the author and the American Academy of Religion.

*How can one call the belly of the whale image "worldwide" on the basis of two ex-
amples? If one looks at the entries following motif F 911.4, Jonah: Fish (or water
monster) swallows a man, we do not find worldwide distribution. There are no
references to sub-Saharan Africa or to aboriginal Australia, for example. Do peoples who have never seen a whale have traditional myths recounting the adventures
of a hero in the "belly of a whale"? Highly unlikely. Campbell did not consult the
Motif-Index. Like most universalists, he is content to merely assert universality
rather than bother to document it. This is one reason why he appeals to kindred
spirits in the humanities who speak blithely about the nature of man with data drawn
exclusively from Western cultures. Anyone who knows the story of Jonah can relate
to Campbell's claim that the belly of the whale is a worldwide image. It is undoubtedly comforting to think that all mankind shares common myths and metaphors,
but the empirical facts don't support such an illusion.*

   *If Campbell's generalizations about myth are not substantiated, why should stu-
dents consider his work? Because he is such a well-known popularizer of mythology,
he has attracted a large following outside the academy, and even some university
students are intrigued by his universalistic approach. For this reason, an assess-
ment of his theory of myth is included. Robert A. Segal of the Program in Religious
Studies, Louisiana State University, has written a critique of Campbell's work. The
original essay was entitled "Joseph Campbell's Theory of Myth: An Essay Review of
his Oeuvre." Readers may wish to consult Campbell's writings for themselves to
make their own judgment about the validity and utility of his approach. For more
of Segal's writings on myth, see his masterful "In Defense of Mythology: The History
of Modern Theories of Myth," Annals of Scholarship 1 (1980), 3–49. For further
references to the vast hero-pattern scholarship, see Alan Dundes, "The Hero Pattern and the Life of Jesus," in Interpreting Folklore (Bloomington, Ind., 1980), pp.
223–61.*

The publication in 1943 of *Where the Two Came to Their Father* (Campbell, 1943), the text of a Navaho myth, marked at once the first work in
the Bollingen Series and the first work on myth by Joseph Campbell,
who contributed a commentary to the text of the myth. The publication in 1974 of *The Mythic Image* (Campbell, 1974) marks both the final,
one-hundredth work in the Bollingen Series and the crowning, whether
or not final, work by Campbell on myth. In the thirty intervening years
the Bollingen Series has published ninety-eight other works on a variety of cultural topics but on myth and religion above all. In the same
period Campbell has published four books, all on myth. His most popular book has been *The Hero with a Thousand Faces* (1949), an analysis of
hero myths, which he regards as the most fundamental myths. His
tome has been the four-volume *The Masks of God* (1959–68), in which
he traces the evolution of primitive, Oriental, Occidental, and "creative" mythology. *The Flight of the Wild Gander* (1969), a collection of essays, and *Myths to Live By* (1972), a series of public lectures, are lesser
works which serve to illustrate his major themes. In addition to coauth-

oring a "Skeleton Key" to the mythic-like *Finnegans Wake* (1944), Campbell has edited a number of works, notably the writings of Heinrich Zimmer (Campbell, 1946–55) and selected papers from the *Eranos-Jahrbücher* (Campbell, 1954–64). What all these efforts have in common is not only their subject—myth—but also a generally Jungian approach to it—an approach shared, not coincidentally, by the Bollingen Series itself, which numbers several distinguished Jungians among its authors and which in fact takes its name from that of the Swiss village where Jung had his private retreat.

The Mythic Image represents no departure from Campbell's past approach to myth. Indeed, his approach has remained basically unaltered since his first book. The distinctiveness of *The Mythic Image* is its art work. It illustrates visually the same themes which Campbell has illustrated verbally throughout his career. Because it is a summary, albeit a pictorial one, of Campbell's lifelong views, a consideration of those views seems the most appropriate way of treating it.

In all his writings Campbell offers a veritable revelation which, if heeded, can save modern man from his despair. Campbell offers his revelation with passion but also with modesty, for it is not new. It is the wisdom of primitive and ancient man, and it is to be found in myths, which modern man has blindly dismissed because he has misunderstood them. Rightly understood, they can save him from his spiritual plight.

The following extended passage from *Myths to Live By* best captures Campbell's message:

> Now the peoples of all the great civilizations everywhere have been prone to interpret their own symbolic figures literally. . . . However, today such claims can no longer be taken seriously by anyone with even a kindergarten education. And in this there is serious danger. For not only has it always been the way of multitudes to interpret their own symbols literally, but such literally read symbolic forms have always been . . . the supports of their civilizations, the supports of their moral orders, their cohesion, vitality, and creative powers. . . . With our old mythologically founded taboos unsettled by our own modern sciences, there is everywhere in the civilized world a rapidly rising incidence of vice and crime, mental disorders, suicides and dope addictions, shattered homes, impudent children, violence, murder, and despair. . . . Is the conscientious teacher . . . to be loyal first to the supporting myths of our civilization or to the "factualized" truths of his science? Are the two, on level, at odds? . . . We must now ask whether it is not possible to arrive *scientifically* at such an understanding of the life-supporting nature of myths that, in criticizing their archaic features, we do not misrepresent and disqualify their necessity. . . . Traditionally, . . . mythic beings and events

are generally regarded and taught as facts. . . . When these stories are interpreted, though, not as reports of historic fact, but as merely imagined episodes projected onto history, . . . the import becomes obvious; namely, that although false and to be rejected as accounts of physical history, such universally cherished figures of the mythic imagination must represent facts of the mind. . . . Myths, according to Freud's view, are of the psychological order of dream. . . . Both, in his opinion, are symptomatic of repressions of infantile incest wishes. . . . And thus Freud, like Frazer, judged the worlds of myth, magic, and religion negatively, as errors to be refuted, surpassed, and supplanted finally by science. . . . An altogether different approach is represented by Carl G. Jung, in whose view the imageries of mythology and religion serve positive, life-furthering ends. . . . They are telling us in picture language of powers of the psyche to be recognized and integrated in our lives, powers that have been common to the human spirit forever, and which represent that wisdom of the species by which man has weathered the milleniums. Thus they have not been, and can never be, displaced by the findings of science, which relate rather to the outside world. . . . (1972, 8–13)

Put summarily, Campbell's claims are these: (1) that modern society is in turmoil; (2) that it is in turmoil because modern man finds life meaningless; (3) that modern man finds life meaningless because he is bereft of myths, which alone make life meaningful; (4) that modern man is bereft of myths because science, the belief in which virtually defines modern man, has refuted myths taken literally; (5) that the real meaning of myth is not, however, literal but symbolic; (6) that the symbolic meaning of myth is psychological; (7) that the psychological meaning of myth is Jungian; (8) that read in symbolic, psychological, Jungian fashion, myth is compatible with science and so is acceptable to modern man; and (9) that when accepted, myth gives meaning to life and can thereby restore tranquility to society.

It is useful to examine each of these claims in order. Modern society, says Campbell first, is in turmoil. As evidence he cites "a rapidly rising incidence of vice and crime, mental disorders, suicides and dope addictions, shattered homes, impudent children, violence, murder, and despair." Assume that there actually is increasing turmoil in modern society. Campbell asserts, second, that its cause is the sense of meaninglessness modern man experiences. Surely, however, there has been equal, if not greater, turmoil in ages when people believed in myths and so presumably experienced no meaninglessness. Why, then, need the cause of the present turmoil be man's existential plight? Insofar as the turmoil is social, might it not have a social cause? Is there any reason to assume that the cause is sublime rather than mundane? What at any rate is the exact relationship between a cause so sublime and an effect so mundane? To none of these questions does Campbell supply an answer. He simply takes for granted the causal connection.

Campbell maintains next that man finds life meaningless because he has no myths. Why, one might ask, does Campbell single out myths? Why is man's travail not ascribable to the absence of, say, rituals or of religion generally? Do myths alone provide meaning?

To be sure, Campbell does associate myths with rituals and usually links myths to religion. Rituals, he says, "are the enactments of myths, and by participating in the rite one is participating in the myth and consequently activating the accordant structures and principles within one's own psyche. Without some kind of ritual enactment the whole thing fails to get inside the active aspect of one's system . . ." (Kisly 1976, 75). As closely tied to myths as rituals are, they are still only the means of inculcating myths, where the meaning lies. Because there are alternative views of ritual—for William Robertson Smith (1889), for example, myth serves ritual, not vice versa; for Mary Douglas (1966, 1970) ritual, not myth, gives meaning to life—Campbell's subordination of ritual to myth requires justification, and he fails to supply it.

As with ritual, so with religion generally: Campbell typically ties but subordinates it to myth. Modern man's despair stems from his loss of not religion as a whole but only myth. Because there are alternative views of religion—for Mircea Eliade (1959), for example, religion generally, not just myth, gives meaning to life—Campbell must justify his own view, and again he fails to do so.

According to Campbell, modern man has no myths because science has made belief in them impossible—at the literal level. For myth taken literally amounts to primitive science, to an explanation of the physical world in outdated, supernatural terms. Campbell himself, however, counts as myths themes and ideologies which in no way involve the supernatural—for instance, the myth of the American frontier, the myth of Aryan supremacy, and Marxism. Are not these myths therefore compatible with science? Why, then, can they not provide modern man with literal alternatives to myths involving the supernatural? Campbell does not say.

Yet assume that all myths involve the supernatural and that science therefore precludes the acceptance of them literally. This position is a familiar one and in Rudolf Bultmann (1953, 1958) finds its classic formulation. Campbell expresses this view uninhibitedly: "Let us ask therefore: What can the value or meaning be of a mythological notion which, in the light of modern science, must be said to be [taken literally] erroneous, philosophically false, absurd, or even formally insane?" (1969, 126).

To be acceptable to the scientific outlook of modern man myth must be interpreted symbolically. Campbell does not, however, justify a symbolic interpretation on pragmatic grounds: that myth must accommodate modern man. On the contrary, he, like Bultmann, contends, and this contention is his next claim, that the true meaning of myth is symbolic: "It must be conceded . . . that whenever a myth has been taken literally its sense has been perverted . . ." (1959, 27). For both Campbell and Bultmann the conflict, or would-be conflict, between myth and science offers an opportunity, not a justification, for reinterpreting myth. The justification is the nature of myth itself.

One significant difference between Campbell and Bultmann is that Campbell offers no justification for deeming the true nature of myth symbolic. It is one thing to appeal to the true meaning of myth to justify a symbolic reading. It is another thing to justify a symbolic reading as the true one. The justifications which Bultmann offers for his interpretation of, specifically, the New Testament are scarcely persuasive, but at least he offers some. Campbell offers none. Once again, he takes his claim for granted.

Even if Campbell were able to justify his claim that the meaning of myth is symbolic, he would still have to justify his further claim that the particular symbolic meaning of myth is psychological. Here Campbell is like Bultmann, not unlike him. Bultmann may offer arguments, convincing or not, that the meaning of myth is symbolic, but he offers no arguments that the particular symbolic meaning of myth is, for him, existential. He simply pronounces it so. Campbell does the same, simply pronouncing the symbolic meaning of myth psychological: "When these stories are interpreted, though, not as reports of historic fact, but as merely imagined episodes projected onto history . . . the import becomes obvious; namely, that although false and to be rejected as accounts of physical history, such universally cherished figures of the mythic imagination must represent facts of the mind . . ." (1972, 10).

Even if Campbell were able to justify his claims that the meaning of myth is symbolic and that the symbolic meaning of myth is psychological, he would still have to justify his yet further claim that the particular psychological meaning of myth is Jungian. In the long passage initially cited Campbell does not, it is true, say explicitly that the psychological meaning of myth is Jungian. Rather, he contrasts the negative meaning Freud finds in myth to the positive meaning Jung finds.

Freud, he explains, regards myth as the disguised fulfillment of repressed sexual desires. Jung, by contrast, sees myth as the hidden expression of unrecognized spiritual desires. Clearly, however, Campbell's view of myth is much like Jung's. For both, myths not only, as for
Freud, concern man rather than the world but also concern the spiritual side of man and give meaning to life.

At times Campbell almost explicitly endorses Jung's interpretation
of myth. For example, having noted his own interpretation of myths as
archetypes, or universal patterns, he says, "The psychologist who has
best dealt with these, best described and best interpreted them, is Carl
Jung . . ." (1972, 216). If only in the light of his editing of *The Portable
Jung* (Campbell, 1971), papers from the *Eranos-Jahrbücher*, and the
writings of Heinrich Zimmer, Campbell would seem a likely Jungian.
Nevertheless, he invariably maintains some distance from Jung—usually, as in the present quotation, by praising Jung rather than by allying
himself with him.

Even if qualified, Campbell's Jungian stance requires less an acknowledgment than a justification. Why is a Jungian interpretation of
myth preferable to, most conspicuously, a Freudian one? According to
Campbell, Freud's interpretation is inadequate, and inadequate because it ignores the meaning of myth for believers:

> No functioning mythological system can be explained in terms of the
> universal images of which it is constituted. These images are developed
> largely from such infantile imprints as those which we have just re-
> viewed and constitute merely the raw material of myth. They carry the
> energies of the psyche into the mythological context and weld them to
> the historical task of the society, where the symbols function, not in the
> way of a regressive recall of the spirit to the joys and sorrows, desires
> and terrors of little Oedipus . . . but rather as releasers and directors of
> the energies into the field of adult experience and performance. (1959, 91)

In other words, Freud's reduction of myth to its infantile, sexual origins cannot account for its adult, spiritual meaning for believers.

Incontestably, Freud, unlike Jung, neglects the adult, spiritual meaning of myth for believers, though for Jung as well as for Freud the
meaning is unconscious. The issue neglected by Campbell, however, is
whether the adult, spiritual meaning of myth is the true one. Campbell
may think that it is, but he must prove that it is. He cannot, once again,
take his claim for granted. He must refute Freud's theory.

Instead, he merely dismisses it, just as he does the theories of all
other rivals to Jung. He dismisses the theories of historians and anthropologists, both of whom, he says, deem the meaning of myth par-

ticular—to each age or society—rather than universal. He dismisses theories which deem the meaning of myth universal but literal—the theory, unnamed by him, of, for example, Eliade (1954, 1963). He dismisses theories which deem the meaning of myth universal and symbolic but nonpsychological—the theories of Edward Tylor (1871), Bultmann, and Claude Lévi-Strauss (1955, 1969–73), for example. Campbell's Jungian interpretation may, of course, be correct, but he must prove it so—by proving alternative theories inadequate and Jung's theory adequate.

Yet Campbell presents one more argument for not just his Jungian interpretation of myth in particular but his overall capacity to interpret myth, whatever his interpretation. He maintains that his lifelong comparativist study of myth has given him the perspective both necessary and sufficient to understand myth: "What I would suggest is that by comparing a number [of myths] from different parts of the world and differing traditions, one might arrive at an understanding of their force, their source and possible sense" (1972, 24). Speaking specifically of archetypes, he says, more boldly, "All my life, as a student of mythologies, I have been working with these archetypes, and I can tell you, they *do* exist and are the same all over the world" (1972, 216).

That the study of a phenomenon worldwide provides the key to its meaning is the standard contention of comparativists, but a fallacious contention it is. To assert that the study itself of a phenomenon evinces its meaning is to presuppose that the theory which explains it exists within the phenomenon, awaiting discovery. Otherwise the mere study of the phenomenon would not be decisive. In actuality, however, one brings a tentative hypothesis to bear on a phenomenon and tests it. One does not derive a hypothesis, let alone an automatically correct one, from the phenomenon, as the comparativist claim to privileged access necessarily assumes.

There are several ways of demonstrating the fallaciousness of Campbell's professed comparativist procedure. First, his amassing of myths from all over the world presupposes that the meaning of myth is universal. For Campbell to argue that his survey of myths worldwide discloses their meaning is to beg the fundamental question: whether their meaning is universal. For him to appeal in response to the universal similarities among myths is to beg the same question, which is not whether those similarities exist but whether they, rather than the differences, harbor the meaning of myth.

Second, the scrutiny of myths worldwide by other comparativists has yielded theories wholly different from Campbell's—the theories of Eliade, Tylor, Lévi-Strauss, and Freud, for example. Since the sheer study, or putatively sheer study, of myths yields a variety of theories, and often incompatible ones, it clearly does not suffice to yield the true one. The study of myths worldwide not only, then, may be unnecessary to secure the true theory of myth but certainly is insufficient. The existence of so many different theories culled from the same general sources suggests, moreover, if it does not prove, that the theories offered are imposed and not derived.

Third, the existence of rival theories aside, Campbell's own theory far exceeds the conclusions derivable from simply the study of myths. Myths themselves fail to reveal not only that their meaning is universal but also that it is symbolic, psychological, and Jungian. Campbell says that his lifelong study of myths has convinced him that archetypes exist. But surely the study itself of myths reveals the existence of universal similarities at only the literal, narrative level. It does not reveal their symbolic, psychological, spiritual nature—the Jungian sense of "archetypes." Only speculation does, and speculation transcends plain study.

Finally, even if the plain study of myths yielded Campbell's theory, and his theory only, he would still have to validate it by testing. Yet he suggests that his theory not only derives from the myths themselves but is self-validating as well. The existence of rival theories merely compounds the necessity of validating it.

Having claimed that the meaning of myth is universal, symbolic, psychological, and Jungian, Campbell claims, penultimately, that, when so understood, myth is compatible with science and is therefore acceptable to modern man. Insofar as myth for Campbell is really about man rather than the world, it does not rival science and thus is presumably compatible with it. But insofar as myth is about the spiritual side of man, its scientific credibility is tenuous.

Assume, however, the scientific acceptability of Campbell's theory. His final claim is that myth, properly understood, not only is acceptable to modern man but also, when accepted, gives meaning to life and can thereby end the turmoil facing modern society. Just as it is scarcely clear how the cause of social unrest need or even can be man's experience of meaninglessness, so it is far from clear how the solution need or, more important, can be the recovery of meaning. If Campbell, like Eliade and Bronislaw Malinowski (1926), were to take myth literally, as an explanation and even justification of the world, its capacity to solve social problems would be easier to grasp. Since, however, he insists that myth is symbolic and denies that it concerns external reality at all, the gap between it and the problems it is supposed to alleviate remains wide.

In summary so far, Campbell vaunts a number of bold claims about myth but fails to substantiate any of them. He asserts that myth, correctly understood, provides an antidote to the turmoil of modern society, but he fails to prove that the degree of turmoil in modern society is unprecedented; that modern society is in turmoil because modern man finds life meaningless; that modern man finds life meaningless because he has no myths; that myths alone give meaning to life; that modern man has no myths because his belief in science precludes his acceptance of them at the literal level; that the real meaning of myth is not, however, literal but symbolic; that the symbolic meaning of myth is psychological; that the psychological meaning of myth is Jungian; that when thus understood, myth accommodates science and so is acceptable to modern man; and that when accepted, myth gives meaning to life and can thereby allay the turmoil of modern society. Instead of arguments, Campbell makes assertions.

As irksome as Campbell's dogmatism is, even more irksome is his own violation of it. His assertion that the meaning of myth is symbolic he never qualifies, but he does qualify his seemingly uncompromising pronouncement that its symbolic meaning is psychological, whatever the particular psychology involved. Because his qualifications occur throughout his writings, and frequently within the same book, no change in his thought can account for them.

On the one hand Campbell declares continually, as in the opening quotation, that the true meaning of myth is psychological. To understand myth is to recognize that its subject matter is not the world but man, and not man's consciousness but his unconscious:

> For they [myths] are not historical. That much is clear. They speak, therefore, not of outside events but of themes of the imagination. . . . In short, these holy tales and their images are messages to the conscious mind from quarters of the spirit unknown to normal daylight consciousness, and if read as referring to events in the field of space and time . . . they will have been misread and their force deflected. . . . (1972, 24)

In deeming the meaning of myth psychological Campbell deems its meaning not only inner rather than outer but also universal rather than particular. He therefore denies that either the historian or the anthropologist can understand its meaning:

> It is of first importance not to lose sight of the fact that the mythological archetypes . . . cut across the boundaries of these cultural spheres. . . . No amount of learned hair-splitting about the differences between Egyptian, Aztec, Hottentot, and Cherokee monster-killers [in myths] can obscure the fact that the primary problem here is not historical or ethno-

logical but psychological—even biological; that is to say, antecedent to
the phenomenology of the cultural styles; and no amount of scholarly
jargon or apparatus can make it seem that the mere historian or anthropologist is dealing with the problem at all. (1969, 47–48)

On the other hand Campbell says various times, if much less often,
that the meaning of myth is either universal or particular, in which
case the historian or the anthropologist would be privy to one of its
meanings:

> We may therefore think of any myth or rite either as a clue to what may
> be permanent or universal in human nature (in which case our empha-
> sis will be psychological, or perhaps even metaphysical), or on the other
> hand, as a function of the local scene, the landscape, the history, and the
> sociology of the folk concerned (in which case our approach will be eth-
> nological or historical). (1959, 461)

Occasionally, Campbell says that myth is understandable only as both
particular and universal (1959, 462). He even states outright that "there
is no such thing . . . as an uncommitted psychology of man qua 'Man,'
abstracted from a specific historical field" (1969, 104)—a considerable
departure from his already cited claim, and in the same book, that "no
amount of scholarly jargon or apparatus can make it seem that the
mere historian or anthropologist is dealing with the problem at all"
(1969, 48).

Just, then, as Campbell ordinarily deems the meaning of myth psychological rather than historical or anthropological, yet at times deems
its meaning historical or anthropological as well as psychological, so
he ordinarily deems the meaning of myth psychological rather than
metaphysical, yet at times deems its meaning metaphysical as well as
psychological. On the one hand his rejection of a literal reading of
myth constitutes a rejection of any outer meaning. When, then, he
says, for example, that "mythologies, having sprung from the psyche,
point back to the psyche" and that "anyone seriously turning within
will, in fact, rediscover their references to himself" (1972, 266), he surely
implies that the meaning of myth is exclusively psychological.

On the other hand Campbell says several times that the meaning of
myth is metaphysical as well as psychological. In other words, myth is
about not just man but also the world:

> And so, to grasp the full value of the mythological figures that have come
> down to us, we must understand that they are not only symptoms of the
> unconscious . . . but also controlled and intended statements of certain

spiritual principles, which have remained as constant throughout the course of human history as the form and nervous structure of the human physique itself. Briefly formulated, the universal doctrine teaches that all the visible structures of the world—all things and beings—are the effects of a ubiquitous power out of which they rise . . . and back into which they must ultimately dissolve. (1949, 257)

Myth thus manifests not merely the human unconscious, as one would have otherwise assumed, but also the invisible essence of reality itself.

Having alternatively pronounced myth a psychological rather than historical or anthropological phenomenon, a historical or anthropological as well as psychological phenomenon, a psychological rather than metaphysical phenomenon, and a metaphysical as well as psychological phenomenon, Campbell offers an additional pair of views: that no single correct interpretation of myth exists, and, rather differently, that all interpretations of myth are equally correct:

There is no final system for the interpretation of myths, and there will never be any such thing. Mythology is like the god Proteus. . . . (1949, 381)

Mythology has been interpreted by the modern intellect as a primitive, fumbling effort to explain the world of nature (Frazer); as a production of poetical fantasy from prehistoric times, misunderstood by succeeding ages (Müller); as a repository of allegorical instruction, to shape the individual to his group (Durkheim); as a group dream, symptomatic of archetypal urges within the depths of the human psyche (Jung); as the traditional vehicle of man's profoundest metaphysical insights (Coomaraswamy); and as God's Revelation to His children (the Church). Mythology is all of these. The various judgments are determined by the viewpoints of the judges. (1949, 382).

If no one conclusive interpretation of myth exists, and if all interpretations are equally correct, then the advocacy of any interpretation reflects only the bias of its advocate. Campbell's advocacy of a Jungian interpretation is therefore no longer an assertion of the one true meaning of myth, as one would have supposed, but simply an expression of his personal preference.

If Campbell's statements about the meaning of myth contradict or at least qualify one another, his statements about the cause and function of myth run askew to one another. Campbell presents at least five different explanations of the cause of myth. Myth, he says variously, is the product of: (1) the fear of death (1972, 20); (2) the experience of society (1972, 20–21); (3) the experience of the world (1972, 21–22); (4) the imprintings of socially produced signals (1959, chaps. 1–2; 1972, 44–45, 216–21); and (5) the inherited archetypes of the collective uncon-

scious (1972, 216–17). These causes of myth are not incompatible, but
they are discontinuous.

Similarly, Campbell provides at least six different explanations of the
function of myth. Myth, he says, serves: (1) to justify society (1970,
140–41; 1972, 8–9, 222; Kisly 1976, 72); (2) to integrate man with society
(1959, 466–67; 1972, 8–9); (3) to integrate man with the world (1943, 59,
83; 1970, 138–40; 1972, 221; Kisly 1976, 72); (4) to explain the world
(1970, 140; 1972, 221; Kisly 1976, 72); (5) to convey socially produced signals which enable man to adjust to life crises (1949, 10–11; 1959, chaps.
1–2; 1969, 52–59; 1970, 141–42; 1972, 219, 222; Kisly 1976, 72); and (6) to
convey messages from the collective unconscious (1972, 13, 24). Most
of these functions correspond to the causes Campbell enumerates,
and the disparity among them corresponds as well.

Campbell no more proves that these varied causes and functions of
myth are the true ones than he proves that the changing meanings he
unravels are the true ones. He bases his assertions not on arguments
but on examples, examples enlisted from cultures and disciplines of
all kinds—from the East as well as the West, from primitive as well as
modern societies, and from the arts as well as religion. Yet as impressive as his array of examples is, it does not suffice. For well-nigh every
example he cites is interpretable in one or more of the other ways he
arbitrarily rejects—literally rather than symbolically, sociologically
rather than psychologically, sexually rather than spiritually, as a particular rather than a universal. In sum, for all his lifelong devotion to
myth, Campbell has yet to prove that his interpretation of myth is
correct.

WORKS CONSULTED

Bultmann, Rudolf. 1953. "New Testament and Mythology." In *Kerygma and
Myth: A Theological Debate*, ed. Hans Werner Bartsch, trans. Reginald H.
Fuller, vol. 1, 1–44. London.
———. 1958. *Jesus Christ and Mythology*. New York.
Campbell, Joseph. 1943. Commentary to *Where the Two Came to Their Father:
A Navaho War Ceremonial*. Given by Jeff King, recorded by Maud Oakes.
Bollingen Series no. 1, 51–84. New York.
———. 1944. *A Skeleton Key to "Finnegans Wake,"* with Henry M. Robinson.
New York.
———. 1946–55. Edited the works of Heinrich Zimmer: *Myths and Symbols in
Indian Art and Civilization*. Bollingen Series no. 6. New York, 1946. *The King
and the Corpse*. Bollingen Series no. 11. New York, 1948. *Philosophies of In-
dia*. Bollingen Series no. 26. New York, 1951. *The Art of Indian Asia*. Bollingen
Series no. 29. New York, 1955.

————. 1949. *The Hero with a Thousand Faces*. Bollingen Series no. 17. New York.

————. 1952. Edited *The Portable Arabian Nights*. New York.

————. 1954–68. Edited *Papers from the Eranos Yearbooks*. Trans. Ralph Manheim. Bollingen Series no. 30. Vol. 1, *Spirit and Nature*. New York, 1954. Vol. 2, *The Mysteries*. New York, 1955. Vol. 3, *Man and Time*. New York, 1957. Vol. 4, *Spiritual Disciplines*. New York, 1960. Vol. 5, *Man and Transformation*. New York, 1964. Vol. 6, *The Mystic Vision*. Princeton, N.J., 1968.

————. 1959–68. *The Masks of God*. Vol. 1, *Primitive Mythology*. New York, 1959. Vol. 2, *Oriental Mythology*. New York, 1962. Vol. 3, *Occidental Mythology*. New York, 1964. Vol. 4, *Creative Mythology*. New York, 1968.

————. 1969. *The Flight of the Wild Gander: Explorations in the Mythological Dimension*. New York.

————. 1970. Edited *Myths, Dreams, and Religion*. New York.

————. 1971. Edited *The Portable Jung*. New York.

————. 1972. *Myths to Live By*. New York.

————. 1974. *The Mythic Image*. Bollingen Series no. 100. Princeton, N.J.

Clarke, Gerald. 1972. "The Need for New Myths." *Time* 99, no. 3, 50–51.

Douglas, Mary. 1966. *Purity and Danger*. London.

————. 1970. *Natural Symbols*. London.

Eliade, Mircea. 1954. *The Myth of the Eternal Return*. Trans. Willard R. Trask. Bollingen Series no. 46. New York.

————. 1959. *The Sacred and the Profane*. Trans. Willard R. Trask. New York.

————. 1963. *Myth and Reality*. Trans. Willard R. Trask, New York.

Kisly, Lorraine. 1976. "Living Myths: A Conversation with Joseph Campbell." *Parabola* 1, no. 2, 70–81.

Lévi-Strauss, Claude. 1955. "The Structural Study of Myth." *Journal of American Folklore* 68, 428–44.

————. 1969–73. *Introduction to a Science of Mythology*. Trans. John and Doreen Wrightman. Vol. 1, *The Raw and the Cooked*. New York, 1969. Vol. 2, *From Honey to Ashes*. New York, 1973.

Malinowski, Bronislaw. 1926. *Myth in Primitive Psychology*. London.

Smith, William Robertson. 1889. *Lectures on the Religion of the Semites*. Edinburgh.

Tylor, Edward B. 1871. *Primitive Culture*. 2 vols. London.

Earth-Diver:
Creation of the Mythopoeic Male

ALAN DUNDES

*The Jungian approach to myth should not be confused with the Freudian approach.
One may disagree with both Jungian and Freudian theories, but one should be
aware of their distinctive differences. The Jungians call their discipline "analytical
psychology" so as not to be confounded with Freudians, who speak of "psycho-
analysis." Jungian theory, as presented in the preceding essays, assumes the existence of precultural, pan-human archetypes that are manifested in such mental
phenomena as myths. It is difficult to imagine how Jungian archetypes, believed to
be universal, can be reconciled with the anthropological tenet of cultural relativism. In contrast, Freudian theory can be.*

*According to Freudian theory, there is a relationship, perhaps causal, perhaps
only correlational, between the initial conditions of infancy and early childhood
(with respect to parent-child relations, sibling relations, etc.) and adult projective
systems, which include myth. Insofar as conditions of early childhood may vary
from culture to culture, so adult projective systems, including myth, may also vary.
The Freudian notions of symbolism, displacement, condensation, projection, etc.,
may be operative in all cultures, but the particular symbols and the specific projections will be culturally relative. While the Jungian archetypes are never fully
knowable, according to Jung himself, the hypothetical Freudian isomorphism or
parallelism between infantile conditioning (weaning, toilet training, etc.) and adult
projections in a given culture can be empirically tested. Either there is a correspondence or there is not.*

*Studies in the distribution of myths reveal that it is not a matter of choosing
between universals and cultural relativity. There is no myth that is universal, no
myth which is found among all the peoples of the earth. Even the widespread flood
myth seems to be absent in sub-Saharan Africa. By the same token, there is no myth
that is limited to a single culture. Most myths are found among related peoples. One
can speak of South American Indian myths, North American Indian myths (some
are common to both North and South America), African myths, Indo-European
myths. Since myths are not universal, those espousing universalist theories must
explain the lacunae in distribution. If archetypes are innate and "genetic," why aren't
the same myths found in all cultures?*

*If Freudian theory is valid, then how can one explain the existence of the same
myth in different cultures? If myths are a projection of infancy, then does that mean*

Reprinted from the *American Anthropologist* 64 (1962), 1032–50, by permission of the
American Anthropological Association. Not for further reproduction.

that cultures sharing the same myths must also share the same crucial formative elements of infantile conditioning?

One of the most widespread myth types in native North America is the earth-diver creation myth (motif A 812), as was demonstrated by Anna Birgitta Rooth's comparative survey. However, the earth-diver is also found in Asia and in eastern Europe, but not in Africa nor in aboriginal Australia. For additional studies of earth-diver not cited in the following essay, see H. de Charencey, Une Légende cosmogonique (Havre, 1884); Sarat Chandra Mitra, "On the Cosmological Myth of the Birhors and Its Santali and American Indian Parallels," Journal of the Anthropological Society of Bombay 14 (1929), 468–78; L. Walk, "Die Verbreitung der Tauchmotifs in den Urmeerschöpfungs (und Sintflut-) Sagen," Mitteilungen der Anthropologischen Gesellschaft in Wien 63 (1933), 60–76; Wilhelm Schmidt, "Das Tauchmotif in der Erdschöpfungsmythen Nordamerikas, Asiens und Europas," in Mélanges de linguistique et de philologie (Paris, 1937), pp. 111–22; and Mircea Eliade, "Mythologies asiatiques et folklore sud-est européen. I. Le Plongeon cosmogonique," Revue de l'histoire des religions 160 (1961), 157–212.

For other Freudian studies of myth, see Géza Róheim, The Gates of the Dream (New York, 1952); Philip Slater, The Glory of Hera (Boston, 1968). Most psychoanalysts tend to limit their investigations of myth to classical myths or biblical texts. For an entry to the extensive psychoanalytic literature on myth, see Justin Glenn, "Psychoanalytic Writings on Classical Mythology and Religion: 1909–1960," The Classical World 70 (1976), 225–47. See also the multi-volume reference work by Alexander Grinstein, Index of Psychoanalytic Writings (New York, 1950–).

Few anthropologists are satisfied with the present state of scholarship with respect to primitive mythology. While not everyone shares Lévi-Strauss's extremely pessimistic opinion that from a theoretical point of view the study of myth is "very much the same as it was fifty years ago, namely a picture of chaos" (1958, 50), still there is general agreement that much remains to be done in elucidating the processes of the formation, transmission, and functioning of myth in culture.

One possible explanation for the failure of anthropologists to make any notable advances in myth studies is the rigid adherence to two fundamental principles: a literal reading of myth and a study of myth in monocultural context. The insistence of most anthropologists upon the literal as opposed to the symbolic interpretation, in terms of cultural relativism as opposed to transcultural universalism, is in part a continuation of the reaction against nineteenth-century thought, in which universal symbolism in myth was often argued, and in part a direct result of the influence of two dominant figures in the history of anthropology, Boas and Malinowski. Both these pioneers favored studying one culture at a time in depth, and both contended that myth was essentially nonsymbolic. Boas often spoke of mythology reflecting culture, implying something of a one-to-one relationship. With this view, purely descriptive ethnographic data could be easily culled from the mythological material of a particular culture. Malinowski argued along similar lines: "Studied alive, myth, as we shall see, is not symbolic, but a direct expression of its subject matter" (1954, 101). Certainly, there is much validity in the notion of mythology as a cultural reflector, as the well-documented researches of Boas and Malinowski demonstrate. However, as in the case of most all-or-nothing approaches, it does not account for all the data. Later students in the Boas tradition, for example, noted that a comparison between the usual descriptive ethnography and the ethnographical picture obtained from mythology revealed numerous discrepancies. Ruth Benedict (1935), in her important introduction to *Zuni Mythology*, spoke of the tendency to idealize and compensate in folklore. More recently, Katherine Spencer has contrasted the correspondences and discrepancies between the ethnographical and mythological accounts. She also suggests that the occurrence of folkloristic material which contradicts the ethnographic data "may be better explained in psychological than in historical terms" (1947, 130). However, anthropologists have tended to mistrust psychological terms, and consequently the pendulum has not yet begun to swing away from the literal to the symbolic reading of myth. Yet it is precisely the insights afforded by advances in human psychology which open up vast vistas for the student of myth. When anthropologists learn that to study the products of the human mind (e.g., myths) one must know something of the mechanics of the human mind, they may well push the pendulum towards not only the symbolic interpretation of myth but also towards the discovery of universals in myth.

Freud himself was very excited at the possibility of applying psychology to mythology. In a letter to D. E. Oppenheim in 1909, he said, "I have long been haunted by the idea that our studies on the content of the neuroses might be destined to solve the riddle of the formation of myths . . ." (Freud and Oppenheim 1958, 13). However, though Freud was pleased at the work of his disciples Karl Abraham and Otto Rank in this area, he realized that he and his students were amateurs in mythology. In the same letter to Oppenheim he commented: "We are lacking in academic training and familiarity with the material." Unfortunately, those not lacking in these respects had little interest in psychoanalytic theory. To give just one example out of many, Lewis Spence, in his preface to *An Introduction to Mythology*, stated: "The theories of Freud and his followers as to religion and the origin of myth have not been considered, since, in the writer's opinion, they are scarcely to be taken seriously." What was this theory which was not to be taken seriously? Freud wrote the following: "As a matter of fact, I believe that a large portion of the mythological conception of the world which reaches far into the most modern religions, is *nothing but psychology projected to the outer world.* The dim perception (the endopsychic perception, as it were) of psychic factors and relations of the unconscious was taken as a model in the construction of a *transcendental reality*, which is destined to be changed again by science into *psychology of the unconscious*" (1938, 164). It is this insight perhaps more than any other that is of value to the anthropologist interested in primitive myth.

There is, however, an important theoretical difficulty with respect to the psychoanalytic interpretation of myth. This difficulty stems from the fact that there are basically two ways in which psychoanalytic theory may be applied. A myth may be analyzed *with* a knowledge of a particular myth-maker, or a myth may be analyzed *without* such knowledge. There is some doubt as to whether the two methods are equally valid and, more specifically, whether the second is as valid as the first. The question is, to employ an analogy, can a dream be analyzed without a knowledge of the specific dreamer who dreamed it? In an anthropological context, the question is: can a myth be interpreted without a knowledge of the culture which produced it? Of course, it is obvious that any psychoanalyst would prefer to analyze the dreamer or myth-maker in order to interpret more accurately a dream or myth. Similarly, those anthropologists who are inclined to employ psychoanalysis in interpreting myths prefer to relate the manifest and latent content of myths to specific cultural contexts. However, this raises another important question. Do myths reflect the present, the past, or both? There are some anthropologists who conceive of myths almost exclusively in terms of the present. While tacitly recognizing that traditional myths are of considerable antiquity, such anthropologists, nevertheless, proceed to analyze a present-day culture in terms of its myths. Kardiner's theory of folklore, for instance, reveals this bias. Speaking of the myths of women in Marquesan folklore, Kardiner observes, "These myths are the products of the fantasy of some individual, communicated and probably changed many times before we get them. The uniformity of the stories points to some common experience of all individuals in this culture, not remembered from the remote past, but currently experienced." According to Kardiner, then, myths are responses to current realities (1939, 417, 214). Roheim summarizes Kardiner's position before taking issue with it. "According to Kardiner, myths and folklore always reflect the unconscious conflicts of the present generation as they are formed by the pressure brought to bear on them by existing social conditions. In sharp contrast to Freud, Reik, and myself, a myth represents not the dim past but the present" (1940, 540).

The evidence available from folklore scholarship suggests that there is remarkable stability in oral narratives. Myths and tales re-collected from the same culture show considerable similarity in structural pattern and detail despite the fact that the myths and tales are from different informants who are perhaps separated by many generations. Excluding consideration of modern myths (for the myth-making process is an ongoing one), one can see that cosmogonic myths, to take one example, have not changed materially for hundreds of years. In view of this, it is clearly not necessarily valid to analyze a *present-day* culture in terms of that culture's traditional cosmogonic myths, which in all likelihood date from the prehistoric *past*. An example of the disregard of the time element occurs in an interesting HRAF [Human Relations Area Files]-inspired cross-cultural attempt to relate child-training practices to folk tale content. Although the tales were gathered at various times between 1890 and 1940, it was assumed that "a folk tale represents a kind of summation of the common thought patterns of a number of individuals . . ." (McClelland and Friedman 1952, 245). Apparently common thought patterns are supposed to be quite stable and not subject to cultural change during a fifty-year period. Thus just one version of a widely diffused North American Indian tale type like the Eye Juggler is deemed sufficient to "diagnose the modal motivations" of the members of a culture. Nevertheless, Kardiner's theoretical perspective is not entirely without merit. Changes in myth do occur and a careful examination of a number of variants of a particular myth may show that these changes tend to cluster around certain points in time or space. Even if such changes are comparatively minor in contrast to the over-all structural stability of a myth, they may well serve as meaningful signals of definite cultural changes. Thus, Martha Wolfenstein's comparison of English and American versions of Jack and the Beanstalk (1955) showed a number of interesting differences in detail, although the basic plot remained the same. She suggested that the more phallic details in the American versions were in accord with other cultural differences between England and America. Whether or not one agrees with Wolfenstein's conclusions, one can appreciate the soundness of her method. The same myth or folk tale can be profitably compared using versions from two or more separate cultures, and the differences in detail may well illustrate significant differences in culture. One thinks of Nadel's (1937) adaptation of Bartlett's experiment in giving an artificial folk tale to two neighboring tribes in Africa and his discovery that the variations fell along clear-cut cultural lines, rather than along individualistic lines. However, the basic theoretical problem remains unresolved. Can the myth as a whole be analyzed meaningfully? Margaret Mead in commenting briefly on Wolfenstein's study begs the entire question. She states: "What is important here is that Jack and the Beanstalk, when it was first made up, might have had a precise and beautiful correspondence to the theme of a given culture at a given time. It then traveled and took on all sorts of forms, which you study and correlate with the contemporary cultural usage" (Tax 1953, 282). The unfortunate truth is that rarely is the anthropologist in a position to know when and where a myth is "first made up." Consequently, the precise and beautiful correspondence is virtually unattainable or rather unreconstructible. The situation is further complicated by the fact that many, indeed the majority of myths are found widely distributed throughout the world. The historical record, alas, only goes back so far. In other words, it is, practically speaking, impossible to ascertain the place and date of the first appearance(s) of a given myth. For this reason, anthropologists like Mead despair of finding any correspondence between over-all myth structure and culture. Unfortunately, some naive scholars manifest a profound ignorance of the nature of folklore by their insistent attempts to analyze a specific culture by analyzing myths which are found in a great many cultures. For example, the subject of a recent doctoral dissertation was an analysis of nineteenth-century German culture on the basis of an analysis of the content of various Grimm tales (Mann 1958). Although the analyses of the tales were ingenious and psychologically sound, the fact that the Grimm tales are by no means limited to the confines of Germany, and furthermore are undoubtedly much older than the nineteenth century, completely vitiates the theoretical premise underlying the thesis. Assuming the validity of the analyses of the tales, these analyses would presumably be equally valid wherever the tales appeared in the same form. Barnouw (1955) commits exactly the same error when he analyzes Chippewa personality on the basis of a Chippewa "origin legend" which, in fact, contains many standard North American Indian tale types (Wycoco). It is clearly a fallacy to analyze an international tale or widely diffused myth *as if* it belonged to only one culture. Only if a myth is known to be unique, that is, peculiar to a given culture, is this kind of analysis warranted. It is, however, perfectly good procedure to analyze the differences which occur as a myth enters another culture. Certainly, one can gain considerable insight into the mechanics of acculturation by studying a Zuni version of a European cumulative tale or a native's retelling of the story of Beowulf. Kardiner is at his best when he shows how a cultural element is adapted to fit the basic personality structure of the borrowing culture. His account of the Comanche's alteration of the Sun Dance from a masochistic and self-destructive ritual to a demonstration of feats of strength is very convincing (1945, 93).

The question is now raised: if it is theoretically only permissible to analyze the differentiae of widely diffused myths or the entire structure of myths peculiar to a particular culture, does this mean that the entire structure of widely diffused myths (which are often the most interesting) cannot be meaningfully analyzed? This is, in essence, the question of whether a dream can be analyzed without knowledge of the dreamer. One answer may be that to the extent that there are human universals, such myths may be analyzed. From this vantage point, while it may be a fallacy to analyze a world-wide myth as if it belonged to only one culture, it is not a fallacy to analyze the myth as if it belonged to all cultures in which it appears. This does not preclude the possibility that one myth found in many cultures may have as many meanings as there are cultural contexts (Boas 1910b, 383). Nevertheless, the hypothesis of a limited number of organic human universals suggests some sort of similar, if not identical, meaning. It should not be necessary to observe that, to the extent that anthropologists are scientists, they need not fear anathematic reductionism and the discovery of empirically observable universals. The formula $e = mc^2$ is nonetheless valid for its being reductionistic.

A prime example of an anthropologist interested in universals is Kluckhohn. In his paper, "Universal Categories of Culture," Kluckhohn contends that "the inescapable fact of cultural relativism does not justify the conclusion that cultures are in all respects, utterly disparate monads and hence strictly noncomparable entities" and that "valid cross-cultural comparison could best proceed from the invariant points of reference supplied by the biological, psychological, and socio-situational 'givens' of human life" (1953, 520, 521). Of even more interest is Kluckhohn's conviction that these "givens" are manifested in myth. In "Recurrent Themes in Myths and Mythmaking," he discusses "certain features of mythology that are apparently universal or that have such wide distribution in space and time that their generality may be presumed to result from recurrent reactions of the human psyche to situations and stimuli of the same general order" (1959, 268). Kluckhohn's recurrent themes appear somewhat similar to Freud's typical dreams. Although Freud specifically warned against codifying symbolic translations of dream content and, although he did clearly state his belief that the same dream content could conceal a different meaning in the case of different persons or contexts, he did consider that there are such things as typical dreams, "dreams which almost every one has dreamed in the same manner, and of which we are accustomed to assume that they have the same significance in the case of every dreamer" (1938, 292, 39). While there are not many anthropologists who would support the view that recurrent myths have similar meaning irrespective of specific cultural context, that does not mean that the view is false. For those who deny universal meanings, it might be mentioned that the reasons why a particular myth has widespread distribution have yet to be given. The most ardent diffusionist, as opposed to an advocate of polygenesis or convergence, can do little more than show how a myth spreads. The how rarely includes the why. In order to show the plausibility of a symbolic and universal approach to myth, a concrete example will be analyzed in some detail.

One of the most fascinating myths in North American Indian mythology is that of the earth-diver. Anna Birgitta Rooth, in her study of approximately 300 North American Indian creation myths, found that, of her eight different types, earth-diver had the widest distribution. Earl W. Count, who has studied the myth for a number of years, considers the notion of a diver fetching material for making dry land "easily among the most widespread single concepts held by man" (1952, 55). Earth-diver has recently been studied quite extensively by the folklorist Elli Kaija Köngäs (1960), who has skillfully surveyed the mass of previous pertinent scholarship. The myth as summarized by Erminie Wheeler-Voegelin is:

> In North American Indian myths of the origin of the world, the culture hero has a succession of animals dive into the primeval waters, or flood of waters, to secure bits of mud or sand from which the earth is to be formed. Various animals, birds, and aquatic creatures are sent down into the waters that cover the earth. One after another animal fails; the last one succeeds, however, and floats to the surface half dead, with a little sand or dirt in his claws. Sometimes it is Muskrat, sometimes Beaver, Hell-diver, Crawfish, Mink who succeeds, after various other animals have failed, in bringing up the tiny bit of mud which is then put on the surface of the water and magically expands to become the world of the present time (1949, 334).

Among the interesting features of this myth is the creation from mud or dirt. It is especially curious in view of the widespread myth of the creation of man from a similar substance (Frazer 1935, 4–15). Another striking characteristic is the magical expansion of the bit of mud. Moreover, how did the idea of creating the earth from a particle of dirt small enough to be contained beneath a claw or fingernail develop, and what is there in this cosmogonic myth that has caused it to thrive so in a variety of cultures, not only in aboriginal North America but in the rest of the world as well?

Freud's suggestion that mythology is psychology projected upon the external world does not at a first glance seem applicable in the case of the earth-diver myth. The Freudian hypothesis is more obvious in other American Indian cosmogonic conceptions, such as the culture hero's Oedipal separation of Father Sky and Mother Earth (Roheim 1921, 163) or the emergence myth, which appears to be man's projection of the phenomenon of human birth. This notion of the origin of the emergence myth was clearly stated as early as 1902 by Washington Matthews with apparently no help from psychoanalysis. At that time Matthews proposed the idea that the emergence myth was basically a "myth of gestation and of birth." A more recent study of the emergence myth by Wheeler-Voegelin and Moore makes a similar suggestion en passant, but no supporting details are given (1957, 73–74). Roheim, however, had previously extended Matthews's thesis by suggesting that primitive man's conception of the world originated in the pre-natal perception of space in the womb (1921, 163). In any event, no matter how close the emergence of man from a hole in Mother Earth might appear to be to actual human birth, it does not appear to help in determining the psychological prototype for the earth-diver myth. Is there really any "endo-psychic" perception which could have served as the model for the construction of a cosmogonic creation from mud?

The hypothesis here proposed depends upon two key assumptions. The two assumptions (and they are admittedly only assumptions) are: (1) the existence of a cloacal theory of birth, and (2) the existence of pregnancy envy on the part of males. With regard to the first assumption, it was Freud himself who included the cloacal theory as one of the common sexual theories of children. The theory, in essence, states that since the child is ignorant of the vagina and is rarely permitted to watch childbirth, he assumes that the lump in the pregnant woman's abdomen leaves her body in the only way he can imagine material leaving the body, namely via the anus. In Freud's words: "Children are all united from the outset in the belief that the birth of a child takes place by the bowel; that is to say, that the baby is produced like a piece of faeces" (1953, 328). The second assumption concerns man's envy of woman's childbearing role. Whether it is called "parturition envy" (Boehm) or "pregnancy envy" (Fromm), the basic idea is that men would like to be able to produce or create valuable material from within their bodies as women do. Incidentally, it is this second assumption which is the basis of Bruno Bettelheim's explanation of puberty initiation rites and the custom of couvade. His thesis is that puberty rites consist of a rebirth ritual of a special kind to the effect that the initiate is born anew *from males*. The denial of women's part in giving birth is evidenced by the banning of women from the ceremonies. Couvade is similarly explained as the male's desire to imitate female behavior in childbirth. A number of psychoanalysts have suggested that man's desire for mental and artistic creativity stems in part from the wish to conceive or produce on a par with women (Jones 1957, 40; Fromm 1951, 233; Huckel 1953, 44). What is even more significant from the point of view of mythology is the large number of clinical cases in which men seek to have babies in the form of feces, or cases in which men imagine themselves excreting the world. Felix Boehm makes a rather sweeping generalization when he says: "In all analyses of men we meet with phantasies of anal birth, and we know how common it is for men to treat their faeces as a child" (1930, 455; see also Silberer 1925, 393). However, there is a good deal of clinical evidence supporting the existence of this phantasy. Stekel (1959, 45), for example, mentions a child who called the feces "Baby." The possible relevance of this notion to the myth of the origin of man occurred to Abraham (1948, 320), Jung (1916, 214), and Rank (1922, 54). Jung's comment is: "The first people were made from excrement, potter's earth and clay" (cf. Schwarzbaum 1960, 48). In fact, Jung rather ingeniously suggests that the idea of anal birth is the basis of the motif of creating by "throwing behind oneself" as in the case of Deucalion and Pyrrha. Nevertheless, neither Abraham, Jung, nor Rank emphasized the fact that anal birth is especially employed by men. It is true that little girls also have this phantasy, but presumably the need for the phantasy disappears upon the giving of birth to a child. (There may well be some connection between this phantasy and the widespread occurrence of geophagy among pregnant women [Elwin 1949, 292, n. 1].)

Both of the assumptions underlying the hypothesis attempting to explain the earth-diver myth are found in Genesis. As Fromm points out (1951, 234), the woman's creative role is denied. It is man who creates and, in fact, it is man who gives birth to woman. Eve is created from substance taken from the body of Adam. Moreover, if one were inclined to see the Noah story as a gestation myth, it would be noteworthy that it is the man who builds the womb-ark. It would also be interesting that the flood waters abate only after a period roughly corresponding to the length of human pregnancy. Incidentally, it is quite likely that the Noah story is a modified earth-diver myth. The male figure sends a raven once and a dove twice to brave the primordial waters seeking traces of earth (cf. Schwarzbaum 1960, 52, n. 15a). In one apocryphal account, the raven disobeys instructions by stopping to feast on a dead man, and in another he is punished by having his feathers change color from white to black (Ginzberg 1925, 39, 164). Both of these incidents are found in American Indian earth-diver myths (Rooth 1957, 498). In any case, one can see that there are male myths of creation in Genesis, although Fromm does not describe them all. Just as Abraham, Jung, and Rank had anal birth without pregnancy envy, Fromm has pregnancy envy without anal birth. He neglects to mention that man was created from dust. One is tempted to speculate as to whether male creation myths might be in any way correlated with highly patriarchal social organization.

Of especial pertinence to the present thesis is the clinical data on phantasies of excreting the universe. Lombroso, for example, describes two artists, each of whom had the delusion that they were lords of the world which they had excreted from their bodies. One of them painted a full-length picture of himself naked, among women, ejecting worlds (1895, 201). In this phantasy world, the artist flaunting his anal creativity depicts himself as superior to the women who surround him. Both Freud and Stekel have reported cases in which men fancied defecating upon the world, and Abraham cites a dream of a patient in which the patient dreamed he expelled the universe out of his anus (Freud 1949b, 407; Stekel 1959, 44; Abraham 1948, 320). Of course, the important question for the present study is whether or not such phantasies ever occur in mythical form. Undoubtedly, the majority of anthropologists would be somewhat loath to interpret the earth-diver myth as an anal birth fantasy on the basis of a few clinical examples drawn exclusively from Western civilization. However, the dearth of mythological data results partly from the traditional prudery of some ethnographers and many folklorists. Few myths dealing with excretory processes find their way into print. Nevertheless, there are several examples, primarily of the creation of man from excrement. John G. Bourke (1891, 266) cites an Australian myth of such a creation of man. In India, the elephant-headed god Ganesh is derived from the excrement of his mother (Berkeley-Hill 1921, 330). In modern India, the indefatigable Elwin has collected quite a few myths in which the earth is excreted. For instance, a Lanjhia Saora version describes how Bhimo defecates on Rama's head. The feces is thrown into the water, which immediately dries up, and the earth is formed (1949, 44). In a Gadaba myth, Larang the great Dano devoured the world, but Mahaprabhu "caught hold of him and squeezed him so hard that he excreted the earth he had devoured. . . . From the earth that Larang excreted, the world was formed again" (1949, 37). In other versions, a worm excretes the earth, or the world is formed from the excreta of ants (1949, 47; 1954, 9). An example closer to continental North America is reported by Bogoras. In this Chukchee creation myth, Raven's wife tells Raven to go and try to create the earth, but Raven protests that he cannot. Raven's wife then announces that she will try to create a "spleen-companion" and goes to sleep. Raven "looks at his wife. Her abdomen has enlarged. In her sleep she creates without effort. He is frightened, and turns his face away." After Raven's wife gives birth to twins, Raven says, "There, you have created men! Now I shall go and try to create the earth." Then "Raven flies and defecates. Every piece of excrement falls upon water, grows quickly, and becomes land." In this fashion, Raven succeeds in creating the whole earth (Bogoras 1913, 152). Here there can be no doubt of the connection between pregnancy envy and anal creation. Unfortunately, there are few examples which are as clear as the Chukchee account. One of the only excremental creation myths reported in North America proper was collected by Boas. He relates (1895, 159) a Kwakiutl tale of Mink making a youth from his excrement. However, the paucity of American Indian versions does not necessarily reflect the nonexistence of the myth in North America. The combination of puritanical publishing standards in the United States with similar collecting standards may well explain in part the lack of data. In this connection it is noteworthy that whereas the earlier German translation of Boas's Kwakiutl version refers specifically to excrement, the later English translation speaks of a musk-bag (1910a, 159). Most probably ethnographers and editors alike share Andrew Lang's sentiments when he alludes to a myth of the Encounter Bay people "which might have been attributed by Dean Swift to the Yahoos, so foul an origin does it allot to mankind" (1899, 166). Despite the lack of a great number of actual excremental myths, the existence of any at all would appear to lend support to the hypothesis that men do think of creativity in anal terms, and further that this conception is projected into mythical cosmogonic terms.

There is, of course, another possible reason for the lack of overtly excremental creation myths, and this is the process of sublimation. Ferenczi, in his essay "The Ontogenesis of the Interest in Money" (1956), has given the most explicit account of this process as he traces the weaning of the child's interest from its feces through a whole graduated series of socially sanctioned substitutes ranging from moist mud, sand, clay, and stones to gold or money. Anthropologists will object that Ferenczi's ontogenetic pattern is at best only applicable to Viennese type culture. But, to the extent that any culture has toilet training (and this includes any culture in which the child is not permitted to play indiscriminately with his feces), there is some degree of sublimation. As a matter of fact, so-called anal personality characteristics have been noted among the Yurok (Posinsky), Mohave (Devereux), and Chippewa (Barnouw, Hallowell). Devereux (1951, 412) specifically comments upon the use of mud as a fecal substitute among the Mohave. Moreover, it may well be that the widespread practices of smearing the body with paint or daubing it with clay in preparation for aggressive activities have some anal basis. As for the gold-feces equation, anthropologists have yet to explain the curious linguistic fact that in Nahuatl the word for gold is *teocuitlatl*, which is a compound of *teotl*, "god," and *cuitlatl*, "excrement." Gold is thus "excrement of the gods" or "divine excrement" (Saville 1920, 118). This extraordinary confirmation of Freudian symbolism, which was pointed out by Reik as early as 1915, has had apparently little impact upon anthropologists blindly committed to cultural relativism. (See also Roheim 1923, 387. However, for an example of money-feces symbolism in the dream of a Salteaux Indian, see Hallowell 1938.) While the gold-feces symbolism is hardly likely in cultures where gold was unknown, there is reason for assuming that some sort of sublimation does occur in most cultures. (For American Indian instances of "jewels from excrements" see Thompson 1929, 329, n. 190a. In this connection, it might be pointed out that, in Oceanic versions of the creation of earth from an object thrown on the primeval waters, as found in Lessa's recent comprehensive study [1961], the items thrown include, in addition to sand, such materials as rice chaff, betel nut husks, and ashes, which would appear to be waste products.) If this is so, then it may be seen that a portion of Ferenczi's account of the evolutionary course of anal sublimation is of no mean importance to the analysis of the earth-diver myth. Ferenczi states: "Even the interest for the specific odour of excrement does not cease at once, but is only displaced on to other odours that in any way resemble this. The children continue to show a liking for the smell of sticky materials with a characteristic odour, especially the strongly smelling degenerated produce of cast off epidermis cells which collects between the toes, nasal secretion, ear-wax, and the dirt of the nails, while many children do not content themselves with the moulding and sniffing of these substances, but also take them into the mouth" (1956, 273). Anyone who is familiar with American Indian creation myths will immediately think of examples of the creation of man from the rubbings of skin (Thompson 1955, motif A 1263.3), birth from mucus from the nose (motif T 541.8.3), etc. The empirical fact is that these myths do exist! With respect to the earth-diver myth, the common detail of the successful diver's returning with a little dirt under his fingernail is entirely in accord with Ferenczi's analysis. The fecal nature of the particle is also suggested by its magical expansion. One could imagine that as one defecates one is thereby creating an ever-increasing amount of earth. (Incidentally, the notion of creating land masses through defecation has the corollary idea of creating bodies of water such as oceans through micturition [motif A 923.1]. For example, in the previously mentioned Chukchee myth, Raven, after producing the earth, began to pass water. A drop became a lake, while a jet formed a river.)

The present hypothesis may also serve to elucidate the reasons why Christian dualism is so frequently found in Eurasian earth-diver versions. Earl Count considers the question of the dualistic nature of earth-diver as one of the main problems connected with the study of the myth (1952, 56). Count is not willing to commit himself as to whether the earth-diver is older than a possible dualistic overlay, but Köngäs agrees with earlier scholars that the dualism is a later development (Count 1952, 61; Köngäs 1960, 168). The dualism usually takes the form of a contest between God and the devil. As might be expected from the tradition of philosophical dualism, the devil is associated with the body, while God is concerned with the spiritual element. Thus it is the devil who dives for the literally lowly dirt and returns with some under his nails. An interesting incident in view of Ferenczi's account of anal sublimation is the devil's attempt to save a bit of earth by putting it in his mouth. However, when God expands the earth, the stolen bit also expands, forcing the devil to spit it out, whereupon mountains or rocks are formed (Köngäs 1960, 160–61). In this connection, another dualistic creation myth is quite informative. God is unable to stop the earth from growing and sends the bee to spy on the devil to find a way to accomplish this. When the bee buzzes, in leaving the devil to report back to God, the devil exclaims, "Let him eat your excrement, whoever sent you!" God did this and the earth stopped growing (Dragomanov 1961, 3). Since the eating of excrement prevented the further growth of the earth, one can see the fecal nature of the substance forming the earth. In still another dualistic creation myth, there is even an attempt made to explain why feces exists at all in man. In this narrative, God creates a pure body for man but has to leave it briefly in order to obtain a soul. In God's absence, the devil defiles the body. God, upon returning, has no alternative but to turn his creation inside out, which is the reason why man has impurities in his intestines (Campbell 1956, 294). These few examples should be sufficient to show that the dualism is primarily a matter of separating the dross of matter from the essence of spirit. The devil is clearly identified with matter and in particular with defecation. In a phrase, it is the devil who does the dirty work. Thus Köngäs is quite right in seeing a psycho-physical dualism, that is, the concept of the soul as being separable from the body, as the basis for the Christian traditional dualism. However, she errs in assuming that both the creator and his "doppelgänger" are spiritual or concerned with the spiritual (1960, 169). Dualism includes one material entity and, specifically in earth-diver dualism, one element deals with dirt while the other creates beauty and valuable substance from the dirt.

It should be noted that earth-diver has been previously studied from a psychoanalytic perspective. Géza Róheim, the first psychoanalytic anthropologist, made a great number of studies of the folklore and mythology of primitive peoples. In his earlier writings, Róheim tended to follow along the lines suggested by Freud, Abraham, and Rank in seeing folk tales as analogous to dreams (1922, 182), but later, after he discovered, for example, that the Aranda word *altjira* meant both dream and folk tale (1941, 267), he began to speculate as to a more genetic relationship between dream and folk tale or myth. In a posthumously published paper, "Fairy Tale and Dream" (1953a), this new theory of mythology and the folk tale is explained. "To put this theory briefly: It seems that dreams and myths are not merely similar but that a large part of mythology is actually derived from dreams. In other words, we can not only apply the standard technique of dream interpretation in analyzing a fairy tale but can actually think of tales and myths as having arisen from a dream, which a person dreamed and then told to others, who retold it again, perhaps elaborated in accord with their own dreams" (1953a, 394; for a sample of Róheim's exegesis of what he terms a dream-derived folk tale, see 1953b). The obvious criticism of this theory has been made by E. K. Schwartz in noting that "one can accept the same psychoanalytic approach and techniques for the understanding of the fairy tale and the dream, without having to accept the hypothesis that the fairy tale is nothing else but an elaboration of a dream" (1956, 747–48). Thus Schwartz, although he lists twelve characteristics of fairy tales which he also finds in dreams, including such features as condensation, displacement, symbolism, etc., does conclude that it is not necessary to assume that fairy tales are dreams. Róheim, in *The Gates of the Dream*, a brilliant if somewhat erratic full-length treatment of primitive myth and dream, had already addressed himself to this very criticism. He phrases the criticism rhetorically: "Then why assume the dream stage, since the unconscious would contain the same elements, even without dreams?" His answer is that the dream theory would explain not only the identity in content but also the striking similarity in structure and plot sequence (1951, 348). Actually, the fundamental criticism is not completely explained away. There is no reason why both dream and myth cannot be derived from the human mind without making the myth only indirectly derived via the dream.

Róheim's theory comes to the fore in his analysis of earth-diver. In fact, he even states that the earth-diver myth is "a striking illustration of the dream origin of mythology" (1951, 423). Róheim has assumed the existence of what he calls a basic dream in which the dreamer falls into something, such as a lake or a hole. According to Róheim, this dream is characterized by a "double vector" movement consisting both of a regression to the womb and the idea of the body as penis entering the vagina. In interpreting the earth-diver as an example of this basic dream, Róheim considers the diving into the primeval waters of the womb as an erection. Of considerable theoretical interest is Róheim's apparent postulation of a monogenetic origin of earth-diver: "*The core of the myth is a dream actually dreamed once upon a time by one person.* Told and retold it became a myth . . ." (1951, 428). Actually, Róheim's overall theory of the dream origin of myth is not at all necessarily a matter of monogenesis. In fact, he states that it is hardly likely as a general rule that an original dream was dreamed by one person in a definite locality, from which the story spread by migration. Rather, "many have dreamed such dreams, they shaped the narrative form in many centers, became traditional, then merged and influenced each other in the course of history" (1951, 348).

The validity of Róheim's interpretation of earth-diver depends a great deal on, first of all, his theory of the dream origin of myth and, secondly, the specific nature of his so-called basic dream. One could say, without going so far as to deny categorically Róheim's theoretical contentions, that neither the dream origin of myth nor the existence of the "basic dream" is necessary for an understanding of the latent content of the earth-diver myth. Curiously enough, Róheim himself anticipates in part the present hypothesis in the course of making some additional comments on earth-diver. In discussing the characteristic trait of the gradual growth of the earth, Róheim cites an Onondaga version in which he points out the parallelism between a pregnant woman and the growing earth. From the point of view of the present hypothesis, the parallelism is quite logically attributable to the male creator's

desire to achieve something like female procreativity. Thus the substance produced from his body, his baby so to speak, must gradually
increase in size, just as the process of female creativity entails a gradually increasing expansion. (Here again, the observation of the apparently magically expanding belly of a pregnant woman is clearly a human universal.) Róheim goes on to mention what he considers to be a
parallel myth, namely that of "the egg-born earth or cloacal creation."
As will be shown later, Róheim is quite correct in drawing attention to
the egg myth. Then following his discussion of the Eurasian dualistic
version in which the devil tries to keep a piece of swelling earth in his
mouth, Róheim makes the following analysis: "If we substitute the rec-
tum for the mouth the myth makes sense as an awakening dream con-
ditioned by excremental pressure" (1951, 429). In other words, Róheim
does recognize the excremental aspects of earth-diver, and, in accordance with his theory of the dream origin of myth, he considers the
myth as initially a dream caused by the purely organic stimulus of the
need to defecate. Róheim also follows Rank (1912, 1922, 89) in interpreting deluge myths as transformations of vesical dreams (1951, 439–
65). Certainly, one could make a good case for the idea that some folk
tales and myths are based upon excremental pressures, perhaps originally occurring during sleep. In European folklore, there are numerous examples, as Freud and Oppenheim have amply demonstrated, of
folk tales which relate how individuals attempt to mark buried treasure only to awake to find they have defecated on themselves or on
their sleeping partners. It is quite possible that there is a similar basis
for the Winnebago story reported by Radin (1956, 26–27) in which
Trickster, after eating a laxative bulb, begins to defecate endlessly. In
order to escape the rising level of excrement, Trickster climbs a tree,
but he is forced to go higher and higher until he finally falls down right
into the rising tide. Another version of this Trickster adventure is found
in Barnouw's account of a Chippewa cycle (1955, 82). The idea of the
movement being impossible to stop once it has started is also suggested in the previously cited Eurasian account of God's inability to
stop the earth's growth. That God must eat excrement to stop the
movement is thematically similar to another Trickster version in which
Trickster's own excrement, rising with flood waters, comes perilously
close to his mouth and nose. However, the fact that there may be "excremental pressure myths" with or without a dream origin does not
mean that excremental pressure is the sole underlying motivation of
such a myth as earth-diver. To call earth-diver simply a dream-like
myth resulting from a call of nature without reference to the notions of

male pregnancy envy and anal birth theory is vastly to oversimplify the psychological etiology of the myth. Róheim, by the way, never does reconcile the rather phallic interpretation of his basic dream with the excremental awakening dream interpretation of earth-diver. A multicausal hypothesis is, of course, perfectly possible, but Róheim's two interpretations seem rather to conflict. In any event, Róheim sees creation myths as prime examples of his dream-myth thesis. He says, "It seems very probable that creation myths, wherever they exist, are ultimately based on dreams" (1951, 430).

The idea of anal creation myths spurred by male pregnancy envy is not tied to the dream origin of myth theory. That is not to say that the dream theory is not entirely possible but only to affirm the independence of the two hypotheses. In order to document further the psychological explanation of earth-diver, several other creation myths will be very briefly discussed. As already mentioned, Róheim drew attention to the cosmic egg myths. There is clinical evidence suggesting that men who have pregnancy phantasies often evince a special interest in the activities of hens, particularly with regard to their laying of eggs (Eisler 1921, 260, 285). The hens appear to defecate the eggs. Freud's famous "Little Hans," in addition to formulating a "lumf" baby theory, also imagined that he laid an egg (1949b, 227–28). Lombroso (1895, 182) mentions a demented pseudo-artist who painted himself as excreting eggs which symbolized worlds. Ferenczi, moreover, specifically comments upon what he calls the "symbolic identity of the egg with faeces and child." He suggests that excessive fondness for eggs "approximates much more closely to primitive coprophilia than does the more abstract love of money" (1950, 328). Certainly the egg-creation myth is common enough throughout the world (Lukas 1894), despite its absence in North America. It is noteworthy that there are creations of men from eggs (motifs T 542 or A 1222) and creation of the world from a cosmic egg (motif A 641). As in the case of feces (or mud, clay, or dirt), the cloacal creation is capable of producing either men or worlds or both.

Another anal creation myth which does occur in aboriginal North America has the spider as creator. The Spider myth, which is one of Rooth's eight creation myth types found in North America, is reported primarily in California and the Southwest. The spider as creator is also found in Asia and Africa. Empirical observation of spiders would quite easily give rise to the notion of the spider as a self-sufficient creator who appeared to excrete his own world, and a beautiful and artistic world at that. Although psychoanalysts have generally tended to interpret the spider as a mother symbol (Abraham 1948, 326–32; cf. Spider Woman in the Southwest), Freud noted at least one instance in folklore where the thread spun by a spider was a symbol for evacuated feces. In a Prussian-Silesian tale, a peasant wishing to return to earth from heaven is turned into a spider by Peter. As a spider, the peasant spins a long thread by which he descends, but he is horrified to discover as he arrives just over his home that he could spin no more. He squeezes and squeezes to make the thread longer and then suddenly wakes up from his dream to discover that "something very human had happened to him while he slept" (Freud and Oppenheim 1958, 45). The spider as the perfect symbol of male artistic creativity is described in a poem by Whitman entitled "The Spider." In the poem, the spider is compared to the soul of the poet as it stands detached and alone in "measureless oceans of space" launching forth filament out of itself (Wilbur and Muensterberger 1951, 405). Without going into primitive Spider creation myths in great detail, it should suffice to note that, as in other types of male myths of creation, the creator is able to create without any reference to women. Whether a male creator spins material, molds clay, lays an egg, fabricates from mucus or epidermal tissue, or dives for fecal mud, the psychological motivation is much the same.

Other cosmogonic depictions of anal birth have been barely touched upon. As Ernest Jones has shown in some detail (1951, 266–357), some of the other aspects of defecation such as the sound (creation by thunder or the spoken word), or the passage of air (creation by wind or breath), are also of considerable importance in the study of mythology. With respect to the latter characteristic, there is the obvious Vedic example of Pragapati, who created mankind by means of "downward breathings" from the "back part," cited by Jones (1951, 279). One account of Pragapati's creation of the earth relates the passing of air with the earth-diver story. "Prajapati first becomes a wind and stirs up the primeval ocean; he sees the earth in the depths of the ocean; he turns himself into a boar and draws the earth up" (Dragomanov 1961, 28). Another ancient male anal wind myth is found in the Babylonian account of Marduk. Marduk conquers Tiamat by the following means: "The evil wind which followed him, he loosed it in her face. . . . He drove in the evil wind so that she could not close her lips. The terrible winds filled her belly" (Guirand 1959, 51). Marduk then pierces Tiamat's belly and kills her. The passage of wind by the male Marduk leads to the destruction of the female Tiamat. Marduk rips open the rival creator, the belly of woman, which had given birth to the world. There is also the Biblical instance of the divine (af)flatus moving on the face of the waters. Köngäs (1960, 169) made a very astute intuitive observation when she suggested that there was a basic similarity between the spirit of God moving upon the primeval water and the earth-diver myth. The common denominator is the male myth of creation whereby the male creator uses various aspects of the only means available, namely the creative power of the anus.

Undoubtedly anthropologists will be sceptical of any presentation in which evidence is marshalled à la Frazer and where the only criteria for the evidence appears to be the gristworthyness for the mill. Nevertheless, what is important is the possibility of a theory of universal symbolism which can be verified by empirical observation in the field in decades to come. Kluckhohn, despite a deep-seated mistrust of pan-human symbolism, confesses that his own field work as well as that of his collaborators has forced him to the conclusion that "Freud and other psychoanalysts have depicted with astonishing correctness many central themes in motivational life which are universal. The styles of expression of these themes and much of the manifest content are culturally determined but the underlying psychological drama transcends cultural difference" (Wilbur and Muensterberger 1951, 120). Kluckhohn bases his assumptions on the notion of a limited number of human "givens," such as human anatomy and physiology. While it is true that thoughts about the "givens" are not "given" in the same sense, it may be that their arising is inevitable. In other words, man is not born with the idea of pregnancy envy. It is acquired through experience, that is, through the mediation of culture. But if certain experiences are universal, such as the observation of female pregnancy, then there may be said to be secondary or derived "givens," using the term in an admittedly idiosyncratic sense. This is very important for the study of myth. It has already been pointed out that from a cultural relativistic perspective, the only portion of mythology which can be profitably studied is limited to those myths which are peculiar to a particular culture or those differences in the details of a widely diffused myth. Similarly, the literal approach can glean only so much ethnographic data from reflector myths. Without the assumption of symbolism and universals in myth, a vast amount of mythology remains of little use to the anthropologist. It should also be noted that there is, in theory, no conflict between accepting the idea of universals and advocating cultural relativism. It is not an "either/or" proposition. Some myths may be universal and others not. It is the all-or-nothing approach which appears to be erroneous. The same is true for the polygenesis-diffusion controversy; they also are by no means mutually exclusive. In the same way, there is no inconsistency in the statement that myths can either reflect or refract culture. (The phrase was suggested by A. K. Ramanujan.) Lévi-Strauss (1958, 51) criticizes psychoanalytic interpretations of myth because, as he puts it, if there's an evil grandmother in the myths, "it will be claimed that in such a society grandmothers are actually evil and that mythology reflects the social structure and the social relations; but should the actual data be conflicting, it would be readily claimed that the purpose of mythology is to provide an outlet for repressed feelings. Whatever the situation may be, a clever dialectic will always find a way to pretend that a meaning has been unravelled." Although Lévi-Strauss may be justified insofar as he is attacking the "Have you stopped beating your wife?" antics of some psychoanalysts, there is not necessarily any inconsistency stemming from data showing that in culture A evil grandmothers in fact are also found in myth, while in culture B conscious norms of pleasant grandmothers disguise unconscious hatred for "evil" grandmothers, a situation which may be expressed in myth. In other words, myths can and usually do contain both conscious and unconscious cultural materials. To the extent that conscious and unconscious motivation may vary or be contradictory, so likewise can myth differ from or contradict ethnographic data. There is no safe monolithic theory of myth except that of judicious eclecticism as championed by E. B. Tylor. Mythology must be studied in cultural context in order to determine which individual mythological elements reflect and which refract the culture. But, more than this, the cultural relative approach must not preclude the recognition and identification of transcultural similarities and potential universals. As Kluckhohn said, "The anthropologist for two generations has been obsessed with the differences between peoples, neglecting the equally real similarities—upon which the 'universal culture pattern' as well as the psychological uniformities are clearly built" (Wilbur and Muensterberger 1951, 121). The theoretical implications for practical field work of seeking psychological uniformities are implicit. Ethnographers must remove the traditional blinders and must be willing to collect *all* pertinent material even if it borders on what is obscene by the ethnographer's ethnocentric standards. The ideal ethnographer must not be afraid of diving deep and coming up with a little dirt; for, as the myth relates, such a particle may prove immensely valuable and may expand so as to form an entirely new world for the students of man.

REFERENCES CITED

Abraham, Karl. 1948. *Selected Papers on Psycho-Analysis*. The International Psycho-Analytical Library no. 13. London.

Barnouw, Victor. 1955. "A Psychological Interpretation of a Chippewa Origin Legend." *Journal of American Folklore* 68, 73–85, 211–23, 341–55.

Benedict, Ruth. 1935. *Zuni Mythology*. Columbia University Contributions to Anthropology no. 21. New York.

Bettelheim, Bruno. 1955. *Symbolic Wounds*. London.

Berkeley-Hill, Owen. 1921. "The Anal-Erotic Factor in the Religion, Philosophy and Character of the Hindus." *International Journal of Psycho-Analysis* 2, 306–38.

Boas, Franz. 1895. *Indianische Sagen von der nord-pacifischen Küste Amerikas*. Berlin.

———. 1910a. *Kwakiutl Tales*. Columbia University Contributions to Anthropology no. 2. New York.

———. 1910b. "Psychological Problems in Anthropology." *American Journal of Psychology* 21, 371–84.

Boehm, Felix. 1930. "The Femininity-Complex in Men." *International Journal of Psycho-Analysis* 11, 444–69.

Bogoras, Waldemar. 1913. *Chuckchee Mythology*. Jesup North Pacific Expedition Publications no. 8.

Bourke, John G. 1891. *Scatalogic Rites of All Nations*. Washington, D.C.

Campbell, Joseph. 1956. *The Hero with a Thousand Faces*. New York.

Count, Earl W. 1952. "The Earth-Diver and the Rival Twins: A Clue to Time Correlation in North-Eurasiatic and North American Mythology." In *Indian Tribes of Aboriginal America*. ed. Sol Tax. Selected Papers of the 19th International Congress of Americanists. Chicago.

Devereux, George. 1951. "Cultural and Characterological Traits of the Mohave Related to the Anal Stage of Psychosexual Development." *Psychoanalytic Quarterly* 20, 398–422.

Dragomanov, Mixailo Petrovic. 1961. *Notes on the Slavic Religio-Ethical Legends: The Dualistic Creation of the World*. Russian and East European Series, vol. 23. Bloomington, Ind.

Eisler, Michael Joseph. 1921. "A Man's Unconscious Phantasy of Pregnancy in the Guise of Traumatic Hysteria: A Clinical Contribution to Anal Erotism." *International Journal of Psycho-Analysis* 2, 255–86.

Elwin, Verrier. 1949. *Myths of Middle India*. Madras.

———. 1954. *Tribal Myths of Orissa*. Bombay.

Ferenczi, Sandor. 1950. *Further Contributions to the Theory and Technique of Psycho-Analysis*. International Psycho-Analytical Library no. 11. London.

———. 1956. *Sex in Psycho-Analysis*. New York.

Frazer, James George. 1935. *Creation and Evolution in Primitive Cosmogonies*. London.

Freud, Sigmund. 1938. *The Basic Writings of Sigmund Freud*. New York.

————. 1949a. *Collected Papers*. Vol. 2. London.

————. 1949b. *Collected Papers*. Vol. 3. London.

————. 1953. *A General Introduction to Psycho-Analysis*. New York.

Freud, Sigmund and D. E. Oppenheim. 1958. *Dreams in Folklore*. New York.

Fromm, Erich. 1951. *The Forgotten Language*. New York.

Ginzberg, Louis. 1925. *The Legends of the Jews*. Vol. I. Philadelphia.

Guirand, Felix. 1959. "Assyro-Babylonian Mythology." In *Larousse Encyclopedia of Mythology*. New York.

Hallowell, A. Irving. 1938. "Freudian Symbolism in the Dream of a Salteaux Indian." *Man* 38, 47–48.

————. 1947. "Myth, Culture and Personality." *American Anthropologist* 49, 544–56.

Huckel, Helen. 1953. "Vicarious Creativity." *Psychoanalysis* 2, no. 2, 44–50.

Jones, Ernest. 1951. *Essays in Applied Psycho-Analysis, II*. International Psycho-Analytical Library no. 41. London.

————. 1957. "How to Tell Your Friends from Geniuses." *Saturday Review* 40 (August 10), 9–10, 39–40.

Jung, Carl Gustav. 1916. *Psychology of the Unconscious*. New York.

Kardiner, Abram. 1939. *The Individual and His Society*. New York.

————. 1945. *The Psychological Frontiers of Society*. New York.

Kluckhohn, Clyde. 1953. "Universal Categories of Culture." In *Anthropology Today*; ed. A. L. Kroeber. Chicago.

————. 1959. "Recurrent Themes in Myths and Mythmaking." *Proceedings of the American Academy of Arts and Sciences* 88, 268–79.

Köngäs, Elli Kaija. 1960. "The earth-diver (Th. A 812)." *Ethnohistory* 7, 151–80.

Lang, Andrew. 1899. *Myth, Ritual and Religion*. Vol. I. London.

Lessa, William A. 1961. *Tales from Ulithi Atoll: A Comparative Study in Oceanic Folklore*. University of California Publications Folklore Studies no. 13. Berkeley and Los Angeles.

Lévi-Strauss, Claude. 1958. "The Structural Study of Myth." In *Myth: A Symposium*, ed. Thomas A. Sebeok. Bloomington, Ind.

Lombroso, Cesare. 1895. *The Man of Genius*. London.

Lukas, Franz. 1894. "Das Ei als kosmogonische Vorstellung." *Zeitschrift des Vereins für Volkskunde* 4, 227–43.

Malinowski, Bronislaw. 1954. *Magic, Science and Religion and Other Essays*. New York.

Mann, John. 1958. "The Folktale as a Reflector of Individual and Social Structure." Ph.D. diss., Columbia University.

Matthews, Washington. 1902. "Myths of Gestation and Parturition." *American Anthropologist* 4, 737–42.

McClelland, David C. and G. A. Friedman. 1952. "A Cross-Cultural Study of the Relationship Between Child-Training Practices and Achievement Motivation Appearing in Folk Tales." In *Readings in Social Psychology*, ed. G. E. Swanson, T. M. Newcomb, and E. L. Hartley. New York.

Nadel, S. F. 1937. "A Field Experiment in Racial Psychology." *British Journal of Psychology* 28, 195–211.

Posinsky, S. H. 1957. "The Problem of Yurok Anality." *American Imago* 14, 3–31.

Radin, Paul. 1956. *The Trickster.* New York.

Rank, Otto. 1912. "Die Symbolschichtung im Wecktraum und ihre Wiederkehr im mythischen Denken." *Jarhbuch für Psychoanalytische Forschungen* 4, 51–115.

———. 1922. *Psychoanalytische Beiträge zur Mythenforschung.* 2nd ed. Leipzig.

Reik, Theodor. 1915. "Geld und Kot." *Internationale Zeitschrift für Psychoanalyse* 3, 183.

Róheim, Géza. 1921. "Primitive Man and Environment." *International Journal of Psycho-Analysis* 2, 157–78.

———. 1922. "Psycho-Analysis and the Folk-Tale." *International Journal of Psycho-Analysis* 3, 180–86.

———. 1923. "Heiliges Geld in Melanesien." *Internationale Zeitschrift für Psychoanalyse* 9, 384–401.

———. 1940. "Society and the Individual." *Psychoanalytic Quarterly* 9, 526–45.

———. 1941. "Myth and Folk-Tale." *American Imago* 2:266–79.

———. 1951. *The Gates of the Dream.* New York.

———. 1953a. "Fairy Tale and Dream." *The Psychoanalytic Study of the Child* 8, 394–403.

———. 1953b. "Dame Holle: Dream and Folk Tale (Grimm No. 24)." In *Explorations in Psychoanalysis*, ed. Robert Lindner. New York.

Rooth, Anna Birgitta. 1957. "The Creation Myths of the North American Indians." *Anthropos* 52, 497–508.

Saville, Marshall H. 1920. *The Goldsmith's Art in Ancient Mexico.* Indian Notes and Monographs. New York.

Schwartz, Emanuel K. 1956. "A Psychoanalytic Study of the Fairy Tale." *American Journal of Psychotherapy* 10, 740–62.

Schwarzbaum, Haim. 1960. "Jewish and Moslem Sources of a Falasha Creation Myth." In *Studies in Biblical and Jewish Folklore*, ed. Raphael Patai, Francis Lee Utley, Dov Noy. American Folklore Society Memoir 51. Bloomington, Ind.

Silberer, Herbert. 1925. "A Pregnancy Phantasy in a Man." *Psychoanalytic Review* 12, 377–96.

Spence, Lewis. [1921]. *An Introduction to Mythology.* New York.

Spencer, Katherine. 1947. *Reflection of Social Life in the Navaho Origin Myth.* University of New Mexico Publications in Anthropology no. 3.

Stekel, Wilhelm. 1959. *Patterns of Psychosexual Infantilism.* New York.

Tax, Sol, et al., eds. 1953. *An Appraisal of Anthropology Today.* Chicago.

Thompson, Stith. 1929. *Tales of the North American Indians.* Cambridge.

———. 1955. *Motif-Index of Folk-Literature.* Bloomington, Ind.

Wheeler-Voegelin, Erminie. 1949. "Earth Diver." In *Standard Dictionary of Folklore, Mythology and Legend*, vol. I, ed. Maria Leach. New York.

Wheeler-Voegelin, Erminie, and Remedios W. Moore. 1957. "The Emergence Myth in Native North America." In *Studies in Folklore*, ed. W. Edson Richmond. Bloomington, Ind.

Wilbur, George B., and Warner Muensterberger, eds. 1951. *Psychoanalysis and Culture.* New York.

Wolfenstein, Martha. 1955. "'Jack and the Beanstalk': An American Version." In *Childhood in Contemporary Cultures*, ed. Margaret Mead and Martha Wolfenstein. Chicago.

Wycoco (Moore), Remedios. 1951. "The Types of North-American Indian Tales." Ph.D. diss., Indiana University.

The Story of Asdiwal

CLAUDE LÉVI-STRAUSS

Less controversial than Jungian and Freudian approaches to myth is the structural study of myth. There are basically two forms of what is commonly termed structural analysis with respect to folk narrative. One type seeks to delineate the sequential compositional structure of a narrative. This approach is associated with Vladimir Propp's Morphology of the Folktale *(Austin, 1968). The second attempts to reveal the paradigms of binary oppositions underlying a given narrative. Claude Lévi-Strauss, professor of social anthropology at the Collège de France, is the originator and principal advocate of this approach.*

Lévi-Strauss's pioneering research began with his paper "The Structural Study of Myth" (which included a controversial analysis of the Oedipus story) in the Jour-nal of American Folklore in 1955, followed by his brilliant exegesis of a Tsimshian tale, "The Story of Asdiwal," which he presented as his inaugural lecture on assuming his chair of anthropology in 1959. Then came a monumental four-volume Introduc-tion to a Science of Mythology: *vol. 1,* The Raw and the Cooked *(New York, 1969); vol. 2,* From Honey to Ashes *(New York, 1973); vol. 3,* The Origin of Table Manners *(New York, 1978); vol. 4,* The Naked Man *(New York, 1981). In this tour de force, Lévi-Strauss analyzes scores of South American (and some North American) Indian myths. Lévi-Straussian paradigms tend to revolve around binary oppositions and the meaning of narrative structure. As is commonly the case with most anthropolo-gists who consider folk narrative, the analysis inevitably turns out to be based on kinship relations, in some form or other.*

For an overview of the different structural approaches to folk narrative, see Alan Dundes, "Structuralism and Folklore," Studia Fennica *20 (1976), 75–93. For a useful survey of the huge array of structural studies of folk narrative including myth, see Danish folklorist Bengt Holbek's "Formal and Structural Studies of Oral Narratives: A Bibliography," in* Unifol, Årsberetning 1977 *(Copenhagen, 1978), pp. 149–94. For a critique of Lévi-Strauss's analysis of Asdiwal, see L. L. Thomas, J. Z. Kronenfeld, and D. B. Kronenfeld, "Asdiwal Crumbles: A Critique of Lévi-Straussian Myth Analysis,"* American Ethnologist *3 (1976), 147–73. For a further entry into the abundant*

From *Structural Anthropology*, vol. 2, by Claude Lévi-Strauss, translated by Monique Layton. © 1973 by Claude Lévi-Strauss. Reprinted by permission of the author; Basic Books, Inc., Publishers; and Penguin Books Ltd. (Though the full essay runs to p. 197, only pp. 146–65 are reprinted here.) This essay was originally published under the title "La Geste d'Asdiwal," in *Annuaire, 1958–1959*, École pratique des hautes études, Section des sciences religieuses (Paris, 1958), pp. 3–43. It was republished in *Les Temps Modernes*, No. 179 (March 1962). "The Story of Asdiwal" was first published in English in Edmund Leach, ed., *The Structural Study of Myth and Totemism* (London: Tavistock, 1967), pp. 1–47. Nicholas Mann translated it from French and Monique Layton has for the most part relied upon Mann's translation.

*scholarship devoted to Lévi-Strauss's structural approach to myth, see François H.
Lapointe and Claire C. Lapointe,* Claude Lévi-Strauss and His Critics: An International Bibliography of Criticism (1950–1976) *(New York, 1977). See also Simon
Clarke, "Lévi-Strauss's Structural Analysis of Myth,"* Sociological Review 25 (1977),
743–74; *John Peradotto, "Oedipus and Erichthonius: Some Observations of Paradigmatic and Syntagmatic Order,"* Arethusa 10 (1977), 85–101; *and Michael P. Carroll, "Lévi-Strauss on the Oedipus Myth: A Reconsideration,"* American Anthropologist 80 (1978), 805–14.

This study of a native myth from the Pacific coast of Canada has two
aims. First, to isolate and compare the *various levels* on which the
myth evolves: geographic, economic, sociological, and cosmological—
each one of these levels, together with the symbolism proper to it,
being seen as a transformation of an underlying logical structure common to all of them. And, second,* to compare the *different versions* of
the myth and to look for the meaning of the discrepancies between
them, or between some of them; for, since they all come from the same
people (but are recorded in different parts of their territory), these
variations cannot be explained in terms of dissimilar beliefs, languages,
or institutions.

The story of Asdiwal, which comes from the Tsimshian Indians, is
known to us in four versions, collected some sixty years ago by Franz
Boas and published in the following books: *Indianische Sagen von der
Nord-Pacifischen Küste Amerikas* (Berlin, 1895); *Tsimshian Texts*, Smithsonian Institution, Bureau of American Ethnology, no. 27 (Washington,
1902); *Tsimshian Texts* (G. Hunt, co-author), Publications of the American Ethnological Society, n.s., vol. 3 (Leyden, 1912); and *Tsimshian Mythology*, Smithsonian Institution, Bureau of American Ethnology, 31st
Annual Report, 1909–1910, (Washington, 1916).

We shall begin by calling attention to certain facts which must be
known if the myth is to be understood.

The Tsimshian Indians, with the Tlingit and the Haida, belong to
the northern group of cultures on the Northwest Pacific Coast. They
live in British Columbia, immediately south of Alaska, in a region
which embraces the basins of the Nass and Skeena rivers, the coastal
region stretching between their estuaries, and, further inland, the land
drained by the two rivers and their tributaries. Both the Nass in the
north and the Skeena in the south flow in a northeast-southwesterly
direction, and they are approximately parallel. The Nass, however, is

---

*The second portion of this essay is not reprinted here. —ED. NOTE slightly nearer north–south in orientation, a detail which, as we shall see, is not entirely devoid of importance.

This territory was divided among three local groups, distinguished by their different dialects: in the upper reaches of the Skeena, the Gitskan; in the lower reaches and the coastal region, the Tsimshian themselves; and in the valleys of the Nass and its tributaries, the Nisqa. Three of the versions of the myth of Asdiwal were recorded on the coast and in Tsimshian dialect (Boas 1895, 285–88; Boas and Hunt 1912, 71–146; Boas and Hunt 1916, 243–45, and the comparative analysis, 792–824); the fourth was recorded at the mouth of the Nass, in Nisqa dialect (Boas 1902, 225–28). It is this last which, when compared with the other three, reveals the most marked differences.

Like all the people on the northwest Pacific Coast, the Tsimshian had no agriculture. During the summer, the women's work was to collect fruit, berries, plants, and wild roots, while the men hunted bears and goats in the mountains and sea lions on the coastal reefs. They also practiced deep-sea fishing, catching mainly cod and halibut, but also herring nearer the shore. It was, however, the complex rhythm of river fishing that made the deepest impression upon the life of the tribe. Whereas the Nisqa were relatively settled, the Tsimshian moved, according to the seasons, between their winter villages, which were situated in the coastal region, and their fishing places, either on the Nass or the Skeena.

At the end of the winter, when the stores of smoked fish, dried meat, fat, and preserved fruits were running low, or were even completely exhausted, the natives would undergo periods of severe famine, an echo of which is found in the myth. At such times they anxiously awaited the arrival of the candlefish, which would go up the Nass (which was still frozen to start with) for a period of about six weeks in order to spawn (Goddard 1934, 68). This would begin about March 1, and the entire Skeena population would travel along the coast in boats as far as the Nass in order to take up position on the fishing grounds, which were family properties. The period from February 15 to March 15 was called, not without reason, the "Month when Candlefish is Eaten," and that which followed, from March 15 to April 15, the "Month when Candlefish is Cooked" (to extract its oil). This operation was strictly taboo to men, whereas the women were obliged to use their naked breasts to press the fish. The oil-cake residue had to be left to become rotten from maggots and putrefaction and, despite the pestilential stench, it had to be left in the immediate vicinity of the dwelling houses until the work was finished (Boas and Hunt 1916, 44–45, 398–99).

Then everyone would return by the same route to the Skeena for the second major event, which was the arrival of the salmon fished in June and July (the "Salmon Months"). Once the fish was smoked and stored away for the year, the families would go up to the mountains, where the men would hunt while the women laid up stocks of fruit and berries. With the coming of the frost in the ritual "Month of the Spinning Tops" (which were spun on the ice), people settled down in permanent villages for the winter. During this period, the men sometimes went off hunting again for a few days or a few weeks. Finally, toward November 15, came the "Taboo Month," which marked the inauguration of the great winter ceremonies, in preparation for which the men were subjected to various restrictions.

Let us remember, too, that the Tsimshian were divided into four nonlocalized matrilineal clans, which were strictly exogamous and divided into lineages, descent lines, and households: the Eagles, the Ravens, the Wolves, and the Killer Whales; also, that the permanent villages were the seat of chiefdoms (generally called "tribes" by native informants); and, finally, that Tsimshian society was divided into three hereditary castes with bilateral inheritance of caste status (each individual was supposed to marry according to his rank): the "Real People" or reigning families, the "Nobles," and the "People," which comprised all those who (failing a purchase of rank by generous potlatches) were unable to assert an equal degree of nobility in both lines of their descent (Boas and Hunt 1916, 478–514; Garfield 1939, 173–74; Garfield, Wingert, and Barbeau 1951, 1–34; Garfield and Wingert 1966).

Now follows a summary of the story of Asdiwal taken from Boas and Hunt (1912) which will serve as a point of reference. This version was recorded on the coast at Port Simpson in Tsimshian dialect. Boas published the native text together with an English translation.*

Famine reigns in the Skeena valley; the river is frozen and it is winter. A mother and her daughter, both of whose husbands have died of hunger, both remember independently the happy times when they lived together and there was no dearth of food. Released by the death of their husbands, they simultaneously decide to meet, and they set off at the same moment. Since the mother lives down-river and the daughter up-river, the former goes eastwards and the latter westwards. They both travel on the frozen bed of the Skeena and meet halfway.

Weeping with hunger and sorrow, the two women pitch camp on the bank at the foot of a tree, not far from which they find, poor pittance that it is, a rotten berry, which they sadly share.

*Boas's translation is paraphrased rather than cited by Lévi-Strauss. —ED. NOTE

During the night, a stranger visits the young widow. It is soon learned that his name is Hatsenas,[1] a term which means, in Tsimshian, a bird of good omen. Thanks to him, the women start to find food regularly, and the younger of the two becomes the wife of their mysterious protector and soon gives birth to a son, Asdiwal (Asiwa, Boas 1895; Asi-hwil, Boas 1902).[2] His father speeds up his growth by supernatural means and gives him various magic objects: a bow and arrows, which never miss, for hunting, a quiver, a lance, a basket, snowshoes, a bark raincoat, and a hat—all of which will enable the hero to overcome all obstacles, make himself invisible, and procure an inexhaustible supply of food. Hatsenas then disappears and the elder of the two women dies.

Asdiwal and his mother pursue their course westward and settle down in her native village Gitsalasert, in the Skeena Canyon (Boas and Hunt 1912, 83). One day a white she-bear comes down the valley.

Hunted by Asdiwal, who almost catches it thanks to his magic objects, the bear starts to climb up a vertical ladder. Asdiwal follows it up to the heavens, which he sees as a vast prairie, covered with grass and all kinds of flowers. The bear lures him into the home of its father, the sun, and reveals itself to be a beautiful girl, Evening-Star. The marriage takes place, though not before the Sun has submitted Asdiwal to a series of trials, to which all previous suitors had succumbed (hunting wild goat in mountains which are rent by earthquakes, drawing water from a spring in a cave whose walls close in on each other, collecting wood from a tree which crushes those who try to cut it down, a period in a fiery furnace). But Asdiwal overcomes them all, thanks to his magic objects and the timely intervention of his father. Won over by his son-in-law's talents, the Sun finally approves of him.

Asdiwal, however, pines for his mother. The Sun agrees to allow him to go down to earth again with his wife, and gives them, as provisions for the journey, four baskets filled with inexhaustible supplies of food, which earn the couple a grateful welcome from the villagers, who are in the midst of their winter famine.

In spite of repeated warnings from his wife, Asdiwal deceives her with a woman from his village. Evening-Star, offended, departs, followed by her tearful husband. Halfway up to heaven, Asdiwal is struck down by a

1. Hatsenas (Boas and Hunt 1912), Hadsenas (Boas 1895). It is a bird like the robin (*Turdus migratorius*) but not a robin (Boas and Hunt 1912, 72–73). According to Boas, it sings, "hō, hō" and its name means "luck" and describes a bird sent as a messenger from heaven (1895, 286). One is reminded of the black bird (*Ixoreus naevius*) which is indeed a winter bird, with a strange and mysterious call (Lévi-Strauss 1971, 438–39, 447).

In this work, which has no linguistic pretentions, the transcription of native terms has been simplified to the extreme, keeping only those distinctions which are essential in avoiding ambiguities among the terms quoted.

2. The name of Asdiwal certainly has several connotations. The Nass form, *Asi-hwil*, means "crosser of mountains" (Boas 1902, 226). But cf. also "*Asdiwal*," "to be in danger" (Boas and Hunt 1912, 257) and *Asewaelgyet*—a different name for and special variety of the thunderbird (Barbeau 1950, vol. 1:144–45, vol. 2:476).

look from his wife, who disappears. He dies, but his loss is at once re-
gretted and he is brought back to life by his celestial father-in-law.

For a time, all goes well. Then, Asdiwal once again feels a twinge of
nostalgia for earth. His wife agrees to accompany him as far as the earth,
and there bids him a final farewell. Returning to his village, the hero
learns of his mother's death. Nothing remains to hold him back, and he
sets off again on his journey downstream.

When he reaches the Tsimshian village of Ginaxangioget, he seduces
and marries the daughter of the local chief. To start with, the marriage is
a happy one, and Asdiwal joins his four brothers-in-law on wild goat
hunts which, thanks to his magic objects, are crowned with success.
When spring approaches, the whole family moves, staying first at Metlakatla, and then setting off by boat for the river Nass, going up along the
coast. A head wind forces them to a halt and they camp for a while at
Ksemaksén. There, things go wrong because of a dispute between Asdiwal and his brothers-in-law over the respective merits of mountain-
hunters and sea-hunters. A competition takes place—Asdiwal returns
from the mountain with four bears that he has killed, while the brothers-
in-law return empty-handed from their sea expedition. Humiliated and
enraged, they break camp, and, taking their sister with them, abandon
Asdiwal.

He is picked up by strangers coming from Gitxatla, who are also on
their way to the Nass for the candlefish season.

As in the previous case, they are a group of four brothers and a sister,
whom Asdiwal wastes no time in marrying. They soon arrive together at
the River Nass, where they sell large quantities of fresh meat and salmon
to the Tsimshian, who have already settled there and are starving.

Since the catch that year is a good one, everyone goes home: the Tsimshian to their capital at Metlakatla and the Gitxatla to their town Laxalan,
where Asdiwal, by this time rich and famous, has a son. One winter's
day, he boasts that he can hunt sea lions better than his brothers-in-law.
They set out to sea together. Thanks to his magic objects, Asdiwal has a
miraculously successful hunt on a reef, but is left there without food or
fire by his angry brothers-in-law. A storm gets up and waves sweep over
the rock. With the help of his father, who appears in time to save him,
Asdiwal, transformed into a bird, succeeds in keeping himself above the
waves, using his magic objects as a perch.

After two days and two nights the storm is calmed, and Asdiwal falls
asleep exhausted. A mouse wakes him and leads him to the subterranean home of the sea lions whom he has wounded, but who imagine
(since Asdiwal's arrows are invisible to them) that they are victims of an
epidemic. Asdiwal extracts the arrows and cures his hosts, whom he
asks, in return, to guarantee his safe return. Unfortunately, the sea lions'
boats, which are made of their stomachs, are out of use, pierced by the
hunter's arrows. The king of the sea lions therefore lends Asdiwal his
own stomach as a canoe and instructs him to send it back without delay.

When he reaches land, the hero discovers his wife and his son inconsolable. Thanks to the help of this good wife (but bad sister, for she carries out the rites which are essential to the success of the operation), Asdiwal makes killer whales out of carved wood and brings them to life. They break open the boats with their fins and bring about the shipwreck and death of the wicked brothers-in-law.

But once again Asdiwal feels an irrepressible desire to revisit the scenes of his childhood. He leaves his wife and returns to the Skeena valley. He settles in the town of Ginadâos, where he is joined by his son, to whom he gives his magic bow and arrows, and from whom he receives a dog in return.

When winter comes, Asdiwal goes off to the mountains to hunt, but forgets his snowshoes. Lost, and unable to go either up or down without them, he is turned to stone with his lance and his dog, and they can still be seen in that form at the peak of the great mountain by the lake of Ginadâos (Boas and Hunt 1912, 71–146).

Let us keep provisionally to this version alone in order to attempt to define the essential points of its structure. The narrative refers to facts of various orders: first, the physical and political geography of the Tsimshian country, since the places and towns mentioned really do exist; second, the economic life of the natives which, as we have seen, governs the great seasonal migrations between the Skeena and Nass valleys during the course of which Asdiwal's adventures take place; third, the social and family organizations, for we witness several marriages, divorces, widowhoods, and other connected events; and lastly, the cosmology, for, unlike the others, two of Asdiwal's visits, one to heaven and the other below the earth, are of a mythological and not of an experiential order.

First of all, let us consider the geographical aspects.[3]

The story begins in the Skeena Valley, when the two heroines leave their villages, one upstream, the other downstream, and meet halfway. In the version that Boas recorded at the Nass estuary, it is stated that the meeting place, this time on the Nass, is called Hwil-lê-ne-hwada, "Where-They-Meet-Each-Other" (Boas 1902, 225).

After her mother's death, the young woman and her son settle in her native village (i.e., her father's, where her mother had lived from the time of her marriage until her husband's death), the downstream village. It is from there that the visit to heaven takes place. This village,

---

3. The map on p. 303, more precise and more complete than the one published in the previous editions of this work, was kindly given me by Professor Wilson Duff of the University of British Columbia in Vancouver, to whom I wish here to express my gratitude. The names of places are easily identifiable in spite of a transcription slightly different from that of Boas.

called Gitsalasert, "People of the [Skeena] Canyon," is situated not far
from the modern town of Usk (Garfield 1939, 175; Boas and Hunt 1912,
71, 276; cf. Krause 1956, 214–15: "Kĭtselāssin," on the Skeena River). Although the Tsimshian dialect was spoken there, it was outside the
"nine towns" which, strictly speaking, formed the Tsimshian province
(Boas and Hunt 1912, 225).

On his mother's death, Asdiwal continues his journey downstream,
that is to say, westward. He settles in the town of Ginaxangioget, where
he marries. This is in Tsimshian country proper on the lower reaches
of the Skeena. Ginaxangioget is, in fact, a term formed from the root of
git = "people" and gi.k = "hemlock tree," from which comes Ginax-
angi.k, "the people of the firs" (Garfield 1939, 175). Ginaxangioget was
one of the nine principal towns of the Tsimshian (Boas and Hunt 1916,
482–83).[4]

When Asdiwal leaves with his in-laws for the Nass to fish candlefish
there, they go first to the Skeena estuary, then take to the sea and stop
at the capital city of the Tsimshian, Metlakatla. A recent town of the
same name, founded by natives converted to Christianity, is to be
found on Annette Island in Alaska (Beynon 1941; Garfield, Wingert, and
Barbeau 1951, 33–34). Old Metlakatla is on the coast, north of Prince
Rupert and halfway between the Skeena and the Nass estuaries. Ksemaksén, where the first quarrel takes place, and where Asdiwal is first
abandoned by his brothers-in-law, is also on the coast, a little further
north.

The Tsimshian-speaking tribe called Gitxatla, which is independent
of those centers around Metlakatla, forms a group of islanders living
on McCauley, Porcher, and Dolphin islands, across and south of the
Skeena estuary. Their name comes from git, "people," and qxatla,
"channel" (Garfield 1939, 175; Boas and Hunt 1916, 483).[5] Having traveled from east to west, Asdiwal accompanies them to the Nass, that is
to say in a south–north direction, then in the opposite direction, to
"their town," offshore from which (and probably to the west, since it
was a deep-sea expedition) the visit to the sea lions takes place.

From there, Asdiwal returns to the Skeena—this time from west to
east. The story ends at Ginadâos (or perhaps Ginadoiks, from git, "people," na, "of," doiks, "rapid current"), the name of a torrent which flows
into the Skeena (Garfield 1939, 176).[6]

4. Swanton gives "Kinagingeeg, near Metlakatla" (1952, 606); cf. Krause 1956, 214–15:
Kin-nach-hangik, "on the peninsula near Fort Simpson."
5. Swanton gives Kitkatla, "on Porcher Island" (1952, 607).
6. Boas gives Ginadâiks, "one of the nine towns of the Tsimshian" (Boas and Hunt
1912, 223); cf. Kinnatōiks "on the Tsimshian peninsula near Fort Simpson" (Krause 1956,
214–15).

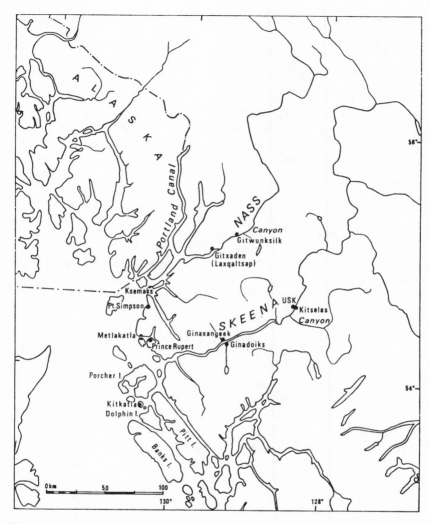

Map 6

Let us now consider the economic aspect. The economic activities brought to notice by the myth are no less real than the geographical places and the populations evoked in the preceding paragraphs. Everything begins with a period of winter famine such as was well known to the natives in the period between mid-December and mid-January, before the moment when, theoretically, the spring salmon arrived, which was just before the arrival of the candlefish, the period called "the interval" (Boas and Hunt 1916, 398–99). After his visit to the heavens, Asdiwal takes part in the spring migration to the Nass for the candlefish season; then we are told of the return of the families to the Skeena in the salmon season.

These seasonal variations—to use Marcel Mauss's expression—are on a par with other, no less real differences emphasized by the myth, notably that between the land hunter (personified by Asdiwal, born on the river and upstream, i.e., inland) and the sea hunter (personified first by the People of the Firs who live downstream on the estuary, and then, still more clearly, by the inhabitants of Porcher and Dolphin islands).

When we move on to the sociological aspects, there is a much greater freedom of interpretation. It is not a question of an accurate documentary picture of the reality of native life, but a sort of counterpoint which seems sometimes to be in harmony with this reality, and sometimes to part from it in order to rejoin it again.

The initial sequence of events evokes clearly defined sociological conditions. The mother and daughter have been separated by the latter's marriage, and since that time each has lived with her own husband in his village. The elder woman's husband was also the father of the younger woman, who left her native village to follow her own husband upstream. We can recognize this as a society in which, while having a system of matrilineal filiation, residence is patrilocal, the wife going to live in her husband's village; and one in which the children, although they belong to their mother's clan, are brought up in their father's home and not in that of their maternal kin.

Such was the situation among the Tsimshian. Boas emphasizes it several times: "In olden times it was customary for a great chief to take a princess from each tribe to be his wife. Some had as many as sixteen or eighteen wives," which would clearly be impossible if a man had to live in his wife's native village. More generally, says Boas, "There is ample evidence showing that the young married people lived with the young man's parents," so that "the children grew up in their father's home" (Boas and Hunt 1916, 355, 529, 426; cf. 420, 427, 441, 499–500).

But, in the myth, this patrilocal type of residence is quickly undermined by famine, which frees the two women from their respective obligations and allows them, upon the death of their husbands, to meet (significantly enough) halfway. Their camping at the foot of the tree on the bank of the frozen river, equidistant from up-river and down-river, presents a picture of a matrilocal type of residence reduced to its simplest form, since the new household consists only of a mother and her daughter.

This reversal, which is barely hinted at, is all the more remarkable because all the subsequent marriages are going to be matrilocal, and thus contrary to the type found in reality.

First, Hatsenas's marriage with the younger woman. Fleeting though this union between a human being and a supernatural being may be, the husband still lives in his wife's home, and therefore in her mother's home. The matrilocal trend is even more apparent in the version recorded on the Nass. When his son Asi-hwil has grown up, Hatsenas (who here is called Hôux) says to his wife: "Your brothers are coming to look for you. Therefore I must hide in the woods." Shortly thereafter, the brothers come, and leave again, laden with supplies of meat given to the women by their protector. "As soon as they left, Hôux returned. The [women] told him that their brothers and uncles had asked them to return home. Then Hôux said, 'Let us part. You may return to your home; I will return to mine.' On the following morning, many people came to fetch the women and the boy. They took them to Gitxaden. The boy's uncles gave a feast and his mother told them the boy's name, Asi-hwil" (Boas 1902, 227).

Not only does the husband seem an intruder—regarded with suspicion by his brothers-in-law and afraid that they might attack him—but, contrary to what happens among the Tsimshian and in other societies characterized by the association of matrilineal filiation and patrilocal residence (Boas and Hunt 1916, 423; Malinowski 1922), the food gifts go from the sister's husband to the wife's brothers.

Matrilocal marriage, accompanied by antagonism between the husband and his in-laws, is further illustrated by Asdiwal's marriage to Evening-Star; they live in her father's home, and the father-in-law shows so much hostility toward his son-in-law that he sets him trials which are deemed to be fatal.

Matrilocal, too, is Asdiwal's second marriage in the land of the People of the Firs, which is accompanied by hostility between the husband and his brothers-in-law because they abandon him and persuade their sister to follow them.

The same theme is expressed in the third marriage in the land of the People of the Channel, at any rate to start with. After Asdiwal's visit to the sea lions, the situation is reversed: Asdiwal recovers his wife, who has refused to follow her brothers and was wandering in search of her husband. What is more, she collaborates with him to produce the "machination"—in the literal and the figurative sense—by means of which he takes revenge on his brothers-in-law. Finally, patrilocality triumphs when Asdiwal abandons his wife (whereas in the previous marriages it had been his wife who had abandoned him) and returns to the Skeena where he was born, and where his son comes alone to join him. Thus, having begun with the story of the *reunion of a mother and her daughter*, freed from their affines or *paternal kin*, the myth ends with the story of the *reunion of a father and his son*, freed from their affines or *maternal kin*.

But if the initial and final sequences on the myth constitute, from a sociological point of view, a pair of oppositions, the same is true, from a cosmological point of view, of the two supernatural voyages which interrupt the hero's "real" journey. The first voyage takes him to the heavens and into the home of the Sun, who first tries to kill him and then agrees to bring him back to life. The second takes Asdiwal to the subterranean kingdom of the sea lions, whom he has himself killed or wounded, but whom he agrees to look after and to cure. The first voyage results in a marriage which, as we have seen, is matrilocal, and which, moreover, bears witness to a maximal exogamous separation (between an earthborn man and a woman from heaven). But this marriage will be broken up by Asdiwal's infidelity with a woman of his own village. This may be seen as a suggestion of a marriage which, if it really took place, would neutralize matrilocality (since husband and wife would come from the same place) and would be characterized by an endogamous proximity which would also be maximal (marriage within the village). It is true that the hero's second supernatural voyage, to the subterranean kingdom of the sea lions, does not lead to a marriage. But, as has already been shown, this visit brings about a reversal in the matrilocal tendency of Asdiwal's successive marriages, for it separates his third wife from her brothers, the hero himself from his wife, their son from his mother, and leaves only one relationship in existence: that between the father and his son.

In this analysis of the myth, we have distinguished four levels: the geographic, the techno-economic, the sociological, and the cosmological. The first two are exact transcriptions of reality; the fourth has nothing to do with it; and in the third real and imaginary institutions are interwoven. Yet in spite of these differences, the levels are not separated out by the native mind. It is rather that everything happens as if the levels were provided with different codes, each being used according to the needs of the moment, and according to its particular capacity, to transmit the same message. It is the nature of this message that we shall now consider.

Winter famines are a recurrent event in the economic life of the Tsimshian. But the famine that starts the story off is also a cosmological theme. All along the Northwest Pacific Coast, in fact, the present state of the universe is attributed to the havoc wrought in the original order by the demiurge Giant or Raven (Txamsen, in Tsimshian) during travels which he undertook in order to satisfy his irrepressible voracity. Thus Txamsen is perpetually in a state of famine, and famine, although a negative condition, is seen as the *primum mobile* of creation.[7] In this sense we can say that the hunger of the two women in our myth has a cosmic significance. These heroines are not so much legendary persons as incarnations of principles which are at the origin of place names.

One may schematize the initial situation as follows:

mother	daughter
elder	younger
downstream	upstream
west	east
south	north

The meeting takes place at the halfway point, a situation which, as we have seen, corresponds to a neutralization of patrilocal residence and to the fulfillment of the conditions for a matrilocal residence which is as yet only hinted at. But since the mother dies on the very spot where the meeting and the birth of Asdiwal took place, the essential movement, which her daughter begins by leaving the village of her marriage "very far upstream" (Boas and Hunt 1912, 71), is in the direction east–west, as far as her native village in the Skeena Canyon, where she in her turn dies, leaving the field open for the hero.

Asdiwal's first adventure presents us with an opposition—that of heaven and earth—which the hero is able to surmount by virtue of the intervention of his father, Hatsenas, the bird of good omen. The latter is a creature of the atmospheric or middle heaven and consequently is well qualified to play the role of mediator between the earth-born Asdiwal and his father-in-law the Sun, ruler of the highest heaven. Even so, Asdiwal does not manage to overcome his earthly nature, to which he twice submits, first in yielding to the charms of a fellow countrywoman and then in yielding to nostalgia for his home village. Thus there remains a series of unresolved oppositions:

low	high
earth	heaven
man	woman
endogamy	exogamy

7. For a summary and comparative analysis of all the texts which have been listed as referring to the greed of the demiurge, see Boas and Hunt 1916, 636ff.

Pursuing his course westward, Asdiwal contracts a second matrilocal marriage which generates a new series of oppositions:

mountain hunting	sea hunting
land	water

These oppositions, too, are insurmountable, and Asdiwal's earthly nature carries him away a third time, with the result that he is abandoned by his wife and his brothers-in-law.

Asdiwal contracts his last marriage not with the river dwellers, but
with islanders, and the same conflict is repeated. The opposition continues to be insurmountable, although at each stage the terms are
brought closer together. This time it is in fact a question of a quarrel
between Asdiwal and his brothers-in-law on the occasion of a hunt on
a reef on the high seas; that is, on land and water at the same time. In
the previous incident, Asdiwal and his brothers-in-law had gone their
separate ways, one inland and on foot, the others out to sea and in
boats. This time they go together in boats, and it is only when they
land that Asdiwal's superiority is made manifest by the use he makes
of the magic objects intended for mountain hunting:

> It was a very difficult hunt on account of the waves which swept past
> [the reef] in the direction of the open sea. While they were speaking
> about this, [Asdiwal] said: "My dear fellows, I have only to put on my
> snowshoes and I'll run up the rocks you are talking about." He succeeds
> in this way, whilst his brothers-in-law, incapable of landing, stay shame-
> facedly in their boats. (Boas and Hunt 1912, 125–26).

Asdiwal, the earth-born master of the hunt finds himself abandoned
on a reef in high seas. He has come to the furthest point in his westward journey; so much for the geographic and economic aspects. But
from a logical point of view, his adventures can be seen in a different
form—that of a series of impossible mediations between oppositions
which are ordered in a descending scale: high and low, water and
earth, sea hunting and mountain hunting, and so forth.

Consequently, on the spatial plane, the hero is completely led off his
course, and his failure is expressed in this *maximal separation* from
his starting point. On the logical plane, he has also failed because of
his immoderate attitude toward his brothers-in-law, and because of his
inability to play the role of a mediator, even though the last of the oppositions which had to be overcome—between the types of life led by
the land hunters and sea hunters—is reduced to a *minimal separation*. There would seem to be a dead end at this point; but from neutral
the myth goes into reverse and its machinery starts up again.

The king of the mountains (in Nass dialect, Asdiwal is called Asi-hwil, which means "Crosser of Mountains") is caught on a caricature of a mountain, one that is doubly so because, on the one hand, it is nothing more than a reef and, on the other, it is surrounded and al-most submerged by the sea. The ruler of wild animals and killer of bears is to be saved by a she-mouse, a caricature of a wild animal.[8] She makes him undertake a *subterranean journey*, just as the she-bear, the supreme wild animal, had imposed on Asdiwal a *celestial journey*. In fact, the only thing that is missing is for the mouse to change into a woman and to offer the hero a marriage which would be symmetrical to the other, but opposite to it. Although this element is not to be found in any of the versions, we know at least that the mouse is a fairy: Lady Mouse-Woman, as she is called in the texts, where the word *ksem*, a term of respect addressed to a woman, is prefixed to the word denoting a rodent. Following through the inversion more systemati-cally than had been possible under the preceding hypothesis, this fairy is an old woman incapable of procreation—an "inverse wife."

And that is not all. The man who had killed animals by the hun-dreds goes this time to heal them and win their love.[9] The bringer of food (who repeatedly exercises the power he received from his father in this respect for the benefit of his family) becomes food, since he is transported in the sea lion's stomach.[10]

Finally, the visit to the subterranean world (which is also, in many respects, an "upside-down world") sets the course of the hero's return; for from then onward he travels from west to east, from the sea toward the mainland, from the salt water of the ocean to the fresh water of the Skeena.

This overall reversal does not affect the development of the plot, which unfolds up to the final catastrophe. When Asdiwal returns to his people and to the initial patrilocal situation, he takes up his favorite occupation again, helped by his magic objects. But he *forgets* one of them, and this mistake is fatal. After a successful hunt, he finds himself trapped halfway up the mountain side: "Where might he go now? He

8. As the smallest mammal to appear in mythology, and also because in the mythol-ogy of the Northwest Coast the mouse represents the land animal at its most modest level: that of domestic life. The mouse is in fact the domestic animal of the earth. With this distinction, she is entitled to the tiny offering of fat which drips from woolen ear ornaments when they are thrown into the fire in her honor.

9. "The love of the master of the sea lions and of his whole tribe increased very much" (Boas and Hunt 1912, 133).

10. The Tsimshian of the Nisqa group "look to the river (Nass) for their food supply, which consists principally of salmon and candlefish. Indeed, it is owing to the enor-mous numbers of the latter fish that run in to spawn in the early spring that the name Nass, meaning 'the stomach or food depot' has been given to the river" (Emmons 1910).

could not go up, he could not go to either side" (Boas and Hunt 1912, 145). And on the spot he is changed to stone, that is to say, paralyzed, reduced to his earth-born nature in the stony and unchangeable form in which he has been seen "for generations."

The above analysis leads us to draw a distinction between two aspects of the construction of a myth: the sequences and the schemata.

The sequences form the apparent content of the myth, the chronological order in which things happen: the meeting of the two women, the intervention of the supernatural protector, the birth of Asdiwal, his childhood, his visit to heaven, his successive marriages, his hunting and fishing expeditions, his quarrels with his brothers-in-law, and so forth.

But these sequences are organized on planes at different levels of abstraction in accordance with schemata, which exist simultaneously, superimposed one upon the other; just as a melody composed for several voices is held within bounds by two-dimensional constraints: first by its own melodic line, which is horizontal, and second by the contrapuntal schemata, which are vertical. Let us then draw up an inventory of such schemata for this present myth.

1. *Geographic schema*. The hero goes from east to west, then returns from west to east. This return journey is modulated by another one, from the south to the north and then from the north to the south, which corresponds to the seasonal migrations of the Tsimshian (in which the hero takes part) to the River Nass for the candlefish season in the spring, then to the Skeena for the salmon fishing in the summer.

2. *Cosmological schema*. Three supernatural visits establish a relationship between terms thought of respectively as "below" and "above": the visit to the young widow by Hatsenas, the bird of good omen associated with the atmospheric heavens; the visit by Asdiwal to the highest heavens in pursuit of Evening-Star; and his visit to the subterranean kingdom of the sea lions under the guidance of Lady Mouse-Woman. The end of Asdiwal, trapped in the mountain, then appears as a *neutralization* of the intermediate mediation established at his birth but which even so does not enable him to bring off two further extreme mediations (the one between heaven and earth considered as the op-

position low/high and the other between the sea and the land considered as the opposition east/west).

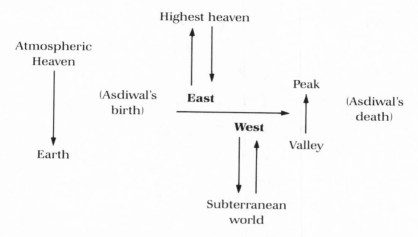

3. *Integration schema*. The above two schemata are integrated in a
third consisting of several binary oppositions, none of which the hero
can resolve, although the distance separating the opposed terms gradually dwindles. The initial and final oppositions, high/low and peak/
valley, are "vertical" and thus belong to the cosmological schema. The
two intermediate oppositions, water/land and sea hunting/mountain
hunting, are "horizontal" and belong to the geographic schema. But
the final opposition, peak/valley, which is also the narrowest contrast,
brings into association the essential characteristics of the two preceding schemata: it is "vertical" in form, but "geographical" in content.[11]
Asdiwal's failure (he is trapped half way up the mountain because he
forgot his snowshoes) thus takes on a significance geographical, cosmological, and logical.

When the three schemata are reduced in this way to their bare es-
sentials, retaining only the order and amplitude of the oppositions,
their complementarity becomes apparent.

Schema 1 is composed of a sequence of oscillations of constant amplitude: east – north – west – south – east.

Schema 2 starts at a zero point (the meeting halfway between upstream and downstream) and is followed by an oscillation of medium

11. The double aspect, natural and supernatural, of the opposition between peak
and valley, is already in the myth, since the hero's perilous situation results from an
earthquake caused by the gods. [This episode occurs in another Tsimshian text included
in the second portion of this essay, not reprinted here. —ED. NOTE]

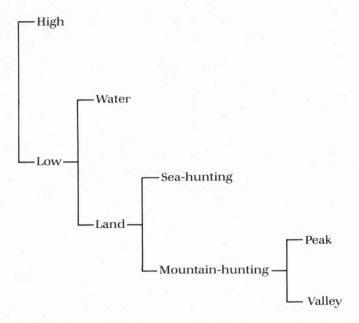

amplitude (atmospheric heavens–earth), then by oscillations of maximum amplitude (earth–heaven, heaven–earth, earth–subterranean
world, subterranean world–earth) which die away at the zero point
(halfway up, between peak and valley).

Schema 3 begins with an oscillation of maximum amplitude (high–
low) which dies away in a series of oscillations of decreasing amplitude
(water–land; sea hunting–mountain hunting; valley–peak).

4. *Sociological schema.* To start with, the patrilocal residence pre-
vails. It gives way progressively to the matrilocal residence (Hatsenas's
marriage), which becomes deadly (Asdiwal's marriage in heaven), then
merely hostile (the marriage in the land of the People of the Firs), before weakening and finally reversing (marriage among the People of
the Channel) to allow a return to patrilocal residence.

The sociological schema does not have, however, a closed structure
like the geographic schema, since, at the beginning, it involves a mother
and her daughter; in the middle, a husband, his wife, and his brothers-
in-law; and, at the end, a father and his son.[12]

12. As we shall later see, the apparent gap in the cycle is explained by the fact that in
the story of Waux, Asdiwal's son, the closure will be the result of a matrilateral marriage
which ends in a terminal situation: husband and wife without children. [This note refers
to the portion of the essay not reproduced here. —ED. NOTE]

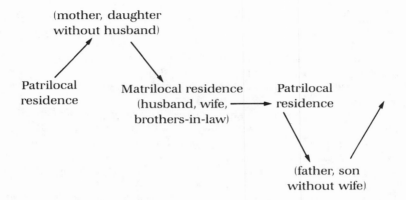

(mother, daughter without husband)

Patrilocal residence

Matrilocal residence (husband, wife, brothers-in-law) → Patrilocal residence

(father, son without wife)

5. *Techno-economic schema.* The myth begins by evoking a winter famine; it ends with a successful hunt. In between, the story follows the economic cycle and the seasonal migrations of the native fishermen.

Famine → Fishing for Candlefish → Salmon Fishing → Successful Hunt

6. *Global integration.* If the myth is finally reduced to its two extreme propositions, the initial state of affairs and the final, which together summarize its operational function, then we end up with a simplified diagram.

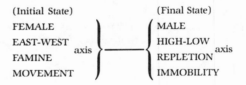

(Initial State)
FEMALE
EAST-WEST
FAMINE   } axis
MOVEMENT

(Final State)
MALE
HIGH-LOW
REPLETION   } axis
IMMOBILITY

Having separated out the codes, we have analyzed the structure of the message.

REFERENCES

Barbeau, M. 1950. *Totem Poles*. National Museum of Canada, *Anthropological Series 30*, no. 119, 2 vols. Ottawa.

Beynon, W. 1941. "The Tsimshians of Metlakatla." *American Anthropologist*, n.s., 43.

Boas, F. 1895. "Indianische Sagen von der Nord-Pacifischen Küste Amerikas," in *Sonder-Abdruck aus den Verhandlungen der Berliner Gesellschaft für Anthropologie, Ethnologie und Urgeschichte, 1891–1895*. Berlin.

———. 1902. *Tsimshian Texts*. Smithsonian Institution, Bureau of American Ethnology, Bulletin no. 27. Washington, D.C.

———, ed. 1911. *Handbook of American Indian Languages*. Smithsonian Institution, Bureau of American Ethnology, no. 40, 2 vols. Washington, D.C.

Boas, F., and Hunt, G. 1912. *Tsimshian Texts*. Publications of the American Ethnological Society, n.s., vol. 3. Leyden.

———. 1916. *Tsimshian Mythology*. Smithsonian Institution, Bureau of American Ethnology, 31st Annual Report, 1909–1910. Washington, D.C.

Durlach, T. M. 1928. *Relationship Systems of the Tlingit, Haida and Tsimshian*. Publications of the American Ethnological Society, vol. 11. New York.

Emmons, G. T. 1910. "Niska," in *Handbook of American Indians North of Mexico*. Smithsonian Institution, Bureau of American Ethnology, Bulletin no. 30, 2 vols. Washington, D.C.

Garfield, V. E. 1939. *Tsimshian Clan and Society*. University of Washington Publications in Anthropology. vol. 7, no. 3. Seattle.

Garfield, V. E., and Wingert, P. S. 1966. *The Tsimshian Indians and their Arts*. Seattle.

Garfield, V. E., Wingert, P. S., Barbeau, M. 1951. *The Tsimshian: Their Arts and Music*. Publications of the American Ethnological Society, vol. 18. New York.

Goddard, P. E. 1934. *Indians of the Northwest Coast*. American Museum of Natural History, Handbook Series no. 10. New York.

Krause, A. 1956. *The Tlingit Indians: Results of a Trip to the Northwest Coast of America and the Bering Straits*, trans. E. Gunther. Seattle.

Lévi-Strauss, C. 1971. *Mythologique IV: L'Homme nu*. Paris.

Malinowski, B. 1922. *The Sexual Life of Savages in North-Western Melanesia*, 2 vols. New York.

Swanton, J. R. 1952. *Indian Tribes of North America*. Smithsonian Institution, Bureau of American Ethnology, Bulletin no. 145. Washington, D.C.

The World Conception of Lajos Ámi, Storyteller

SÁNDOR ERDÉSZ

*In reviewing the various theories of myth, one may begin to wonder what the ulti-
mate goal of myth study is or should be. Are the origins of myth or the geographic
spread of particular myths the principal research objectives of mythologists? Or
should questions of function or structure or psychological symbolic meaning take
precedence? Each mythologist will answer according to his or her own intellectual
predilections. It is true that any approach that yields insight is obviously worthwhile. Yet there is probably consensus among mythologists that among all the possible reasons for studying myth surely one of the most important is to gain access
to how man perceives his world. It is not easy to get inside another person's mind
to discover the features of worldview. Often worldview is not consciously or formally articulated per se. One cannot simply approach a prospective informant and
ask point blank, "Can you please tell me about your worldview?" any more than
one can ask the same informant to describe in detail the grammar of the language
he or she speaks.*

*If myth and other genres of folklore do encapsulate principles of worldview and
values, then they represent valuable sources for the understanding of cognitive systems be they universal or culturally relative. This is one reason why Lévi-Strauss's
approach to myth is so important. Regardless of whether one agrees with every
feature of his analysis, one can only applaud his attempt to relate the content or
structure of the narrative he studies to the content and structure of the culture as
a whole.*

*In the following fascinating study, a Hungarian folklorist interviews a gifted peas-
ant storyteller and discovers that the storyteller's conception of the world appears
to be largely drawn from or parallel to the world described in folktales. Although
technically the narratives in question are folktales and not myths, the data gleaned
from the remarkable interview is often cosmogonic and mythical in nature. (For
that matter, the story of Asdiwal is not a proper myth either; it is a folktale or
legend.)*

Originally the term worldview *in academic parlance tended to be limited to
matters of cosmogony, but in later usage it has come to refer to the way a people
perceives the world and their place in it. In this regard, the reader may be able
to extrapolate principles of Hungarian peasant worldview from the cosmogonic
details provided by Lajos Ámi. For example, it becomes increasingly clear that
Lajos Ámi believes man's place is severely limited by time and place (and perhaps*

Reprinted from *Acta Ethnographica* 10 (1961), 327–44, by permission of the author
and the Ethnographical Institute of the Hungarian Academy of Sciences.

class structure). Striking metaphors abound demonstrating that one cannot break through boundaries. The "natural" limitations include a place where the sun's rays cannot reach, a North Pole so frozen that an airplane could not fly over it, and a firmament so thick that the mythical sky tree could not penetrate it. A somewhat sad metaphor for peasant life under such conditions is one of stunted growth. The sky tree, unable to grow straight up to and through the firmament, is forced to curve thirteen times under the sky. This is both cosmogonic worldview and an acute, perhaps unwitting, perception of a peasant's (limited) possibilities for growth or mobility in Hungary. Incidentally, the tale of the sky-high tree is a standard folktale, especially popular in Hungary though found elsewhere in eastern Europe and Germany. It is classified by folklorists as Aarne-Thompson tale type 468, The Princess of the Sky-Tree. See Stith Thompson, The Types of the Folktale, *2nd ed. (Helsinki, 1961). For a thorough comparative study of the tale, see Linda Dégh, "The Tree That Reached Up to the Sky (Type 468)," in Linda Dégh, ed.,* Studies in East European Folk Narrative *(Bloomington, Ind., 1978), pp. 263–316.*

For a survey of anthropological research on worldview, see Michael Kearney, "World View Theory and Study," Annual Review of Anthropology *4 (1975), 247–70. For more about Lajos Ámi's worldview, see Sándor Erdész, "The Cosmogonical Conceptions of Lajos Ámi, Storyteller,"* Acta Ethnographica *12 (1963), 57–64. For a remarkable account of a worldview system, see Marcel Griaule,* Conversations with Ogotemmêli: An Introduction to Dogon Religious Ideas *(Oxford, 1965).*

In December 1958, I became acquainted with Lajos Ámi, a storyteller in Szamosszeg (Szatmár County). During the following year I taped 243 folktales and 13 legends from him. This material is sizeable not only numerically but also in length. His story material almost entirely comprises the complete range of story types known in the northeastern part of our country. His extraordinary story material is due to his incomparable memory. He is able to recall almost word by word the folktales and other stories heard until 1918. We can get acquainted with the ancient world concept of Lajos Ámi not only from his material, which exceeds the stories of the Thousand and One Nights, but also from his own world of imagination, since he spoke about his individual interpretation of the *structure of the world* during our conversations. Naturally there is no difference between Ámi's mythical impression of the world and the world concept in his stories, for both ideas as nourished by the realm of Hungarian folk-belief.

Lajos Ámi was born on October 2, 1886, in Vásárosnamény. His father, György Ámi, was the gypsy smith of the town. His mother originated from a Hungarian peasant family. Already his father was ignorant of the Gypsy language. As a small child he got to Szamosszeg because of the early death of his father. His stepfather, Imre Balogh, a bricklayer, was a very good storyteller, and Lajos Ámi learnt all his tales by the time he was six or eight years old. He was fourteen when he became an apprentice in the brick factory at Szatmárnémeti. Vince Bunkó, a stoker of Italian background, must have been also a great master of storytelling because he not only taught L. Ámi how to fire bricks but more than 100 folktales as well. Lajos Ámi stayed in Szatmárnémeti until he was eighteen. After this he worked at various jobs for two years. In 1907 he was recruited to the Hussars of Nyíregyháza. After being discharged, in 1911 he married. A child which died after a few days was born to them. They didn't have any more.

Even though he struggled and worked a lot during the Horthy régime, he could not obtain more than 1½ acres of land until the time of the Liberation in 1945. During the re-allotment of land in 1945, he got six acres. He didn't farm alone for long. He became a charter member of the Dózsa Cooperative Farm of Szamosszeg in 1949. He has been retired as a cooperative member since January 1, 1960.

Lajos Ámi never learned how to read and write, but he taught an entire village community with his tales. In the cooperative he is still telling stories, especially during group activity. He also goes to tell stories at the peasants' houses. On August 20, 1959, the Cabinet of the Hungarian People's Republic bestowed the title of "Master of Folk Arts" on Lajos Ámi in recognition of his activity in preserving the folk tradition. In the first days of 1959, after we taped the tales and autobiography of Lajos Ámi, we had a long discussion about the *structure of the world.* We publish the most essential parts of the conversation material as follows:

"Describe how the world is arranged."

"Well, according to me the world looks like this: the world is round like an apple. The world is divided into parts by great rivers called ocean."

Later it becomes clear that the expression "world" refers to the universe. The world in which we live is flat as a disk.[1] He answered my question concerning where the center of the world is.

"It is stated that the beginning and the end of the world, no matter from where they measure it, is equidistant from Budapest. Therefore Budapest is said to be the center of the world."

"What holds the firmament?"

1. In the story entitled "The Lead Friar, Who Cast the Forest in Tin, and the Old Woman," the old woman says: "Well because of you I put one of my feet at one end of the world and my other foot at the other end." This section refers to the disk-shaped world also.

"In my opinion the firmament is set down on the rim of the earth as a tent when it is placed. It is in that shape like a tent when it is fastened on the earth with stakes. The firmament doesn't have to be fastened down because it is supported by the Earth. The firmament is so low at this point that the swallow has to drink water kneeling on the black cottonweed." [2]

"What is the 'black cottonweed'?"

"It's a sort of green plot of grass, but the green became black because the sun couldn't shine under the angle of the sky. They call it black cottonweed because it cannot become green. For the sun can't reach there to make it green under those eaves."

According to L. Ámi there are ice mountains in the north and glass mountains in the east.

"There are mountains as high as the sky in the Arctic Ocean. They couldn't break through them since the time of creation because they are made of ice. According to my estimation, as I know it from the stories, there has to be a glass mountain some place far away in the East, because they went through the Glass Mountain to find 'aranyi-fjitó madár'" [the golden bird, who is able to make someone a youth with its song].

"Why can't someone walk off the Earth?"

"In my opinion no mortal human being from the countries we know has ever been at the edge of the world. I believe that no one has ever found the edge of the world yet. They cannot walk to the edge of the world, either in the North, the East or the West. They even tried to cross the North Pole with an airplane. They got so frozen that they couldn't break through it."

"How far is the edge of the world?"

"Well, I couldn't say anything definite about it, but there was a knight whose horse was doing one million kilometers a minute, and after seven days and seven nights he only reached the Glass Mountain.

2. In the story of L. Ámi entitled "Little King Miklós Couldn't Find a Fine Native Woman to Marry," we can read the following about the wanderings of the hero: "When he got to the end of the world where the swallow drinks water kneeling on the black cottonweed because he wasn't able to straighten up, he found an old-looking house there."

Thus this way somebody would be able to count how many thousands of kilometers the distance is."

"What do you think the firmament is made of?"

"In my judgment the firmament is of pure gold.[3] I use the example of lightning, when someone looks up he sees such brightness, like pure gold. That is the real firmament, visible during lightning. In other words, the lightning separates the thick layer of air and permits us to see a strip of the shining firmament."

"Did anyone see the firmament at close quarters?"

"They went so high with an airplane into the thick layer of air that people couldn't see them even with magnifying glasses, and when they looked up they said: 'Yea, they have gotten into the firmament!' But it wasn't true. No mortal human being can get into it. Even if they accidentally could go so high that they would reach the firmament, they wouldn't have enough time to make a hole in it because it may not be so thin. For it stood in its place the same way for hundreds of thousands of years. Therefore I guess that it has to have such thick walling that no human being could cut through it."

"According to this, the Sky-High Tree could only reach the firmament and couldn't have penetrated it?"

"That's right. It went beyond the thick layer of air until it reached the firmament, the real gold firmament, and there the Sky-High Tree was stopped. We tell in the story that it curved thirteen times under the firmament because it should have grown more. Being unable to puncture the golden firmament, it couldn't straighten up any more."[4]

"What is the world held by so that it wouldn't fall?"

3. The expression "tiszta vont arany" (pure gold) was used in the sense of "termés arany" (native gold) by L. Ámi.
4. L. Ámi begins the story entitled "The Pear Tree of the King's Gate Whose Fruit Was Always Stolen" in the following manner: "So there was such a pear tree in the gate of the king which curved 13 times under the sky." In his story entitled "The Man Who Said He Had No Master," we find the text: "Do you see how tall this mountain is? It covers 14,000 acres, but its top curved three times under the sky because it couldn't straighten up." In the story called "Old King Attila," the coachman reported to the young king that: "I really became scared because such thick blue flames rose above the top of the tree in the forest that even the sky was becoming sooty."

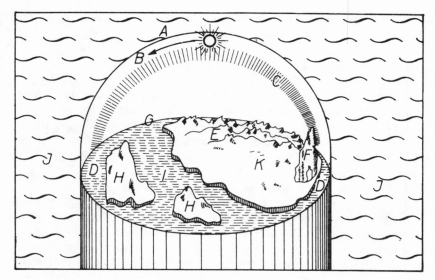

Figure 1
The Middle World after L. Ámi. A: the firmament; B: the orbit of the Sun;
C: the thick layer of air; D: the places where the sun rises and sets; E: the Ice
Mountains; F: the Glass Mountains; G: the edge of the world; H: the conti-
nents; I: the sea; J: the sea within the universe; K: the Hole of the World.

"In my estimation the firmament and the Earth stand on water. I
emphasize the firmament and the Earth, for if the Earth didn't rest on
water we wouldn't be able to dig a well. And I've always heard that the
water of the sea is under us. The fact that water also has to be above us
on the firmament is proven by the driving rain which falls in certain
places and the whole country is destroyed where the downpour occurs. Therefore it is true that there is water over us, above the firmament, and there is water under us" (Fig. 1).

Between the firmament and the surface of the Earth there is a thick
layer of air. This stratum sometimes becomes so thick that "one can
hardly see his way, though it is a bright day, for the clouds cover the
area and the sun cannot shine on the Earth."

The celestial bodies revolve under the firmament on the thick layer
of air. Every heavenly body "runs its own course, but not in the sky, we
only say so. The thick layer of air supports the sun, moon and stars."

Not only does the thick layer of air support the celestial bodies, but
also the water. "Under the sun there are waters which they call clouds.
These are held by a thick layer of air. Their name is only cloud water.
They are also called rain clouds. These are as large as the sea."

"What proves that there is water above the thick layer of air?"

"The proof is in the small frogs and little fishes which we find on the ground after a rain. There are animals, newts, small fish and frogs in the water supported by the thick layer of air above us. There are even bigger ones. One-pound fish can be found after a greater rain."

"Do you think someone could go there with a boat?"

"Of course someone could go there with a boat! It is possible because there the water is just like the sea water, or the Szamos or Tisza Rivers."

"You meant that the sun goes under the firmament and is borne by the thick layer of air. But where is the sun when it is dark at night?"

"Many people question how it is that the sun comes up in the east and goes down in the west, and on the following morning it comes up in the east in its own place. It has its own orbit. When the sun goes to the edge of the world, it sneaks under the earth into the water, takes a bath and then it comes back to the east. Thus in the morning it is in its place again, and from there it has to make the same trip it took at night. From under the earth and under the water it returns to its usual place" (Fig. 2).

"According to this, does the sun go into the water at night?"

"Yes, it goes in the water. It goes under the Earth and under the water so that in its watery orbit it would wash off all the sinning it took upon itself during the day and all the curses of bad people it had to hear.[5] The sun orbits under the Earth and in the sky just as one thinks of a wheel as turning."

"Since nothing goes by itself, what propels the sun?"

"It goes like a jet plane. The sun is self-propelled and never stops. If the sun once stopped it could not start again."

5. In the story entitled "The Bear Who Drank Water for Seven Years But Couldn't Swallow a Drop," the king promised the hand of his daughter to the one who can find the moon. The hero of the story found the vanished celestial body on the bottom of the sea and wanted to throw it back to the sky. The moon pleaded in this way: "Let me stay for at least one more year, so that I could bathe enough for it would make me rested! I don't hear so many dirty words, for some people, including you too, can curse among the people more than others. I heard you cursing also a great many times."

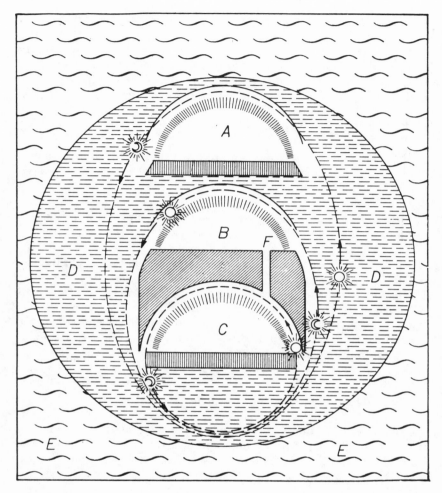

Figure 2
The Universe after L. Ámi. A: the upper world; B: the middle world; C: the
world below; D: the sea within the universe; E: the sea which supports the
world; F: the Hole of the World.

"Does the moon also sink in the water?"

"Yes, it also sinks in the water. It orbits around the whole world at all
the places where it is on duty.[6] So the moon has the same orbit as the
sun. When the sun sets in the west the moon rises in the east."

6. In the story entitled "Little King Miklós Couldn't Find a Fine Native Woman to

This is all L. Ámi told us about our world, or more exactly about the "middle world."

According to his imagination there is a world under us, just as big as ours. "I heard that covered by a layer of earth between the waters there are just as many living people under the earth as here in the upper layer." The under world has its own firmament too.

Through the "Hole of the World" it is or rather it was possible to descend to the world beneath. The "Hole of the World" is somewhere in Russia, but nobody knows its exact location any more. In the hole there is a ladder just as in the smokestacks of factories. It happened that the dragons kidnapped the king's daughter. "When the dragons were taking the king's daughter under the Earth, they had the ladder kicked off by the magic steed so that the girl couldn't be followed." But the knight still rescued the princess. "There wasn't any ladder in the whole world, but they made a device out of a barrel which they lowered by a rope."

L. Ámi relates the thickness of the Earth also to the period necessary to lower the knight. "The Earth is so deep that no one can realize it, for the rope with the barrel took one day and one night to be lowered into Dragon Land.[7]

"According to this is it possible that there are still dragons there?"

"Well, maybe dragons are there and maybe other peoples too. Let's suppose that our continent is here. We are Hungarians. Next to us there are Czechoslovakia, Serbia and Roumania. Already these are other peoples."

"Therefore is it possible that another country is next to Dragon Land?"

"Yes, it is possible that there is another."

"Where could hell be? Is it under the Earth too?"

Marry," one star tells the hero of the tale: "Well, quickly climb on my back. We are almost late because I have to go on duty tonight for I have to take my place."

7. In L. Ámi's story entitled "Peter Húzom Didn't Find Anyone Stronger Than Himself," we can read the following: "There was a tree, the root of which was 10,000 kilometers long. János Erős pulled it out at once. The Hole of the World was down there. Going down two thousand kilometers there was the Highwaymen's Cave of the 'Bakarasz' (Tom Thumb)." "The Magicians Were Never Afraid" is the title of his story in which mention is again made of the trip to the world below. "The one-headed dragon went down to the bottom of the well. He left his 365 heads placed at the foot of the well. He collected all the princesses, countesses and baronesses. He brought them back to the well, and they pulled them up by the lift of the well."

"Yes, hell is there some place next to Dragon Land."

"What produces the light for those living in the under world?"

"Through our continent the dragons went into Russia in order to take the sun from the sky. I know about the dragon king telling János Pálinkás, 'We will take your sun from this part of the world so that we would have two and we wouldn't ever have darkness.' A sun would have risen after their sun had set, if they had been able to take it. Only the moon would have been left for us. But they could not take it because János Pálinkás caused them to burn in great numbers."

"Does the sun go over the Land of the Dragons or under it when it sets here?"

"Yes, it passes under their land. It goes under the two countries, under the two worlds. The world at its edge is similar to a tent. There our sun goes down into the bottomless waters. The dragons' sun sets the same way even though it is below us. It revolves under the water and then comes back to the sky. Their sun goes on the lower sky and ours on the higher" (Fig. 2).

The upper world and the middle world are the same. Over the firmament above us live the same amount of people as in the middle world.

"Uncle Ámi, you already said that there is a sun, a moon and stars in the lower world as in the middle world, how is it in the upper world?"

"We already know that the dragons have their own sun. We also have our own sun, moon and stars in the middle world. As I see it they also have to have their own sun above, for the ones who left from here as holy men to move into Heaven live as angels above. Therefore they, too, have the same kind of sun as we have. The stars shine above their heads, and the moon is having the same orbit just as in our part of the world."

There is a giant milky lake in the upper world. "In that Milk Lake the angels who deserve to be allowed to fly in Heaven bathe. The water of the Milk Lake belongs to Paradise. I know about this because all the people heard that the water of the Milk Lake exists."

"How did this new world come into being?"

"Well as I know it from heresay, when the Father Almighty created the original couple, Adam was made first. Adam got bored in Paradise. Therefore God took one of Adam's ribs out and created a woman called Eve." After the fall in Paradise the Creator told Adam the following: "Neither you nor Eve have a place in Paradise from now on. I will open the gate and throw you out. Live in blood and sweat because you brought sin to humanity. Then he grabbed the hands of Adam and Eve and threw them out of the Garden of Eden. They landed down on this Earth, but they didn't get hurt at all."[8]

"Where was this door?"

"It was above the firmament and it still is. It opens when a soul has to appear."

"Do you know above what country this door could be?"

"Well, I can't say this for certain, but I know that Adam and Eve fell someplace between Vienna and Buda. Therefore the door could be above that area."

The above conception of the world makes it apparent that L. Ámi is an unusual folk character. He didn't get this world concept readymade. Based on his own observation combined with tale and other traditional elements, he formed a system out of it himself. Since he was forced to work in his early childhood instead of study, he didn't learn how to read and write. Unavoidable illiteracy excluded him from possibilities of a higher scholastic training. Therefore he could gain his knowledge only from oral tradition. L. Ámi referred to two sources of knowledge when he was speaking about his religious imagination. His notions "I know it from stories" and "As I heard it" show that his world of imagination was formed partly by his own tales and partly by the traditions preserved by the community. The community cut off from books also interprets the phenomena of the world by interpolating supernatural power and fictional elements. The comment of L. Ámi "I know it from hearing," first of all means that even this community is interested in the structure of the world, in the question of soul, etc.,

8. Kálmány enumerates more examples that Paradise is in the upper world according to the realm of Hungarian folk belief and that the fall of the first couple also occurred in the celestial region above us (Kálmány 1893, p. 43). According to a Vogul datum, similar to the notion of L. Ámi, the first couple was lowered from the sky by a rope (Munkácsy 1896, p. 135).

from day to day. Especially during the long winter nights, they exchanged their opinions based on tradition which they formed about this matter. In other words the concept of the world which L. Ámi probably heard in his early childhood was a topic of conversation. These beliefs and primitive religious fantasies, which he was already acquainted with in his childhood, are still embedded in his thinking today.

While learning the extensive story material he became familiar with the world of tales. Thus the stories themselves also greatly helped him to formulate an individual concept about the world. L. Ámi senses this when he says, "If someone knows how to interpret, he knows how things go on in the world even from the tales."

The outstanding storytellers believe the tales. The related miraculous stories are thought by them to have once occurred. According to M.-Fedics, the great storyteller who died in 1938, "The tales all happened to the ancient people."[9] J. Varga, a storyteller of Nyírvasvári, in answer to my question whether the things told in his tales once happened, said: "Of course they happened. Once there were miracles like this. Now there is a different system, but we still have scientists who invent everything." J. Varga finds support for his tales in science, while other storytellers in faith. L. Ámi, according to his own individual opinion, believes the reality of his tales.

The memory of an historical event and natural disaster doesn't vanish without a sign. These dates are the indispensable supports of the chronology of the people. The 1848 Freedom Fight against the Austrians, the Great Famine of 1863, etc., cannot be erased from the memory of the people. They also relate the other less important dates. Regarding the question of the reality in tales, L. Ámi also refers to historical events. L. Ámi experienced the difference between the world of tales and the world of reality. No miraculous things happen in the world of reality, while in the world of tales the hero is surrounded by creatures possessing supernatural power, by speaking animals, by charms and the magic power of the spoken word. The reason why this is not so is explained by him as follows: "The curse doesn't work since 1848." According to him the spoken word had such power before 1848 that if somebody damned another it immediately took effect. Before 1848 witches and magicians who were able to change men into animals and other things travelled around the world. Even devils had supernatural power. There was a change in 1848. No miraculous things happened since that time. L. Ámi himself tells why: "No things like

9. Ortutay 1940, "Introductory Study," p. 67.

these happen today. God refused the power from the Devil and took away the curses from men. If God had allowed these, there already wouldn't be a single healthy person on this earth. Such miracles don't happen since 1848. Nobody can do such things as they did before."

The above statement of L. Ámi relates not only to folktales but also to the beliefs. Thus he holds the tales and superstitious stories to be true previous to 1848. Therefore the story world of L. Ámi is not a desired *dream world*[10] but the reality of old times which had taken place in the land belonging to the present Hungary.

In connection with the examination of the background of folktales, J. Honti writes: "If we want to discover the history and the meaning of the special structure of the world found in tales, we have to pay attention to the ancient mythical and religious world concepts."[11] This recognition led to the collection and elaboration of the singular world concept of L. Ámi, the storyteller.

Until the beginning of the eighteenth century the question of the shape of the Earth and the existence of the celestial sea were among the debated theses of cosmology. Naturally the mythical world concept didn't entirely vanish. It is preserved by the people's memory in many areas, even if only in slight traces.

Honti opposes those who consider the world concept in tales as surviving phenomena of the ancient mythical world concept and according to whom the tale is dragging the material of dead traditions along. He considers that the background of tales is alive at all times. Thus on the basis of the world concept in tales, we can suppose the existence of the mythical world concept, nevertheless the two world images are in agreement with each other. It is regrettable that, having no other means, he proves the existence of the mythical world concept through the Medieval scholastic world concept, which is not quite convincing. We are in a more favourable position because at the present time we can make an effort to observe the structure of the world in tales through a comparison of the mythical world concept of Lajos Ámi.

The debate in connection with the shape of the Earth was ended by Magellan's trip around the world. To the people cut off from the chance of gaining scientific knowledge, the *world* was still held as a palm-sized microcosmos, which one was able to visually comprehend. It is not accidental that the conceptions held about the Earth being disk-shaped and the hemispherical sky could have developed independently of each other without any reciprocal effect.

The purpose of our paper was only to introduce the magical world

10. Honti 1940, p. 4.　　11. Honti 1940, p. 311.

concept of a storyteller, but because of the importance of parallels we consider it necessary to introduce a few choice examples from Hungarian material first of all.

L. Ámi drew a colourful picture about the edge of the world and the lowness of the firmament. We can find the tale formula of the swallow who drinks water while kneeling in two folktales collected by J. Berze Nagy.[12] However, Berze Nagy incorrectly states that this formula signifies such a place "which is beyond the borders of reality."[13] S. Dömötör was also unable to give the correct explanation of this question.[14] L. Vajda, who made comparative studies based on world-wide text material, was the first to recognize the meaning of the tale formula of the swallow who drinks water kneeling.[15] L. Ámi, as we saw, gives specific information relating to this. The formula comes from a primitive imagination in which the firmament folding over the Earth at the edge of the world has to be very low. F. Jóni, storyteller, said, in his tale entitled "The Frog King," "Where the swallow drinks the water kneeling on the black cottonweed," but Jóni is already ignorant of the meaning of the tale formula.

Logically, where the Earth is imagined as a flat disk, the notion concerning the edge of the Earth and the joining of Heaven and Earth can be found. According to the popular tradition of Göcsej: "The edge of the world is where the firmament joins the Earth."[16] One Székely folktale says that the edge of the world is where "the curtains of the sky are lowered."[17] In these traditions the edge of the Earth means the edge of the world at the same time; thus they imagine the world in this shape. The end of the world, according to L. Ámi, is unapproachable because the low sky *would fall on the person who sees it*. I found a similar belief in Nyírgyulaj (a town in Szabolcs County) in November of 1959. They told that St. David fiddles in the moon. No one may look at him. If the fiddle string breaks, *it will strike out the person's eye*. When the gods made the firmament out of stone the "Golds" of northeastern Siberia started to fear that it *may fall on them*. Therefore the gods hid the stone (the firmament) from the peoples' eyes with air.[18] Probably this fear of a falling sky belongs to the components of Eastern origin among our popular realm of beliefs.

Different peoples have a similar opinion about the edge of the world.

12. Berze Nagy 1907, p. 274; Berze Nagy 1940, p. 99.
13. Berze Nagy 1940, p. 488.
14. Dömötör 1948, p. 57; Berze Nagy 1940, p. 99. Dömötör, not knowing the second datum of Berze Nagy, writes, "The expression is an individual peculiarity of a single storyteller, therefore it isn't a characteristic feature of our tales from the Lowland."
15. Vajda 1953, p. 250. Vajda's statement is perfectly identical to the idea of L. Ámi.
16. Gönczi 1914, p. 181.   17. Berze Nagy 1943, p. 240.   18. Harva 1938, p. 59.

A. Ipolyi refers to a Slavic folktale in Hungary. In this story the prince "reaches the Glass Mountain, slippery as ice, standing at the edge of the world."[19] According to the Vogul and Ostyak realm of belief, the Earth is surrounded by a mountain range and this mountain range is called Ural. Caucaus (Kaf) is defined in the Arabian and Turkish dictionaries as a mountain located at the edge of the world.[20]

In his work published in 1854, A. Ipolyi was the first who referred to the world concept preserved by the Hungarian popular traditions. He analyzed the two meanings of the word "világ" ("world" in Hungarian). First the word "világ" is associated to time, such as "Török világ" (Turkish period) and "Kuruc világ" (the times of Francis Rákóczi), etc. The other "világ" is special. According to the latter interpretation other worlds besides ours also exist. He states that the Hungarian word "világ" also means universe in addition to the more restricted earthly or heavenly world.[21] We saw that "világ" also refers to the universe according to L. Ámi.

The conception of waters which surround the universe can be found in the world view of several other peoples. The idea of the world floating on water is inseparable from the notion of the sea above and under us. Troels-Lund writes that, according to the world concept of Thales, the Earth floats as a disk on the ocean. The arched sky is on top of these. Above everything there is again the water which produces the rain.[22] Anaximandros was convinced that the Earth freely floats on water. Among the Central and North Asian peoples a conception is known that beneath and around our Earth there is an infinite primeval sea.[23]

L. Ámi is convinced that the same water which is horizontally extending in the sea is above the firmament. For example, the "bottomless deep sea" in our world is a part of the waters within the universe. The horizontally extending sea (Letter I, Fig. 1) and the sea within the universe are interconnected (Letter D, Fig. 2). L. Ámi also believes in an external sea, but it is located outside of the universe and in this the universe floats (Letter E, Fig. 2).

According to L. Ámi there is one more layer of water between the firmament and the Earth. The idea of water above us is general in the Medieval Christian cosmology, and they even maintained that "the natural place of water is above the Earth."[24] The Orotšon Tunguz believe that in the water above us there swims a great fish, creating thunder with its fins and wind with its tail.[25] We have to mention here

19. Ipolyi 1929, p. 130.   20. Harva 1938, p. 23.   21. Ipolyi 1939, p. 77.
22. Troels-Lund 1913, p. 95.   23. Harva 1938, p. 22.   24. Honti 1940, p. 316.
25. Harva 1938, p. 206.

the opinion of the Samoyedes that the Jenissei originates in a great lake lying in the sixth celestial layer.[26]

The primitive ideas of a water above are known throughout the world, but the opinion of L. Ámi has its own peculiar feature, for it supposes different celestial oceans both on the thick layer of air and above the firmament. Actually we witness the intermingling of the attitude of the scholastic world concept and our folktales which took their origin in the East.

The vertical and horizontal world concepts in tales (to which J. Berze Nagy first called attention)[27] can be equally found in the tales of L. Ámi, even in the mixed form.[28] In the case of L. Ámi, this mixing of world concepts takes place only in his tales. In his mythical world concept other worlds can be found exclusively in the vertical division.

Let's talk about the other worlds.

The Christian teaching of the existence of a Heaven above us and a Hell below became fairly general all over Europe. But the idea of a three-fold world is fairly common among the peoples who believe in shamanism. The Sojots imagine the world to be three disks, set upon one another, among which the Earth is in the middle. The Jakuts also distinguish an upper, middle and lower world.[29] Among the Altaic peoples we may consider the world concept with six, nine, twelve and sixteen layers more common. We could derive the attitude of the world concept of L. Ámi from the Christian view of nature, if we did not consider the ones told about the thick layer of air.

According to L. Ámi the thick layer of air extends between the sky and the Earth in the three worlds. This layer is not ordinary air, but a somewhat solid glass-like material, for the celestial bodies would not be able to travel on it. From the stories of L. Ámi it becomes understandable that the black cloud, or rather the thick layer of air, signifies an important and solid celestial layer in the world concept of the

26. Harva 1938, p. 21.
27. Berze Nagy 1943, p. 239.
28. In the story by L. Ámi entitled "The Golden Bird, Who Is Able to Make Someone a Youth with Its Song," Laurel Land is beyond the Glass Mountain, even though in his mythical world concept the Glass Mountain is at the edge of the world. János Erös, in the story entitled "The Man Who Had No Master," marries the daughter of the king of the devils somewhere in Hungary as the result of a unilateral decision. His father-in-law caught him by a trick and took him into the Land of the Devils which lay on a horizontal plane, but there they still speak about Hungary as a country which is in the upper world. In the tale entitled "Come Here, Brothers! I Don't Know What This Man Wants to Say," István Kiss arrives at Curley Land to visit his younger sister, after a trip which he also took in a horizontal direction. During the conversation his brother-in-law said: "Well, we understand that we are not as ruddy *as the people who live in the upper part of the world*, because we only eat bread made from rice here in Curley Land."
29. Harva 1938, p. 25.

storyteller.[30] If we pay attention to the three thick layers of air besides the three levels of worlds, then L. Ámi's perspective of the world becomes similar to the Eastern six-layered comprehension of the world concept.

Ideas of a multi-layered world are fairly widespread among the Hungarian folk beliefs.[31] On the basis of the popular legends and myths, A. Ipolyi tries to fit the seven-layered universe into Hungarian mythology. The copper, silver and gold forests, the underground palaces of dragons, the inhabitation of Hell by devils, the land of fairies, and the homeland of the sisters-in-law—the Sun, Moon and Wind—all may be found in the different worlds. In the stories written about the Sky-High Tree the climbing shepherd boy found a city on every branch. According to A. Ipolyi every branch means a layer of the earth.[32]

L. Ámi's concept is different from the Christian concept even in not assigning the other worlds to Heaven and Hell. To him, Hell means one of the countries in the world below. L. Ámi's idea concerning the upper and lower worlds agrees with the realm of Hungarian folktales and with the religious ideas of our Eastern relatives.

The upper worlds are superior to our world in all religious ideas. L. Ámi says that the inhabitants of the upper world bathe in the Milk Lake. In the Hungarian idiom they use the colloquial expression "tejbevajba fürdik" ("he bathes in milk and butter") to express that someone is prosperous. We can get acquainted with the concept of a milk lake from the Altaic Tartar shaman songs and also from other religious ideas.[33] The Milk Lake frequently occurs in Hungarian folktales too.

The ideas about the celestial strata can be found most completely in the type of folktales about the *Sky-High Tree*. They all begin with a shepherd boy's attempt to climb the tree in the king's garden. On the way up he discovers green pastures, castles and churches on the several levels. This story form was first compared by S. Solymossy to the realm of belief of the Siberian shamanist peoples, stating that the motif of the Sky-High Tree can be classed with our ancient remembrances which came with us from the East before the original conquest of the present Hungary.[34]

In the realm of belief of the Siberian peoples the idea of the Sky-

30. In L. Ámi's story entitled "The Man Who Said He Had No Master," mention is made about a hero who "banged his head on a black cloud."

31. During my field work at Újfehértó (Szabolcs County) in November of 1960, L. Rátkai, a 47-year-old shepherd, said: "The worlds under and above us are innumerable and we, too, live in one of the layers."

32. Ipolyi 1929, p. 78.

33. Harva 1938, pp. 170, 556.

34. Solymossy 1922, p. 43.

High Tree also can be found. As a tent is supported by a pole, the sky, in their opinion, rests on a tree as if it were a giant pole too. In the folk legends of the Jakuts, the Siberian Tatars,[35] this tree reaches and supports the sky. The notion that this tree reaches beyond the seven celestial layers can also be found in the Jakut folk legends.[36]

It also occurs in the imagination of the Altaic peoples that the top of the giant pine tree which grows in the center of the Earth reaches up to the house of Bai Ülgön in the sixteenth celestial layer.[37] Therefore the Eastern analogies of the Sky-High Tree can be divided into two groups. In the first group the Tree of the World reaches the firmament; in the other it reaches the celestial layers. L. Ámi's Tree of the World can be classified in the former group, for its top only reaches the sky, and its top is even bent because it wasn't able to straighten up. This image can be found in a Csángómagyar folktale of Zajzon (Transylvania) where "there was such a large cherry tree in the courtyard of the count that *it had to bend against the sky*."[38] According to Berze Nagy this tree has the same role as the Jakuts' Sky-Supporting Tree of the World.[39]

According to both the shamanistic peoples and the Hungarian folktales, this World Tree is a way in which someone can get into the upper regions. L. Ámi also believes that there is a door between Vienna and Buda at the pinnacle of the sky. We frequently find these door-like openings in Hungarian folktales.

We may read about the hero of a Csángómagyar folktale from Tatrang. "On the sixth day he reached the sky. There at *the gate of the sky* he found a very old man."[40] In other stories we find the door on the tree trunk. This door means the opening which leads to the upper world.

The Altaic peoples call this opening a chimney through which the shamans travel from one region to another.[41] The Buryats also call the opening on the sky the *Door to Heaven*, and they interpret the openings of the individual celestial layers to be exactly above one another vertically.[42]

The openings which connect the celestial layers can be found not only above but also below. G. Kiss mentions fifty-seven Hungarian versions of number 301 story type, in which the hero descends through the hole leading into the world below.[43] The opening leading to the lower world is the *Hole of the World*, frequently occurring in the stories of L. Ámi too. This image may also be found in the world con-

35. Berze Nagy 1958, p. 129.   36. Harva 1938, p. 76.   37. Berze Nagy 1958, p. 129.
38. Horger 1908, p. 422.   39. Berze Nagy 1958, p. 136.   40. Horger 1908, p. 376.
41. Harva 1938, p. 53.   42. Harva 1938, p. 54.   43. Kiss 1959, p. 253.

cept of the Altaic peoples. They call the opening which leads to the world below *the Smokehole of the Earth*. The Jakut shamans have a round shaped iron plate with a hole in it hanging on their clothing, and this plate symbolizes the hole in the center of the Earth.[44]

Regarding the ways leading to the other worlds, L. Ámi distinguishes between the upper and lower world. According to him only the souls divorced of matter may get into the upper world, while into the world below even flesh and blood people may also gain access; all who are able to go down through the hole of the world, in other words.[45] In contrast with the upper world, L. Ámi considers the lower world to be the organic continuation of our world where living beings similar to us dwell.

It is interesting that L. Ámi imagines the orbiting of the sun in the same way as the ancient Greeks, who held the opinion that "die Sonne an jeden Abend im Westen in den Wellen des Ozeans unterging, segelte sie auf diesem im Laufe der Nacht wieder zurück, um am nächsten Morgen rein gewaschen im Osten aufzustehen."[46] The opinion of Anaximandros was already somewhat different. He thought that during the night the sun proceeds across the sky of the other world which is the mirror reflection of our world. On the other hand, according to L. Ámi, every world has its own celestial bodies, and the suns and moons of all three celestial layers pass under the lower world (Fig. 2).

Let us return to the story of L. Ámi already mentioned above in which there is a reference about a way leading across the Glass Mountain. The hero who set off on a journey for the golden bird, who is able to make someone a youth with its song in "Babérország" (Laurel Land), dines with an old beggar at the foot of the Glass Mountain. The latter said: "My son, finish eating, because the Glass Mountain is going to open in a few hours and we have to go through it. So when it opens we have to be by the middle of the Glass Mountain." Both the Buryats and the Gilyaks reckon that the sky is shaped like an upside-down cauldron and is in continuous motion. While it is moving, an opening is caused between the rim of Heaven and Earth through which the legendary hero of Buryat may also get through. They believe that the sun leaves the world at the opening of the Earth.[47] As we can see, L. Ámi's

---

44. Harva 1938, p. 26.

45. In 1552 Sebestyén Tinódi Lantos, on the basis of Thuróczi's Chronicles, worked up Lőrinc Tar's Journey to Hell (Tinódi-Emlékkönyv 1956, pp. 95–98). In the story Lőrinc Tar went to the Underworld in human form and returned in the manner of the hero of story type 301.

46. Troels-Lund 1913, p. 94.

47. Harva 1938, pp. 35–36, and Solymossy 1929, p. 143.

view preserves the Eastern religious elements. The motif of the periodical split of the Glass Mountain, which is at the end of the world, preserves this memory of sunset and its departure from the world (or rising).

We can see that the world concept of the storyteller is derived from two sources. Through one tradition it is preserving the medieval Christian or even older world concept, and it reconciles these with the view of world concepts in the Hungarian folktales. Possessing this modest material we may not undertake to observe every historical, etymological, etc., constituent of the world concepts. Probably later the collection of similar folk characters' opinion may create a basis for a more general investigation of world concepts.

BIBLIOGRAPHY

Berze Nagy, J. 1907. *Népmesék Heves- és Jász-Nagykun-Szolnok megyéböl* (Folktales from Heves and Jász-Nagykun-Szolnok Counties). Vol. 9, *Magyar népköltési gyüjtemény* (Collection of Hungarian Folk Poetry). Budapest.

Berze, Nagy, J. 1940. *Baranyai magyar néphagyományok* (Hungarian Folklore of Baranya County), vol. 2. Pécs.

Berze, Nagy, J. 1943. *Mese* (Tales). Vol. 3, *A magyarság néprajza* (The Ethnography of the Hungarians), 3rd ed., 226–89. Budapest.

Berze Nagy, J. 1958. *Égigérö fa* (The Sky-High Tree). Pécs.

Dömötör, S. 1948. "Egy értelmetlennek látszó mesekezdö formulánkról" (Concerning an Apparently Nonunderstandable Story Beginning Tale Formula). *Magyar nyelvör* 72, 57–59. Budapest.

Gönczi, F. 1914. *Göcsej s kapcsolatos Hetés vidékének és népének összevontabb ismertetése* (A More Concise Description of Göcsej and the Allied Hetés Area). Kaposvár.

Harva, U. 1938. *Die religiösen Vorstellungen der altaischen Völker.* FF Communications, vol. 125. Helsinki.

Honti, J. 1940. "A népmese háttere" (The Background of Folktales). *Ethnographia* 51, 308–20.

Honti, J. n.d. *Az ismeretlen népmese* (The Unknown Folktale). n.p.

Horger, A. 1908. *Hétfalusi csángó népmesék* (The Csángó Folktales of Hétfalu). Vol. 10, *Magyar népköltési gyüjtemény* (Collection of Hungarian Folk Poetry). Budapest.

Ipolyi, A. 1929. *Magyar mythologia* (Hungarian Mythology). Vol. 2, 3rd ed. Budapest.

Kálmány, L. 1893. *Világunk alakulásai nyelvhagyományainkban* (The Formation of Our World Through Our Language Traditions). Szeged.

Kiss, G. 1959. "A 301-es mesetípus magyar redakciói" (The Hungarian Redactions of the 301 Story Type). *Ethnographia* 70, 253–68.

Munkácsi, B. 1896. Vogul népköltési gyüjtemény (Collection of Vogul Folk Poetry). Vol. 1. Budapest.

Ortutay, Gy. 1940. Fedics Mihály mesél (Mihály Fedics Narrates). Vol. 1, Új magyar népköltési gyüjtemény (Collection ot New Hungarian Folk Poetry). Budapest.

Solymossy, S. 1922. "Keleti elemek népmeséinkben" (Oriental Elements in Our Folk-tales). Ethnographia 33, 30–44.

Solymossy, S. 1929. "Magyar ösvallási elemek népmeséinkben" (Hungarian Primitive Religious Elements in Our Folktales). Ethnographia 40, 133–52.

Tinódi-Emlékkönyv. 1956. Szombathely.

Troels-Lund, T. 1913. Himmelsbild und Weltanschauung im Wandel der Zeiten. 4th ed. Leipzig.

Vajda, L. 1953. A pigmeusok harca a darvakkal (The Pygmies' Battle with the Crane). Ethnographia 64, 242–56.

The Myth of Washington

DOROTHEA WENDER

The study of myth is a serious enterprise, but that shouldn't mean that it cannot also be fun. Scholars in nearly every part of the academy sometimes take themselves just a bit too seriously, and it is well to be reminded of this. Theories of myth, it turns out, can occasionally be as bizarre as the myths they purport to explain. It would be tempting to subject the theories of myth to the same kind of rigorous and not-so-rigorous analysis that has been applied to myths. One could then have a Freudian analysis of a Lévi-Straussian analysis or equally a structural study of a Freudian study, to mention just two of numerous possible combinations. Such a trend would have no end. If we had a Freudian analysis of a Lévi-Straussian analysis, we could certainly analyze that Freudian analysis according to Lévi-Straussian structural principles. Rather than carrying this infinite series of analyses any further, let us turn to an unusual overview of theories of myth written by Dorothea Wender, professor of classics at Wheaton College in Norton, Massachusetts. Aside from the fact that the story of George Washington would be classified by folklorists as a legend, not a myth—remember Professor Bascom's essay with which this volume began—the various proposed readings of the story are exemplary.

Euhemerists, of course, still insist that George Washington, the culture hero of the American people, was a real man. It is the purpose of this paper to put to rest that view, once and for all. On the face of it, it would seem not unreasonable to assume that a kernel of historical truth must lie somewhere beneath the myths about Washington; this assumption, however, is baseless, since *every detail* of the Washington myth can be analyzed and shown to be symbolic by at least one approved method of myth-analysis.

I. THE CHERRY TREE AND THE AXE: EATING THE GOD IN AMERICA

In the first place, Washington is clearly a faded god, not a man since his name is patently derived from the city of Washington (Washing-

Reprinted from *Arion*, n.s. 3 (1976), 71–78, by permission of the author and the Trustees of Boston University.

town: place of ritual cleanliness), just as Athene's is from Athens. That he is not only a city-patron but an agricultural deity can be seen from his association with trees, particularly the cherry tree. He has wooden teeth; he cuts down a cherry tree in his youth; cherry trees are a prominent feature of his city's beauty, and every year, in the spring, a cherry blossom festival is held, in which (putative) virgins, designated as cherry blossom "princesses," ride through the city in triumph. Surely these maidens represent the new birth of vegetation, just as the hoary old men (called, appropriately, "senators") who nominate and frequently ride with them, represent the leafless, wrinkled boughs of the forest in winter. And when does the festival take place? A short time after another rite, the "Birthday" (or more accurately re-birth day) of the annually resurrected Washington, the personification of the cherry tree.

Can we not see in this annual rite, and in the story of the hatchet and the cherry tree, traces of an earlier, more barbaric ritual in which chosen maidens were annually cut down, sacrificed in honor of the cherry tree spirit, in order to insure the regeneration of the vernal blossoms? Surely we can, and evidence of even grosser enormity is provided by the annual ritual of "eating the god" on this re-birth day: I refer, of course, to the consumption of cherry pie, which clearly represents a now-forgotten practice of cannibalism, in which the human representatives of the cherry-spirit were consumed in a ritual meal.

Washington's role as a dying and reviving eniautos-daemon is probably most clearly seen in these cherry tree rites and myths, but he functions, too, as the patron of certain *rites de passage* involving the crossing of water. Traces of this ancient function can be clearly seen in the myths of his crossing the Delaware river and throwing a silver dollar across the Potomac. Both these myths undoubtedly refer to initiation rites: that the Delaware crossing is a purely ritual and not "historical" tale can be seen from the fact that in pictorial representations the year-god is portrayed standing up in the boat, blessing the gaily costumed priests and initiates who accompany him. If the voyage and river were envisioned as "real," a "real" commander would surely have known enough to remain seated in a rocking boat.

Initiation ritual is probably found, also, in the dollar-across-the-Potomac story, but another annual rite is perhaps also suggested here: rainmaking. The dollar, like rain, is silvery, and also might remind one of the "riches" attendant upon well-watered crops. It is tossed over the river (by a human representative of Washington), and falls on the fertile Virginia soil; by sympathetic magic this procedure was intended to stimulate the spring rains, with moisture drawn from the swollen rivers, to fall in like manner upon the thirsty farmland. Washing-town (the town bathed by spring rains) is still a place of mysteriously inspiring loveliness every spring, when the cherry trees clothe themselves in those fleecy mantles that mimic the recently melted snow; the Washington Monument, with its crude likeness of a tree, still reminds us of our tall deity; Mount Vernon, the "vernal" holy precinct where lies the "tomb" of the everliving tree spirit, still echoes with the voices of the past, and the dollar—no longer, it is true, sacred and silver but now a mere faded shred of paper—still bears the likeness of the cherry tree god, and still compels the ungrudging worship of the faithful.

II. THE CASE OF LITTLE GEORGE

In the Story of little George we find yet another clear-cut case of the Family Romance. In the first place, the hero is born in *Virgin*-ia: since he cannot bear to think of himself as the product of sexual union between his beloved mother and hated father, the mythmaker invests his birth with fantasied purity. This infantile wish for the mother's chastity can be seen more clearly in the repeated emphasis in the story on cherries—"cherry" being a slang word for the hymen. When little George attacks a "cherry tree" with his "little hatchet," the infantile fantasy of deflowering the pure mother is expressed in symbolic form. But the hated father, by forgiving little George, ridicules the child's diminutive "weapon." The father then dies, immediately gratifying little George's murderous fantasies, but leaving a residue of neurotic guilt in the hero's developing superego. Eventually little George reaches physical maturity and becomes a surveyor ("one who watches")—presumably, this fascination with watching refers to the child's envious observation of the primal scene. Thus we can see that little George, although technically a man, is still fixated in the Oedipal phase, perhaps because of the early death of the father. He marries a mother-surrogate (a widow with children), but is himself unable to be a father. He compensates for this inability to achieve full sexual maturity by becoming a soldier, the most "masculine" profession, but we can see the difficult and unsatisfactory nature of this form of sublimation in the Valley Forge episode. Valleys clearly represent the female genitalia, and a forge is a hot place; hence little George attempts to accommodate himself to mature sexuality, but fails. Due to his infantile neurosis, he "freezes" (cannot perform adequately) in the "hot valley." Eventually, however, he stops "freezing" and goes on to "win the war" against King George (a surrogate for the hostile father). The bugaboo of the "father" is at last defeated for all time, and little George usurps his place. At last he wins the gratification which his infantile ego had been unable to achieve by more usual means: he becomes famous for "sleeping" in various beds, retires to *Mount* Vernon ("mount" is another sexual slang word), and is eventually memorialized, not by a little hatchet, but by a giant erect phallos of marble. Little George no longer, the triumphant ego is now called the Father of his Country.

III. BAKED BEANS BOURRÉE
("With a heigh-ho, Derry Derrida!")

The preceding interpretations of the *Geste de Washington* are of course "true." Since human minds universally operate in a bipolar way and accomplish transformations similarly, *every* interpretation of a still-living myth is "true" and should be considered as one more variant of the myth in question. Our interpretation, too will be "true" in the same way, and could in turn be "truly" interpreted by us as yet another variant; our second interpretation could then again be treated as still another "true" version, and so on, as on the Quaker Oats box. . . .

But let us examine our key myth, G^1.

G^1: George and the Cherry Tree

The culture-hero George Washington receives a small axe from his father. He uses the axe to cut down a cherry tree. G's father angrily demands to know the culprit. George confesses and is not only forgiven, but rewarded with a display of paternal affection.

In the preceding tale, the most puzzling feature is that the young miscreant is rewarded rather than punished for his act of wanton destruction. Not until we realize that this myth is really about the origin of cream cheese will we understand the reasoning behind this anomaly, but because of the tale's extreme reticence on the subject of cream cheese it will be necessary first to examine another closely related set of myths, G$^{2,3,4,5.}$ $\cdots$ . . . .

The name "George" (Greek $\gamma\varepsilon\omega\rho\gamma\acute{o}\varsigma$) means "farmer," and "Washington" (Washing-town) seems to refer to the cleansing of a city, the ultimate cultural product, by means of celestial (rain) water, the ultimate natural product. The opposition between town and water ($\rightarrow$ culture vs. nature) is therefore mediated by the farmer George, who, by means of the introduction of cultivated plants, reconciles the bipolarity inherent in his surname.

George : Washing : town : : :
cultivated plants : water : city : : :
farming : nature : culture

In variants G^{12} and G^{13} (the crossing of the Delaware and the Dollar over the Potomac) we find some interesting inversions. In G^{12} a boat made of wood (organic, above-ground material) crosses a river; George goes to the other side. The situation is reversed in G^{13}, where a dollar made of silver (inorganic, below-ground material) crosses the river, and George stays on the near side.

$$Delaware \rightarrow Potomac$$
$$boat \rightarrow dollar^{(-1)}$$
$$George\ goes \rightarrow George\ stays^{(-1)}$$

Once again, we find the farmer-hero in a mediating position between water ($\rightarrow$ nature) and dollar $\rightarrow$ boat ($\rightarrow$ culture). . . .

In the story, G^7, of George as surveyor, we find still another sort of mediation: just as a farmer uses tools (cultural products) to work *under* the earth (nature), a surveyor uses tools to "look *over*" the earth . . . and the story of George's wooden teeth (G^{32}) presents the mediatory role of the farmer in still another code, the gustatory. The wooden teeth are a transformation of the metal "teeth" of the plow; as George masticates his food in order to make it digestible, so the plow chews up the earth to make it produce edible plants. Thus, wooden teeth: mastication: farming. . . .

A pair of similar but inverted tales are found in G^{28} (Valley Forge) and G^5 (Mount Vernon).

$$down \rightarrow up^{(-1)}$$
$$Valley \rightarrow "Mount"^{(-1)}$$
$$winter \rightarrow spring\ ("Vernon")^{(-1)}$$
$$soldiering \rightarrow farming^{(-1)}$$

Thus farming, seen as the mediator between culture and nature (between washing and ton), itself becomes one pole of a new set of opposites. . . .

When we compare our key myth (G^1) with a related tale (G^{128}) of the cherry trees planted in the city of Washington after the hero's death, we find a particularly striking set of inversions:

G^1	G^{128}

Washington (hero) $\rightarrow$ Washington (city)
natural setting (farm in Virginia) $\rightarrow$ civilized environment$^{(-1)}$
cherry tree destroyed $\rightarrow$ cherry trees planted$^{(-1)}$
hatchet   planting spade
(destructive cultural product) $\rightarrow$ (restorative cultural product)

In other words, in G^1 the hero Washington uses a cultural product to destroy nature in a natural setting; in G^{128} the city Washington uses a cultural product to restore nature in a civilized setting. . . .

We are now ready to consider the three major geographical areas found in the *Geste de Washington*. Virginia, a farming area in the south, the home of cherry trees (cherries →a natural raw food) is in bipolar opposition to Massachusetts, an industrial area in the north, the home of baked beans (an extreme form of cooked food). The hero mediates between these poles: he farms in Virginia, and takes command of the continental army in Massachusetts. The opposition between farming and soldiering (noticed before in the Valley Forge-Mount Vernon pair of tales) is now mediated by a new profession, politics, in a new geographical location, Philadelphia. Philadelphia is the perfect mediating city, midway between urban North and rural South, home of Philly cream cheese, a natural food made palatable by nature's method of cooking, controlled decay. The accompanying diagram will perhaps make the interpretation clearer.

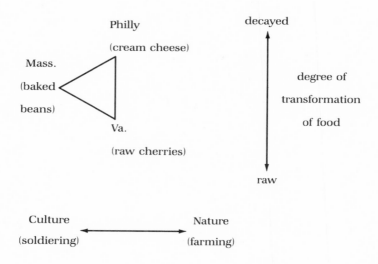

We have seen that the hero Washington mediates between nature and culture by being a farmer, and then between farming and soldiering by being a president; just so Philadelphia mediates between Virginia and Massachusetts, both in the geographic and the culinary codes. In conclusion we must cite one last set of transformations, which should amply confirm the validity of this interpretation:

Mass. → soldiering → baked beans → First in War
Va.   → farming   → raw cherries → First in Peace
Philly → politics   → cream cheese → First in the Hearts
                                                     of his Countrymen!

To sum up: it seems clear from the extreme fruitfulness of all the methods of interpretation used that the tale of Washington is an unusually good example of pure myth, untainted by the chancy quirks of history.

Suggestions for Further Reading in the Theory of Myth

Abrahamsson, Hans. 1951. *The Origin of Death: Studies in African Mythology*. Studia ethnographica Upsaliensia, no. 3 (1951), 1–176. A detailed comparative consideration of some fifteen different African myth types accounting for the origin of death, accompanied by maps showing distribution patterns of the myths.

Baumann, Hermann. 1936. *Schöpfung und Urzeit des Menschen im Mythus der afrikanischen Völker*. Berlin. 435 pp. A comparative consideration of the principal myths of Africa with some attention to nineteenth-century theories such as solar mythology.

———. 1959. "Mythos in Ethnologischer Sicht." *Studium Generale* 12, 1–17, 583–97. A helpful survey of the structure and function of myth in non-Western societies.

Bidney, David. 1953. "The Concept of Myth." In *Theoretical Anthropology*, 286–326. New York. A philosophical consideration of the truth and validity of myth with particular reference to such factors as belief and symbolism.

Boas, Franz. 1940. *Race, Language and Culture*. New York. 647 pp. This collection of more than sixty of Boas's published papers includes a number that articulate his approach to myth, e.g., "The Development of Folk-tales and Myths" (1916), pp. 397–406; "The Growth of Indian Mythologies" (1895), pp. 425–36; "Dissemination of Tales Among the Natives of North America" (1891), pp. 437–45; and "Mythology and Folk-tales of the North American Indians" (1914), pp. 451–90.

Buess, Eduard. 1953. *Die Geschichte des mythischen Erkennens*. Munich. 228 pp. In this survey by a Swiss theologian at the University of Basel, myth as a category of thought is examined with special reference to the Bible. Included is a historical summary of myth conceptualizations (pp. 85–105), emphasizing the scholarship in classics and history of religion.

Chase, Richard. 1949. *Quest for Myth*. Baton Rouge, La. 150 pp. A literary-historical survey of myth theories. Myth is defined as a form of literature.

Cohen, Percy S. 1969. "Theories of Myth." *Man* 4, 337–53. A survey of functionalist, Freudian, and Lévi-Straussian approaches to myth from an anthropological perspective.

Douglas, Wallace W. 1953. "The Meanings of 'Myth' in Modern Criticism." *Modern Philology* 50, 232–42. A consideration of the usage of the term by liter-

343

ary critics drawing attention to the opposition between a presumed mytho-poeic world of emotions and feelings and the factual world of logic and reason.

Eliade, Mircea. 1963. *Myth and Reality*. New York. 204 pp. One of the many works by this author treating the role of myth in ancient sacred and modern secular contexts. Myths are looked at with respect to their patterning and their functioning as rites of renewal even in disguised form in the contemporary world.

————. 1973. "Myth in the Nineteenth and Twentieth Centuries." In Philip P. Wiener, ed., *Dictionary of the History of Ideas*, vol. 3, 307–18. New York. A review of the major contributions to myth scholarship.

Feldman, Burton, and Robert D. Richardson. 1972. *The Rise of Modern Mythology 1680–1860*. Bloomington, Ind. 564 pp. A useful compilation of annotated excerpts from Fontenelle, Vico, Banier, and dozens of other writers who referred to myth, ending with E. A. Poe, Melville, and Thoreau.

Fischer, J. L. 1963. "The Sociopsychological Analysis of Folktales." *Current Anthropology* 4, 235–95. A lengthy survey of approaches to the study of folk narrative including myth.

Fontenrose, Joseph. 1966. *The Ritual Theory of Myth*. Folklore Studies no. 18. Berkeley and Los Angeles. 81 pp. A trenchant critique of the myth-ritual approach.

Frazer, J. G. 1930. *Myths of the Origin of Fire*. London. 238 pp. A comprehensive comparative consideration of fire origin myths from many cultures.

Gordon, R. L., ed. 1981. *Myth, Religion & Society: Structuralist Essays*, by M. Detienne, L. Gernet, J.-P. Vernant, and P. Vidal-Naquet. Cambridge. 306 pp. Translations of twelve studies by leading French classicists applying the principles of structuralism to ancient Greek mythology.

Greenway, John L. 1977. *The Golden Horns: Mythic Imagination and the Nordic Past*. Athens, Ga. 226 pp. A literary and social-historical approach to Nordic myths as sources of national consciousness and identity.

Hartlich, Christian, and Walter Sachs. 1952. *Der Ursprung des Mythosbegriffes in der modernen Bibelwissenschaft*. Tübingen. 191 pp. A historical account of the development of the concept of myth, especially as it became a factor in theological studies of the Bible.

Hautala, Jouko. 1961. "Gedanken über Mythen und einige andere Arten von traditionellen Erzählungen." *Studia Fennica* 9, 3–29. A Finnish folklorist reviews and wrestles with the term *myth* as defined in religious studies and folklore scholarship.

Hiatt, L. R., ed. 1975. *Australian Aboriginal Mythology*. Canberra. 213 pp. This volume contains six sophisticated structural anthropological essays on myths from various Australian native societies, emphasizing connections between myth and social organization.

Honko, Lauri. 1970. "Der Mythos in der Religionswissenschaft." *Temenos* 6, 36–67. A critical discussion of the role of myth in religion with references to numerous contemporary theoretical writings.

Hudson, Wilson M. 1966. "Jung on Myth and the Mythic." In Wilson M. Hudson, ed., *The Sunny Slopes of Long Ago*, Publications of the Texas Folklore Society no. 33, 181–97. Dallas. The best brief scholarly introduction to Jung's approach to myth.

Jensen, Adolf E. 1963. *Myth and Cult Among Primitive Peoples*. Chicago. 349 pp. A study of the ritual functioning of myth in non-Western societies.

Jung, C. G., and C. Kerényi. 1963. *Essays on a Science of Mythology*. New York. 200 pp. First published in German in 1941, this introduction to the Jungian approach includes two essays by each co-author.

Kerényi, Karl. 1939. "Was ist Mythologie?" *Europäische Revue* 15, 557–72. A classical mythologist influenced by Jung reviews myth definitions and also proposes the term *mythologem* as a basic unit or mythic theme (somewhat analogous to Jung's *archetype*).

Kirk, G. S. 1970. *Myth: Its Meaning and Functions in Ancient and Other Cultures*. Berkeley and Los Angeles. 299 pp. A consideration of theories of myth with applications, especially the approach of Lévi-Strauss to classical Greek and Near-Eastern narratives, for example, Gilgamesh.

Kluckhohn, Clyde. 1942. "Myths and Rituals: A General Theory." *Harvard Theological Review* 35, 45–79. An important review of the alleged relationship between myth and ritual with examples drawn from Navaho materials.

Krappe, Alexander H. 1938. *La Genèse des mythes*. Paris. 359 pp. A general comparative overview of myth themes with emphasis on classical and Indo-European texts.

Lanczkowski, Günter. 1968. "Neuere Forschungen zur Mythologie." *Saeculum* 19, 282–309. An erudite review of trends in myth scholarship with special emphasis on its connections with religion.

Lévy-Bruhl, Lucien. 1983. *Primitive Mythology: The Mythic World of the Australian and Papuan Natives*. St. Lucia, Queensland. 332 pp. A translation of the 1935 philosophical work that sought to explore the nature of "primitive" thought as manifested in myth.

Littleton, C. Scott. 1973. *The New Comparative Mythology*. 2nd ed. Berkeley and Los Angeles. 271 pp. An introduction to the voluminous writings of George Dumézil on Indo-European mythology.

Malinowski, Bronislaw. 1926. *Myth in Primitive Psychology*. London. 128 pp. An eloquent plea for the functional study of myth in cultural context.

Monro, D. H. 1950. "The Concept of Myth." *The Sociological Review* 42, 115–32. A discussion of myth as rationalization and its connection with ideology.

Niles, Susan A. 1981. *South American Indian Narrative: Theoretical and Analytical Approaches*. New York. 183 pp. A valuable annotated bibliographical listing of the major studies of South American Indian narrative including myth.

Okpewho, Isidore. 1983. *Myth in Africa: A Study of Its Aesthetic and Cultural Relevance*. Cambridge. 305 pp. An interesting critique of myth theory in the light of African material by a Nigerian scholar but marred by a confusion of myth with such other forms of oral narrative as folktale and epic.

Patai, Raphael. 1972. *Myth and Modern Man*. Englewood Cliffs, N. J. 359 pp. A somewhat popularized attempt to find examples of myth in modern life with some reference to the standard scholarship.

Peradotto, John. 1973. *Classical Mythology: An Annotated Bibliographical Survey*. Urbana, Ill. 76 pp. In this useful booklet published by the American Philological Association some 212 books are listed and briefly but critically reviewed.

Rank, Otto. 1922. *Psychoanalytische Beiträge zur Mythenforschung*. Leipzig. 184 pp. A selection of several of Rank's Freudian essays analyzing creation myths.

Righter, William. 1975. *Myth and Literature*. London. 132. pp. A useful overview of the role of myth in literature with myth defined in part as a "significant story."

Rogerson, J. W. 1974. *Myth in Old Testament Interpretation*. Beiheft zur Zeitschrift für die alttestamentliche Wissenschaft no. 134. Berlin. 206 pp. A marvelously lucid and well-written analysis of the role of myth scholarship in biblical criticism.

Róheim, Géza. 1953. *The Gates of the Dream*. New York. 554 pp. A partisan but sometimes brilliant Freudian approach to myth, deriving it from a basic dream with analysis of myth text examples drawn from all over the world.

Ruthven, K. K. 1976. *Myth*. London. 104 pp. An introduction to myth with special emphasis on the relationship of myth to literature.

Schubert, Rose. 1970. *Methodologische Untersuchungen an Ozeanischem Mythenmaterial*. Studien zur Kulturkunde 24. Wiesbaden. 237 pp. A technical consideration of more than eight hundred texts resulting in a detailed delineation of five Oceanic myth types.

Sebeok, Thomas A., ed. 1958. *Myth: A Symposium*. Bloomington, Ind. 110 pp. A reprinting of a special issue of the *Journal of American Folklore* 78 (1955) devoted to myth, including Richard M. Dorson's "The Eclipse of Solar Mythology" (pp. 15–38) and "The Structural Study of Myth" (pp. 50–66) by Claude Lévi-Strauss.

Segal, Robert A. 1980. "In Defense of Mythology: The History of Modern Theories of Myth." *Annals of Scholarship* 1, 3–49. A sophisticated probing examination of the myth theories of Tylor, Malinowski, Radcliffe-Brown, Jung, Freud, Eliade, Lévy-Bruhl, Lévi-Strauss, Bultmann, Frazer, Harrison, and Hooke.

Slater, Philip E. 1968. *The Glory of Hera: Greek Mythology and the Greek Family*. Boston. 513 pp. An imaginative but controversial psychoanalytic interpretation of Greek myths in the light of presumed Greek family interpersonal dynamics.

Steblin-Kamenskij, M. I. 1982. *Myth*. Ann Arbor. 150 pp. Translated from Russian, this work views myth from an evolutionary perspective in which it allegedly reflects an early period of primitive consciousness. This treatment of Eddic myths is introduced by an essay by Edmund Leach.

Usener, Hermann. 1904. "Mythologie." *Archiv für Religionswissenschaft* 7, 6–32.

A survey of nineteenth-century approaches to myth in the context of the history of religion.

Van Gennep, Arnold. 1910. "Was ist Mythus?" *Internationale Wochenschrift für Wissenschaft, Kunst, und Technik* 4, 1167–74. After reviewing the usual definitional difficulties, the author concludes that myth is a narrative that occurs in tandem with ritual.

Vickery, John B., ed. 1966. *Myth and Literature: Contemporary Theory and Practice*. Lincoln, Neb. 391 pp. An anthology of some thirty-four reprinted essays treating "myth" in such authors as Faulkner, Kafka, and Zola, with myth mostly being employed as a synonym for pattern, theme, or archetype.

Vries, Jan de. 1961. *Forschungsgeschichte der Mythologie*. Freiburg. 381 pp. One of the most comprehensive historical surveys of myth-theory scholarship.

Waldthausen, Heide Margaret. 1978. "The Analysis of Myth: Some German Contributions." *Reviews in Anthropology* 5, 443–56. A review essay focusing primarily on a special issue of *Paideuma* 22 (1976) devoted to myth analysis.

Wardman, A. E. 1960. "Myth in Greek Historiography." *Historia* 9, 403–13. A review of the attitudes towards myth as found in Greek historical writings by Herodotus, Thucydides, and others.

Index

Designer:	Eric Jungerman
Compositor:	G & S Typesetters, Inc.
Printer:	Vail-Ballou Press
Binder:	Vail-Ballou Press
Text:	10/12 Zapf Book Light
Display:	Zapf Book Demi
	Zapf Book Light Italic